THE LAST MEDICI

TO

MY FATHER AND MOTHER

THE LAST MEDICI

Harold Acton

'And no birds sing!'

THAMES AND HUDSON

© Harold Acton, 1932, 1958, 1980

First published 1932; revised edition 1958;
illustrated edition 1980

This book was designed and produced
by John Calmann and Cooper Ltd, London

Published in the USA in 1980
by Thames and Hudson, Inc.

ISBN: 0-500-25074-X

Library of Congress Catalog Card Number: 80-50687

Printed in Great Britain
by Morrison and Gibb Ltd, Edinburgh

CONTENTS

CONTENTS

CONTENTS

CHAPTER XVIII

CHAPTER XIX

CHAPTER XX

CHAPTER XXI

CHAPTER XXII

CHAPTER XXIII

CHAPTER XXIV

CHAPTER XXV

CONTENTS

CHAPTER XXVI

CHAPTER XXVII

LIST OF ILLUSTRATIONS

All the pictures are in Florence unless otherwise stated. The author and publishers are most grateful to the following who supplied photographs: Alinari (A), Fototeca Italiana-Firenze, Scala (S), Paolo Tosi (T), Alexander Zielcke (Z).

INTRODUCTION TO
THE ILLUSTRATED EDITION

his new edition of *The Last Medici*, which was published
originally by Faber and Faber in 1932, is distinguished from its
predecessors by the addition of profuse illustrations. These
have been chosen as visual aids to the text, images of the Florentine
background, the various country houses of the Medici Grand Dukes
and the gardens they created, the elaborate ceremonies and festivities
for special occasions, and the physical aspects of the protagonists.

Some of the great country houses, such as Pratolino and Lappeggi,
have all but disappeared; Poggio Imperiale, thus named by the Grand
Duchess Maria Maddalena of Austria who bought it in 1622, has been
transformed; and it is due to the engravings of Stefano Della Bella and
of Giuseppe Zocchi rather than to verbal descriptions that we may
visualize them in their prime. In several instances photographs have
been included for purposes of comparison. The Pitti Palace has been
enlarged but it was never finished according to Buontalenti's plan to
round off the piazza with projecting wings. After the destruction of
Pratolino in 1814 many of its statues were moved to the Boboli
gardens, whose vast amphitheatre was often used for the theatrical
performances described in the text.

As Giuseppe Zocchi was the most scrupulous recorder of post-
Medicean Florence and its outskirts, Justus Sustermans was the leading
portraitist of the Medici during his long life. It was not his fault if his
portraits are somewhat monotonous, for the seven children of Cosimo
II and Maria Maddalena of Austria inherited their mother's Habsburg
features, which were blended with those of the Bourbons in the offspring of Cosimo III and Marguerite-Louise d'Orléans. Sustermans
made no attempt to flatter the princely models whose effigies he has
printed on our retina.

Born in Antwerp in 1597, he was apprenticed to Willem de Vos for
seven years, after which he was trained in Paris by the court painter
François Pourbus II, a meticulous fellow Fleming. In 1619 he went

to Florence with the Belgian weaver Pieter Fevère, who had been invited by Cosimo II to superintend his tapestry factory. So impressed was Cosimo by Sustermans's portrait of Fevère that he appointed him court painter with a monthly salary, board and lodging, in 1620. From then until he died in 1681 at the age of eighty-four Sustermans depicted all the Medici of that period, in some cases again and again. Vittoria della Rovere posed for him in many guises—as the Madonna, a Vestal Virgin, Saints Margaret, Helen and Victoria, as well as her voluminous self. Though he was a friend of Rubens and Van Dyck he had none of their panache and glitter, but few painters have left so many realistic likenesses of a single dynasty during the course of three reigns. If the features failed to inspire him he concentrated on the costume, on satin, lace and velvet and the patina of damascened armour. At his best, as in his head of Galileo, he seems to have been influenced by Velazquez. Albeit a steady favourite for sixty years he made no enemies at a court where jealousy was rife.

Sustermans had no Florentine competitors in his iconographical field. Carlo Dolci's portrait of the widowed Vittoria della Rovere is a notable exception, for he was mainly obsessed with religious subjects—hence his fascination for the dowager and her bigoted son. A post-humous bust of the same dowager inlaid with semi-precious stones is a unique product of the *pietre dure* (or Florentine mosaic) workshops. The face was carved in chalcedony. Giuseppe Antonio Torricelli, the artist, claimed that it was the first life-size hardstone portrait ever made.

When Florentine sculpture was in the doldrums Cosimo III had the good sense to send promising students to Rome under the tutelage of Ciro Ferri. They returned as from a rejuvenation treatment in the "new Roman manner", Baroque with a sober Tuscan difference.

In spite of his fatal blemishes as a sovereign Cosimo III evinced surprising flair in his patronage of sculptors. Giovanni Battista Foggini, some of whose portrait-busts we reproduce, was appointed "first sculptor" in 1687 with the same house and foundry in Borgo Pinti which Giambologna and the two Taccas had occupied, and in 1695 he was also appointed "first architect". Massimiliano Soldani Benzi was appointed "master of the mint" in 1688, where he revived the art of casting medals, besides a quantity of bronze sculpture, free-standing groups of figures and reliefs. Both Foggini and Soldani have been restored to critical favour since the revaluation of the Baroque.

Foggini was responsible for the splendid reliefs on the tomb of St Francis Xavier at Goa, and he trained a skilful generation of sculptors and architects. The rare portrait-bust of Marguerite-Louise which we are privileged to reproduce—rare because Cosimo had no wish to be reminded of his cantankerous spouse—if not by Foggini is a product of his studio. Soldani married a daughter of Sustermans and held his post at the mint for forty prolific years.

The Grand Prince Ferdinando, who predeceased his father in 1713 at the age of fifty, was a more enthusiastic and discriminating patron of art than Cosimo III. Alessandro Magnasco's *Hunting Scene* is an eloquent example of his taste in reaction against the pietistic preferences of his father. Both Ferdinando and his wife Violante of Bavaria appear in this "hunting scene", probably at Pratolino; Ferdinando jokingly points his gun at a buffoon relieving himself behind a bush while Violante in a plumed hat lowers the gun with a restraining hand. It is the record of a whimsical moment such as a camera might capture today, but how much more vital! Dr H. Voss has suggested that the glum youth behind the Prince might be Magnasco's self-portrait and that the dark-haired fellow behind the Princess is Sebastiano Ricci, whose brother Marco painted the trees in the background. Sebastiano was fruitfully employed by Ferdinando at this period.

Even if the dates do not coincide Magnasco must have appealed to Gian Gastone, whose penchant for the bizarre was more acute than his elder brother's. The picture of the last Grand Duke in his bedroom is of singular interest but it makes one regret that Magnasco never tackled a subject so worthy of his style and temperament. According to Lanzi, he was more highly esteemed by foreigners than by his own countrymen.

I have to thank Mr John Calmann for the great pains he has taken in the production of this book, and Mr and Mrs John Clark of Scala Editrice for their valuable assistance in providing the coloured illustrations.

11 FEBRUARY, 1980

INTRODUCTION

It is already a quarter of a century since this book was published, and I was twenty-five years old when I finished writing it. That was by no means a propitious period for the publication in England of books about Italy. There had been a glut of these during the Edwardian era, and satiety was followed by a certain disgust, which was consciously or subconsciously due to political reasons. So the glorious Risorgimento had led to Mussolini! What would the English friends of Mazzini and Garibaldi have had to say? Even at that time Mrs Browning had had her doubts:

> *But Italy, my Italy,*
> *Can it last this gleam?*
> *Can she live and be strong?*
> *Or is it another dream*
> *Like the rest we have dreamed so long?*

That Italy would live and be strong was palpably certain, but the immediate outlook was dismal, and those who had loved her with an ardour none the less deep for being sentimental felt jilted and betrayed. Gloomily they relegated their well-thumbed Augustus Hares and Trevelyans to some remote and dusty shelf and boycotted new publications except those dealing with the fine arts. The ultra-sentimental became Fascists, and I have often wondered if Mrs Browning herself would not have acclaimed the *Duce* and the march on Rome like various gentle Englishwomen of my acquaintance who had survived the Victorian age.

In Italy, on the other hand, my book would give official umbrage, for only the heroic achievements of the past were meet to be recalled, and those who had lived dangerously since the days of ancient Rome were lauded, somewhat monotonously, to the skies. What chance had I to obtain a hearing with a chronicle of decadence? 'Hang up no more withered wreaths in the sanctuary of life,' wrote Nietzsche, who had also written that aphorism which confronted one, with local variants, on every other wall: 'The secret of a joyful life is to live dangerously.' Was I not hanging up another withered wreath in the sanctuary of life?

Thus neither in England nor in Italy could I hope to win popular approval with *The Last Medici* in 1932. But youth is perverse, and one writes for one's own delectation. To be candid, I was fascinated by the prodigious pageantry as well as by the ferment of fine arts of seventeenth-century Italy, whose virtues were being rediscovered after the usual cycle of neglect. With all the enthusiasm of a neophyte I rallied to the still-disputed cause of the baroque. And I wished to produce a baroque piece of literature (the expression was less hackneyed then, but I can find no substitute) for which the decline and fall of the Medici seemed to provide a perfect subject, about which very little was known.

All students of history were more or less familiar with the early Medici. All visitors to Florence must have seen Benozzo Gozzoli's frescoes of the cavalcade of the Three Kings to Bethlehem which leave an indelible impression of their physical distinction and splendour. There was no dearth of literature on the subject since the publication of William Roscoe's pioneer biography of Lorenzo the Magnificent in 1796. The success of this work was unusual: the demand for it increased faster than the booksellers could supply it. 'Accordingly,' we are told, 'the first edition went rapidly off, and the author shortly afterwards received from Messrs. Cadell, of the Strand, the very liberal offer of 1,200 *l.* for the copyright, which he at once accepted. A second edition was immediately published, and this, in 1799, was followed by a third.' The veteran Lord Orford sent Roscoe a fervent letter of congratulation; Lord Bristol invited him to Italy, offering him, at the same time, the use of his apartments at Rome or at Naples; Lord Lansdowne 'not only expressed his full approbation of the work in a letter to Mr Roscoe, but also took an opportunity of publicly eulogizing it in the House of Lords'; and Mr Mathias, author of the once-popular *Pursuits of Literature*—(Lady Blessington has left a delightful vignette of this eccentric in *The Idler in Italy*)—thus celebrated his achievement in a poem:

But hark! what solemn strains from Arno's vales
Breathe raptures wafted on the Tuscan gales!
Lorenzo rears again his awful head,
And feels his ancient glories round him spread;
The Muses, starting from their trance, revive,
And, at their ROSCOE'S bidding, wake and live.

Soon Italian, German and French translations appeared, and an American edition, printed in Philadelphia, sold like hot cakes. Roscoe's classic paved the way for other excellent books about Lorenzo: von Reumont's exhaustive and exhausting biography, Edward Armstrong's masterly monograph, still the best in my opinion, E. L. S. Horsburgh's detailed study, and dozens more. Recently there has been a lull, but it is bound to pass. As Armstrong wrote, 'no biography of Lorenzo will ever be definitive, for the questions in dispute are rather of feeling than of fact'. Books about other members of the family followed. Walter Pater and J. A. Symonds in England, Carducci, del Lungo and Villari in Italy, stimulated a gargantuan appetite for more.

While the supply met the demand, one must confess that it was predominantly stodgy. The Medici were so closely identified with their native city that their biographies tended to become treatises on Florence. And the political history of Florence is of minor importance; what matters supremely is its culture. It is as inspiring patrons of art and literature that the Medici will live, not as Machiavellian manipulators of Italian diplomacy. Jacob Burckhardt, whose *Civilization of the Renaissance in Italy* (1860) has never been surpassed, perceived this fact which too many have since forgotten: 'If we seek to analyse the charm which the Medici of the fifteenth century, especially Cosimo the Elder (d. 1464) and Lorenzo the Magnificent (d. 1492) exercised over Florence and over all their contemporaries, we shall find it lay less in their political capacity than in their leadership in the culture of the age.' To understand this leadership, which nobody has questioned, it is necessary to know something about their private lives and characters. Yet most of their biographers are reticent on the subject. Janet Ross's *Lives of the early Medici as told in their correspondence* (1910) is therefore invaluable, and it is a pity that it has found no successors in England. Personally, I would exchange half the insipid nineteenth-century biographies for this human record. Colonel G. F. Young's two volumes, *The Medici* (1909), of which there are numerous editions, remains the most convenient general history of the dynasty in English and as such has not been superseded; in Italian Pieraccini's massive *La Stirpe de' Medici di Cafaggiolo* supplements the eight volumes of Galluzzi's *Istoria del Granducato* (1781) with a meticulous diagnosis of all the family diseases. But until the publication of the present volume no history of the dynasty's decline had been produced, and nothing more luminous on the subject has come to light since then.

Of my critics I had no cause to complain. On the whole they were friendly; they were even flattering. I remember with gratitude Miss Rebecca West's appreciation. In those days writers lived in terror of Miss West's reviews. But my moral detachment was considered rather shocking, for a writer on historical subjects was expected to deliver a moral verdict even when it was implicit in his narrative. I happened to view history, or this chosen patch of it, as a landscape with figures advancing and retreating under different lights and shadows. The seventeenth-century Tuscan landscape I strove to depict, not broadly like the modern Impressionists, but with 'period' fidelity and niceness of finish; the figures I hoped to group so as to include variety and incident. Relying mainly on contemporary witnesses for the finish, I submerged myself in my subject, or fancied I had. With the aid of direct quotations I tried to let my readers see Cosimo III and his family as they were seen by their contemporaries.

In the 1920's the Florentine Archives were far less crowded than they are to-day. I was privileged in this respect, for I enjoyed the luxury of a little table all to myself, piled with old court diaries and other documents from which I made extracts more copious than would ever suit my purpose under the spell of their pulsating actuality: those from Settimanni alone would have filled a volume. Perusing these now, I wonder at my zest, for I had plenty of other temptations to distract me. When, after a deal of procrastination, the book was published, I washed my hands of it and went to Peking. There I remained until 1939, and in all those years I seldom gave the Medici a thought. I had fallen in love with a city unlike any in Europe; I had surrendered to the serene influence of the civilization which permeated it and to the charm of Chinese courtesy, a courtesy of the heart. There was no discord in this harmony until the Japanese invasion, but I have described some of this in my *Memoirs*. Events in Europe gave it a finer edge: I knew it could not last. . . .

After the war it was my first home, Florence, that claimed me. The sensations of childhood recaptured were all the more acute after so eventful an absence. My earliest interests revived with a redoubled force as I gazed towards the city from the garden of La Pietra. Suddenly the whole valley with the Duomo in its midst sparkled as if it had been washed by a golden shower. And the past became the present in that moment. What had this to do with the Medici, my reader may ask. In Florence the Medici are omnipresent. My book dealing with their swansong and decline had long been out of print and people began to ask me about it. According to the booksellers it was frequently in demand, but even second-hand copies were scarce. I suspect it was thanks to Mr Bernard Berenson, who spoke of it in terms of the most generous praise, that various publishers approached me, but these requested me to add new material of a sensational kind; otherwise it was in danger of passing unnoticed amid the host of brave new publications. I might add more hair-raising anecdotes about Gian Gastone for the benefit of sexual psychologists, or quote from his brother's correspondence with famous painters and musicians for the benefit of art historians and musicologists. But after careful consideration I concluded that these would be mere frills and furbelows; they might even destroy the unity of my narrative. A few additions I have made here and there, but they are not sensational. Some were suggested by a recent publication, Dottoressa Anna Maria Crinò's *Fatti e Figure del Seicento Anglo-Toscano*, which contains a mass of interesting documents, including a letter to Cosimo III from Lord Stafford while a prisoner in the Tower, thanking him for a gift of 'most excellent Wine, at this time, when I am under so great a Charge of Treason, and in prison for it'.

What the book needed, rather, was complete revision. At first I was impelled to rewrite the whole; I had changed—who does not?—since my light-hearted twenties. Its faults, very glaring to me, were due to youthful exuberance; but so, perhaps, were its merits. However, I have pruned most of the purpler passages of which I was once so proud and deleted others which struck me as juvenile excrescences. The substance remains the same but the form, I hope, is neater.

In the original preface I refer to the corridor running from the Uffizi to the Pitti Palace which used to be adorned with Medicean portraits. Sections of this were destroyed by the Germans when they blew up all the Florentine bridges save the Ponte Vecchio in 1944, and in order to block the latter demolished most of the surrounding buildings, 'the heart of Dante's Florence'. It has yet to be restored to its pristine condition, so that the modern visitor will seek out those pictures in vain. I for one hope that they will eventually be replaced. In the meantime students of Medicean iconography must rest content with the collection of portraits on the ground floor of the Riccardi Palace. Mr Frederick Hartt has left a memorable account of the Hitlerian holocaust in his *Florentine Art under Fire* (Princeton, 1949), when the mansion of the Grand Dukes of Tuscany resembled some tragic slum: 'There was only one source of water in the palace, and there were six thousand refugees who had come to find shelter in these massive walls after the Germans had evacuated the whole section of the city along the riverbanks. Even the royal apartments had been put to use to accommodate this tide of human misery, and the romantic walks of the Boboli Gardens were used as a public toilet. It was months before the gardeners got them clean again.' Fortunately the Pitti suffered no structural damage; the roofs and windows shattered by shellfire and explosions were soon repaired.

And now, as this goes to press, I have received a letter from Mr Berenson which he kindly permits me to quote: 'I am happy to hear that you are preparing a new edition of your *Last Medici*. It is a work of art and not a mere chronicle of irrelevant facts. I beg you not to alter a jot or tittle except of course for purely stylistic reasons. Do not dream of sticking on rags and tags of petty little documents that have been discovered since the first edition appeared.'

With this message from the venerable Sage of Settignano I feel emboldened to sail on.

Florence, 9 February, 1958.

PREFACE

On the subject of Florence, monumental works abound: it is even discouraging to consider them: the labours of so many patient lives screwed in their ponderous leaden coffins. How many pilgrims have died of exhaustion on that labyrinthine road leading, inevitably, to the House of Medici. The last word has not been uttered: more elaborate, more heavily-ballasted tomes are sure to follow. For as Dr Burckhardt wrote in his evergreen *Civilization of the Renaissance in Italy*: 'The most elevated of all political thought and the most varied forms of human development are found united in the history of Florence, which in this sense deserves the name of the first modern state in the world.' And: 'It will be an object of thought and study to the end of time.'

The Renaissance is admittedly the most interesting period of Italian history, Florence the most typical state, Lorenzo de' Medici its most typical citizen. The Florentine voice was then at its strongest and best and its echoes still drown all others in that noble city. So it is chiefly with the Medici of the Renaissance that historians have been preoccupied, and with the rise, the glorious supremacy of this family to whose fortunes, even in Italy, there is no exact parallel.

I shall therefore make no apology for failing to retrace their career. The facts are too familiar—that they were originally bankers by profession who gently, without military resources or experience of war, established a despotism which, with two interruptions, lasted for three centuries; that they established it when Florence was the intellectual capital of Europe; provided Rome with two great Popes, France with two great Queens; and that Medicean blood has flowed into every great dynasty in Europe.

The decline and end of this family are less familiar. In England it was long considered proper to leave the private lives of the last Medici in a discreet mist, as doomed ornamental beings, mere occupants of a remarkable museum: exotic fish hidden behind seaweed, stirring languidly in a subaqueous current of history—melancholy, ineffectual.

21

True, the Rev. Mark Noble and Colonel G. F. Young have allotted them chapters. In Italy, of course, it is otherwise, as any bibliography of the Medici would show: from Professor Gaetano Pieraccini we may discover their most trivial ailments; Giuseppe Conti has left us a mine of miscellaneous information; M. Rodocanachi has thoroughly explored the exploits of the Grand Duchess Marguerite-Louise, while the question of the Tuscan Succession has been minutely dealt with in many a treatise.

The object of the present volume, a compilation rather than a history, is to render some account of these last Medici and the Florence of their time, avoiding dissertations on the tortuous and complicated question of the Tuscan Succession. In the monumental works (to paraphrase a remark of the late Signor Biagi's), few of us have found that which forms the irresistible attraction of the past: those facts and details which, in a single sentence or anecdote, explain the secret of a whole age or people better than do all the pages historians and philosophers ever wrote.

I hope to be forgiven, then, if I have sacrificed much of the outer to that inner history which describes the individual and desires the unique: a twisted nose, one eye larger than the other, the habit of eating chicken to the sound of flutes, a preference for satyrs to sylphs, etc.

The famous corridor leading from the gallery of the Uffizi to the Pitti Palace may give rise to curious and even fantastic speculations. The student of so-called 'human' physiognomies would here be in his element, confronted on either side—and it is a very long corridor that rambles over the Ponte Vecchio—confronted with so formidable a collection of mediocre portraits.

On the left side as he proceeds, the pupil of Lavater will surely pause. These are not for the ordinary tourist, who will pass on. They are not for him who would seek to discover some imaginary ancestry. Indeed, there is such a surfeit of faces that the mind may pardonably become blurred, weary of fishing for facts from the annals of bygone ages, weary of trying to identify each recovered fact and pin it on to a portrait here or there—wherever he may chance to reconcile some familiar historical incident with the visage staring from the wall. But the pupil of Lavater, if not as extinct as the ichthyosaurus, is almost as rare to-day. Physiognomy has been replaced by many, and more exciting, intellectual pastimes since the days of the pundit from Zürich.

It is not the conscious, but the subconscious, amongst other things, that counts (we are told): in some circles the face has come to be considered a mask, rather than an expression of personality, each trait of which can be manipulated so as to conceal the inward character. Even if we are to accept the fashionable current theories, these Medicean masks are more than strangely related to one another. There is such an insistent assertion of certain features, such a repetition of eyes, noses, lips and jowls, that the total impression is one of purposeful monotony. It is almost boring at the outset. But it ceases to be so, after they are subjected to a more careful scrutiny.

The painters responsible for these records seldom attain to any high standard of portraiture or aesthetic realization: they are, with a few exceptions, second-rate, and shrouded in decent mystery. The *pictor* remains properly *ignotus*.

Many years ago some researches were made in this direction: we were none the worse for some knowledge of the models who had been drawn from their obscurity. Thus were we brought acquainted with several members of the Medici family who do not often come to light in the chronicle of great events, but who are by no means less interesting for that reason.

Unfortunate ladies who had been strangled, melancholy children who were poisoned before they reached the age of puberty, were able to smile on the world again, now that they and their titles had been recognized in the long corridor leading from the Uffizi to the Pitti Palace.

Here may the same people be perceived during the different stages of their lives when it behoved them to pose for another portrait, as for a photograph nowadays. Marguerite-Louise d'Orléans, before she had been soured by her matrimonial adventure in Tuscany; Anna Maria Luisa, the pathetic last descendant of the Medici family, before she married the Elector Palatine; Cardinal Francesco Maria, as he would have liked to be seen, youthful and florid, a frolicking prelate of doubtful celibacy, before the miserable marriage with Eleonora Gonzaga that saddened his latter years.

These portraits are as characteristic of the seventeenth-century Medici as the Lelys at Hampton Court of the seventeenth-century Stuarts, and the women of Charles II's reign, even unto the proud display of their bosoms, have much of the same monotony. And it is strange to compare the portraits of these Medici with those of the earlier branch, with the Renaissance-faces of Lorenzo and Giuliano, and the grandsons and great-grandsons of Cosimo *Pater Patriae*. For the Bourbon has intruded. There is no longer the same austerity: instead, a ponderous sensuality becomes more and more apparent, rigid in the beginning of the seventeenth century and kept under firm control, as in the faces of Austrian and Spanish nobility, but later loosening into a thicker voluptuousness, curdling into flaccid folds until, finally, a terrible senile lust asserts itself. Decay sets in. The muscles that were taut have let themselves go. The heavy eyelids droop more than ever now, the loose and flabby lips completely drop, like some pulpy fruit, bursting and over-ripe: only the nose retains its mighty prominence. But for this indomitable bulwark all the features sag, and no amount of pride will succeed in pulling them together. The over-emphasis of each weakness: the triumph of matter over mind, of exultant fleshiness (never has the spirit surrendered to such an extent as this, one exclaims) accumulates so as to form the most gruesome of caricatures.

The decadence of the Medici family—the word is here employed in its historic sense alone, and as in de Gourmont's conclusion to an enlightening essay on the subject: *'l'idée de décadence n'est donc que l'idée de mort naturelle'*—this decadence began with a faint indication. Externally it began with Francesco and Ferdinando, the sons of Cosimo I, and with the gradual subjection of Tuscany to the House of Hapsburg. A spectacle not devoid of a certain morbid fascination.

Of all the minor causes, chiefly political, that led to the disappearance of the Medici, a summary would be a waste of words, since the major causes can be compressed into one alone—death. Such a truism as this, Pasquale Villari observed, requires no demonstration. But their death was not without its harmony and beauty. It was truly 'Medicean'. Their last years rolled by with a tremendous outward pomp. The period itself was an ironical *chiaroscuro* of magnificent and sordid interludes. Their funerals verily were gorgeous, and their sepulchres of porphyry are almost gay in their luxurious elaboration.

The death-rattle was first audible in 1670, when Cosimo III came to the Tuscan throne. During the first years of the eighteenth century it had become very loud indeed. At length it ceased with Gian Gastone, in 1737. His sister, Anna Maria Luisa, lingered till 1743, a ghost on sufferance.

I

The Birth of Cosimo III – Character of Ferdinando II
—His Enthusiasms – Scientific Development

A question whether the illustrious House of Medici might be brought, quite prematurely, to an end, was almost raised before the birth of Cosimo III.

The Grand Duchess Vittoria della Rovere had experienced two painful catastrophes. Her first son Cosimo had been born on a chilly Tuesday, the twentieth of December, 1639. On Wednesday this infant died, and on Thursday a Florentine chronicled in his diary: The Most Serene little dead Prince was exposed to the public in the Chapel of the Pitti Palace, clothed in a royal mantle of silver satin, with a crown set upon his tiny head. Then by night was he privily borne to his burial in a small coffin, and accompanied by Marchese Colloredo, the chief major-domo, in a carriage to the Church of San Lorenzo, where he was held in view of the people for nearly two hours. The infant had only breathed for twenty-four hours. Smallpox, which the Grand Duchess contracted previously in August, had been the cause of this calamity. She recovered: a year and half later, on Friday the thirty-first of May, 1641, and at two o'clock in the morning, she was delivered again of a child.

The Grand Duchess had been in travail for nineteen hours beforehand. Hardly was the child baptized in the midwife's arms before it went to Paradise, we read. 'On the first of June, the little corpse of the defunct Princess, having been duly exposed to the public in the Chapel of the Pitti, comely as an angel (which she is even now in Paradise) was conveyed to San Lorenzo, where her brother had also been buried. Engraven in Latin on her tombstone are the simple words: You who read ask not my name. I was a little daughter to Ferdinando II, Grand Duke of Tuscany, and having entered this life, and been duly baptized, then gladly sought the heavenly existence.'

Again the Grand Duchess recovered. Her brother-in-law, Prince

Leopoldo, informs Prince Mattias constantly of her condition: 'Her Highness bears it well, considering that the fever is not yet abated; and I may assure your Highness that she has weathered a powerful hurricane.' And a week later he writes that she is in such repaired health that there is not even a trace of fever in her milk.

But when a tradition of unsuccessful deliveries begins, it is likely to continue. Moreover in Florence it was a matter of common knowledge that there had been discords in her conjugal life. Vittoria was proud and haughty; and Ferdinando's tastes, alas, were not exclusive. Of the Grand Duke's four brothers, Francesco had died while serving in the Imperial army; and the others had too many of the self-indulgent qualities of bachelors to marry. The prospects for an heir were not auspicious.

It was during the one troubled period of the Grand Duke Ferdinando's otherwise tranquil reign, to the beat of drums as it were, that the Grand Duchess became pregnant for the third time. For the absurd 'War' of Castro was then in progress; troops were being gathered and reviewed at Prato and Montepulciano. Captain Fracasso in his gay plumed paraphernalia stalked the Via Larga again. The Florentines were restive. Would the Grand Duchess present them, on this occasion, with an abortion? And would she perish of it? Perchance it was the mother's turn to die. . . .

While the Florentines were cynically speculating, on August 14th, 1642, the Grand Duchess was happily delivered for the third time. A son and heir: the dynasty was safe. The mother did not leave her apartments in the Pitti until September 29th, when, followed by a fine cavalcade and train of coaches filled with bejewelled ladies of quality, she repaired in state to the Cathedral. There all the hundreds of tall wax candles were lit, and a solemn Mass was chanted to the accompaniment of four choirs. The twilight of the sacristies became a dazzling midday. All banners were unfurled; the bells pealed rhythmically on; Florence rejoiced.

After a sumptuous dinner, the Grand Duchess visited the shrine of the SS. Annunziata, and the miraculous picture of Gabriel bringing the news to the Blessed Virgin was uncovered. It is said to have been completed by an angel, while the artist, who deemed himself unworthy to paint the Mother of our Lord, had fallen asleep in the midst of his prayers. Some attributed it to St Luke. Whoever it was, remarked John Evelyn, infinite is the devotion of both sexes to it. To this day the picture is considered so sacred that it is only exhibited upon special occasions, great festivals of the Church, when it is scarcely visible for the crowds of ardent worshippers. John Evelyn saw the SS. Annunziata in 1644, two years after Cosimo's birth; it was then 'so enriched by the devotees, that none in Italy, save Loreto, is said to exceed it'. The miraculous picture, he wrote, 'is always covered with three shutters, one of which is of massy silver; methinks it is very brown, the forehead and cheeks whiter, as if it had been scraped. They report that those who have the honour of seeing it never lose their sight—happy then we!'

In the beginning of 1642 Galileo died. It was appropriate, and almost symbolical, that the greatest scientist in Tuscany should be extinguished in the year of the last Cosimo's birth.

Cosimo III's youth was spent in the serenest period of the Granducato. The State of Tuscany was purely monarchical and despotic. Florence had relapsed into the condition of political coma and intellectual activity that became it so well; existence was agreeable and various.

In European politics his father's maxim might well have been *Tenir peu de place, et en changer peu.* After a successful skirmish and treaty with the bustling and interfering Barberini, the Grand Duke Ferdinando II had gained a superficial military credit, and the esteem, for what that was worth, of Italian and foreign princes. Pope Urban VIII had been compelled to revoke the sentence of excommunication he had pronounced against Ferdinando's brother-in-law, the Duke of Parma, and to restore Castro to his enemy. The Papal treasury was almost drained. Urban was overcome by such distress at the signing of the treaty that he fell into a swoon, and only recovered to die shortly after. He prayed that heaven would avenge him on the godless princes who had forced him into war (twenty-five men had perished at the great battle of Mongiovino), and expired at the age of seventy-six on July 28th, 1644.

Innocent X was appointed his successor mainly by the influence of Ferdinando's uncle, old Cardinal Carlo, at the Conclave, so that he could not help being partial to the Medici.

Ferdinando had also gained the certain knowledge that he possessed neither resources nor military organization sufficient to allow him to take part in any protracted war. This knowledge he transmitted to his son.

Florence had long ceased to be sacred to Mars and his tradition. In this respect it resembled the other Italian States, with the exception of Piedmont. The distinguished Bishop of Salisbury, Dr Burnet, travelling through Italy in 1685, remarked that 'the frontiers, both of the Spaniards and the Venetians, as well as those of the other Princes of Italy, show that they are not very apprehensive of one another; and when one passes through those places, which are represented in history as places of great strength, capable of resisting a long siege, he must admit that the sight of them brings the idea that he had conceived of them a great many degrees lower. For Lombardy, which was so long the seat of war, could not stand out against a good army now so many days as it did then years.'

After Ferdinando's conflict with the Barberini, the Medici abstained from further military enterprises. Little else would they do in politics henceforth but profess a placid neutrality.

Various potentates might send them ambassadors with petitions for men or for gold. Perhaps they would receive a casket of rare unguents, powders and essences for their pains. Such testimonies of Ferdinando's regard would alternate with pipes of Montepulciano. But always to their demands for more material assistance they would receive a firm response—with sundry polite expressions—to the effect that the Grand Duke would be ready enough to comply, whenever there was a serious emergency or risk of invasion.

Ferdinando had only to steer a lukewarm, unambitious course between France, Austria and Spain, and this he did with considerable skill and equanimity. Because of his neutrality he had a reputation for profound wisdom and knowledge of statecraft. Enjoying this prestige under peaceful conditions, Ferdinando decided to encourage the sciences and arts in the bountiful tradition of his ancestors.

We may see him to the life at close quarters, standing or sitting, in a series of grandiose portraits by Justus Sustermans, who, from the reign of Cosimo II to that of Cosimo III, resided in Florence and painted all the living members of the Medici. Ferdinando II, the fifth

Grand Duke of Tuscany, is portrayed in a variety of attitudes and costumes. The effect of majesty is achieved in many ways—by the aid of
swirling satin cloaks trimmed with hot miniver and delicate frozen lace;
or the sweeping hat of a cavalier bedecked with ostrich plumes; or of
flashing decorative armour—a bold breastplate admirable for exploit-
ing reflections—and a marshal's baton like a telescope. Usually the
broad red cross of the Grand Master of the Order of Santo Stefano hangs
handsomely above the gently bulging paunch. Other accessories no
less important have been called in, such as the Roman toga, and we may
smile a little at the painter's laudable attempts to supply the deficiencies
of his good patron's phiz, and lend him a more formidable aspect. For
the lymphatic nose, bulbous above the nostrils, the upturned black
moustache, reminiscent of bygone French gendarmes, the drooping,
moist lower lip inherited from his Hapsburg mother, together with
the double chin, belie the would-be Roman effect.

Ferdinando II was nowise formidable, unless he lost his temper. In
his person, as they put it, he partook of the German; but the heroic
armour, the military pose, was not quite appropriate. He had inherited
none of the cast-iron features and qualities of his ancestor Cosimo I. He
was a frugal and canny Tuscan, with a great deal of dangling good-
nature about him, studious, yet fond of practical joking. During the
plague of 1630, while all the wealthier citizens either fled or secluded
themselves in their country houses, Ferdinando, then twenty years of
age, remained with his brothers in the city, doing all in his power to
relieve the general distress. His people never forgot it.

Primarily attached to his family concerns, he called his brothers to
collaborate with him in the government, and to take part in the intimate
life of the Court. He was fortunate in Mattias, who distinguished himself as a general in the Imperial army during the Thirty Years War and
finally settled down to govern Siena; and in Leopoldo, whose discrimination and knowledge of science, art and literature was famous
throughout Europe. We are told that Ferdinando and Leopoldo 'nurtured the same passions, and together formed one will and desire'. But
all Ferdinando's tact was required to keep on good terms with the
eldest, Gian Carlo, who began life as a generalissimo of the Spanish
Seas and a grandee of Spain, and ended it as a prelate who would not
have been out of place in the *Satyricon*. The Pope described him as the

most virile of the Medicean princes. Ferdinando preferred to close his eyes and ears to the Cardinal's too-visible and loud licentiousness. An anecdote of his youth already denoted certain symptoms of the Grand Duke's easy, tolerant nature. On a cold winter's evening he was warming himself by a fire in his apartment, when his mother, the Archduchess Maria-Maddalena, paid him an impromptu visit.

She told him with dismay that she had suddenly discovered the existence of a particular carnal abuse in Florence; among people, moreover, of distinct parts, power and social standing. In spite of whatsoever virtues they might possess, she was determined to have them all severely punished, and submitted a long list of offenders to his scrutiny.

When the Grand Duke had read it, he remarked that this information did not suffice. There were others of similar tendencies he could append to her list. And taking a quill, he added his name in capitals. The Archduchess said he had done this merely to save the guilty, but that she would have them chastised all the same. The Grand Duke inquired to what punishment she chose to condemn them, and she replied with some vehemence: 'They must be burned.' So the Grand Duke, flinging the list into the fire, said: 'There they are, Madame, punished just as you have condemned them.'

As Galluzzi pointed out, a characteristic of the times was that kings and princes were exempt from that high standard of morals which was expected from their subjects, and excesses were part of their grandeur and independence. The Grand Duke's separation from his wife 'was not suffered to outrage public opinion', however, and all appearances of respect were carefully preserved towards each other. The cause of Ferdinando's long estrangement from his wife after Cosimo's birth was known to have been a handsome page, Count Bruto della Molara. The Grand Duchess was naturally indignant when she surprised her husband and his page in the midst of forbidden dalliance, and promptly left the room without a word. The Tuscan could wink at such wantonness; but he could not pardon arrogance and officious bigotry. Vittoria combined the latter with an icy reserve; her character was diametrically opposed to Ferdinando's, and consequently she was disliked by her subjects as cordially as her husband was beloved.

The Grand Duchess is said to have repented of her dudgeon later and to have attempted, in vain, a reconciliation. She vented her spleen on the pages: she called in Jesuit preachers to denounce their scandalous practices from the pulpit. But Bruto, with the Grand Duke's connivance, succeeded in compromising at least one of these Jesuits, who was forced to leave the country in disgrace.

Ferdinando's economy formed a contrast with his brother the Cardinal Gian Carlo's extravagance. It seems to have struck contemporary travellers. Sir John Reresby, who went to Florence in 1654, wrote: 'He does not think it below him to play the merchant, and his great frugality, withal, makes him—and not without reason—esteemed the richest Prince in Italy: of which last it is evidence sufficient, I mean of his frugality, that he boards with his cook: that is, he agrees with him by the week to provide for him daily so many dishes of meat for his own table, most of his servants being put to board wages.' And John Evelyn: 'In this Palace (the Pitti) the Grand Duke ordinarily resides, living with his Swiss Guards after the frugal Italian way, and even selling what he can spare of his wines, at the cellar under his very house: wicker bottles dangling over even the chief entrance into the Palace, serving for a vintner's bush.'

But his frugality—('there is not perhaps in the world,' wrote Goldsmith, 'a people less fond of this virtue than the English')—besides being a necessity after the plague of 1630, was also a notable Tuscan trait; it does not signify that Ferdinando was avaricious.

The Florentines were partial to pageantry: they invested their civic pride in their festivals, and it is to the Florentines that we are indebted for the earliest *feux de joie*, or fireworks, as we less poetically call them. They originated at the feasts of St John the Baptist and the Assumption, when wooden structures adorned with painted statues, whose mouths and eyes spouted beautiful flames, were set up in the squares. Ferdinando was prodigal of shows to impress the popular imagination, apart from the festivals that had been held in Florence yearly ever since the green days of the Republic; with their races of chariots, barbs and greyhounds; their games of *calcio*, a decorative and stately forerunner of football; and their jousts. Minute descriptions of such entertainments fill the pages of contemporary diaries, but, like the catalogues of auctions, they are stilted and cold: they convey little of that enchantment, less of that thrill, experienced by the Florentine public. We see them closer in the engravings of Callot and della Bella. For in the

Seicento men sought above all, as Corrado Ricci pointed out,[1] to satisfy a craving peculiar to that age, for aesthetic astonishment, for something to marvel at in music, metre or marble. It is permanently reflected and crystallized in their architecture—in Bernini's monuments as in Marini's poems. From every pile that was raised, the private citizen pined for some new gush of surprise: he longed to be caught unawares by some dexterous audacity. A building, unless it administered a definite shock like an electrical fish, was more or less voted a failure.

During Ferdinando's reign the festivals increased in splendour and elaboration. The character of the mediaeval tournament had altered: tilting was mingled now with mythological fantasies, fables sung in recitative style, with fireworks, fountains of bubbling wine and intricate architectural machines; it was coupled with music, dances, drama and song. The finest artists—men of the calibre of the Buontalenti (called *delle Girandole*, of the catherine wheels), the Tacca, the Parigi[2] —were to dedicate the best part of their genius to these ephemeral forms of art.

Ferdinando had always some demonstration of this kind up his sleeve, as it were, to amaze his guests after a banquet, and dazzle their eyes with his wealth: the banks of the Arno would be illuminated and barges of musicians would float up to serenade them; or a tourney would be given by torchlight on Piazza Santa Maria Novella, accompanied by masquerades and chariots full of energetic violinists.

Between these extravagant entertainments, Ferdinando lived as retired as was consistent with the situation of a prince, and relaxed from the cares of state in one of his innumerable country houses, preferably at Poggio Imperiale and Artimino.

The woods within reach of his villas were plentifully stocked with red deer, roe deer, fallow deer, wolves, goats, foxes, porcupines, hares, pheasants, partridges, boufles (or buffaloes), wild boars and other quarry. There he regularly pursued the healthful exercise of the chase, and the Court diaries preserve perhaps even more minute information on this topic than about his entertainments. When Sir John Reresby visited Poggio a Caiano, Ferdinando had just made a paddock-course

---

[1] *Architettura Barocca in Italia.* Bergamo, 1912.

[2] As Bernini in Rome, Torelli and Baccio del Bianco in Madrid, and Inigo Jones in England.

1 Ferdinando II by Justus Sustermans. Palazzo Pitti

2 *(above)* View of Florence from Pignone by Gaspar van Wittel, called Vanvitelli.
Palazzo Pitti

3 *(opposite)* Cardinal Carlo de'Medici, uncle of Ferdinando II,
by Sustermans. Palazzo Pitti

4 *(above)* Venus fountain at the Villa La Petraia by Giambologna
5 *(opposite)* Fountain in the grotto at Castello

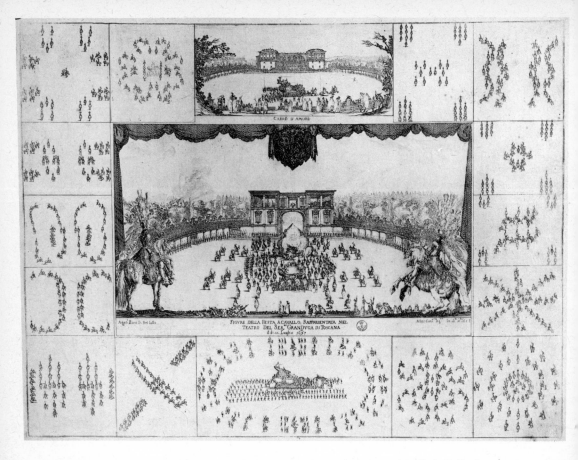

6 *(above)* Masque on horseback in the amphitheatre of the Boboli Gardens,
July 1637, engraved by Stefano Della Bella

7 *(left)* View of Florence,
drawing by Lanci.
Gabinetto di Disegni e delle stampe

8 *(opposite)* The staircase
in the garden of
Poggio a Caiano

9 The amphitheatre in the Boboli Gardens

10 A joust in the Piazza Santa Croce,
attributed to the school of Vasari.
Palazzo Vecchio

11 *(above)* The façade of Poggio a Caiano

12 *(opposite)* Cardinal Gian Carlo
de'Medici, brother of Ferdinando II,
by Sustermans. Lucca, Pinacoteca

13 The Grand Duchess Vittoria della Rovere, wife
of Ferdinando II, by Carlo Dolci. Palazzo Pitti

14 Ferdinando II in oriental costume
by Sustermans. Palazzo Pitti

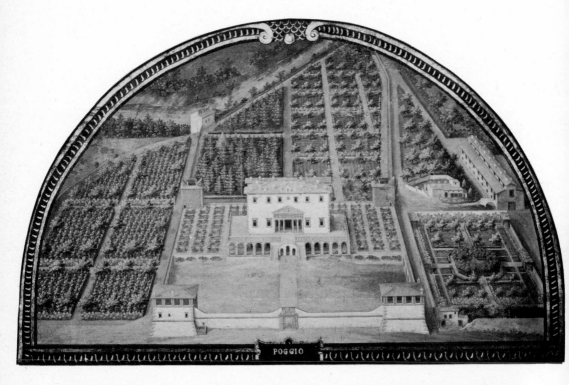

POGGIO

La Real Villa del Poggio a Caiano.

21.

15 *(opposite above)* Poggio a Caiano,
seventeenth-century lunette
painted by Justus Utens.
Museo di Firenze com'era

16 *(opposite below)* Poggio a Caiano,
engraving after Giuseppe
Zocchi published in 1744.
Museo di Firenze com'era

17 *(above)* Poggio a Caiano:
the rear façade

18 *Madonna and Child* by Carlo Dolci. Palatina

in the park 'by the direction of Signior Bernard Guascoigne,[1] an Italian who, having served our late King (Charles I) in his wars, carried the pattern from England.' 'There,' he says, 'we found the Duke diverting himself in the morning, who, after his return to dinner, according to his usual civility to strangers, sent us two dishes of fish (being Friday) and twelve bottles of excellent wines, to our inn.'

His enjoyment of hunting, fishing and playing at skittles or bowls was rational; he enjoyed them only in ratio to his successes. According to eye-witnesses he did not actually distinguish himself in any one of them, but it was always arranged to appear as if he did. When he won at bowls he would boast of it for days, and remain in the best of humours. He liked to fancy that he played a better game than the inn-keeper Catello, a famous bowling champion of that period. This conceit was diplomatically pandered to. For his courtiers, knowing how soon the Grand Duke's mildness and moderation could be transformed into a sudden gust of fury, would bribe Catello beforehand, when they heard that their sovereign, free from gout, was in the bowling mood. And the champion would have to feign an ignominious defeat.

There was a relative well-being in commerce and agriculture, and a continual influx to Florence of distinguished foreigners. The Medicean Court was still a lodestone to the intellectual. The Grand Duke Ferdinando, and Leopoldo, his more cultured brother, attracted the finer scientists and scholars by their generosity and sympathy with the anti-Aristotelian trend of the times. And the spirit of Rabelais, as it were, was wafted over Tuscany before the advent of that grimmer ghost—in the background dimly discernible—to loom over the reign of Cosimo III: the ghost of Ignatius of Loyola.

The characteristics of Florentine life during the first half of the Seicento were an extensive gaiety and Bohemianism; and these gave birth to the best literature of the age, to that burlesque poetry and prose which is still so kicking, so alive. Everywhere you looked there was evidence of this gaiety: on the steps of Santa Maria del Fiore, before Santa Croce or on the bridge of Santa Trinità, where the *improvvisatori* sweated verses from every pore; at the meetings of the Crusca, where

---

[1] Sir Bernard Gascoigne (1614–1687), otherwise Bernardo Guasconi, diplomatist and soldier, of Florentine birth. He fought in England for Charles I, and was created Sir Bernard Gascoigne in 1661.

an academician[1] would pronounce a dissertation on the president's nose; puns and anagrams were cunningly intermingled and exploded in the houses of Dati, Redi and other littérateurs. And likewise in the halls of the Medici. One might go so far as to say that no serious matter was dealt with, no problem solved without a reaction of rollicking repartee. The general feeling was: with all your heart, blood and guts, *lude, bibas et edas; post mortem nulla voluptas*. Or, as it has been loosely translated: 'Eat, drink and play at leisure; for after death's no pleasure.' There was an epidemic of *bisboccia*, a term whose syllables express the sense: gross feeding, heavy drinking and a prompt answer to the calls of lust.

The result, instead of an abatement of vigour, was a fermentation in every field, fanned by science into general fecundity. Sweet music was now composed for every instrument; painters frescoed the interiors and exteriors of whole churches and palaces with their riotous visions: complicated perspectives swarming with foreshortened and elongated figures in ecstatic attitudes—deceptive tricks of *chiaroscuro*, bituminous shadows and sudden shafts of light. The most esteemed painters and architects were those who could work fastest. Luca Giordano owed half his immense reputation to his speed. He was called *il Fulmine della Pittura*, and the Proteus of painting, but above all, *Luca fa presto*. The last name clung to him from an anecdote to the effect that Luca, when obliged to take refreshment, did not leave his work but, gaping like a young bird, gave notice to his father of the calls of hunger. Where-upon, always on the watch, the old man promptly supplied him with nourishment, at the same time repeating with affectionate solicitude: 'Hustle, my boy!'—*Luca fa presto*.

Barometers vied with thermometers, and each scientific brain was set in motion like a pendulum: now it swung towards the new telescope, now towards the artificial incubation of eggs. Never were odes and sonnets poured out in such liquid profusion. They were scattered like winged sperm upon the air.

The eccentric Giovanni da San Giovanni is the most fervid, fertile and representative Florentine painter of the period. Since, like the Grand Duke, his patron, he suffered from gout and could only use his legs with difficulty, he was accustomed to paint from a tub which, drawn upwards by means of two ropes passed through holes in the ceiling,

---

[1] I.e., Annibale Caro.

served him for a scaffold. Giovanni lived through only thirty-six years of the Seicento, but his gay allegorical frescoes on cupolas and façades, like those on the Palazzo Mariani in Piazza S. Croce (where his aim, in which he succeeded, was to set forth the charms of woman) define much of the aesthetic spirit of these years.

His time was divided between painting such subjects as the 'Expulsion of the Sciences from Greece' and the invention of some elaborate practical joke; he even carried practical jokes into his painting. On the walls of Pratolino, for instance, he depicted certain nymphs castrating Ghianni, the Grand Duke's dwarf, in the guise of a satyr tied to a tree. They are doing it with surgical thoroughness: a pretty picture, as a contemporary remarks. An impudent servant of Giovanni's appears as the Devil in the Badia, and a courtier, who gave himself airs, as another goatish satyr, in a room of the Pitti. It is perhaps for this reason that the worthy Abate Lanzi wrote of Giovanni da San Giovanni: he carried the famous dictum of Horace, 'All is allowable', to excess, and often preferred whim to art.

A posse of other artists, with Lorenzo Lippi of Florence and Salvator Rosa of Naples to the fore, were almost as preoccupied with poetry as with painting. Indeed, there was so much multiplying and interbreeding of talent, that to estimate the genius of these men one does not know whether to turn to one of Salvator's savage landscapes or to one of his equally savage satires; to Lorenzo Lippi's delineation of 'St Saverio recovering from the claws of a crab the Crucifix which he had dropped into the sea' or to his *Malmantile Racquistato*, the long mock-heroic poem once dear to every Tuscan for its 428 pages 'full of not only Tuscanisms, but Florentinisms',[1] 'the delight of the philologist, remarkable for embalming much local folk-lore, and so many local phrases as to be shorter than its own glossary'.[2] Lorenzo Lippi, like his friend Salvator, professed to write poetry as he spoke, and to paint what he observed. If he strictly adhered to his maxim, he spoke in puns, acrostics and anagrams, and saw an allegory in every face and cloud.

It was the moment of the Mock-Heroic, for which Alessandro Tassoni had set the fashion with *La Secchia Rapita* (The Rape of the Bucket). Gabriello Chiabrera, with his Pindarics and Anacreontics,

[1] Janet Ross. *Old Florence and Modern Tuscany.*
[2] Richard Garnett. *Italian Literature.*

reformed the Italian ode, or canzone, and swelled the lyrical afflatus until we are given the perfect dithyramb, *Bacchus in Tuscany* by Francesco Redi, an erudite writer on Natural History, and court physician, who employed himself otherwise in extracting salts from the ashes of vegetables. No hard-and-fast line had yet been drawn between literature and science. The versatility of those productive men appears overwhelming. One talent, one profession did not suffice.

The creative artist was never more cunningly merged with the clown. Salvator Rosa scored two of his greatest successes in the Commedia dell' Arte as Coviello, the roystering braggart, and Pascariello, the sharp, roguish, rapid *valet de place*. He even developed his Coviello into two personages, Coviello 'Formica', and Coviello 'Patacca', which have remained in the repertory of Neapolitan masks. Sometimes it is impossible to differentiate: behold the clown! behold the creative artist! Often each quality was detrimental to its component, but in the rare exceptions—and it is with the rare exceptions that posterity, after all, is concerned—this combination made for some superlative achievement.

Historians have a conspicuous tendency to idealize the fifteenth and sixteenth centuries, and to depreciate the seventeenth. Distance would seem to make their hearts grow fonder. According to them the Quattrocento was a halcyon period of strong, cheerful, active life, of refreshing breezes and pure mountain air—whereas the Seicento was degraded, a miserable swamp of devitalization, despair and unhealthy excitement. The phenomenon of 'Seicentismo' or 'Marinismo' spelled blight. But let us examine the previous centuries impartially and inquire: were these less theatrical? Were they devoid of brutality, fanaticism, high-sounding nonsense; of nepotism, pedantry, ostentation?

During the early years of the Seicento, Galileo had given a far-reaching stimulus to the study of science. The telescope reached upward and its crystal eye observed the shape and motions of remotest stars. In Florence an adventurous coterie cropped up and flourished, whose chief ambition was to penetrate the mysteries of nature. It did not suffice them simply to fall down and worship, as of old, in that vast temple. Taking stock of their ideas, the learned discovered that they were surfeited with scholastic metaphysics—the quaint potpourri of

Aristotle and St Athanasius that had been imposed upon them. They were determined to deduce the truth from the observation of facts, and to disperse error by the force of experimental knowledge. Italy's strength lay here. With its new conquests of science and reason, its rebellious aspirations, its cerebral erethism, the seventeenth provided for the *éclaircissement* of the eighteenth century, and paved the way for modern life and thought. European man had turned from searching for the secrets of his soul to the problem of his earthly dwelling-place.

The Grand Duke Ferdinando and his brother Leopoldo were lured by the fascination of Galileo's teaching. The improvement of scientific instruments, and the invention of new lenses for telescopes, were to become their favourite occupations. We are told that even the gravest cares of government, such as Ferdinando's conflict with the Barberini, were not allowed to interfere with his cherished experiments, which he practised in his private apartments. Evangelista Torricelli da Modigliana, who invented the barometer, was his 'chief philosopher and mathematician'. Famiano Michelini, whose astronomical observations were shared by Ferdinando, was professor in mathematics to Princes Gian Carlo and Leopoldo, while Prince Mattias studied under one of Galileo's closest friends, Maestro Niccolo Aggiunti of Borgo S. Sepolcro.

Orders poured from the palace for new and improved telescopes, barometers, thermometers and hygrometers. The traveller Lassels noticed many 'weather glasses, which are most curious' in the Grand Duke's bedchamber, and Sir John Reresby divers mathematical devices in the by-chambers of the Pitti: 'one demonstrating the perpetual motion; another, that either by land or sea, if you see the fire of a cannon, or hear the report, and desire to know at what distance it is from you, it infallibly shows it, as they say, to a quarter of a mile, by the knocking of a leaden plummet, fastened by a string against the wood of the instrument; with many others'.

The knowledge thus gained was not to be a mere end in itself. Ferdinando and Leopoldo wished to popularize their *strumentino*, or 'little instrument', as they called the thermometer, and use it for practical purposes. Not only throughout Tuscany, but even from abroad, they were kept informed by correspondents of the changes in temperature. Leopoldo took a thermometer in his coach while travelling from

Florence to Rome in March, 1668, and in his account of that journey he noted the different degrees of atmospheric temperature with which he came in contact.

Some of Ferdinando's thermometers were intended to register the variations of the temperature of air, others to mark those of liquids, and he had a quantity of special ones for baths. During the winter a 'little instrument' was hung in every room of the royal apartments.

Ferdinando was fascinated by heat in general (the caloric) and the propagation of sound: he even attempted the Egyptian manner of hatching chickens by means of artificial and graduated heat, and sent for two Copts to give him a demonstration of this process. When he wintered at Pisa, which boasts the first anatomical theatre and first botanical garden in Europe (both created before the middle of the sixteenth century), he spent many hours in the laboratory adjoining the latter—the 'cradle of Tuscan chemistry'. Winter was then the finest season at Pisa, mild as an English spring. The neighbouring Apennines had not then been cleared of their woods, so the city was screened from sharp east winds. The Medici annually fled there for Christmas from the cold of the capital. During Lent they stayed at Leghorn because they could have the best fish there, and at the cheapest rate.

'I imagine,' writes Prince Mattias to Ferdinando in 1631, wishing to discover how to produce a certain pomade of jessamine for the hair, 'that your Highness is now become a perfect alchemist and marvellous distiller, since with such pleasure you pursue your curiosity to the laboratory. . . .'

Flattering courtiers may have exaggerated the talents of Ferdinando and Leopoldo; there were detractors, on the other hand, who wrote of the Grand Duke that, 'having lavished large sums on researches and the manufacture of instruments, he thought he had gained the right to say, and have it said, that these were of his own invention'. But original documents, such as the 'Registers of experiments performed and observed by the Grand Duke Ferdinando II' in the first volume of Cimento manuscripts, and Redi's 'Observations of vipers', disprove this accusation.

Leopoldo founded the famous Academy of the Cimento in 1657 to bring the scientists at the Medicean Court together, to organize and concentrate their labours in search of scientific truth. There were ten members: Vincenzo Viviani, Alfonso Borelli, Antonio Oliva, Francesco Redi, Carlo Dati, Carlo Rinaldini, Alessandro Marsili, Paolo and Candido del Buono and Lorenzo Magalotti, its genial secretary. Its motto was *Provando e Riprovando* (proving and proving again); its insignia a furnace with three crucibles. The members assembled in the Pitti, on which occasions the Grand Duke and his family mingled as equals with the humblest of them. The first report of their experiments, which includes those on the supposed incompressibility of water, the gravity of bodies and the property of electrical matter, was published in 1666. It is a substantial monument.

Francesco Redi was their most spirited spokesman, and in his writings he took infinite pains to destroy the superstition still current among men of gentle birth and education. So far the scientists had been too servile to tradition: they believed much nonsense hallowed by antiquity. If some venerable author asserted that steeples were capable of flying through space, they were willing to suppose it.

How can they swallow such statements, asks Redi, when the same author frequently contradicts himself. Thus, in one passage, Pliny the naturalist says that no bee will ever touch flesh. Elsewhere, he writes: 'an you fear that bees lack nourishment, set some dried raisins and crushed figs, or the raw flesh of a fowl, within close range. . . .'

And when the most incongruous opinions about a subject are held by each time-honoured authority, where shall the credulous tradition-lover turn? Will mere chance determine his choice? Several Greek and Latin authorities concur that bees can be engendered by the putrefied body of a bull. But if some conscientious apiarist should seek to fill his hive, consider his embarrassment! For Columella teaches us that the entrails alone have the virtue of engendering bees. According to another, the beast should be buried, except his horns, which must be left exposed to air: from these, if severed at the right moment, a winged swarm will escape. One poet maintains that the corpse should be covered with thyme; Pliny suggests that straw from stable-litter should be substituted. From Virgil (at the end of his fourth book of Georgics) we gather that the bull's burial is a vain precaution: enough to leave it in the open. Another distinguishes between bees that are born of flesh and bees that issue from the brain or spine; the former constitute the proletariat, the latter the queen bees and aristocracy. Redi quotes no fewer than twenty-two contemporaries who believe these pretty fables: he is even ready to extend the list of them.

Now Redi, and the members of the Cimento, pronounce their decisions only when they are founded on facts, controlled by the senses and aided by all the instruments at the disposal of science. Redi's mission was to fight the credulity of his contemporaries: it mattered not whether the authority they relied on were ancient or modern. In his 'Observations of vipers' he began with denouncing the ancients.

The naturalist of old time wrote that vipers had an inconceivable horror of the ash-tree and its shadow. Put some vipers in a circle of such trees, and they would rather let themselves be burned alive on the spot than escape between them. And elsewhere: surround a serpent with betony leaves, and it will lash itself madly with its tail, and perish soon afterwards. Redi would see for himself. After several experiments he ascertains that beeches and betony leaves, far from producing such drastic effects, are often sought by vipers as a solace. Aristotle claims that spiders do not lay. After a long and minute examination Redi concludes that they are oviparous.

Redi and his friends did not shrink from the most repulsive ordeals to test such assertions. According to Gallienus you cannot eat a viper without being consumed by terrible thirst. A somewhat sickly friend of Redi's was gracious enough to oblige him by submitting himself to this diet. At various hours of the day he absorbed either a broth of these reptiles, or some bread that had been sprinkled with their dried and pounded flesh, or even the whole body of one, washed down with wine in which a viper had been preserved. Yet he proved no thirstier than before. As for their gall, a drop of it was deemed fatal to the most robust of men. Avicenna thought all antidotes were useless in such a contingency and many respected worthies shared his opinion. A certain Jacopo Sozzi, however, dissolved some gall in half a glass of cold water, and drank it down intrepidly without suffering any ill consequence. Since everybody believed, despite his protestations, that he had rendered himself poison-proof with mithridate beforehand, they tried the experiment on some cocks, two pigeons, a dog, a peacock, a turkey and a swan. But these were equally impervious.

Aulus Gellius advised anyone bitten by a serpent not to consult a good doctor, but a good musician. An active antidote would prove infinitely less effective than the strains of an harmonious instrument under the hand of a true artist. A violinist would work wonders. Others were not so easy to verify. How can the average mortal account for the curious romance with which some ancients invested the viper and marine eel?

The viper, having embellished himself, wanders along by the sea-shore in the hottest rays of the sun, and with passionate hissing beckons to his love. While she lifts her head from the billows and makes for the shore, he, in cautious anticipation, rejects his venom and deposits it on a rock—otherwise the beloved will die soon after the nuptials. Later the gallant returns for his venom. If he is unable to find it, despair will consume him and put an end to his days.

After these examples from hoary antiquity Redi turns to the moderns and their blind faith in remedies imported from distant lands, whose exoticism appealed to the imagination. Many a strange panacea was introduced into Italy at this time by some philanthropic missionary. Such missionaries flocked into the Pitti from all parts of the world, and the Grand Duke received them so hospitably that they compared him with Alcinous; and vouchsafed their most precious secrets in return.

One of these, Antonio Morera, Canon of the Cathedral of Goa, recommended the following: collect some white bristles from the tails of elephants and bind yourself a bracelet thereof; you will then be secure from vertigo, and the pestilential air of swamps will cease to harm you. This was a current remedy in the Empire of Siam and the Island of Ceylon. But somehow the bracelet lost its efficacy in Florence.

The same Canon told Redi that in the mountains of Malabar there were sombre birds which carried little stones of varied form and hue in their bellies. These, when placed in the centre of the forehead, would promptly banish a headache of any description. Don Morera induced Redi to try this cure when he was suffering from one of his chronic megrims. The obstinate pain, however, lasted twenty-four hours, as usual. The worthy priest was lost in astonishment. Evidently Redi was an exception, the most unfortunate of mortals—unless headaches were not accounted the same in Europe as in Asia. 'In any case,' he added, 'these stones must possess some admirable virtue, else why should Nature have caused them to develop in an organ of winged creatures? We know that Nature never acts without an aim.' Morera would not hear of a less recondite but more plausible explanation: the birds had swallowed them.

A discalced Carmelite, D. Philippe de la Trinité, claimed that the bones of a certain fish would stop any sort of haemorrhage. The proof? A viceroy of the Indies had been wounded in an artery by a clumsy surgeon, whereupon it had sufficed him to press a tooth of this animal between his fingers, and the copious flow of blood was stanched. The bones had an additional property: they were a powerful weapon against temptations of the devil. This recipe was also tried, with negative results. There was no reason to question the good father's sincerity: he had merely been uncritical, too ready to lend an ear to seductive legends. Such gullibility demanded exploitation, and there were plenty of quacks abroad; Redi warned Kircher[1] and other naturalists against them. For instance, there was a foreign clockmaker in Florence who told the Grand Duke: 'In my native land the skins of many are insensitive to the discharge of a pistol or arquebuss. This is the result of a magic formula, also of medicinal herbs and stones endowed with a special virtue. I do not speak from hearsay: I can claim to have seen it.' Some of his listeners scoffed, so the clockmaker sent for one of his compatriots, a soldier, who, like Siegfried, was reputed invulnerable, and the Grand Duke soon had him put to the test. Boldly the man bared his chest, and some excited scientists were about to fire when Ferdinando begged them to aim at a less delicate part of his anatomy. This was fortunate, for the poor fellow had to be carried off to hospital. He had been duped like the clockmaker, the experiment having worked elsewhere. But on that previous occasion the bullets had been tinkered with so as to graze the skin without piercing it. At the Pitti there was no trickery, and the weapons were normally charged.

The Cimento only lasted ten years.[2] There were the usual smoulder-

[1] Esperienze intorno a diverse cose naturali e particolarmente a quelle che ci son portate dall'Indie. Lettera al p. A. Chircher della Cia di Gesù.

[2] Examples of astrolabes, quadrants, glass vases and tubes employed in these tests may still be seen, together with some of Galileo's most valuable instruments —such as his first thermometer, the first microscope invented by him and his lodestone magnet; the two telescopes he constructed in 1609 when he held the Chair of Mathematics at Padua, by one of which he 'discovered' the satellites of Jupiter—in the Florentine Museum of Natural History. Many were exhumed from remote corners of the Pitti, covered with cobwebs and dirt, and entirely forgotten. Among these was the large orrery, arranged according to the Ptolemaic

ing jealousies: Borelli and Viviani quarrelled about the 'movement and stability of the earth', Oliva and Rinaldini left Florence, and Leopoldo, perhaps rather tired of trying to restore peace and order among these irascible rivals, left for Rome to become a Cardinal at the age of fifty.

Other scientific academies had preceded it at Naples, Rome and Palermo, but this, the father of our own Royal Society, was the first to respond with alacrity and to practise Galileo's great precept: to deduce the laws of Nature by facts of observation which have been proved by the severest tests of experiment.

system, which was later cleaned and repaired. This unique instrument was made between 1588 and 1593 by Antonio Santucci, the cosmographer of the Grand Duke Ferdinando I. 'The central globe,' as the Horners remark (Susan and Joanna Horner: *Walks in Florence and its Environs*, Vol. II, 1884), 'is of peculiar interest, owing to the fact that the great freshwater lakes Albert and Victoria Nyanza in Africa, near the White Nile, are marked upon it, which for a considerable period after this globe was made, were entirely forgotten, and only brought into notice in our own time by the explorations of Captain Speke in 1858, and of Sir Samuel Baker in 1864.'

Other instruments continued to be used long after the Cimento was extinguished. A powerful crystal lens made by Bresanz of Dresden is exhibited in the Museum, which was used by Averani and Targioni, the pupils of Viviani and Redi, in their experiments on the combustibility of the diamond, and of other precious stones. Later it was employed by Sir Humphry Davy in his researches into the chemical components of the diamond. Such an instrument as this goes to prove that Ferdinando lavished his large sums with sagacity.

II

*Cosimo III in Early Youth – The Florentine Court
– Cardinal Gian Carlo – Projects for Cosimo's Marriage
– Marguerite-Louise d'Orléans*

The Grand Duke would have liked to give his son a modern scientific education. But the Grand Duchess objected, and he took the line of least resistance in the matter. Anything for peace. Vittoria had a bevy of priests intriguing at her heels and an influential confessor. Their one idea being to pave the way for a dogmatically docile successor, they advised her to keep Cosimo well away from astrolabes and such dangerous heretical toys. Volunnio Bandinelli of Siena, a theologian better calculated to form a priest than a good prince, was appointed his tutor. His mark on Cosimo's juvenile mind was an enduring one, and long after 1655, when Bandinelli was created a Cardinal by Alexander VIII, an intimate correspondence continued between master and pupil. Those who attempted afterwards 'to make him shed the yoke of that servile education', such men of culture as Milton's friend Carlo Dati, and Magalotti, the secretary of the Cimento, were foiled. When his uncle Leopoldo invited him to take part in the meetings of the Cimento, the blasé young Prince did not blush to observe, with a deprecating gesture, that he considered his attendance in that society a waste of time.

In his early youth it seemed as if Cosimo were cut out for a sportsman. The child, at any rate, was a precocious shot. On January 14th, 1654, Prince Gian Carlo wrote to Mattias from Pisa: 'To-day I have a piece of news that should surprise you. . . . The young Prince has killed a goose in mid-air.' At the age of eleven and a half we read that Cosimo, having fired five times at some running pigs with his little arquebus, charged only with one ball, killed four, to everybody's delight.

He was then, according to the Lucchese ambassador, a fine sturdy boy with a bright complexion: 'he succeeds wonderfully in everything to which he is applied: his manner of receiving royal ministers, and his neat rejoinders, are quite above his tender years'. At the age of fourteen he was seen on horseback for the first time in public. Two years later, as he was galloping at Poggio Imperiale beside his riding master, he fell and hurt a leg, but the accident was not a serious one. Subsequently we hear less of his riding.

A change seems to have taken place in his character about the time of his accident, of which the next Lucchese ambassador gives the first inkling in 1659. 'The Prince,' he writes, 'now in his seventeenth year, exhibits the symptoms of a singular piety . . . he is dominated by melancholy beyond all that is usual, and in this he differs from his father. The Grand Duke is affable with all men, easily moved to laughter and ready with a jest, whereas the Prince is never seen to smile. The people attribute this to an imperious and reserved disposition, from which they do not foresee any desirable consequences.'

Cosimo was very seldom inclined to converse with the ladies, although he was civil enough in saluting them. As for dancing, he would have endorsed the opinions of Cicero and Lord Chesterfield about 'that silly exercise'—that *Nemo sobrius saltat*. The courtiers were naturally perplexed. Here was a robust young man, in all the bloom of adolescence, shunning their society for that of dingy priests. The choral chant of the Church was the only form of music he could endure, and he had a lasting abhorrence for the songs of females.

Before he had reached the age of eighteen he had been zealous in visiting the holy places of La Verna, Camaldoli and Vallombrosa, and at every shrine had left numerous tokens of piety behind him. He never let a day go by without hearing at least one or two Masses, reciting the Offices of the Virgin, and reading some 'holy' book.

When Cosimo was eighteen, his father and mother became reconciled after their long estrangement. No more was heard of the handsome Count Bruto della Molara. A second son, the future Cardinal Francesco Maria, was the fruit of this tardy reconciliation.

Ferdinando hoped to enjoy domestic tranquillity henceforth. Still, he could not but be disconcerted by the gloom of Cosimo's disposition. The young man was forever at his devotions. His father perceived with concern that only monks and friars put him socially at ease; with all others he showed himself dumb and reserved. Only the salvation of his soul seemed to occupy his mind.

The legends of the martyrs, then, of many a saint not in the Roman breviary; the histories of miracles; the two hundred and thirty questions of Albert le Grand: Cosimo considered these far more consequential than all the experiments of the Cimento put together. With regard to certain saints whose influence is enduring this might have been so, but Cosimo was still too callow to make distinctions and he suffered from a precocious spiritual pride or self-righteousness.

Despite a penchant for ceremony, Cosimo never disguised his contempt for the Court around him, and this, with the exception of Spain, was the least licentious in Europe. Futile points of precedence assumed the supreme importance of State affairs and formed the chief topic of conversation.

Cardinal Gian Carlo's Court was very different. All those young bloods, virtuosi, makers of mirth, the rumours of whose riotous living rendered them unacceptable to the Grand Duchess, found refuge there from boredom, and joined his hunting and gambling parties. Like his uncles, Don Lorenzo and Cardinal Carlo, his life was dedicated to pleasure. His high clerical position was never allowed to stand in the way of amusement; he was given, as they said, headlong to the pleasures of Venus: if there was a beautiful woman to be found in Florence, he was determined to enjoy her favours at any time and cost.

Raised to the purple at the age of thirty-four, after an unfortunate love affair and a term as 'Generalissimo of the Spanish Seas', he had been unable, from the very beginning, to resign himself to the game of keeping up appearances. Sustermans has left fine portraits of this bold and factious young prelate, who had 'the long hair and curls usually associated in our minds with the cavaliers of that period in England'. The jaunty angle of his *berretta* betokens his dandyism.

Alexander VII deputed him as legate *a latere*, with Cardinal Frederick of Hesse-Darmstadt, because they were both brothers of sovereign princes, to escort Christina of Sweden on her entry to Rome at the head of a great cavalcade.

Although His Holiness had told her that so great was the value of her conversion it was celebrated in heaven by a greater festival than was visible on earth, he soon decided that her influence on young prelates was insufficiently edifying. He objected to the freedom and ease marking her intercourse with Gian Carlo, and insisted that on future visits to the Queen he was to be accompanied by Cardinals older than himself. Gian Carlo, who had been raised to the purple for political reasons, resented what he considered unnecessary interference. Finally the Pope complained that Gian Carlo was too young and handsome for his office and requested Ferdinando to recall him to Florence.

A plague had spread along the coast of Spain, Sardinia and Naples; now it threatened Rome, and served as a pretext for Gian Carlo's departure. Ferdinando, having gained from previous experience, took such precautions that Florence remained immune. Mattias, who was governing Siena, saw that the frontiers were well guarded: communication with Rome was cut off, and correspondence with Alexander ceased. Christina of Sweden herself, who was on her way to France at the time, was not admitted into Leghorn.

So Gian Carlo returned to his Florentine banquets and hunting parties, to cultivate his garden—and, above all, to cultivate the ladies. Ferdinando had made him a gift of that garden in the Via della Scala where the members of the Platonic Academy had held their sublunary debates. Gian Carlo made it gorgeous with giants and grottoes, and fantastic with fountains and exotic flora: curious plants from the pensile gardens of Babylon pushed their trembling, twisting leaves from vases worthy of the Muse of Gongora. It became the orchard of his orgies. But the garden is now demolished; so we must needs rely on Sir John Reresby's account.[1]

'The form of it,' he wrote, 'is rather long than square, graced with several rare greens, and waterworks, after the manner of Italy. On one side is a close walk, with greens; wherein, while you think to walk securely, by the turning of a key you are assailed by a shower of rain rising out of the ground, all the length of the walk. At the end of this walk is a grotto, from whose sides, enamelled with stones of all colours and shells of fish, springs forth water in several places, as also from the top and bottom. In the midst of this garden is a house of pleasure, and truly so; the Cardinal here usually giving rendezvous to his mistresses. The upper rooms are furnished with fine pictures, the lower with statues and waterworks. Near to the house stands the statue of a giant,

---

[1] *Travels of Sir John Reresby*. London, 1904.

of great esteem, being twenty feet high; his posture is holding a pitcher above his head with both arms, catching the water that falls out of it with his mouth.'

But the cognomen wherewith a botanist will christen a flower is seldom worthy, generally unintelligible. Gian Carlo, remembering some feature of a mistress, came to draw fine comparisons among the petals—between the pale, the pert and the vaporous one, the brazen, the buxom and the frail—came to call one Giralda, and others Cepparella, Cappona, Frescobalda, after the various beauties who had disturbed him, who still disturbed him strangely. More dusky than the rest was Ottomanna, the daughter of the Turkish Grand Signior: she had fled from Constantinople with one of her brothers, to be baptized in the Christian faith. The brother became a Dominican friar and faded away; Ottomanna married and settled down in Florence, though the fact that she became acquainted with the Cardinal indicates that the Moslem strain in her was not extinguished in the Baptistry. Perhaps an iris, slowly unfolding its petals to the light, was given her name in the garden of Via della Scala. On the other hand, we might conjecture that Cepparella was an indoor flower with tiny, visible veins: she so suddenly shrivelled and died. But even in death, it is said, she was so beautiful that her cold corpse tempted all that saw it to prurience, and haunted them with they knew not what atrocious grace. The sexton who buried her said that Cardinal Gian Carlo, remembering the convulsions of that ivory body, came to look once more; and overcome by so much beauty, entered the vault and lay with her for the last time.

La Cepparella must have bequeathed her name to the Cardinal's orchids.

If this garden constituted his playground, it also set the scene for an occasional tragedy. Gian Carlo was the dragon of this Hesperides, and a jealous dragon. Since his return from Rome, homicides and murderous attacks occurred in Florence with disagreeable frequency. They were never referred to at Court, and as the Grand Duke was afraid of his brother, he let them pass, even when Cavaliere Luna, who had been a favourite page of his, happened to be drowned in the Cardinal's pond. All Florence knew the facts. Luna had been the Cardinal's rival in a love affair, and his Eminence, resenting it, decided somewhat conventionally to invite him to dinner.

There was a small island in the middle of his garden fishpool; an elysian spot, delicately shaded with trees. From here, while dining, one could throw morsels to the aged carp, and watch them break the tranquil water's brim, wrinkle it with their snouts. Perhaps they would leap into the cool air, for on summer evenings the thin-winged almost invisible gnats were ever dizzily swarming an inch or so above the surface. On this islet the table was elaborately served, and Luna sat among the privileged guests. The sun's heat was tempered by now, and from the rich twilight deepening down the avenues, a breeze brought with it some of the fragrance of slumbering blossoms.

With toasts, recitations and speeches, the wine had flowed abundantly. Night fell, and the dews, and the candles guttered over the napery. Luna's neighbour, a courtier of the Cardinal's, involved him in a lengthy disquisition and kept plying him with liquor the while. When the last course was over, and the other diners had wandered off to amuse themselves in different corners of the garden—or simply to hear the nightingales—the two were left still arguing together. Presently Luna and his neighbour rose from their seats. A wooden board without railings served as a rustic bridge to the mainland; and as they were about to cross it his companion gave the lurching Luna a push. There was hardly a splash. He might have slipped in by accident. Some time had been given him to sink ere the aggressor set up a hue and cry for help. At the belated call a few drunken guests assembled to enquire what was the matter. The corpse of poor Luna was finally extricated from the weeds and the Cardinal was, of course, disconsolate.

We have said that, like his uncles Don Lorenzo and Cardinal Carlo, Gian Carlo lived for pleasure. But whatever their little failings, none of these were enemies of the mind. The amenities of life were practised by them as an exceedingly fine art. The sublime and the vile touched hands. They were prompt to recognize, and make a good use of, talent. An artist was still regarded as something of a rarity, and treasured accordingly. Salvator Rosa had been presented to Gian Carlo in Rome, and the young Cardinal found in the works, character and humour of Salvator much that accorded with his own. 'He soon conceived for him one of those violent *engouements* which the great are apt to mistake for friendship, and invited him to Florence. Salvator's arrival in Florence was a triumph. The Grand Duke and the Princes of his house received him, not as an hireling, but, as he had frankly painted himself—as one whose principles and genius placed him beyond the possibilities of dependence. An annual income was assigned to him, during his residence in Florence, in the service of the Court, besides a stipulated price for each of his pictures; and he was left perfectly unconstrained, and at liberty to paint for whom else he pleased.'[1]

Don Lorenzo, who alone of this trio remained a private gentleman of leisure, had revived the fashion for theatricals. By conferring his patronage on two societies of players, who styled themselves the 'Inflamed' (*Infuocati*) and the 'Immovable' (*Immobili*), and by lending them his apartments for rehearsals, he afforded the Italian theatre, which was a natural growth—like the olive and the vine, it might have been rooted in the soil—some latitude for expansion. Cardinal Gian Carlo, as his successor (for he had always shared his uncle's enthusiasm for comedies), enabled the 'Immovable' to purchase a fullery from the wool guild, in Via della Pergola, where they built a wooden theatre. For the 'Inflamed' he hired a house in Via del Cocomero, now Ricasoli, and requisitioned Ferdinando Tacca to provide it with a new set of scenes. Such was the humble beginning of the popular Florentine theatres of the Pergola and Niccolini.

Other societies, academies as they were solemnly called, may be said to have formed a link between the Court and the citizens outside it, and between the private and public life of the Medici. It was under Ferdinando II's reign that those 'networks of molecular life, countless and multiform' sprang up and spread all over Italy.

So near, yet utterly removed from all this effervescence, it seemed as if the Grand Prince Cosimo, like his favourite painter, Carlo Dolci, who had vowed his pencil to the Virgin, was to become the victim of a pertinacious melancholy. In the case of saintly Carlino, this melancholy made it sometimes impossible to obtain a word from him: all his answers were sighs. On the day of his wedding, when the company were met for the ceremony, he was nowhere to be found. At last he was discovered in the Church of the Santissima Annunziata, prostrate on the steps of the great altar, before a crucifix.[2]

Cosimo was almost as silent, but his silence was more sullen than saintly. That sullenness redeemed him. It was noted significantly that

[1] Lady Morgan. *Salvator Rosa*.   [2] Baldinucci.

the feminine rather than the masculine saints engaged his rapt, adolescent fancy. This was indeed fortunate: the sex was all to the good; besides which Cosimo had a strict sense of filial duty and family responsibility.

The Grand Duke was convinced, in spite of his personal experience, that marriage would cure Cosimo of his unhappy temper, would quicken his languid pulse, and bring him gently down to Tuscan earth. He was young; surely then his nostalgia for the celestial would be satisfied by a princess with sky-blue eyes, by substituting a sweet and tangible girl for one of those intangible angelic phantoms. Ferdinando looked about him: where could such a one be found?

Until Louis XIV could make up his mind to marry, all other arrangements were hovering, like bees, in suspense. Would they sting, or was it honey they had come to distil?

Neither the Queen of France nor the omnipotent Mazarin were in any haste for his nuptials. The Queen agreed with the Cardinal that it was not good for kings to marry young, because they ran the risk of soon having sons too big for them.

Ferdinando anxiously awaited the results of the Peace of the Pyrenees. When this was signed, in November, 1659, Louis abandoned his first love, Maria Mancini, one of the Cardinal's beautiful and witty nieces—'Mazarinettes' as they were called—and married the Spanish Infanta. There was a welcome interval of peace in Europe, but this Franco-Spanish union disturbed the political balance. For all Ferdinando's aversion to the French, he had been studious to cultivate the friendship of Mazarin. He had kept the French Court generously provided with the choicest Tuscan delicacies, wine, fruit and those balsams and essences from his Fonderia, or chemical laboratory, which were so highly prized,—even with human gifts—those musicians and actors who were a perpetual source of amusement to young Louis XIV.

There had been an Italian Scaramouche at Court ever since he could remember. At the age of two, when Louis was in one of his ill-humours, and nothing could suppress his tears and cries, it was a Scaramouche that came to the rescue. If her Majesty, he remarked, would but permit him to hold the Dauphin in his arms, he flattered himself he could placate that royal infant. The Queen was pleased to consent. Whereupon the mime pulled such an effective series of grimaces that the cries soon ceased, and the Dauphin was tickled to mirth—and even more. For he wantonly did his occasions all over the jester's hands and clothes.

Later, as the *Roi Soleil*, Louis condescended to remind Scaramouche of this Rabelaisian incident. In 1653 he asked Ferdinando to send him Tiberio Fiorilli, Molière's tutor, and the greatest Scaramouche that ever was. The vogue for Italian comedies and music in Paris had been fostered by Mazarin and the banished Barberini. Mazarin, whose motto was ever: '*Qui a le coeur, a tout*', studied the power of music on the Queen Mother. It was considerable. She was fascinated by the soothing voice of Leonora Baroni, and above all by the plaintive cadences of Atto Melani. Leonora never left her side, 'ready to warble forth the moment she gave the signal', and Melani impertinently boasted that she could not live without him! She took him with her when she went to Amiens, and wrote awkward letters to Mattias, begging permission to retain him when he already had engagements in Florence. Every other evening, for four hours at a stretch, he sang sad songs in her apartment. For Anne of Austria, like all the Hapsburgs, delighted in lachrymose airs. Mazarin, music and the Queen thus conspired to keep young Louis and Ferdinando on excellent terms.

The Grand Duke had innumerable foreign correspondents and un-official diplomatic agents of every imaginable sort—wandering abbés, monks, astrologers and barber-surgeons—who were paid for secret in-formation 'and occasionally for something worse'. Most of the Italian virtuosi at the French Court were spies—that astonishing Melani among them, who was at the same time a soprano, composer and im-presario, and often played two rôles in the same opera.

It was through one of his secret agents that Ferdinando first heard rumours of an engagement between the young Duke of Savoy and Marguerite-Louise, a daughter of Gaston d'Orléans, the brother of Louis XIII, and, from all accounts, a most eligible bride. He also heard that the Duke of Savoy would probably decide in favour of some Eng-lish princess instead—less well connected, and therefore more modest. Ferdinando pricked up his ears. On May 20th, 1658, his Prime Min-ister, Gondi, was asking Abbé Bonsi, the Tuscan resident in Paris, a score of questions. Who, precisely, was this princess? What was the real nature of these negotiations between Turin and France?

The prospect of being a royal matchmaker smiled eagerly upon Bonsi. 'Mademoiselle d'Orléans,' he replied, 'is thirteen years of age. She has lovely features, brown hair, turquoise eyes, and appears exceedingly sweet and gentle.' Probably he had never set eyes on her. Anxious to add a note of conviction to his portrait, and to show what a connoisseur he was of the 'bewitching fair', this future bishop remarks that 'perhaps she was a little on the short side, and maybe her shoulders were somewhat narrow, but the waters of Bourbon could soon remedy these minor deficiencies'. (Saint-Simon recorded that she was 'tall and very well made'.) Bonsi, however, adds the finishing strokes of lively wit and gracious manner, which brought her to 'a great familiarity with their Highnesses'. These were the very qualities to inflame a young prince, and banish hypochondria; so it seemed to Ferdinando.

Other princesses were offered to his choice, and amongst them one of the exiled Stuarts; but a fear of offending Cromwell induced Ferdinando to reject this proposal.

Marchetti, the Tuscan ambassador to Saxony, had tried to negotiate a marriage between Cosimo and Princess Ermuth Sophia of Saxony, but the girl declared that she would never renounce her Lutheran faith: the dowry, moreover, was found to be 'a mere bagatelle of twenty thousand thalers'; Ferdinando had counted at least on some hundreds of thousands. The negotiations were dropped. But Mazarin heard there was a risk that Cosimo might wed this Saxon princess. It was the dream of his latter years to receive the Papal tiara, and he wanted Tuscan influence in the Conclave. The hour seemed critical. He interviewed Bonsi, who appeared to know nothing of Marchetti's machinations; after snubbing him for his ignorance, he demanded a portrait of Prince Cosimo.

So pleased was he with this overture, that Ferdinando, who knew his Mazarin, immediately sent him several enormous barrels of his choicest wine. Moreover, he let the Cardinal understand that nobody else would receive of this unrivalled vintage. There was a further exchange of compliments and gifts. The King, acting on his minister's advice, sent Cosimo a couple of palfreys. Ferdinando thanked him by despatching one hundred and twenty-four lemons in return, which were considered of the highest excellence.

In Mazarin's interview with Bonsi, all was left vague; no princess was specified. Bonsi had several strings to his bow, the Princess of Orléans, of Nemours, and others beside, such as the three daughters of the Princess Palatine (the Queen of Poland's sister). Mazarin listened patiently, and assured Bonsi that he would have good reason to congratulate himself if he allowed the matter to pass through his hands.

But of all the princesses Bonsi had proposed to Ferdinando, one appeared eligible above the rest: Marguerite-Louise d'Orléans.

Gaston d'Orléans had married his second wife Marguerite, the daughter of François II, Duke of Lorraine, at Nancy in 1631, a secret love-match which his brother Louis XIII refused to recognize. Marguerite-Louise was born of this union, on July 28th, 1645. She was thus nineteen years younger than her step-sister, the famous 'Grande Mademoiselle', Duchesse de Montpensier.

Her early life was spent with her parents at the quiet court of Blois, where the ambitious and irresolute Gaston had had to retire in mild disgrace after the last check suffered by the Fronde, of which he was the apparent leader. The Duchesse, a virtuous woman but a cold wife, cared little for her three daughters. She was devout, and 'punctuated her prayers with continual meals, by way of curing herself of the vapours, which were much increased thereby'. She only saw her children for a hurried ten minutes or so in the morning and evening, and then it was only to say: 'Hold yourselves straight', and 'Keep your heads up'. According to Mademoiselle, these were the sole instructions her children received. 'They loitered about their rooms with a lot of other little girls, and there was not a single soul of any consequence or authority to look after them.'[1] Among the little girls was Louise de la Vallière.

As Ferdinando had been informed, they intended to marry Marguerite-Louise to the Prince of Savoy; but Turin was afraid of this too-lofty alliance, and Gaston was against it, for he hoped to wed his daughter to the King. Public opinion favoured her, and she was actually spoken of as the 'little Queen'.

It was this ambition of Gaston's that had induced Bonsi to put forward other suggestions to Ferdinando. There was her younger sister, Elizabeth—no beauty, but the possessor of lovely blue eyes, sparkling

[1] Mlle de Montpensier. *Mémoires*, viii, p. 376.

with gaiety. . . . Saint-Simon says that she was hunchbacked and excessively deformed. But Ferdinando held firm to the project of marrying Cosimo to Marguerite-Louise; and Bonsi was told to approach her father. In spite of Gaston's ambitions, Bonsi was not repulsed. He received a flattering encomium of Ferdinando.

'I bear great affection towards the Grand Duke,' wrote Gaston; 'I regard him as a very prudent prince and worthy of every grandeur. I shall always be candid about these sentiments, and without adulation declare my esteem for the most judicious prince in Europe; the best informed of world affairs; the most politic in preserving the favour and respect of all potentates; and the most accommodating there is. I speak from the heart: I myself belong to his family (being a son of Maria de' Medici) and am proud of the relationship, notwithstanding the gout I have inherited therefrom.'

Then the Peace of the Pyrenees, and Louis's marriage to the Infanta, put an abrupt end to Gaston's ambitions. Ferdinando could safely enter the arena of negotiations.

There was this drawback. Some of the most reputably beautiful princesses of that age were in fact misshapen, or pock-marked, or likely to be sterile. Ancient diseases flowed with the ancient 'blue blood' in their veins, even as the gout, from century to century, had knotted the Medicean arteries. One could judge then less than ever by outward appearance. Of the princesses Bonsi had proposed as suitable wives for Cosimo, two were discovered to be malformed: the younger sister of Marguerite-Louise, and the Princess Palatine's eldest daughter. Both of these he had recommended with appropriate flourishes. The latter, particularly, would make an admirable spouse, he wrote, although one of her shoulders was situated on a higher plane than the other—a little fault the iron corset would very soon correct. In fact she wore one, like so many other princesses. . . .

This news put Ferdinando, Cosimo, the whole Medicean Court in a flutter. Were all the French princesses crooked? The Grand Duke asked him to be more explicit; he required the names of such princesses as 'had recourse to the industry of tailors' which the Tuscan resident had discreetly failed to mention.

Bonsi resisted manfully. Perhaps, he said, he had been led into error on this account; had spoken by hearsay; had repeated mere gossip. The rumour was certainly exaggerated. Finally he had to admit that the sister of Marguerite-Louise—the very one he had proffered so freely to Cosimo—was afflicted in this unfortunate manner. In trepidation the Grand Duke wondered if Marguerite-Louise were similarly afflicted, now that, thanks to Mazarin, this match was seriously entertained. The matter must be cleared once and for all before he entered upon further negotiations.

With great caution and secrecy he charged Barducci, the Bishop of San Miniato, to obtain all the requisite information. Barducci promptly wrote Madame Gobelin, one of the women most closely attached to Marguerite-Louise, for 'a sincere and true report of her age, her health, the perfection (or imperfection) of her body, and of her figure in particular; whether she were naturally well-shaped or assisted by her tailor; whether her stature were tall or short'.

Madame Gobelin's answer was voluble:

'You do me full justice in believing that I shall render you a truthful account of all you wish to know. Unless I lie, I must protest that the Princess has excellent qualities of heart and brain. She possesses one of the sweetest and truest hearts you could wish for: she is extremely good-natured and lively, without derogating from that rank to which her birth entitles her. She speaks well, has an agreeable tone of voice, sings very pleasantly, plays the spinet with grace, and dances to perfection. She has a lovely figure, and I swear before God that no tailor ever came to assist it. I would lay down my life on that. She is tall, not so tall as some girls of her age, but she is in no way short, and her bosom is one of the finest and fullest there is. Her skin is white and her cheeks are rosy: her eyes very sparkling; her hair brown and abundant: she arranges and dresses it with her own hands, only some women comb it and aid her somewhat. She is merry enough but never hot-headed; very pious and regular in her devotions. . . . She has the gift of winning the hearts of all she receives. . . . She is deeply attached to her sisters, who are also devoted to her. . . .

'I have had the honour of seeing her almost every day since she was born: she was suckled at the breast of a highly virtuous young woman, and she has not yet suffered from any serious illness. A long while ago she had smallpox, which affected her so little that it is scarcely noticeable. She is never given medicines to preserve her naturally good constitution. I believe she has not yet shown signs of what so many maidens have at her age; of this I am not quite certain. . . . I have not inquired, nor did I know whether to mention the subject or not. I cannot admit she is very regular in her daily occupations. She does some fine needlework at some time during the day, and when she plays at cards, tric-trac or chess, she does all these things with great dexterity.'

Bonsi had written: 'She has a horror of the Louvre because of the concourse there, and she assuredly was born to live in Tuscany, where existence is regulated so methodically.'

Ferdinando and Cosimo were reassured; Mazarin was anxious to have the Princess married as soon as possible. Her step-sister Mademoiselle had already wrecked her alliance with Savoy; unable to bear the thought of a younger sister marrying 'in her teeth', she had persuaded the Prince that Marguerite-Louise was deformed. She might play the same trick again! The Duchesse d'Orléans was meanwhile collecting information about the Florentine Court. Bonsi depicted it as a very Eden, where peace and happiness reigned, where festivity succeeded festivity, where there was perfect freedom. Above all he praised the 'admirable personality' of the Grand Duchess Vittoria. He wound up with the declaration that there would be no happier princess in the world than Marguerite-Louise, if she were wedded to Cosimo.

To Cosimo he kept enumerating her manifold virtues and graces: Marguerite-Louise was *belle à ravir*; her skin a dream of whiteness; her hair ravishingly blonde; her movements were wonderfully graceful; her charm was without parallel on earth. And Bonsi succeeded where others had failed, in wakening Cosimo from his torpor. The Prince's desire was to marry; his impatience now exceeded Ferdinando's. Of late he had begun to pay some attention to his toilet. He who had thoroughly despised foppish things became anxious to follow the French fashion in dress.

Bonsi was to procure Cosimo a suit of the finest stuff obtainable: doublet and broad-legged hose, gloves, dancing-shoes, beaver hats with flowing ribbons and plumes, collars and shirts of English stitching, garters, a sword; nothing must be lacking. Particularly the Prince urged Bonsi to send him a nice selection of those modish minor accessories 'which give the finishing dash to a gentleman'. By their magical assistance he felt he could not fail to captivate the French Princess.

Gaston d'Orléans put no obstacles in the way: the Princess herself appeared well disposed towards the marriage; and all would have happened as soon as Mazarin and Bonsi desired, but for the dowry. Mazarin did not deny that it would be a modest one, but he reminded Ferdinando that in lieu of lucre, the Princess had innumerable virtues; that she came of the royal blood of France; that she seemed 'capable of bearing many children'—all of which Bonsi endorsed. 'She will yield such fruits,' he wrote the Grand Duke, 'as will console your old age, and perpetuate Your Highness's pedigree.' Then Gaston died, on February 2nd, 1660, leaving only eight hundred thousand crowns and a pile of debts. No dowry could be conjured out of these. The Infanta's had not yet been paid, and the treasury was exhausted as a result of Fouquet's maladministration.

After her father's death, Marguerite-Louise became the King's ward, which meant that she was entirely in the hands of Mazarin.

III

*Negotiations for Cosimo's Marriage – The Contract Signed
– The Princess's Marriage by Proxy and Journey to Florence*

Throughout these long negotiations Bonsi had insisted on one characteristic of Marguerite-Louise which she completely failed to possess. That was docility. She was so gentle, so tractable, he repeated, while everything about her pointed to the contrary.

She had inherited many qualities from Henri IV, her grandfather; frankness and freedom of speech; energy, a wild love of movement and physical exercise. Her parents, who had cherished the illusion that she would be Queen of France, had encouraged these natural inclinations. She had been taught to ride in early youth, and spent most of her time in hunting and reading frivolous novels. In fact she had all the twinkling animation and lack of restraint, the coquetry and 'high-bred ease' so popular at Court until the advent of Madame de Maintenon. She had been educated, moreover, with an aversion to Spanish haughtiness and Italian gravity.

When Gaston died, the Dowager-Madame left Blois for Paris, where she installed herself in the Luxembourg Palace, then called the 'Orléans'. At first she had pretended to approve of her daughter's engagement to Cosimo, but now she was eager to prevent it. Marguerite-Louise was bored with her environment: she wanted to spread her wings, to expand. When asked why she wished to marry so soon, Marguerite answered that she feared she would otherwise become too *difficile*. She must marry the Prince of Tuscany before she had experienced the delights of Court. Rumours, nevertheless, were beginning to reach her about the dull uniformity of life in Florence. Her fluttering doubts on the subject are echoed in queries to Bonsi. Were any violinists, for instance, to be found in Tuscany?

Bonsi hastened to assure her that Florence was full of exquisite musicians, but that she was quite free to take with her all the violinists she required. Would they—so long as she were not pregnant—allow her to ride, hunt, employ a French doctor, French maids and a French secretary?

Of course, of course, Bonsi replied. None of her wishes would ever be gainsaid. He did not consider promises binding, and he was determined to succeed, regardless of consequences. Once the Princess was safe in Florence, the Medici could mould her to their will.

The Duke of Savoy reconsidered proposing to her: no doubt he had overcome his scruples on discovering that Marguerite-Louise was as sound in wind and limb as any man could wish. But Mazarin staved him off. The 'necessary dispensation' from Alexander VII, the reigning Pontiff, for marrying cousins even so far removed as were Cosimo and Marguerite-Louise arrived on New Year's Eve, together with a gift of lemons; and Bonsi was rewarded with the title of Ambassador Extraordinary to the Grand Duke. The contract was signed on January 24th, 1661. Marguerite's mother had been converted to the match by Turenne and the Duchesse de Guise: Mazarin had disarmed Monsieur, the King's brother (whose opposition was feared because of his affection for the Princess), by a welcome gratuity of fifty thousand crowns.

There had been an exchange of portraits between Cosimo and Marguerite-Louise, and each professed satisfaction with the features of the other. The contract returned from Florence duly signed by father and son, with an addition of gloves and gallantries for which the Grand Duke had sent from Rome, by Marguerite's request. Then Mazarin, the *deus ex machina*, followed Gaston to the grave on March 9th, with his dream of the triple tiara unrealized. When he lay dying his attendants told him that a comet, sure presage of coming evil, had suddenly appeared in the firmament. 'The comet does me too much honour,' Mazarin observed.

Marguerite's mother chose this moment to step forward again with objections. Madame was positive that her daughter was unsuited to the life in Florence, where, as she said, she would enjoy neither liberty, nor amusement, nor revenue worthy her rank. Now that Mazarin was no more, she recovered her audacity. Albeit the contract was signed, she refused to give her consent. The King, on the other hand, was unable to collect the sum promised for her dowry; he suggested that the ambassador should accept an alternative compensation.

Bonsi's troubles were beginning again. He fidgeted and fretted, threatened and protested. After all, the contract had been signed. . . . Finally he acquiesced that the dowry should be paid by instalments. But the Dowager-Madame was a difficult nut to crack. While her daughter appeared willing to marry Cosimo, she had cut off her allowance. But now the Princess was changing her mind. She ceased to be bored with her surroundings; and agreed with her mother, who promptly presented her with five hundred doubloons. Such weather-cocks were women! Now on all occasions Marguerite-Louise bewailed the thought of going so far away, of leaving her dear Paris. The cause was prudently concealed by Bonsi, but it was the common chit-chat at Court. Marguerite-Louise had fallen in love.

Recklessly, without a thought of her Italian fiancé, she was developing a liaison with Prince Charles of Lorraine,[1] her first cousin, whom she had met two years previously at Blois. Madame encouraged the affair, partly from weakness of character, partly to irritate the Court. Yet she must have known that their close consanguinity would stand in the way of marriage. They did not attempt to suppress or hide their tender feelings; and Madame allowed them to go out riding every day and pass blissful hours together undisturbed.

Bonsi, for all his uneasiness, continued to write that the Princess was pining to join her Cosimo. He was beginning to learn more of the character of this 'docile' Princess. She always pouted at him in public, so that he dared not venture near the Luxembourg. To add to his embarrassment, Cosimo's promised gifts had failed to arrive. The Parisians, he said, were pouring ridicule on him and his master: tales were repeated of the Grand Duke's stinginess. Did he not board with his cook, and sell what he could spare of his wines? A French traveller of the period had remarked of the Florentine aristocracy: '*elle sent un peu le bourgeois, comme toute la noblesse de ce pays-là*'. Were not the Medici parvenus, descended from merchants?

Marguerite-Louise was not even allowed to distribute the fifteen thousand crowns that had been sent her for servants' gratuities. Bonsi

[1] The fifth duke of that house, the future defender of Vienna, and 'terror of the Turk'.

had received a special message from Gondi to distribute the sum him-self, since 'women were extravagant and light-headed'. He was further enjoined to make it last until the time of her departure.

Towards the end of March, Madame strained every nerve to prevent the marriage: she implored the King and interceded with the Queen Mother. But Louis had adopted Mazarin's projects as his own, and considered himself bound to see this contract fulfilled. As the time drew nigh Marguerite-Louise worked herself into a frenzy of despair. She declared that the King was a heartless tyrant, and according to her sister, 'raised a furious uproar' to retire to a nunnery, though her tem-perament was scarce in harmony with the veil. Seeing, however, that in spite of all the King stood firm, she betook herself to the Louvre, and besought him on bended knees to release her. He received her graciously, but her prayers left him unmoved: he said that he could not honourably break his word.

Then the Grand Duke's envoy arrived with splendid gifts, and pub-lic opinion veered in Cosimo's favour. Amongst other objects, Mar-guerite-Louise received an exceedingly precious jewelled box. On the lid was a miniature of Cosimo. Albeit he did not appear as an Antinous, this plump, thick-lipped young man, the box was superb. Her vanity was flattered, but that image, as a writer has expressed it, was less precious than the one she carried in her heart.

Marguerite-Louise's marriage was solemnized by proxy in the King's Chapel at the Louvre on Sunday, April 17th, 1661. The Duc de Guise represented Cosimo. As Marguerite-Louise was still in mourning for her father, a limited number were present at the ceremony, among whom were the Queen Mother, the Queen, the Duchesse d'Orléans, Marguerite's three sisters, and Madame (Henrietta of England, who had married the King's brother in March). Bonsi officiated, as Bishop of Béziers. Cosimo had sent a wonderful ring with a diamond worth four thousand crowns but, conforming to the French custom, a simple one was worn in its stead.

The real bridegroom was lying ill in Florence with the measles. But the bells of the city were ringing nevertheless; they rang for three days.

The protection which Louis XIV's greatness promised to the lesser sovereigns connected with his family, made this alliance to be considered at Florence as the most propitious event which could have occurred to the country.

Everyone in Tuscany was preparing to make the Princess feel at home. The Florentine courtiers were all soliciting Bonsi for costumes in the latest French fashion, and Blanchet, the dancing-master, set forth to teach them the latest Parisian dances.

Marguerite-Louise had tasted of the lotos with Prince Charles of Lorraine. Hunting together, tensely alive and dishevelled, eagerly inhaling the fresh breezes, with a loud hallooing and cracking of whips in their ears, as music to feed their love, they had known the voluptuousness that others find in quieter, more sentimental circumstances. While tasting the lotos, Marguerite-Louise had forgotten her fiancé and her future. She had gone through the formalities of marriage as in a dream. Now she discovered that she was Grand Princess of Tuscany.

Marguerite-Louise was in fact the victim of a political treaty: a girl sacrificed to the combined ambitions of a grand duke, a cardinal, a bishop and a king. Her departure for Florence was delayed because Colbert and her mother could not come to terms about the number of her suite.

On May 6th, 1661, her bed was moved to Fontainebleau. Once that essential piece of furniture was on its way, the Princess had to follow. There was a painful separation from her mother, whom she would never see again; Prince Charles accompanied her to the Abbey of Saint Victor, where he remained in the cloister so as not to see her enter the coach which was to carry her off.

At Fontainebleau, where the Princess was invited to spend four days, she banished all forebodings. The pastimes were full of colour and variety—water fêtes, collations, hunting-parties, comedies and concerts. With the King she was rowed along the newly-lengthened canal. The courtiers followed in barques hung with gay streamers, to the 'marvellously loud and delightful' explosions of petards and harmonies of music. 'Lulli's violins' were the essence of every fête. On the evening of her arrival there was a comedy: Molière perhaps was among the performers. On May 10th, their Majesties entertained her to dinner in the Queen's apartment, and the Queen took her to a ball, where her beauty and grace were greatly admired. 'Never,' wrote Madame de Motteville, 'had the Court of France witnessed festivities of so varied a kind as were seen at Fontainebleau that summer.'

Marguerite-Louise continued her journey full of gloom. Tuscany seemed a world beyond the grave.

'She was accompanied,' says the *Gazette*, 'in the King's name by the dowager Duchesse d'Angoulême; in the name of the Duchesse d'Orléans by the Comte and Comtesse de Belloy, with an escort of his defunct Royal Highness's guard, commanded by the Sieur Devisé, their former adjutant; and by the Bishop of Béziers, on behalf of the Grand Duke of Tuscany.'

She was received at the gate of every town with lofty addresses and flowery compliments, harangued and entertained by the mayor, and served with a succulent repast. To the astonishment of Bonsi, she rode a great part of the way: he had never encountered so hoydenish a girl. She stopped a night at Montargis with her step-sister, the Grande Mademoiselle, and insisted on sharing her bed.

'I was much vexed,' Mademoiselle admitted, with her usual candour, 'as I love my comforts and am not accustomed to sleep with anyone. Marguerite-Louise enjoyed my vexation. She fell asleep before I did, which was fortunate, for while she was dreaming, she leapt at my throat. Had I been asleep she would have strangled me. I did not sleep a wink during the rest of the night, from fear lest the dream should recur.'

She took a roundabout route through Mademoiselle's property at Saint Fargeau, some thirty-five miles from Montargis, and rode the whole way there. The result was that she felt unwell on her arrival, and retired immediately to bed. On the morrow, having slept soundly till midday, she sallied out for a walk in the country, accompanied by two of her sister's maids, a valet and some of the King's pages. Her tastes appeared stranger and stranger to Bonsi, who sat up at night, nervously awaiting her return. Bitterly the Bishop was regretting the rôle he had played in this affair. Perhaps she had taken to flight! Mademoiselle did her utmost to calm and reassure him. At two o'clock in the morning she returned, fresh as a daisy, enchanted with the beauties of the landscape, the freakish groves and thickets in the moonlight. For Marguerite-Louise was a romantic in a 'classical' age. Vividly she rhapsodized, describing her adventures. Her little escort had had to leap over a number of hedges and ditches, and she laughed

19 *(previous page)* Statue of Cardinal Leopoldo de'Medici,
brother of Ferdinando II, by G. B. Foggini. Uffizi

20 *(above)* Prince Mattias de'Medici, brother of Ferdinando II,
by Sustermans. Palazzo Pitti

21 *(opposite)* Cardinal Gian Carlo de'Medici by Sustermans.
Palazzo Pitti

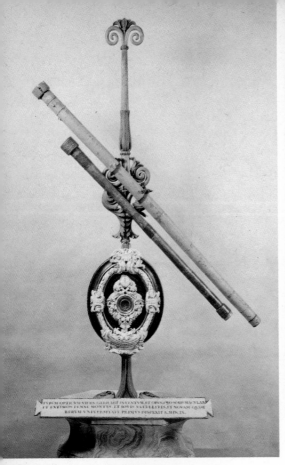

22 *(above left)* Galileo's telescope.
Science Museum

23 *(above right)* Eighteenth-century
brass microscope. Science Museum

24 *(left)* Galileo's astrolabe.
Science Museum

25 *(opposite above)* Instruments for
trepanning the skull.
Science Museum

26 *(opposite below)* Baldassare Lanei's
graphometer. Science Museum

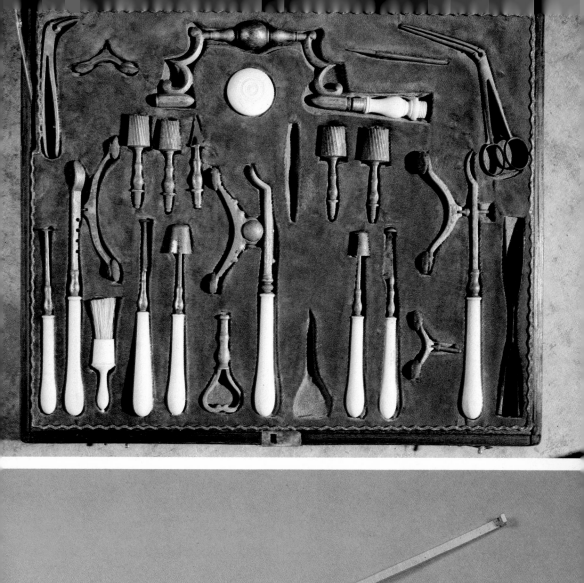
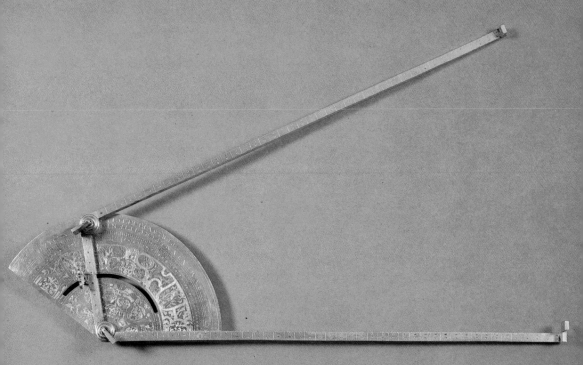

27 *(opposite)* Vittoria della Rovere by Sustermans. Uffizi

28 *(above)* Galileo Galilei by Sustermans. Uffizi

29 Cafaggiolo: a hunting scene, with Cardinal Gian Carlo

30 *(above)* Pratolino: the fountain with the Apennine statue,
etching by Stefano Della Bella.
British Museum, Department of Prints and Drawings

31 *(below)* Pratolino, etching after Zocchi. Museo di Firenze com'era

32 *(opposite)* Pratolino, the gigantic Apennine statue by Giambologna

33 *(above)* Il Trebbio
34 *(opposite)* Fountains in the Boboli Gardens

35 *(above)* Pratolino, lunette by Utens.
Museo di Firenze com'era

36 *(below)* The 'tree-house' at Pratolino,
etching by Stefano Della Bella

37 *(above left)* Ferdinando II
by Sustermans. Palazzo Pitti

38 *(above right)* Prince Francesco
de'Medici, brother of
Ferdinando II, by Sustermans.
Poggio a Caiano

39 *(right)* *The Holy Family*
by Sustermans,
with Vittoria della Rovere as
the Virgin. Palazzo Pitti

40 Cardinal Leopoldo de'Medici by Baciccio. Uffizi

as she told how they had terrified the local peasants who had run away at sight of them, mistaking them for marauders. And so she prattled gaily on till dawn, and a malicious sense of humour lit up in her eyes when the nerve-strained and weary Bishop had begun to doze.

Marguerite-Louise was in no hurry to embrace her husband: at every halting-place she postponed her departure. They were to leave Saint Fargeau on Saturday, but she begged another day's respite. The Bishop dryly remarked that for one so distressed to leave her sister she had already spent a disproportionate amount of time in reconnoitring the neighbourhood alone. On Sunday, as they were setting out for Mass, Mademoiselle was informed that the Prince of Lorraine had arrived. He had sped, all in one stage, directly from Paris. Thrilled and agitated, the Princess tasted the lotos again for one evening, while they dined and played billiards together. But though Prince Charles was in love with her, he was exhausted after his journey; and, alas, was insufficiently ethereal to exist without slumber. He yawned so capaciously that Mademoiselle, who deemed such physical manifestations of fatigue un-gallant, advised him to go to bed.

But the Princess wept all night through, and she was weeping still when the Prince accompanied her next day. He took leave of her at Cosne; and after hearing Mass she parted from Mademoiselle 'with all the tokens of such extreme tenderness that the entire company was moved'. She continued her journey, 'crying aloud for everyone to hear'.

The weather was foul as she approached Marseilles. Some of the heavy luggage-wagons got stuck in the mud. The back wheels were broken, the horses foundered and the Princess complained of a chill. As she entered the town the galleys of Prince Mattias appeared on the crest of the waves, and were saluted by the cannons of Château d'If, near which they cast anchor. The Prince's flotilla consisted of nine ships: three were Florentine, three had been lent by the republic of Genoa and three by the Pope. Prince Mattias, her new uncle-in-law, disembarked incognito to salute her on Cosimo's behalf, 'speaking his own rigmarole, but with considerable eloquence'.

Next day a glittering company emerged from the Italian galleys, and these were also to form the Princess's retinue. Among them, for her special service, were a confessor, two chaplains, four chamberlains, twelve footmen, six equerries, four pages and three dwarfs. Next to those amazing performances in ivory which Prince Mattias had brought from his campaigns in Germany, globes within ornate globes of paper-thin filigree, microscopic achievements as fine as a hair, frigates in full finish of sail, he loved to collect homuncules and watch their ludicrous antics, the more hideous the more prized. Who knows which of these accompanied him to Marseilles: Hippogrifo, Bertoldino or that pearl of deformities, little Bono, whom he had discovered while shooting in the country. 'So small is he that we often lost him in the ditches,' he wrote Gian Carlo, 'eleven years old, with an ugly phiz, nose upturned, thinly scattered tusks for teeth, and an enormous gobbler of fruit. Yesterday he gave us a remarkable proof of this; after consuming about forty cucumbers, a water-melon and thirty figs, he dined in my presence, and then went off with the pages to gorge again.'

Prince Mattias came last in the procession. Marchesa Bentivoglio, the Grand Duchess Vittoria's maid of honour, presented Marguerite-Louise with an agate encircled by precious stones, a fine string of pearls and earrings consisting of five pear-shaped pearls, heaped in an elaborate Florentine salver, on behalf of her mistress.

Then a banquet was given for them, and a comedy composed for the occasion. Finally, before an enormous crowd of spectators, Prince Mattias led Marguerite-Louise upon the high galley which would waft her towards Italy.

Like a great gilded swan it sat upon the sea, ready to carry off its Leda. The sides were sculpted with figures and garlands, glittering with crystal, and the globes and fleurs-de-lis of the Medici. The poop had been transformed into a garden of violets. Within it was upholstered in damask, and carpeted with crimson velvet. It vied with the barge in which the siren Queen of Egypt met and subdued the infatuated Antony.

The first evening they did not sail much farther than the Château d'If, and several bands of musicians serenaded them through the night. The violets poured forth their scent upon a sea so calm that the rows of twenty-eight oars on each side of the galley were in constant motion. The Princess pretended to be indisposed, and rarely left her cabin. It is more likely that she suffered from nostalgia than queasiness, but her misery was none the less acute because of its luxurious setting. Towards the end of the voyage a violent wind arose. The Princess had a gleam of hope: if only it would wreck them! If only a band of corsairs could appear alongside! She recalled the fortunate heroines of novels she had read until her eyes were tired, in the candlelight at Blois. Ah, for a brown-limbed mariner to carry her passive in his arms. . . . But nothing happened: the wind died down, and they scudded over the sparkling waves until, on June 12th, Leghorn was in sight.

IV

The Nuptials of Cosimo III and Marguerite-Louise d'Orléans

It was from Leghorn that the Grand Duke had announced the good news: he had reason to hope for the propagation of his blood, and consequently, for the continuation of his States' prosperity. They were to give the Princess such a welcome that any twinge of homesickness would be utterly dispelled.

The Duchess of Parma, with her children, a train of litters and twenty carriages, went to meet Marguerite-Louise when she disembarked.

A bridge had been set up opposite Pietro Tacca's four Moors in green bronze chained at the feet of Ferdinando I, surrounded by a balustrade, and covered with a rich Turkey carpet, so well adjusted to the galley's level that the Princess was enabled to descend on foot to the roaring of cannon from the fortresses as well as from the nine galleys.

Leghorn was then the leading commercial port of Italy after Genoa. Montesquieu called it 'the masterpiece of the Medicean dynasty'.

The streets through which the bride passed were carpeted with rugs, the houses on either side hung with tapestries and paintings. Four thousand soldiers were lined along the way to the ducal palace. Prince Cosimo was not there to meet her; he had not yet recovered from the measles.

Marguerite-Louise heard Mass; and at night the houses were illuminated by torches, and there were cataracts of fireworks on the piazza. In Italy as in France, it was a similar progression through faintly varied entertainment: only here the flavour was of a coarser, more vivid, more spontaneous character.

On the feast of Corpus Domini, June 15th, 1661, Marguerite-Louise arrived at the Villa Ambrogiana, near Empoli. Here, finally, she met her husband. Even in this moment of moments, Cosimo, a most rigid observer of etiquette, would not bestow upon Marguerite-Louise the first conjugal kiss. Another would have clasped her to his breast, would have uttered perhaps a winning word or two. Cosimo retained his composure. Decorum came before kisses. His measles, contracted, they said, in his zeal to organize ballets on horseback and other diversions for his bride, had only just been cured. A question arose as to how far the young couple should go on their first night together. The Princess's physician declared that although she had once suffered from the measles, a too close contact with her husband at the outset might expose her to it again. Maybe this was unfortunate, but the Princess sighed with relief.

On her way to Florence, at Signa, she met the Grand Duke, accompanied by his brothers, Cardinal Gian Carlo and Prince Leopoldo. Ferdinando, with that courtesy for which he was famous, would not permit her to leave her carriage: 'he greeted her with a thousand marks of respect, joy and friendship, all of which were gracefully reciprocated by the Princess'. She seems to have dissembled her feelings.

For several miles the roads had been watered to keep down the heavy white dust. Marguerite-Louise entered her future capital by night, quietly; all the pomps and ceremonies were reserved for her official entry some days later.

What would you give, after a burning, breathless day in June, winding between hills like prehistoric animals that have been petrified, to come upon Florence thus, after sunset, in the seventeenth century. The gates of the city are opened for you and your equipage, and then are fastened with a resounding clang: you are shut in from puniness, vulgarity. You pass ere long between those lofty palaces, the shrillness of cicadas yet in your ears, your head heavy with odours of aromatic herbs, and the sudden silence and coolness of the streets refresh you as never before: you are roused from your trance—the trance of a lifetime. Here, at last, is the vindication of man: the solid beauty man alone has made: here in these truly Tuscan towers, these leonine façades of rough-hewn stone, bold testimonies of clearness and cleanliness in the starlight.

The Princess entered by the Boboli Gardens, which lie stretched out on the hillside behind the Pitti Palace. The fountains were playing on the terraces of bay and myrtle, and in the alleys white statues of fauns poured water into old sarcophagi; rippling murmurs through the cypress groves deliciously fanned the ear. Was it laughter, music, a serenade? But the Princess never heard them. She was full of dark forebodings, and the stress of accumulated strangeness.

The Grand Duke escorted her to an apartment which, for all her accustomed nonchalance, she found magnificent. She was not seen of the people. Nor did she leave the palace during the next two days. Her time was employed in visiting the galleries, and inspecting Ferdinando's treasures: Hannibal's headpiece, weighing but seven pounds, and yet musket-proof; Charlemagne's sword; the King of China's vest, and other wonders of the Grand Duke's armoury; and the treasures of the Tribuna to follow: the Florentine diamond, weighing a hundred and forty and a half carats, which was then the largest in Europe.[1]

Her French ladies-in-waiting were quite astonished, for 'the Florentines had always been described to them as people devoid of taste'.

The bride and bridegroom made their solemn entry on June 20th, 1661. Marguerite-Louise was received with a splendour exceeding anything Italy had seen for ages. Part of the city had been pulled down to

---

[1] 'This diamond,' wrote Keysler in his *Travels* (1756–1757), 'was the largest in Europe until Mr Pitt, an English gentleman, brought from the East Indies a diamond which exceeded it, which was sold to the Regent of France, and was the most costly and superb jewel belonging to that crown. The sparks which fell from it in cutting, produced Mr Pitt six thousand pounds sterling, and when cut, besides its extraordinary weight of a hundred and forty-four carats, was of a finer water than any diamond that could be produced: whereas the Florentine diamond is of a yellowish water. The Grand Duke was said to have bought his of a Jesuit for seventy-five thousand *scudi* (about 18,750 *l.*); but the father had an exorbitant profit, having given only a single *paolo* (about 7d. sterling) for it on the Piazza Navona, where it was offered for sale as a bit of crystal.' N. P. Willis, on the other hand, who saw it in 1833, writes in his *Pencillings by the Way*: 'It was lost by a duke of Burgundy upon the battlefield of Granson, found by a soldier, who parted with it for five florins, sold again, and found its way at last into the royal treasury of Florence, whence it was brought to Vienna. Its weight is one hundred and thirty-nine and a half carats, and it is estimated at one million forty-three thousand three hundred and thirty-four florins. It looks like a lump of light. Enormous diamonds surround it, but it hangs among them like Hesperus among the stars.' . . . Among all the massive plate curiously chased, the services of gold, the gem-hilted swords, the dishes wrought of solid integral agates, the Florentine diamond was all that Willis coveted: 'the beauty of the diamond was royal. It needed no imagination to feel its value. A savage would pick it up in a desert for a star dropped out of the sky.'

make a fine avenue, and some of the city walls, for the opening of a new door, to be called the Gate of Orléans; the vast base of a column in the Piazza San Marco was removed to clear the way, and the main streets were paved anew. Everywhere porticoes and triumphal arches were raised. 'An imitation theatre in rustic architecture' was erected in Piazza San Gallo with a spacious loggia or open gallery beside it, covered with crimson velvet, and the great awning likewise, to shelter them from the sun. This was where Cosimo and Marguerite-Louise would be crowned, at an altar piled with branching candelabra. Effigies of the great kings of France and symbolical figures with eulogistic mottoes postured on either side of the avenue.

At seven o'clock in the morning, the Princess, accompanied by Mattias, was taken in an ordinary carriage to the Duke of Salviati's villa on the hill of Montughi. There she changed into the embroidered gown of silver cloth and lace head-dress she would wear during the ceremony. Over the gown was sewn 'a chain of diamonds, and forty tapering pearls hanging between them, the whole attached to the shoulders by two pearls the size of a small pigeon's egg.'

She did not leave the Villa Salviati till five o'clock in the afternoon, with a vast retinue. At about thirty steps from the theatre in Piazza San Gallo, Prince Cosimo invited her to leave her carriage. He took her right hand while Mattias took her left, and led her to the altar, before which she knelt on a cushion. The Archbishop of Siena gave her the crucifix to kiss. The Grand Duke then approached, and after receiving the ducal crown from the Archbishop's hands, placed it on the Princess's head. Anon it was replaced by a lighter coronet of pearls, diamonds and rubies. Meanwhile the bells were ringing, the eternal bells of all the Florentine churches, so many sturdy survivors of old republican days; and the cannon were roaring from the fortresses. As the young Princess sat under a dais of silver and gold, the Florentine clergy filed before her to the strains of music.

The procession to the Duomo began. First the twelve macebearers of the Senate in vermilion, followed by a crowd of pages in the Grand Duke's livery. Then the masters of the ceremony, the Marquesses Pietro Corsini and Giovan Vincenzio Salviati, each with twenty pages, some in black velvet and sky-blue, others in green and gold. There were sixteen prelates in all: thirteen bishops and three archbishops in purple and gold, riding two by two, surrounded by heralds and grooms.

The Grand Duke's private German guard marched behind them; then Princes Mattias and Leopoldo with retinue in two tones of scarlet; then Cosimo. The Grand Prince wore black; it served as a finer setting for the gems on his baldric and sword, and on the sleeves of his brocaded doublet. Even his gold spurs were studded with them. He was mounted on a superb horse, and followed by a snow-white palfrey. A hundred footmen surrounded him in scarlet, the colour of the Medici. The Princess followed in an open white-and-silver litter drawn by white mules caparisoned in silver and mounted by two lovely children dressed in white brocade embroidered with gold flowers, white feathers flowing from their caps. Thirty-two young men, selected from the noblest Florentine families, carried the heavy baldachin, an affair of gold cloth fringed with pearls, over her head. The Duchesse d'Angoulême and Comtesse de Belloy followed in a carriage embossed with the arms of France and Tuscany: the fleurs-de-lis in topazes, the balls of the Medici in rubies on a lapis lazuli ground. The retinue came to an end with three hundred coaches filled with nobility.

The Bishop of Fiesole stood waiting for the Prince and Princess at the Cathedral entrance, to sprinkle them with holy water. Then Cosimo led Marguerite-Louise by the hand to the altar, in a haze of gold, and twelve choirs accompanied by musical instruments intoned the *Te Deum*. The Bishop invoked every blessing on the pair, and the moving style of his oratory brought a responsive tear to every eye. When the young apprentices to matrimony returned to the palace 'the cannon of the citadel redoubled its thunder, and spread the news throughout Florence. This was accompanied by continual cheers from the people and other manifestations of extraordinary joy.'

Hoyden though she was, it took Marguerite-Louise a whole day to recover from her fatigue. With one thing and another they had succeeded in tiring her out by June 22nd, on the eve of which, according to the *Gazette*, after a magnificent supper, Marguerite-Louise and Cosimo were led to their chamber, where the Grand Duchess handed the Princess her nightgown. Ferdinando had prepared a nuptial-bed for them whose posts were of silver, 'enamelled in different parts, and embellished with various coloured gems, polished, its value excessive'.

There was little of ecstasy, however, in this consummation. The Princess found her consort awkward and uninteresting. And he very soon grew tired, in excuse of which it was said that the measles had sapped his strength. She did not have to submit to his caresses often. For, on July 18th, Bonsi wrote to Fouquet: 'The Prince has only couched with her three times, and every time he does not go he sends a valet to tell Madame not to await him. The French ladies and serving-women are quite surprised by these little compliments. . . . They try to divert her, but are much embarrassed because she is always sad, and the Prince and Princess never speak together. Madame finds the life here very strange. . . .' Cosimo meted out his endearments at rare intervals, with clinical exactitude. And behold, the bride was unhappy!

The first of a long and bitter series of scenes occurred on the second night they slept together. Not content with her wonderful wedding gifts, Marguerite-Louise tried to force her husband to give her all the crown jewels. (She was already free to use them in the daily adornment of her person.) Cosimo answered with commendable modesty and prudence that he had no right to dispose of them, since they must be preserved for his successors: they did not truly belong to him. This roused her dormant anger, and she turned upon him with a flood of remonstrance. Amongst other things she told him that she would have been more happily married in the most miserable hut in France than in the Court of Tuscany. Since she had not succeeded in cajoling the crown jewels out of him, she purloined a considerable quantity, which she disposed of to her French attendants, and helped them to escape with the booty. They were overtaken, however, and the jewels recovered, but 'strict measures were rendered necessary to watch over her conduct'. We can judge for ourselves if such incidents were calculated to cure the Prince's neurasthenia.

V

Wedding Festivities – St John the Baptist's Day
– 'Il Mondo Festeggiante' – 'Ercole in Tebe'

The burning of the temple of Ephesus was re-enacted vividly by fireworks over the bridge of Santa Trinità; and Marguerite-Louise watched them from the Corsini Palace, the rockets bursting into clear blue stars; there were races in the thoroughfares, banquets and balls in the Palazzo Vecchio. At one of the latter a French lackey inadvertently jostled a Florentine noble. The Italian, 'to teach him that such liberties were not allowed in Tuscany, clapped him a violent fisticuff in the face, and several others deemed it their duty to follow his example'. Marguerite-Louise was much distressed by this incident.

That open familiarity and ease of manner permitted in France was not tolerated in Florence, where gallantry was nigh invisible: a sigh, a fallen glove, a furtive glance among the most audacious, and even these could end in tragedy. Although her husband hated dancing, Marguerite-Louise intended to remedy this state of affairs.

The races, however, could not be compared with anything in France. They took place regularly in Florence on June 24th, the festival of St John the Baptist, patron of the city. There was the Roman chariot-race on the Piazza Santa Maria Novella and the race of barbs in the Via Maggio. Sir John Reresby, among other travellers, saw and described them. Of the former he wrote: 'about forty yards distant (in the Piazza) are erected two posts, from one of which five or six chariots, according to the number of those that run, start at sound of trumpet, and being to run thrice round to win, he therefore that has driven his course, and first comes to the post whence he started, gains the prize, valued at thirty crowns (an easy price for a man's life): the entangling of the chariots one with another, either to gain ground, or at the turn, frequently overturning them, where, if a driver escape a mischief by the fall, he seldom doth being driven over by the following chariots'.

74

The race of barbs on the following afternoon was run from Porta al Prato to Porta alla Croce, with a rich banner,[1] which had been blessed in the Baptistry, as prize. The Medici witnessed the spectacle from a terrace at the entrance to the Prato. 'The course,' wrote Reresby, 'is performed by barbs, which run without any one upon them, only little iron balls, full of pricks, which, fastened to their backs by a girth, fall down on each side by strings; these, by their motion rising and falling, do the office of spurs.' They covered the ground in about seven minutes, and signals of gunpowder were sent off from the top of Porta alla Croce and the cupola of the Duomo to announce the winner. The Grand Duke then wrote the winner's name on tablets, which he flung to the crowd.

The other ceremonies for St John the Baptist's day were no less novel to Marguerite-Louise—the processions of canons from the Cathedral along the carpeted streets, in their most splendid vestments, bearing the sacred relics: an elbow of St Andrew the Apostle, a nail of the Cross, a thorn from the Crown and divers other fragments of holiness, among which the thumb of St John the Baptist probably occupied the place of honour. They were accompanied not only by 'extraordinary music', but also by citizens impersonating angels and saints. There was a general *Offerta*, or offering of tapers, to the spiritual protector of the town. That of the gentlemen of the Mint was most remarkable: an immense torch on a chariot drawn by oxen. The chariot was forty-three feet high, divided into four compartments 'diminishing in size as they ascended to the skies'. In the niches of the lowest compartment four human beings were placed instead of statues, ecclesiastically garbed, with a child in their midst to represent the infant Baptist. A boy took the rôle of St Stephen in a corresponding niche on the other side. Four youths in lily-white, bearing the Prince's coat of arms on one side and the Mint's on the other, stood in the niches of the second compartment. Later they were replaced by wooden virtues. The third was adorned by four harpies; the fourth with grand-ducal escutcheons. A live statue of St John stood on the summit. He stood

[1] A *palio* of crimson velvet lined with grey miniver and trimmed with ermine and a fringe of silk and gold. It was placed on a triumphal car, of which the lions were so realistically carven as to seem almost alive. This car was drawn by two horses with damask coverings on which the arms of the Medici were embroidered in massy gold.

there every year on this festival, fastened by a leather belt to an iron bar (until 1748, when the Medici were extinct). This impersonator of St John was clad with tiger-skins, his arms and legs bare, a nimbus on his head, and in his hands a long cross, which was tied to the chariot. He earned ten francs and a breakfast for this ordeal. The chariot halted a few minutes and he received a basket, containing a hoop-shaped loaf, two bottles of red and white wine, and some cakes, from a second-storey window. He slung the roll on his arm, and after eating and drinking his fill, threw the remnants and empty wine-flasks to the people below.

Later in the day came the *Festa degli Omaggi*.[1] The Grand Duke sat on a raised platform before the Palazzo Vecchio, and 'received homage and fealty from such as hold countries, forts or castles of him, within his dominions, as also other sorts of tenures, which was performed by their passing severally before him on horseback, vailing (or lowering in token of respect) a banner they carried, being summoned, *viratim*, by the herald'. The piazza seemed a forest of pennons and revolving towers, edifices of wood, cardboard and wax—brilliantly painted and gilded symbols of the tribute paid by the towns which were subject to Florence.

From the spectacular point of view Marguerite-Louise's marriage could not have been better timed.

On July 1st the most memorable of all ballets on horseback, *Il Mondo Festeggiante* ('The World in Festivity'), was given in the vast amphitheatre of the Boboli Gardens, which, with the new tiers of seats along its walls, contained a double number of spectators—about twenty thousand. High pyramids dotted all over with lamps surrounded the amphitheatre at intervals, converting night into a shimmering day.

Here is a summary of that remarkable performance: A curtain was drawn by invisible hands opposite the palace, and between improvised rocks and precipices, a giant heavily advanced, bowed under an enormous sphere. It was Atlas, bearing the world's orb on his nape. Drawn by forces cleverly concealed, he stalked the arena. He halted in the centre, and with a thundering voice announced that Hercules, followed by Phoebus and Cynthia (Sun and Moon), had come down from

[1] Instituted in 1300, and celebrated every year until 1808.

the sky for Cosimo's wedding. Whereupon the sphere cracked like a vast ostrich egg, and all in a few minutes the colossus had changed into the *Atlas* Mountain, with four pretty girls poised on the summit: Europe, America, Asia and Africa; some glad because of the wedding, and others dejected. A noise of martial trumpets then burst upon the tympanum, and echoed along the distant avenues and grottoes. Prince Cosimo rode on to the scene (under the borrowed plumes of Hercules), his palfrey covered with gems, followed by two hundred soldiers in rose-coloured liveries. Then came the Knights of Europe, fifty strong, on foot, holding torches: these were the well-drilled vanguard of the Sun. Phoebus arrived on a glittering chariot, guided by Day and surrounded by Hours. The Knights of America followed. Then Cynthia's car, with the Knights of Asia before it, and those of Africa behind. Cynthia sat enthroned in a white dress, escorted by the twelve nocturnal hours. Her chariot was drawn by four snowy horses, guided by Night, with Slumber marching ahead.

All these drew up in a circle: Prince Cosimo in their midst, a plump and placid cynosure. Meanwhile, the four maids of the mountain, emboldened by the presence of warriors, were expressing their conflicting emotions: finally they quarrelled and declared war on each other. Europe and America invoked the aid of Phoebus: Asia and Africa that of Cynthia. The chariots rumbled off; two camps were formed without more ado, and the contest began. Pistols were fired, there was a clash of swords and, among them all—who dares to doubt it?—Prince Cosimo performed prodigies of valour.

Then from the firmament a mighty thunderclap resounded. A lull, and Jove pronounced: let there be peace! The two squadrons settled into figures of half-moons, and stood by to contemplate the Father of the Gods, descending by a contrivance of clouds. When this contrivance touched the ground, they entered it and disappeared. A chariot finer than the others had arrived for Jove. It was guided by Fate, Pallas, Mars, Eternity, Mercury and a heterogeneous assemblage of other deities, abstractions and knights—to represent the Medicean stars (the Satellites of Jupiter, discovered by Galileo) and the signs of the Zodiac, who all paid honour to Jove.

Jove informed Cynthia that the offspring of the Medici would increase—not to the detriment of Africa and Asia, but to their great advantage, because they would diffuse the Catholic Faith in those far-distant regions. After songs of jubilation from the gods, the chariots of the Sun and Moon came together: Phoebus and Cynthia sat beside each other, inviting the warriors to celebrate the nuptials with merry dances. A paean then arose from a hundred voices, accompanied by a great number of instruments. The ballet on horseback began: a quadrille, in the various figures of which the Prince displayed as much grace as he had done valour in the previous battle-scene.

Il Mondo Festeggiante was thus a series of phantasmagorical *tableaux*, culminating with a tournament: a parade of costumes, horses and glittering armour, interspersed with musical choruses and madrigals. Many arts contributed and merged, as in the Russian ballets of Diaghileff, but on an infinitely more spectacular scale.

This was by no means the last of the festivities. In the theatre of the *Immobili*—that of the Via della Pergola under Cardinal Gian Carlo's patronage—there had been continuous rehearsals for a musical drama, entitled 'Hercules in Thebes'. It was given on July 12th; Jacopo Melani composed the music, and like 'The World in Festivity', the libretto was written by Giovanni Andrea Moneglia, one of the Grand Duke's physicians. But the theatre was small; its capacity for accommodation was limited, so that only nobles and foreigners were admitted. The action was adapted to the mythological taste of the period. Jove prophesies, for instance, as he flies down from clouds of pink and gold, that in centuries to come Cosimo and Marguerite-Louise will have enriched the world with a regiment of heroes. Radiant personifications of Glory and Virtue, seated on separate clouds, sing praises of the bride and bridegroom. In all baroque performances one should note the important rôle of the cloud. It was the wonder and terror of all spectators, helping saints, gods, angels to appear on perilous heights, dizzily poised above the audience. It was the *pièce de résistance* in the absence of which a festival would have been foredoomed to failure. Was not a cloud, moreover, responsible for the first solo accompanied by an orchestra?

The legend of this returns to the age of Cosimo I. His daughter Virginia was to marry Don Cesare d'Este in the Church of Santo Spirito, and he commissioned Buontalenti to invent a machine appropriate for the occasion. This was a vast cloud, suspended from the roof behind the high altar. Within it several singers and musicians, armed with a harp, a guitar, two lyres of different sizes, a psaltery, a violin, a triangle and a bass viol, were cleverly concealed. Caccini, a famous Roman singer and composer, climbed into it among them. As soon as the bride advanced with her retinue, the musicians began to melodize in the machine. At this moment, either because the weight of its occupants strained unduly upon the suspensory cords or the engineers were over-hasty in their excitement, the cloud precipitously descended and opened—so that the audience could catch a glimpse of the musicians, who nervously continued to play, with more resolution than melody. But the sudden violence of the descent had paralysed the singers. Their notes had flown as prematurely as the cloud had opened. Caccini alone, accompanied by an unsteady sort of music, sang on with equanimity. The effect was magnificent, the audience was enraptured. Opera is supposed to have originated with this accident, occasioned by an unruly cloud, in 1586.[1]

The cloud was a great factor of 'Hercules in Thebes'. After an amazing prologue, where Neptune arrived on a chariot drawn by swimming horses, and Pluto on a dragon between tongues of flame (with globes and *nuvole* revolving throughout), five scenes continued the bewildering tradition. Hercules descended to Avernus to liberate Theseus. During his absence Lico, his friend, had vainly attempted to seduce his wife and usurp his kingdom: on his return there was a wonderful 'feigned battle' between Lico's and Hercules's militia. Hercules and his companion Alcestes were followed in their adventures by a hunchbacked servant who constantly interrupted their most eloquent dialogue. His buffoonery and cowardice when they reached the Styx provided the comic relief. The performance ended by the seashore, in the gardens of Venus, with cupids weaving dances in the air, nymphs along the shore and gardeners among the flowers.

We may, with the aid of Stefano della Bella's engravings, conjure some of them dimly, the novel sensations of that world, the splendour

---

[1] The chronicles of the period bear witness to the astonishing success it obtained; also they go some way to prove that what was reported merely as a 'lucky accident' was more probably a daring ruse of Caccini's, to test the effect of a solo on a large and distinguished audience. History and legend coincide in relating that Caccini, alluding to it, would often repeat the words of his song 'Oh happy day!' so that he was nicknamed *Benedetto Giorno* to the day of his death.

of its costumes and stage effects. 'Hercules in Thebes' was extrava-
gantly praised; and enjoyed a very real success. Besides the professional
actors many noble amateurs took part in the battle-scene, and some
transformed themselves into nymphs and cupids for the dances. The
then famous composer of *Orontea*, Abate Cesti, was among the
singers.

'The World in Festivity' died with the celebrations which gave it
birth. But 'Hercules in Thebes' survived under many forms, and was
given in Venice, Rome and Naples. The myth served as an agreeable
pretext to flatter princes far from Herculean, and was adaptable to
topical requirements. In August Florence became tranquil again; its
foreign visitors departed, its richer inhabitants sought the countryside.
Marguerite-Louise was taken to see the pleasure-houses and gardens of
her new kinsfolk, such as Poggio Imperiale, Poggio a Caiano, Pratolino and Castello.

The aquatic surprises at Pratolino delighted her, the mysterious
fountains and hidden jets of water, by whose machinations a visitor
would unexpectedly be soused. Strangers were generally caught near
what was known as Cupid's grotto. For the trick to 'come off' they
had to be tired before reaching it, so that a bench would tempt them to
sit down and rest without suspicion. As soon as they relaxed the seat
sank under the strain of their bodies, out flew the water, and they were
drenched from top to toe. Many of these gardens have perished: nothing is left of those wonders at Pratolino which excited the admiration
of Sir Henry Wotton, Montaigne and other discerning travellers, save
Giovanni da Bologna's colossus of the Apennines.

As the favourite residence of Bianca Cappello it was extolled by
Tasso.[1] Marguerite-Louise went there sixteen years after Evelyn (1645),
whose description is the most concise:

'The house is a square of four pavilions, with a fair platform about
it, balustred with stone, situate in a large meadow, ascending like an
amphitheatre, having at the bottom a huge rock, with water running in
a small channel, like a cascade; on the other side are the gardens. The
whole place seems consecrated to pleasure and summer retirement.
The inside of the Palace may compare with any in Italy for furniture of
tapestry, beds, etc., and the gardens are delicious, and full of fountains.

[1] *Rime*, 360, t. II.

In the grove sits Pan feeding his flock, the water making a melodious sound through his pipe; and a Hercules whose club yields a shower of water, which, falling into a great shell, has a naked woman riding on the backs of dolphins. In another grotto is Vulcan and his family, the walls richly composed of corals, shells, copper, and marble figures with the hunting of several beasts, moving by the force of water. Here, having been well washed for our curiosity, we went down a large walk, at the sides whereof several slender streams of water gush out of pipes concealed underneath, that interchangeably fall into each other's channels, making a lofty and perfect arch, so that a man on horseback may ride under it, and not receive one drop of wet. This canopy, or arch of water, I thought one of the most surprising magnificences I had ever seen, and very refreshing in the heat of the summer. At the end of this very long walk stands a woman in white marble, in posture of a laundress wringing water out of a piece of linen, very naturally formed, into a vast laver, the work and invention of M. Angelo Buonarotti. Hence, we ascended Mount Parnassus, where the Muses played to us on hydraulic organs. Near this is a great aviary. All these waters came from the rock in the garden, on which is the statue of a giant representing the Apennines, at the foot of which stands this villa. Last of all we came to the labyrinth, in which a huge coloss of Jupiter throws out a stream over the garden. This is fifty feet in height, having in his body a square chamber, his eyes and mouth serving for windows and door'.[1]

There were a thousand new and necessary introductions. There was the landscape itself, so different, with its minaret cypresses, sloping vineyards and misty olive-groves, from the long lines of pale elms bending beneath French breezes, the relatively drab foliage and flat cornfields near Blois, or even Paris. Near Florence the landscape seemed consecrated, entrenched, enclosed, subsidiary to man. It would take time to become familiar with such surroundings, and with such dry cicada-shrill heat, after the moister air of more northern summers.

The marriage expenses, including the gifts, amounted to five hundred thousand crowns. The Grand Duke allowed Marguerite-Louise an annual income of thirty thousand francs for clothing and pin-money. And if she had failed to extract the crown jewels from Cosimo, remember she had received:

[1] *The Diary of John Evelyn*, p. 114. The Globe Edition.

A string most marvellously pearl'd:
These pearls indeed should show their pride
Daily to sit upon and ride
The fairest neck in all the world.
Two glistering diamonds of such girth
Almost a county they are worth.
Five pearls all equal, very rare,
Each moulded like a perfect pear,
To deck each lovely curling ear. . . .

with other ornaments which Jean Loret has left unrhymed, un-chronicled.

Louis XIV professed himself delighted with all these arrangements; he wrote to the Grand Duke on July 20th, 1661, addressing him as 'cousin', and thanking him with a full heart.

Ten days later (July 30th) the Venetian ambassador was writing: 'During the wedding festivities the young Princess, in wishing to display her royal grandeur and generosity, has given the Grand Duke and other Princes of this house much cause for displeasure. For they discovered that she has despoiled herself of many precious objects for her personal use and necessity to bestow them upon her ladies and others who have accompanied her from France. The Grand Duchess was very aggrieved about it, and the Grand Duke resented it so deeply that friction and misunderstanding have arisen between them, which persevere. The Prince, her husband, is likewise affected, as he takes great exception to the freedom of his wife's behaviour, which, if customary in France, is very unusual in Italy, as the Princess had previously been warned. They have had several other vexations because of the excessive licence of her household, so that the Princes have been obliged to make her promptly dismiss almost everyone, providing her in the meantime with Florentine subjects, and only those of her French servants who appear the most moderate are suffered to remain.'

On her departure from Paris, Louis XIV had presented her with a silver table-set of great value, with the Medici coat of arms engraved above the lilies thereon. The Grand Duke was disgusted to learn that the Princess had given this to Madame du Belloy before she reached Marseilles, and wrote to France in the hope of recovering it.

The bride refused to appear at a banquet of Cardinal Gian Carlo's because she objected to giving her hand to the Duchess of Innsbruck, saying that she had received no instruction to do so in the memorandum the King had given her before she left France. Afterwards the Grand Duke persuaded her to condescend, on condition that His Majesty were duly informed about it. These dissonances aroused much comment, but it was generally believed that the Princess would settle down to obey her elders, because her character was reputed to be charming and her good nature extreme.

VI

*Cosimo's Domestic Troubles Begin — Death of Cardinal Gian Carlo
— Birth of Prince Ferdinando (1663)*

After the festivities the Court reverted to its habitual slow-moving routine, as if dragged through time by those placid white oxen one meets on the roads of Tuscany. Foreign travellers of that period generally agree with Maximilian Misson. 'Though Florence,' he wrote, 'is certainly one of the finest cities in the world, and has the advantage of a most delicious situation, yet it must appear a very sad and melancholy place to those who are accustomed to enjoy the pleasures of society. Sir D., who, you know, has resided here for several years, is not able to express his uneasiness under the intolerable constraint and eternal ceremonies of this place, and particularly exclaims against the invisibility of the beautiful sex; and indeed these customs can never be endured by any but such as are accustomed to 'em from their infancy.'

Ferdinando turned to his scientific pastimes; Cosimo to his devotions; while Vittoria dabbled in theology. Her husband's experiments had filled the Grand Duchess with morbid apprehensions: she spent more time with priests and money on charitable institutions. Science for such a narrow mind was tantamount to necromancy.

Wedlock did not alter Cosimo. Princess Sophia of Hanover wrote, in 1664: 'He sleeps with his wife but once a week, and then under supervision of a doctor, who has him taken out of bed lest he should impair his health by staying there overlong.'

From all external appearance, however, we learn that in his twenty-third year Cosimo was vigorous, robust and a voracious eater. His manner was reserved and serious, though benign and discursive in audience, always governing his speech with Christian maxims and fear of God. He was appalled by the Duke of Mantua's death,[1] 'which, having occurred in the midst of lascivious intercourse, his Highness

---

[1] Carlo II Gonzaga, who died on September 15th, 1665.

84

spoke of with horror'. His austerity allowed him little indulgence for others: he was angered by the delights outside the narrow boundary of his comprehension. 'Verily,' we read, 'the Prince's continence continues to be remarkable, unlike the licentious customs of this clime. But most of the young men of Florence seem to conceive aversion rather than admiration for this quality, and are amazed that at such a florid age he should not evince more passion for his consort. His talents are estimable. He can converse with intelligence on all matters of government, of war, and even of distant lands.

'The most serene spouse, moreover, is full of frolic. She takes pleasure only in singing, dancing and splendid entertainments.' Rarely were two characters, already contrasted by youthful environment and education, less fitted to agree. Everything conspired against their happiness.

On August 27th (1661) the Venetian ambassador writes: 'The Princess's major-domo, a French gentleman, has been compelled by the Grand Duke's order to enter a carriage unexpectedly, without being given time to change his clothes, and, escorted to Leghorn by several armed men on horseback, was put under the governor's custody for having spoken ill of this house, and also on some other charge. Although he insisted that he should first be allowed to speak to his mistress, they would not give him leave, but severely commanded him never again to set foot in these parts; he was to proceed without delay to France or anywhere else he chose. The Princess is said to have been much upset by this news, although she prudently feigns indifference, as in other circumstances equally distressing.'

Cosimo was not the man to inspire passion. And Marguerite-Louise was no cold cloister-lily: she had encountered her ideal of virile beauty in Prince Charles of Lorraine. Her husband could not play the part of an ardent lover. There was nothing impetuous about his wooing: his caresses were clumsy. He was fleshly without being sensual.

It was Ferdinando, rather than Cosimo, who made efforts to mould Marguerite-Louise's new existence to her liking, to win her affection, and wean her thoughts from Versailles. The great entertainments were followed by all the intimate diversions an Italian *villeggiatura* could offer. But Marguerite-Louise failed to enjoy these domestic revels, and showed it; she was continually comparing them with those at home. The sensations of novelty soon died; nothing could make her forget the fact that she was not in France, and this was the eternal burden of her complaint.

Cosimo was rather to be pitied. He could neither change his temperament and physique, nor transmute Florence into Fontainebleau. When Marguerite-Louise was asked if Florence pleased her, she deliberately answered: 'I should like it much better in France.'

She clung to her native customs, however insignificant. She would never change the signet with which she used to seal her letters as a girl. It was only after prolonged argument that she would dress her pages in the Italian fashion.

Her extravagance was alarming. For instance, the Grand Duke sent her a merchant with a variety of beautiful tissues from which he proposed that she should make a selection. But the Princess liked them equally, and kept them all.

Her household expenses were inconceivable to Ferdinando—an ever-rising tide. More material was required for her dresses than for those of any other woman in his family. Her cook consumed more meat and poultry in a day than his in ten.

Her conduct shocked the Florentines. They thought it immodest to allow lackeys in her room at all hours of the day. They criticized her familiar manner. Mutual misunderstanding made her conscious of her isolation. Doubtless her lack of enthusiasm when they tried to cheer her was dampening. At last it wore out their patience, and they left her almost entirely to her French ladies-in-waiting, who were as homesick and discontented as she was. They ridiculed all that was new to them, and this constant rain of ridicule vitiated her outlook. The kindly and tactful Duchesse d'Angoulême had left in December, and there was nobody to take her place.

'Yesterday,' writes Bonsi to Fouquet, 'I heard a humorous thing. The young Duchess is supremely bored, which they consider very strange here, as they do not know she is enamoured of the young Prince of Lorraine.' . . . In the midst of this boredom Prince Charles appeared, like a visiting angel. The uncle to whom he was heir had sold his states to Louis XIV; Prince Charles had protested and in consequence had been given four days to leave France.

The rumour of his tenderness for Marguerite-Louise had never reached Florence. *En passant* one must remark that Bonsi was a peculiar ambassador: secretive with the Grand Duke, and garrulous with strangers.

The Princess sent her equerry to meet Prince Charles, and he was given a distinguished reception at the Pitti.

The Prince expanded under this hospitality, and told Ferdinando and Cosimo his many troubles, projects and ambitions. They expressed their sympathy and polite encouragement. He had several private interviews with Marguerite-Louise. We may suppose that she opened her heart to him, told him of her sorrows; of the suffocating dullness of the Florentine Court; of her intense repugnance to her husband. They commiserated with each other and the bond between them was consolidated.

The visit of Prince Charles was responsible for Marguerite-Louise's subsequent behaviour: her every thought, her every action, became diverted into a single channel: she would leave Tuscany, by hook or by crook, before she died. It might take her years of scheming to accomplish; she regarded Florence as a prison, and the Medici as her gaolers.

When Prince Charles left her she was disconsolate. Immediately there was an interchange of ardent letters between them. Amongst other effusions Prince Charles sent her 'verses upon his absence', which, according to Bonsi, were 'the most quaint and laughable things in the world'. These happened to be intercepted. No storm followed, only a painful scrutiny. The Grand Duke and Cosimo realized that they could not trust this Princess. They spied on her and her ladies-in-waiting. They went so far as to open her mother's letters. Since their tone was not found satisfactory, Marguerite-Louise was informed that her mother was in good health, but that she was forbidden to communicate with her.

The Princess complained to Louis XIV, whose answer was courteous and non-committal. Cosimo might redouble his attentions; she continued to 'play the devil in a hundred ways'. The Grand Duke was no more successful than Cosimo in his efforts to propitiate her, while the Grand Duchess, who could have made matters easier, 'seemed pleased only in criticizing her French sprightliness, and bringing it to the standard of Italian decorum'. The older sneered at the younger woman, at her French clothes and French frivolity. But they were more than evenly matched. The younger woman had a sarcastic wit. She hinted that her mother-in-law had ulterior motives in 'protecting' so many monks and priests, that she wished to make up for regretted years of chastity. The Grand Duchess took advantage of the Princess's flightiness to irritate both Cosimo and Ferdinando against her.

In January, 1663, Cardinal Gian Carlo died of apoplexy. His death came as an ill-concealed relief to Ferdinando, for doubtless his high blood-pressure had been responsible for increasingly dangerous outbursts of violence. When the Cardinal interfered with the law, Ferdinando closed an eye. To quote from a contemporary chronicler:

'A notoriously cruel assassin was finally captured and imprisoned in the Bargello, and he was sentenced to be hung, drawn and quartered on the following Saturday. His wife, a woman of great beauty, had tried to defend him with distinguished advocates and attorneys, after herself pleading in vain for him. But nothing more could be done: the criminal was condemned.

'Somebody then suggested that she should beg an audience of Cardinal Gian Carlo, who perchance might interest himself in her favour. The Cardinal was immediately fascinated by her; it was Thursday, and that same evening they slept together. On Friday morning His Eminence summoned the Sheriff, and inquired what prisoners he had. The Sheriff enumerated them, and when he came to the murderer in question, the Cardinal told him to have the man conveyed to his presence forthwith, because he wished him to be set at liberty. The Sheriff replied that the man was a most notorious assassin condemned to be executed on the morrow; all Florence knew it and was praying for the suffrage of his soul.

'"Enough!" said the Cardinal, "bring him here at once, or your own head will stand bail for him." The Sheriff went in trepidation to the Grand Duke Ferdinando, and apprised him of what had just occurred. For a while the Grand Duke stood in suspense, and then he told him to "obey the Cardinal, since he is my brother".'

Gout might also have been responsible for Gian Carlo's truculence. Once he stumbled and fell on descending from the Grand Duke's carriage. Ferdinando helped him to rise, inquiring if he had hurt himself. When he said no, the Grand Duke remarked: 'Your Eminence has had a great piece of good luck.' The Cardinal turned and answered roughly: 'Your Highness had a great piece of good luck when he was born before I was.'

He had wrecked his health, not only by fast living, but because he liked everything iced, his food, his wine and even his bed. The doctors warned him to change his habits if he wished to survive. Whereupon the Cardinal asked them how many years they gave him to live if he did so. They answered that having weakened his constitution to such an extent they could not promise him more than a seven or eight years' lease.

'And if I continue my present mode of life, how long would you predict for me?'

'Not more than six or seven months,' the doctors declared.

'In that case,' said Gian Carlo, 'I would rather live seven months and do as I please than seven years of dreary self-denial.'

This accounted for his premature death. He bequeathed all his property to the Grand Duke, who would have none of it, as Gian Carlo had left so many debts. All his furniture was sold to satisfy creditors. By this action, says a diarist, the Grand Duke set his people a bad example, for it used to be considered dishonourable not to accept a heritage, and it became feasible henceforth. The Grand Duke was not impelled by avarice, but because little love had been lost between these two brothers; he had always feared the Cardinal's strange temper, and did not wish to be bothered with his property when he had never enjoyed his affection. He had accepted the best pictures from Gian Carlo's collection during his lifetime and these had enhanced the variety of his gallery.

The only other Cardinal in the family at this time, the Grand Duke's uncle, Carlo, was senile and decrepit, and Ferdinando felt the necessity for another 'hat' in the family. Prince Mattias, who governed Siena, was the next eligible by right, but there had been a marked decline in his health, so Prince Leopoldo became candidate in his stead.

Cosimo and his bride contrived to spend the summer without betraying their inmost feelings. They stayed successively at the villas of Poggio Imperiale, Lappeggi and Castello, where they hunted so long as the season allowed. At last the Grand Duke could count on that 'propagation of his race' for which he yearned.

The Princess, aged nineteen, eyed the prospect of motherhood with little pleasure. She wished to continue riding as before; when prevented from enjoying this favourite pastime, she persisted in setting out for long and strenuous walks. It looked as if she intended to compromise the future of the dynasty. To keep her quiet, they soothed her with promises of the greater freedom she would enjoy in future.

On August 9th, 1663, she gave birth to a son, who was to be christened Ferdinando. The traditional festivities were given in Florence for the firstborn: bonfires in the chief squares; volleys from the fortresses; the bells of the Palazzo Vecchio rang for three days, during which two fountains spurted wine on the Piazza Pitti. The Princes threw money to the multitude assembled before the palace. The *Te Deum* was sung again by six choirs in the Duomo, and 106 prisoners were released from their cells.

The midwife who had come from Paris bled the Princess profusely, to the Italians' astonishment. A few days after her delivery she suffered from a tumour on the breast which necessitated an operation. Her convalescence was slow.

Far from bringing peace, this event led to a crisis. Either the Prince and his family took less trouble to gratify her, now that an heir was assured them, or physical weakness had made the Princess more exacting. She shut herself in her room and declared that she would see nobody. Ferdinando blamed her French servants: they had 'engrossed all her confidence, until the meanest of them were objects of Cosimo's jealousy'; he retaliated by dismissing twenty-eight of them, after loading them with presents. Tuscans were substituted, and thus he also hoped to stem the many slanders that had begun to circulate in France about himself and his family.

VII

Matters were not improved when the Princess's French attendants were dismissed. This action awoke in her a furious
spirit of rebellion, and strengthened her desire to return to
France. Not even the innocent smile of her babe, remarks one biographer, could calm the stricken Princess. She 'quitted that nuptial bed,
which had been provided with so much care, and slept with her nurse,
who was still suffered to remain with her'.

The peace-loving Ferdinando flooded his Parisian envoy with letters. Could not the King restrain this termagant? Louis was annoyed
by the turn that this marriage was taking: it was a blow to his own
vanity. He was determined to bring Marguerite-Louise to repentance.
He sent to Florence the Comte de Sainte-Même, who had been
equerry to her father and now served her mother in that capacity.
Sainte-Même, who had been ordered to rebuke her, became her
champion. He felt sorry for her; spoke eloquently in her favour to the
Grand Duke, and was reprimanded by Louis for doing so.

Louis wrote to Marguerite-Louise, when she repeated her desire to
return to France at any cost: 'I have seen certain letters you wrote to
friends of yours, which have astonished and offended me to an extent
you can judge, if, considering the nature of the ideas that pass through
your head (which could not be more extraordinary), you reflect on the
tenderness I feel for you.'

'I wish,' wrote Louis—'*Je veux*'—and we know the high value that
epitome of all royalty attached to those two words, 'that having had
time to think better of it, and remembering from what blood you are
descended, you will regret ever having entertained such fanciful
notions.'

When the King desired a thing, wrote Madame, he never allowed anything to interfere with his wishes. What he had ordered was to be done immediately, and without comment. But Marguerite-Louise was constantly interfering with his wishes, and Louis XIV could do nothing about it. Sainte-Même had failed in his mission, and Marguerite-Louise continued to harass Cosimo, Vittoria and Ferdinando.

'The Grand Duke has repaired to Poggio Imperiale without touching the city,' wrote the Venetian ambassador on April 12th, 1664. 'He will stay there several days with his Court, the site being well suited to the season, and also to mortify the Princess who remains here alone. Her husband, the Prince, it is believed, will repair to Ambrogiana with a similar purpose. The Cardinal has been unable to reconcile them, not from lack of trying, but because she is deaf to protests and attaches no importance to persons, for it is her usual conceit to say that she has married into a family unequal to hers, and vastly inferior to her proper merit, which pricks the most delicate point of these Princes' sensibility. She is unmoved by the distress of her father-in-law, who would like to be more quiet, and the indignation of her husband, who found her nurse's son in her apartments albeit he had been banished from the Palace. The only fear which perturbs her is that the latter, together with the few Frenchmen still in her service, is about to be sent back to Paris. She has written her mother protesting that she, too, wishes to return to France.'

After Sainte-Même, Louis sent others to the rescue the Sieur d'Aubéville, the Marquis de Bellefonds, and the Duc de Créqui, who arrived on May 16th, 1664, with an injunction to tell the Princess that he would not hear of her return to France. The ambassador had several interviews with the Princess, one of which lasted four hours; and he in turn was subjugated.

Discussing the matter later with the Lucchese envoy, Créqui confided that the Princess was in the right. He seems to have forgotten his orders, for he helped her to draw up a treaty in which she claimed all kinds of prerogatives. It contained twelve articles of which Ferdinando accepted six. In the others the Princess required him to increase her allowance to 100,000 francs; that he should promise not to dismiss her French servants; that one Essigny (who had been dismissed) should be recalled; and that three violinists be added to her band of musicians.

Now if Cosimo decided to use a room near hers, she moved elsewhere, heedless of discomfort; spending the winter in summer apartments, protesting that she would even live in the country to avoid him. She begged Ferdinando to let her live alone in one of his villas.

He had her more carefully watched. All her doors were bolted, except those opening on to the Boboli Gardens. He threatened to shut her in a convent, to which she retorted that he would soon repent it, for she would turn all the nuns topsy-turvy. All Florence remarked upon her absence from the feast of St John the Baptist. She refused to appear because Cosimo had to take part in it.

She showed her contempt for Cosimo on every possible occasion. *À propos* of some trivial incident, she told him before the Nuncio that, not only a poor husband, he was even incapable of being a good groom. Then she discovered another way of insulting the Medici. As if they would poison her, she had her kitchen closed, and only allowed two Frenchmen to cook for her and procure her food. Every dish brought to her table was tasted by her steward before she would touch it herself. The superstition was still current in the seventeenth century that the subtlest of venoms were concocted in Florence: 'The Milanese will teach you to be jugglers; the Bolognese, liars; the Venetian, hypocrites; the Neapolitan will metamorphose you into satyrs for lust; the Florentine instructeth in the artifice of poison; and Rome implungeth you into an impure ocean of idolatry and superstition.' The Florentines, it was said, 'will poison with the smoke of a candle, the smell of a candle, or indeed any way imaginable'. But, if we are to judge from certain experiments witnessed by Pepys and Birch at the Royal Society in 1665, the Florentines had lost their prescriptions. 'And we to Gresham College,' wrote Pepys, 'where we saw some experiments upon a hen, a dogg, and a cat, of the Florentine poison. The first it made for a time drunk, but it come to itself again quickly; the second it made vomitt mightily, but no other hurt. The third I did not stay to see the effect of it, being taken out by Povy. . . .' Birch chronicled that the 'Duke of Florence's poyson' had little effect upon the kitten.

In Florence the conflict between the serene spouses was no longer secret, and in Paris the Princess was pitied for the 'maltreatment' to which she was subjected. Cosimo was advised to absent himself awhile, and prudish as he was, travelled to Venice, reputed then the most frivolous of cities. After he had been there, he received a message

93

at Parma urging him to return. Perhaps the Princess was found more tractable once Cosimo was out of sight: peace was patched up for the time being, and she seemed disposed to give him a good welcome. A family feast was to celebrate his birthday on August 7th.

Shortly after Cosimo's arrival the Venetian ambassador wrote that 'the fondness the Princess had proclaimed for her son, her affability towards her mother-in-law and general semblance of gaiety before her husband's return' were over, and 'the discords waxed more lively than ever. The couple never saw each other. . . . The Princess gave her husband to understand that he need not trouble to seek her, because she would not receive him, and at the same time she wished to remove her belongings, and retire to the uppermost floor of the palace.' The Grand Duke sent Gondi to persuade her to change her mind. But she answered that she refused to acknowledge Cosimo as her husband, and that she was leaving her apartments so as not to be molested. Ferdinando 'pretended to his minister that he could not believe such expressions', and Gondi returned to tell the Princess of the Grand Duke's incredulity. Whereupon Marguerite-Louise, without more ado, took a pen, wrote her own reply, and sent it to her father-in-law. All the rejoicings for Cosimo's birthday were cancelled.

Cosimo had his revenge. When the shooting season began, and the Court migrated to Artimino in September, Marguerite-Louise was moved to Prince Mattias's villa of Lappeggi, which occasioned the pun-loving Florentines to say that she was going '*alla peggio*', from bad to worse. Here she was more closely guarded than ever: at least forty soldiers were detailed to keep an eye on her, and six courtiers to follow her about. These did not prevent her from leading quite a pleasant life. She could indulge to her heart's content in those interminable walks that exhausted her ladies- and gentlemen-in-waiting. She shot those fig-peckers (*beccafichi*) which were the delight of gourmets, and roe-deer (one of which she presented to a Lucchese envoy). Or she assembled the local peasants and bade them dance before her, when she did not dance with them herself. She brought gaiety with her, and soon became popular in the neighbourhood. But she had never been well since her confinement, and a recurrent fever gave her the opportunity to say that the Medici wanted her to die in this unwholesome air, but that she preferred such a fate to living with Cosimo. Prince Leopoldo, whose aversion to the Grand Duchess Vittoria was well known and who therefore must have been more sympathetic to Marguerite-Louise, went in October to see what he could do. But the Princess was obstinate, and the Grand Duke, looking sadly at Francesco Maria, his younger son, and at Ferdinando, his little grandson, said: 'They must be well nurtured, for they are the last hope of my line.'

From Lappeggi, Marguerite-Louise was removed to Poggio a Caiano, some ten miles from Florence. As for Louis XIV, he was still determined to make her return to Cosimo. When she begged him to allow her to retire to a convent in France, he replied that 'a princess of the blood only returned to enter the Bastille, not a convent'.

At this juncture she found another ruse. She now declared that her will having been coerced at the time of her marriage, she could not consider herself the Prince's legitimate wife; in accepting to live with him she had it on her conscience that she was committing an act of concubinage. To cleanse herself from this contamination, she longed to spend the remainder of her days in a convent, provided, of course, it were in France. From this moment Cosimo was a prey to doubts and fears. The idea that he had committed fornication and that his son was a bastard, pursued him like a nightmare. Not even the theologians could ease him. He sought consolation in gluttony. *Aux grands maux les grands remèdes.*

The Grand Monarque was not a whit affected by such arguments. The diplomatists having failed, he turned to the clergy, now that it could be called a matter of religious scruples. Père Cosme Feillet, whom he sent, was a monk of the strict order of St Bernard, remarkable for his dexterity as a confessor and director of conscience. He arrived in December, and addressed three sermons to the Princess, one of which was public. While they lasted the Princess showed every sign of contrition, and her cheeks were flooded with penitential tears. But, as soon as they were over, she recovered her accustomed nonchalance. His eloquence had moved her as a strain of music, superficially. In January he betook himself to Rome and extracted a monitory from the Pope, commanding the Princess to submit to her husband's wishes.

A threat of excommunication troubled her no more than the King's expostulations and the Medici's reproofs. Kindness, flattery, severity— all means were tested. Beside Sainte-Même, d'Aubigny, de Bellefonds,

Créqui, Fr Cosme and the Pope there were the many confessors and theologians, Père de Mouchy of the Oratoire, and the papal Nuncio. But she stuck to her decision.

The Grand Duke continued to keep his daughter-in-law 'in honourable but strict seclusion'. One of the King's messengers was forbidden to give the Princess a letter with which he had been entrusted. Since he refused to hand it to an intermediary, he was obliged to take it back to France unopened. Monsieur de la Croix, a messenger from the Duchesse d'Orléans, fared likewise. Little Ferdinando was weaned when he was eighteen months old, after which his mother was not allowed to go near him.

She pretended to be resigned to her mode of life. As the Venetian ambassador wrote, 'thinking naught of reconciliation, she only attends to such amusements as are suited (if not altogether appropriate to her birth and rank) to a fallen princess (*ad una principessa decaduta*). So she spends her fine days in taking long walks, her rainy ones in dancing with her ladies, and with other young people of the neighbouring villages. Recently she concealed herself with such success that a rumour reached Florence she had fled, and for several hours the princes were much perturbed and had no peace till they heard that she was found. It was certainly one of her pranks, but it proves the trend of her thought, for she said another time she would not hide in jest, and only he that wished to follow her would find her, and then in France.'

'The Princess appears very happy,' reported the Nuncio, 'but the Prince is melancholic.' Although the Grand Duke now realized how ill-assorted they were, he was anxious to bring them together, as much for propagation of the species as for economy of specie.

The Marquise Du Deffand now appeared on the scene. Her mother had been governess to Mademoiselle; her father major-domo to the Comte de Fiesque; and she was separated from her husband, a coarse *roué*, who later took advantage of the favours that fell in her direction.

One day when the Duchesse d'Orléans was complaining to the Duchesse d'Aiguillon[1] that she was at a loss to know whom to send to keep her daughter company, the Duchesse d'Aiguillon promptly exclaimed: '*Grand Dieu*, Madame, how providential! I have one in mind whom it seems He has sent for that purpose, a woman of quality from

---

[1] Niece of the Cardinal, and aunt of the Duc de Richelieu.

Poitou. I have known her for some time; she has much wit and is extremely pious.' The lady was soon engaged and the King entrusted her with two memorials for Marguerite-Louise. They were severely worded.

'If,' he wrote, 'the Princess wishes to be an enemy to her own welfare, glory, and that of the house from which she has the honour to be born, and if, contrary to her promises to the King, . . . she desires with invincible obstinacy to behave in a way which damages her reputation and causes His Majesty acute displeasure . . . she must not find it strange that His Majesty, who is a just Prince, unwilling to take part in capricious and sterile projects, refuses to be concerned in this business in any way whatever. He will leave things to follow their own course. The Grand Duke, who has had so many cogent reasons not to grant her the slightest favour, because of the methods she has chosen to extort them from him, has continually made every allowance for her out of respect for His Majesty. . . . In exchange His Majesty is obliged to side with justice rather than follow those incentives which otherwise the tenderness and proximity of blood would inspire.'[1]

But Marguerite-Louise was as insensitive to the King's threats as to the Grand Duke's friendly advances. Madame Du Deffand left Florence in June, 1665, loaded with gifts, like all who left that munificent Court, while the Princess remained a willing prisoner at Poggio a Caiano, whither she had retired. Here, at least, she said, she would not be disgusted by the sight of faces she abhorred. Yet she was the prey of conflicting moods: she had no desire to adopt a humble tone and beg forgiveness, yet her conscience smote her for all the trouble she had caused. The strain affected her health. Fever returned with vomitings and dysentery. All of a tremble, the Grand Duke and Cosimo hastened to the villa. This they never should have done. Fever makes its victims lucid. The mere sight of them increased her agitation to such an extent that she threatened to hurl something at Cosimo and break his head unless he left her room.

Bernini was in Paris at this time: he had been invited by Colbert to design a façade for the Louvre. In Chantelou's account of the great sculptor-architect's visit to France, there is a reference to Marguerite-

[1] From Fontainebleau, on June 14th, 1664. Signed *Louis*, and, farther down, *De Lionne*.

Louise, which proves the general interest and sympathy she created at home.

One evening the Marquise de Raré came with her daughter to see Bernini.[1] They were struck by the resemblance of his *busto* of the King, and asked him if he had passed through Florence on his way hither. He said yes, and they inquired if he had seen the Princess of Tuscany. He answered no, but that he had seen the Prince, who was very well made. They spoke of the Princess's aversion to him. Whereupon he remarked that whoever tried to examine the matter clearly would find that it was inconsiderable: if one could point out the sore spot, it would be easily mended or removed with two fingers, so to speak; that, after all, a woman should make her glory consist in the virtue of suffering her husband's imperfections, when he had them, were they even the greatest in the world.

'I (Chantelou) rejoined that a Princess of her kind, who had been educated at the Court of France, which is the paradise of women, had every reason to be surprised by the life they lead in Florence. The Marquise added that at the Princess's age one could not have those extraordinary virtues which found their pleasure in duty; that she was only fourteen or fifteen years of age when she left France; that she came of so great a family she had hoped they would show her some consideration. He retorted that the higher one's birth, the greater one's capacity for virtues, which are scarcely ever to be found in vulgar persons; that on the whole what had to be done for this misunderstanding was to pray God for the harmony of their wills; that men were unable to effect it: it must come from above.'

Italian women of quality were then unaccustomed to any physical exertion save that of love; from mother to daughter they had led secluded sedentary lives for centuries, plunged in semi-Oriental indolence. Marguerite-Louise, with her passion for fresh air and outdoor amusement, suffered from headaches and vapours if she was denied them, and dragged her companions out into the fields on all occasions. It was not surprising if, like frail hothouse plants, they suffered from this brutal contact with nature. The year before she had exhausted two of her ladies to such an extent that they had spent the whole winter in

---

[1] *Journal du Voyage en France du Cavalier Bernin par Chantelou.* September 23rd, 1665.

bed. She was always rather selfish, and Madame Du Deffand was treated with as little tenderness as her other ladies.

'Yesterday,' she wrote to the Grand Duke, 'the Princess walked four miles by break-neck mountain paths. I followed her awhile, but the roads frightened me so much that I lagged behind. In the evening she went to bed early, being very tired, though she assured me that she was not. All her ladies were no less weary.'

VIII

First Reconciliation – Birth of Princess Anna Maria Luisa – Quarrels Renewed – Cosimo Sets Forth on His Travels (1667) – Second Reconciliation – Death of Grand Duke Ferdinando II

On October 30th, 1665, after many months of Lappeggi and Poggio a Caiano, the Princess went to Florence under the pretext of visiting her child, and requested an interview with the Grand Duke. Much abashed, she expressed a desire to resume her place in the palace. The Grand Duke courteously replied that she had never been deprived of it. He had been looking forward to her return. But he could not disguise from her the fact that she had done great injury to her husband's conscience. The Princess then inquired what guarantees they would offer about her position at Court, but Ferdinando declined to discuss this question. During the next five days all were agog to know if the Grand Duke would make the next move or leave it to his daughter-in-law. On November 6th, Marguerite-Louise sent word that she was ready to return without stipulations. So the Grand Duchess set off to fetch her from Poggio a Caiano.

Cosimo forgot the scruples she had excited in his devout mind, and welcomed her back with eagerness. All agreed (whatever their opinions of her character) that she was more than ever beautiful. And Cosimo's rigid abstinence during their long separation added a prospective zest to the reunion. He waited at the very threshold of the palace to kiss her, after which they exchanged sweet words, and we read, 'all passed between them even with gallantry in this peace concluded by Love'.

That evening the Prince and Princess attended a comedy, and when the Prince went next morning to wish her a good day, she gave him a most friendly reception. Soon it was no longer necessary for Cosimo tentatively to go and bid her good morrow. Such formalities were dispensed with, and the Grand Duke felt more at ease about the future of his dynasty.

Louis XIV was delighted: 'The best news I could hear from you is that of your reconciliation with my cousin the Prince of Tuscany and all his family. My joy is redoubled to see that this has happened of your own accord, without my being compelled to interpose my authority.'[1]

Madame Du Deffand's tactful advice; the boredom of solitude weighing on her twenty summers; a wish to shine in public, and perhaps a tinge of ambition: these had contributed towards her compliance.

The Court was jubilant. Never had Marguerite-Louise shown herself more amiable, more enchanting. A banquet was given at the Pitti on the day of Epiphany. Prince Mattias was king of the twelfth night, and he took advantage of it to drink a gracious toast to Marguerite-Louise. Her mirth enlivened them even more than the wine which flowed so freely. The Court removed to Pisa for the summer, where the Princess could hunt and fish to her heart's content. The winter was spent in festivity. At a dance which took place during the course of February, 1667, she delighted everyone by her grace in a ballet, and by her beauty when she unmasked. The Grand Duke danced himself, and ladies and gentlemen wore gloves, conforming to the new French fashion. Pampered and petted though she was, her movements were jealously watched. The Medici were never rid of their mistrust. Two of her attendants, Monsieur de Monty and his wife, had suddenly to leave the Court because they were suspected of secretly conveying letters to her.

It was not without repugnance that Marguerite-Louise accepted the consequences of her return. Her mind, despite her amiability, was overcast. When she was with child again there was a renewed outbreak of hectic activity. She galloped about wildly on horseback, and tried to miscarry as before. When such strenuous exercise was forbidden, she went for interminable excursions on foot. Balls and comedies were devised: all the pleasures she usually enjoyed the Medici lavished on her, but she swore she would play the devil with them unless they allowed her to have her way. She began with a hunger strike. She declared that she would die of starvation, but the caprice did not last. An epidemic of influenza added to the Medici's anxieties. In Florence 800 victims died in a week, and Marguerite-Louise had a bad attack of it. Her four physicians applied leeches, which drained her of more than eight ounces of blood, although she was in the eighth month of her pregnancy.

[1] November 23rd, 1665.

Marguerite-Louise must have enjoyed a sturdy constitution, for on August 11th, 1667, she gave birth to a daughter, who was christened Anna Maria Luisa. The virulent abscess returned to her breast, and she caught smallpox in November. All her hair had to be cut off. Despite these ailments, and the ignorance of doctors, she recovered.

And again she passed through a period of dejection in which she saw Cosimo as the sole cause of her misfortune; again there were hurricanes of fury and downpours of tears; and the Grand Duke had recourse to his usual expedient of saving his son from further mortification.

Cosimo set forth on his travels again on October 28th, 1667, towards Germany through the Tyrol. His aunt, the Archduchess, gave him a wonderful reception at Innsbruck, whence he proceeded to Augsburg and Mainz with sixty gentlemen in his suite, although he was travelling incognito. To avoid the plague that was ravaging Swabia, he took a boat to Holland down the Rhine, in spite of the dangers of navigating it at this time of the year. At Amsterdam he stayed with Ferroni, a wealthy Florentine merchant, and was entertained by the Prince of Orange. Holland was then at the summit of her commercial opulence and maritime power. The representatives of the different States came to pay him their respects; all the great scholars, luminaries of literature and philosophy who had elected this country as a fatherland, made it a point of honour to be presented to him, and pretended to be amazed, above all, by his knowledge of Latin. It was still sufficiently rare for a prince to be a good linguist, and to travel any distance from his native land. Cosimo was looked on as quite an exception. The great pensionary, Heinsius, was appointed his guide, and accompanied him everywhere. This eager reception from the Dutch, which was largely due to his father's reputation as a Maecenas and patron of learning, was a big sop to that vanity which his wife had done so much to mortify. He repaired with considerable satisfaction to Hamburg, where he met his uncle Gian Carlo's friend, the brilliant and squalid Christina of Sweden; but it is doubtful whether he appreciated her curious character. Maybe she shocked him, as she did the majority of her contemporaries. He returned, this time travelling by land from Nuremberg to Innsbruck, and reached Florence in May, 1668, after eight months' absence.

His family was pleased with the creditable way he had acquitted himself abroad; even his uncle Leopoldo congratulated him. But his wife's attitude towards him was the same, implacable and unrelenting. She was miserable at his return, and refused to see him. It was even said that she had made several attempts at flight. She had been overheard talking with some gipsies from her window at Poggio a Caiano, in whose band she intended to conceal herself and effect her escape. It was also said that she had contemplated flight to a Bavarian convent, and had learned German for that purpose.

Cosimo came back considerably changed. He was more self-assured, and his health had improved. His pride had been puffed by the plaudits he had received on his travels. Nevertheless he suffered. For he was longing to rehabilitate himself at home, to recover his domestic dignity. His wife's contemptuous treatment of him seemed all the more intolerable. He was naturally morose, and now, so deep was the gloom that settled on him, it was feared he would fall dangerously ill. Only travel could help to distract him: the Grand Duke thought it advisable to send him on a more extensive journey. So Cosimo set sail for Barcelona in September, 1668, with a large suite.

Viceroys and municipalities were all so eager to pay him homage that he did not reach Madrid till October 24th, 1668, where the Regent and King (Charles II) received him in private audience. At Cordova he attended a bullfight, and had the honour to receive the keys of the *toril*. By the end of January he was at Lisbon, whence he went for devotions to Compostella. From there he proceeded to Corunna, where he embarked for England.

Count Magalotti kept elaborate account of all that occurred on the journey and sketches were made by the artists in his suite, wherever Cosimo was received, rested or was detained.[1]

This year, 1669, we read, in Eachard's *Life and Reign of Charles II*, 'began with the reception of the Prince of Tuscany, who in the Portland Frigot from Corunna, after being driven into Kingsale in Ireland, and again into the Isle of Silly, arrived at Plymouth on March 22'.

Pepys caught a first glimpse of him soon after his arrival at Brentford. where 'his highness dined in company with all the gentlemen

---

[1] A translation of his tour through England was published in 1821. Lalande, the famous traveller, who saw the manuscript in the Laurentian Library, wrote: '*Je ne connois aucun exemple (si ce n'est celui du Czar, Pierre le Grand), d'un Prince qui ait voyagé avec tant de curiosité, de goût, et d'utilité.*' (*Voyage en Italie.* Tom. ii, p. 286.)

who had been to wait upon him; and a very great number of people, men, women, and whoever were curious enough to come, were allowed to enter the dining-room'.

'The Prince of Tuscany,' he wrote[1] (much as an Italian might have written of a *Milordo* on his Grand Tour), 'who comes into England only to spend money and see our country, comes into town to-day, and is much expected, and we met him, but the coach passing by apace, we could not see much of him, but he seems *a very jolly and good comely man*.' Evidently Pepys admired the countenance that Cosimo's wife found so repellent. Pepys caught several glimpses of him, on Sunday, 'in the Park, and many very fine ladies, and so home, and after supper to bed'; and again, visiting the Duke and Duchess of York. 'I find that he do still remain incognito, and so intends to do all the time he stays here, for avoiding trouble to the King and himself, and expense also to both.' On April 11th, Easter Day, Pepys took his wife to St James's, 'and there carried her to the Queen's Chapel, the first time I ever did it, and heard excellent music. . . . And going out of the Chapel, I did see the Prince of Tuscany come out, a comely, black, fat man, in a morning suit; and my wife and I did see him this afternoon through a window in this Chapel'. The musicians of the chapel were all Italian, their master being Matteo Battaglia, of Bologna. Italian music was then beginning to invade England, in spite of the Englishman's instinctive distrust (*vide* Pepys's *Diary*) of anything foreign. Lord Brouncker[2] was one of the chief enthusiasts; and Sir William Killigrew was then busy sending to Italy for singers, instrumentalists and scene-painters.

Cosimo was given a very warm reception by Charles and his Court, and by the Universities of Oxford and Cambridge, chiefly it appears for the strange reason that his father was supposed to have protected Galileo against Papal persecution. Cosimo, who certainly did not consider any resistance to Papal authority as one of his family's noblest qualifications, had to hear himself extolled at length on this subject by the most eminent college professors.

There was a rumour that Cosimo aspired to the throne of Poland: albeit without foundation, it enhanced his self-esteem. He refused to give his hand to ambassadors except 'in a third place'—at the Queen's,

[1] *Diary of Samuel Pepys*, vol. VIII, p. 267.
[2] First President of the Royal Society.

for instance. The ambassadors of Spain and Venice tolerated these pretensions, and Cosimo paid a visit to the Spanish ambassadress in return. But the French ambassador, Colbert de Croissy (a brother of the great minister), thought them excessive and kept aloof; he was nettled when consequently his wife did not receive an honour similar to that accorded her Excellency of Spain. But he managed to disguise his feelings, and overwhelmed the Prince with all sorts of other attentions. Cosimo was deceived by them to such an extent that he expressed a desire to visit the French ambassadress. One of his gentlemen was sent to make an appointment. Cosimo presented himself punctually; two gentlemen conducted him upstairs, when a third came to announce that the ambassadress was out. Whereupon Cosimo retired in a rage, 'glaring haughtily at the gentlemen'.

'The accident which befell the Prince of Toscane and the french ambassadore heere made a great noise,' wrote Charles to Madame on May 24th.

On such particulars as giving the hand to ambassadors the amity of nations depended. If at Versailles the rules of ceremonial were not always respected, Louis attached immense importance to their observance among his representatives abroad, and Cosimo was equally sensitive about his own dignity. King Charles himself had found that Colbert's predecessor 'is a man very hardly to be pleased, and loves to raise difficultyes even in the easiest matters'. Cosimo had planned a visit to France as soon as he left England, and his troubles with Marguerite-Louise made it essential that he should create a favourable impression on Louis XIV and his Court.

The Grand Duke, anxious for harmony at all costs, ordered Abbé Gondi, his representative in Paris,[1] to offer the King his own terms of compensation. Cosimo left England on June 1st, in the midst of these delicate negotiations. All except the French ambassador had gone to salute him on the day he took leave of King Charles.

He was therefore obliged to make a détour before entering France. He stopped again at the Hague, where he had left so many friends, Amsterdam, Aix-la-Chapelle and Spa, where the baths were already in vogue. Finally, when Gondi had persuaded Louis to accept the Grand Duke's 'personal apology for the Prince's lack of respect', Cosimo

[1] The son of his Prime Minister, the Bali Gondi.

crossed the frontier at Sedan. After a journey well punctuated with pompous receptions he reached Paris, where the Duc de Vitri received him in the King's name.

First he visited his mother-in-law, the Duchesse d'Orléans. She had offered him lodging, but Cosimo held her largely responsible for his misfortunes, and preferred to stay with the Tuscan resident. The King lavished attentions on him, to repair the humiliation he had previously inflicted. He took him in an open carriage to a review of his troops; showed him his palaces, gardens and monuments, and the solemn ceremony of a royal session of parliament. A comedy was performed for him at Saint-Germain, and last winter's opera was revived. He was invited to a festival at Versailles with the usual diversions which Marguerite-Louise had always loved and Cosimo despised. The King exhibited his skill and grace in a ballet rehearsed especially for the occasion; and one can conceive how this must have surprised the prim young Florentine. For Louis would sometimes appear in no less than five different rôles: in *The Nuptials of Thetis and Peleus*, for instance, he represented Apollo, Mars, a Fury, a Dryad and a courtier, in turn. But his favourite character was undoubtedly that of Apollo.

When his visit came to an end, Louis wrote to Marguerite-Louise: 'Consideration for you alone would have obliged me to give my cousin all the favourable treatment he has received from me. But from what I perceived of his personal qualities, I could not have refused them to his peculiar merit.'

Mademoiselle depicted him with a brush dipped in hydromel.

'He spoke admirably on every topic,' she wrote, 'and was very well acquainted with the mode of life at all the Courts of Europe: in that of France he never made a single blunder.

'His physique was rather plump for a man of his age [25]: he had a fine head, black and curly hair, a large red mouth, good teeth, a healthy ruddy complexion, abundance of wit, and was agreeable in conversation.

'The sight of him,' she added, 'was prejudicial to my sister for having lived on such bad terms with him.' However: 'One cannot' (to quote a letter from Madame[1] to the Electress Sophia) 'trust this worthy Mademoiselle in the least. To-day she tries to pleasure you; to-morrow

---

[1] Charlotte Elizabeth, Princess Palatine, and mother of Philippe d'Orléans, Regent of France.

she seeks to do you an injury. She repeats everything said to her with amplifications. . . .' Mademoiselle shows us none of the defects visible in all the engravings: the heavy, protruding lips, the exaggerated forehead, pointed chin, misshapen ears and dumpy, thick-set body. In his letters home, Cosimo complained that he had met only with haughtiness and pride in France, except from the King. It is interesting to note that he witnessed a performance of *Tartuffe*, in its final form. *Tartuffe* had undergone considerable transformation since its first performance in 1664, when the clerical party who thought they saw, in the satire of religious hypocrisy, an attack upon religion in general, succeeded in getting it banned. But the storm had blown over by 1669, and it had become 'the play of the moment'.

Life again at her irony, could Cosimo have seen the reflection of himself a few years hence. How much did he understand as he looked on at the arch-hypocrite across the footlights? We only know that he ate nothing for supper afterwards, as he felt rather unwell.

He stayed in Paris till September 15th, 1669. The King presented him with a superb tapestry on his departure, and his own sword, with richly-jewelled hilt, saying: 'I do not believe myself to be any the less well guarded, for it is in good hands.' In thanking Louis for the sword, Cosimo is supposed to have declared that he had not sufficient strength to wield it, whereupon Louis replied: 'Our arm shall assist you.'

Cosimo returned to Florence on November 1st, at a time when Marguerite-Louise had never been on such terms of apparent amity with her mother-in-law.

Cosimo had been won over by the King's affability. His view of Versailles with its luxurious distractions—'the apartments full of gamblers, hunting every afternoon, and music in the evening'—had made him more tolerant and more inclined to make concessions to his wife's French tastes.

The spring of 1670 began cheerfully. Cosimo organized a ballet, remembering the one he had seen at Versailles. This represented Acneas's arrival in Latium. Marguerite-Louise was allotted the chief rôle.

The Court was more animated than usual when suddenly the Grand Duke fell ill. His dropsical constitution had not benefited by a tardy and perhaps exaggerated application of the precepts of the Salernian school, which recommended a periodical debauch. The physicians bled him with their usual pertinacity. On May 23rd Settimanni wrote: 'Since the Grand Duke had derived no advantage whatever from the medicine he had taken on the previous day, the cupping-glasses were used again, and another ounce was removed from his bladder. *Polvere Capitale* was forcibly thrust down his nose, and four live pigeons were ripped open and, covered with this same powder, were put on his forehead. A cauterizing iron was later applied to his head, but with no success, and as his condition grew worse towards midday, the Nuncio arrived at the palace and gave him the papal benediction. Next morning, although his pulse was still beating, there was little hope for his life, and his confessor, seeing how very weak he was, had several reliquaries placed about him at ten o'clock. At $13\frac{3}{4}$ o'clock he died, at the age of 59, after a reign of 49 years with the reputation of a very prudent prince, held in great esteem by the other princes of Europe.'

He would have been more lamented by his subjects, adds Settimanni, if his qualities had not been diminished during his time of government by increasingly oppressive taxation. A Mr Style[1] watched the funeral procession from a window of the Strozzi Palace, and left the following account of his death and burial:

'This May 27th, 1670, died the Great Duke Ferdinando, of an apoplexy and dropsy; four days after, his body was embalmed; and lay in very great state eight days, being drest in all his robes; afterwards buried in St Lawrence's, the funeral was very august, beginning about nine; and they were from that time till one in the morning before it was finished; there were 1,500 monks with tapers, all the bishops, and archbishops of his dominions; all the knights of St Stephen in their robes, viz. white satin and crimson velvet. The present Great Duke accompanied by Principe Francesco Maria his brother, their mourning cloaks carried up; after the corpse several led horses and the duke's own pad, an English horse; all the officers of the late Duke, with their broken bastoons, a horse-guard of Germans, beating a dead march; lastly, a great number of coaches with six horses, finished the ceremony. At St Lawrence's chapel door, the Pope's Nuncio and other prelates, received the body, who placed it under a very rich pavilion, while the panegyric was speaking; then put it in the vault.'

[1] Eldest son and heir apparent to Sir Thomas Style, Bart., of Watringbury, Kent, but predeceased his father.

IX

Looking back on Ferdinando's reign, it leaves the image of a prolonged and pleasant autumn. One remembers the various academies hung heavily with ripe and rotting fruit, the external brilliance of his Court—not brilliant in the gilded, glittering sense of Versailles although, from an aesthetic point of view, its festivals were finer and the Florentine genius more virile than the Parisian—then, over all, the mild and benign paterfamilias, for as such his subjects regarded him rather than as a sovereign. Ferdinando and his brothers had notably enriched the Florentine galleries. By his marriage to Vittoria della Rovere he had acquired, amongst other treasures from Urbino, Titian's 'Recumbent Venus' and Raphael's portrait of Pope Julius II. To the numerous antiques he had inherited he added some of the choicest sculpture such as the Hermaphrodite, the *Idolino*, the head of Cicero and the Etruscan Chimera.

In 1640 Pietro da Cortona was summoned to fresco the five large rooms on the first floor of the Pitti, and the Florentine, like the Roman, galleries, began to assume the Seicento surface they still retain.

The confused battles of Salvator Rosa and Borgognone were given pride of place; the minute landscapes of Cornelius Poelemburg pullulated in the Medicean apartments. Now travellers pass them by without a look. Was Beckford the last of Poelemburg's admirers? 'Just such scenery as Poelemburg introduces in his paintings' was high praise from the Caliph of Fonthill.

Generally the religion *à la mode* invaded art: it became the leader of the orchestra. We are in the Italy of the Jesuits, of the Counter Reformation, of Bernini. The horizon had been broadened by a posse of new saints, Francis Xavier, Charles Borromeo, Philip Neri and so forth. The painter's ideal, as we have seen (retained *via* Luca Giordano from Paul Veronese), was to move and astound, to fascinate eye and heart simultaneously. So sentiment is blended with sensuality in a series whose violence caused Smollett to exclaim: 'What a pity it is that the labours of painting should have been so much employed in the shocking subjects of the martyrology. Besides numberless pictures of the flagellation, crucifixion and descent from the Cross, we have Judith with the head of Holofernes, Herodias with the head of John the Baptist, Jael assassinating Sisera in his sleep, Peter writhing on the cross, Stephen battered with stones, Sebastian stuck full of arrows, Laurence frying upon a gridiron, Bartholomew flayed alive, and a hundred other pictures equally frightful.'

The prestige of the Medici had increased politically by Ferdinando's triumph over the Barberini, by his mediation between Louis XIV and Pope Alexander VII who had quarrelled about the privileges of the French embassy in Rome (1664), by his assistance to the Emperor against the Turks, by his reputation as the most cultured and diplomatic prince of his time, and by Cosimo's marriage to Louis XIV's cousin. The succession seemed assured, and his death did not appear so sinister an event in the history of the Medici.

But throughout this gradual autumn, he had pursued the mildewing principles of government established by his forbears: he had taxed everything that was taxable without much solid gain to the treasury. 'This Prince gathers monies on all hands, for at Florence, Leghorn and other places he receives contribution from the *Cortegiane*, or prostitute women, for the toleration and protection he gives them; so that an injury done to any of those infamous persons shall be punished, as if it had been done to the most virtuous in the world.'[1]

'No house or land sold but a good part of the price (at least one tenth) goes to him. No woman married but he hath 8 per cent of her portion. Every one that goes to law pays 2 per cent of what he sues for. Every young heifer that is sold pays a crown; not so much as a basket of eggs comes to market but it pays somewhat for toll.'[2]

[1] J. Gailhard, 1668.
[2] *Travels*, by the late Reverend and Learned Mr John Ray, Fellow of the Royal Society, 1664.

In spite of his economy, he had left the finances depressed. The shadows were descending on Tuscany. England and Holland had been rapidly appropriating the traffic of Portugal and Spain. Their manufactures had crippled those of Italy. Remote were the days when the traders of England, Spain, France and Flanders sent their wool and rough cloths to the Calimala,[1] to be dyed and dressed with that perfection of which the Florentine Guild alone possessed the secret. Other nations had got hold of the key and improved upon that knowledge. The silk and wool industries of Florence had thrived since the eleventh century; that of weaving textiles was said to have been introduced by the Umiliati friars in 1062. Each trade had been carefully regulated, and in their statutes the Guilds had chronicled their methods. Now the Florentines sought to revive their bygone prosperity by an archaeological process of recalling those echoes of the past, the prescriptions of their forefathers, and by preventing the introduction of foreign cloth.

Ferdinando had always been weak in his dealings with the Church. He had been but eleven years old when his father, Cosimo II, died in 1621, leaving his mother (Maria-Maddalena of Austria) and grandmother (Christine of Lorraine), to act as Regents, two ladies who inherited the abnormal religious tendencies of the Valois-Lorraine-Bourbon-Hapsburg ancestry combined. During this interval, the *Tutrici*, as they were called, redoubled their activities in founding convents and multiplying the excessive number of monks and nuns in the Grand Duchy. In deference to Urban VIII, they lost the opportunity of annexing Urbino, which was Ferdinando's by marriage, and allowed the septuagenarian Galileo, who had christened the Satellites of Jupiter 'the Medicean Planets', and so, in the rhetoric of Galluzzi, 'registered the name of this family in the eternal annals of heaven', to be led before the Inquisition.

The air was tainted for many years to come. Eventually it was cleared by the War of Castro, and Ferdinando recovered some dignity; he tried to check the clergy, but the Church was still too powerful in

---

[1] A street that was chiefly inhabited by the wool merchants, corresponding to Bartholomew or Cloth Fair, running out of Smithfield, along the north side of the Priory Church of St Bartholomew, which had been the great cloth mart of England since the time of Henry II.

Florence; and its authority over the minds of Vittoria and Cosimo was preponderant.

Plague and malaria had decreased the population: at this time it counted only 720,594 souls. Grass grew in the streets of Pisa, now crumbling and bleak, with magnificent damp-stained empty palaces. Siena, the solitary hill city, governed by Prince Mattias and an oligarchy of impoverished aristocrats, was almost as sepulchral, with its toy-box battlements and striped towers, 'the concentration of everything mediaeval, and incapable of getting beyond mediaevalism' even towards the end of the Seicento, just as its painters had remained eclectic, their 'way of visualizing' unchanged long after the Renaissance. Leghorn, more plebeian, for all its privileges only had a population of 18,000 at the time of Ferdinando's death. There was peace, but it savoured of the backwater; there was tranquillity, but it savoured of creeping paralysis.

Cosimo III succeeded his father in what has been called the full flush of youth. But what a consumptive flush was his! A devotee to the point of bigotry; intolerant of all free thought; hated by his wife; his existence a round of visits to churches and convents.

Both Grand Duchesses aspired to share with Cosimo the honours of government, and the Florentines were speculating as to which would succeed. It was not easy for Cosimo to forget the humiliations he had suffered from his wife; and her frivolous character disqualified Marguerite-Louise from any serious occupation; whereas his mother had watched over Cosimo's youth and moulded him into his present shape. In politics, as in religion, Vittoria and Cosimo thought and saw alike. The long hours they remained closeted together soon showed that he would let himself be guided by her.

Cosimo assumed his new functions with zeal, and the first acts of his administration were moderate. He seemed more conscientious than his father, and he was determined to appear more magnificent.

Foreign visitors were impressed by the new sovereign. One, Mr Style, wrote at this time: 'Cosimo the 3rd is a prince that hath been a great traveller, and hath visited most of the princes' Courts in Europe, truly deserving the character Homer gave of Ulysses, maintaining him to be the wisest of all the Graecians, using no other argument, but that he hath travelled much and had seen *multorum hominum mores et urbes*, and certainly no prince hath ever read more in the great book of the world than himself. His great riches, his noble palaces, his train and retinue, both of officers and guards, make his Court appear the most splendid of Italy. Besides, he willingly admits of strangers' visits; and if persons of quality, receives them standing, and afterwards sends them a present of wine, sweetmeats et caet.' As an instance of condescension he relates that he had not been long walking in the garden of Poggio Imperiale, with Sir John Finch, before the Grand Duke Cosimo came thither, as his custom was every night, to take the air. 'The resident, seeing that opportunity, was pleased to present me to his Highness, who received me with more civility than if I had been his equal, and spoke much in commendation of England.' Mr Style also mentions his reconciliation to Marguerite-Louise.

At first Cosimo concerned himself with various claims and complaints from his subjects which had been neglected for several years. He encouraged them to apply to him personally; and his decisions were just. He examined the conditions of finance. But this happy zeal did not last and, notwithstanding the difference in their personal conduct, the general system of Ferdinando was adopted and pursued by Cosimo III. Vittoria, who had never been allowed to meddle with the government, was delighted with this fresh outlet for her long-thwarted ambitions: a busybody by nature, she took advantage of Cosimo's apathy, proffered an opinion on every subject, and saw that it was respected. From the Lucchese resident we gather that again Cosimo spent half the day in prayer and left the cares of government to his mother and her favourites. In matters of state, Prince Francesco Maria, his brother, aged eleven, was deputed to receive ambassadors at their coming, and see them off at their departure. None of the elder princes of the family remained alive, except Cardinal Leopoldo, who, chiefly from disgust with his nephew's conduct, resided at Rome.

Vittoria was not content with the substance of power, she wanted the pageantry of it also. An old tradition was revived which admitted her to the *Consulta*, the Grand Duke's privy council: eventually the sessions were held in her apartment. Marguerite-Louise was excluded, but she pretended to be engrossed by her son Ferdinando's education, for he was now seven years old. It seemed as if she had acquiesced in disappointment, as if at last her turbulent spirit was broken. Cosimo believed this to be nothing short of a miracle, yet he was made uneasy by the presence of four French secret agents. Three had been sent by the King, the Duchesse d'Orléans and Mademoiselle; the other was the mysterious Tambonneau, a relative of the Comte de Sainte-Même. Little was known about him but that the Duc de Chaulnes, the King's ambassador at Rome, had sent him 'by command of one more powerful than himself', and that his mission was to drive Marguerite-Louise into competition with her mother-in-law, whose Spanish sympathies were feared.

Cosimo had a sudden panic, and he thought of calling Madame Du Deffand again to his assistance. That admirable woman was now lady of the bedchamber to Marguerite's sister, the Duchesse de Guise. Cosimo had had several meetings with the Marquise in Paris which had confirmed his high opinion of her. In January, 1671, he begged her to obtain leave of the King and the Duchesse de Guise to join him as soon as possible. He bombarded Gondi with letters. He entreated Louis XIV. She alone, he said, could prevent 'the disorders he foresaw in the Grand Duchess's conduct'.

Louis XIV summoned the lady in question and spent two hours conferring with her; he sent for her again a few days later without reaching a decision.

Cosimo became more nervous. Tambonneau had returned to Florence after seeing the Duc de Mazarin, who was suffering from smallpox at Turin. This served as an excuse to prevent him from seeing Marguerite-Louise. But she had contrived to speak to him in the Cascine, then a ducal chase.

Marguerite-Louise was now as determined to enter the *Consulta* as Vittoria was to exclude her from it. The Grand Duchesses quarrelled about precedent, as they had done so often before. A della Rovere, said Marguerite-Louise, was not to set herself on a level with a royal princess of France. And so the cauldron was kept boiling.

Cosimo took his mother's side. The atmosphere was charged with spleen. 'Cosimo found himself between two fires: he was the victim of both women's caprices. His wife reproved him for his sheepish obedience to his mother; his mother spurred him on against her political rival, and urged him to tighten his severity.' In fact, we hear, 'the Pitti Palace had become the devil's own abode, and from morn till midnight only the noise of wrangling and abuse could be heard.' Then on May 24th, 1671, the anniversary of the Grand Duke Ferdinando's death, a second son was born to Marguerite-Louise. He was christened Giovanni Gastone, in memory of Gaston d'Orléans, his maternal grandfather.

That function of child-bearing, which from the Grand Duke's point of view constituted the Grand Duchess's main *raison d'être*, had been adequately fulfilled. Now that Cosimo felt more secure, he need not suffer her whimsies and crotchets longer. The year passed and Louis still hesitated to send Madame Du Deffand.

Marguerite-Louise's mother had become cantankerous with the advancing years; she suspected one of her oldest and most trusted servants of wishing to murder her. Two months after imprisoning him she died, in April, 1672, at the age of fifty-seven. At such a time of bereavement they could not deprive the Duchesse de Guise of her favourite companion.

Gondi's unscrupulous curiosity sustained a hard trial when he was summoned by the Duchesse de Guise to witness the opening of a casket, in which the letters of the deceased were kept. The Duchesse herself had told him that it contained correspondence exchanged, under cover of Madame, between Marguerite-Louise and Prince Charles of Lorraine. There lay the secret of the Grand Duchess's life, with evidence that might deliver his master for ever from his torment. But it was burned under his very nose, as soon as he had recognized the Grand Duchess's large, bold, slanting script. Gondi admitted that his fingers had itched. But he was manacled: Madame Du Deffand was in the room watching him.

At the beginning of 1672, Marguerite-Louise had announced to Louis XIV that her health was gone. She thought she was stricken with cancer of the breast. Unless he wished her to die, he must send her an able physician at once. Louis decided to send her 'Alliot le Vieux', who had attended the Queen Mother for a similar complaint, albeit without success. (For the latter case he had prescribed grains of opium compounded with May dew.) Cosimo tried to dissuade Louis from sending him, but Marguerite-Louise pleaded her cause so ably that Alliot set forth on August 26th. Madame Du Deffand's departure depended on the result of his examination. The Duchesse de Guise did not take her sister's troubles seriously, and declared that she would never allow her dear companion to leave unless the Grand Duchess was quite as ill as she pretended to be.

Madame Du Deffand confessed herself unequal to the task which Cosimo was determined to impose on her, and querulously complained of the advancing season. But towards the end of September, Cosimo grew more insistent. Gondi made a supreme effort, flattered Pomponne until he promised to persuade the King, and wheedled the Duchesse de Guise until she unbended. The doctor arrived on September 23rd; and Cosimo lodged him in the palace, provided him with a carriage, and promised to reimburse all his expenses as the King had done. His diagnosis might profoundly affect Cosimo's future.

That same evening Alliot presented himself to the Grand Duchess. She received him graciously, but refused to explain her symptoms. He returned twice without better success. To have her illness declared so severe that it made her return to France imperative, she needed a confederate rather than a physician. She wanted leisure to convert him to her cause. But she could not procrastinate without confirming her husband's suspicions. So she had to let herself be examined prematurely, as it were.

Alliot's diagnosis was given in all sincerity. He had observed 'a little gland on her bosom, no bigger than half the kernel of a fir-cone, colourless, nowise malignant, and betraying none of the characteristics of a cancer.' 'The artery of the spleen' was beating a little faster than was quite normal, but this was probably due to a generous flow of blood. He concluded that the Grand Duchess's alarms were groundless.

This upset Marguerite-Louise's calculations. When Cosimo announced his joy at the news, she gave him a reception several degrees below zero. She then wrote to Louis: 'The Grand Duke came to inform me in the most scathing language that our worthy Alliot had told him I was feigning illness in order to return with him, which I cannot believe, unless he was bribed. I must own, Sire, that his words offended me to such a point that I treated him as a raving lunatic.'

The cancer hypothesis having failed, she assured Alliot that she was about to die. For five years she had been consumed by unspeakable tortures. Alliot was touched. He perceived that she was sick, not in body but in spirit; and he let himself be drawn into her game.

When he went to take leave of the Grand Duke on October 14th, he mustered sufficient courage to disturb him, but not enough to help Marguerite-Louise. He told him that her constitution stood in great need of cooling and refreshment. He suggested that she should take medicinal waters 'neither too sharp nor over-heating'. Those he had in mind were at Sainte-Reine in Burgundy. To his knowledge Italy could offer none as efficacious.

Cosimo soon showed Doctor Alliot that this was precisely what he did not want and Alliot hastened to retrieve his indiscretion. Nothing could be easier than to transmit these waters to Florence, he added. But Cosimo was still dissatisfied. If the waters proved beneficial, his wife would find an argument to continue with the cure on the spot; if ineffectual, she would attribute it to their removal, and would insist even more on visiting Sainte-Reine. That would never do. The doctor was quick to recant, and received 350 golden louis for his pains.

Whenever Cosimo tried to be affable he met with a ruder rebuff. Marguerite-Louise asked for a set of diamonds; he sent her some. At first she accepted them with pleasure, but after a couple of days sent them back. They were not fine enough, she said; she wanted 'the jewels the late Grand Duke had given her'. She was referring to those she had been allowed to wear on her arrival in Florence, the same they had quarrelled over just after the wedding; they belonged to the crown, and not even Cosimo had the right to dispose of them. When Cosimo refused, she answered that he treated her as a slave he could adorn and despoil at his own caprice. Cosimo retorted that if she had really supposed the jewels belonged to her, she would have taken care not to return them when the late Grand Duke died. He reminded her of her boundless extravagance and of his own boundless generosity. Then they bickered over a chambermaid whom the Grand Duchess found too prepossessing, perhaps because she was a favourite of the dowager's; others said it was not a chambermaid but a handsome Turkish boy whom Cosimo had caused to be baptized—maliciously known as *Cosimino di Camera. . . .*

Irritated, says Galluzzi, by such unceasing disrespect, Cosimo dismissed two German grooms and a French dancing-master, who for some time had formed her privy council. The grooms used to accompany her on horseback when she went for a drive, and kept close beside the carriage-window through which she often conversed with them, to the scandal of malicious Florentines. Her dancing-master, Granmaison, who enjoyed the reputation of a bigamist, was also considered over-familiar with Marguerite-Louise. But she bore their dismissal with equanimity. Her cook became a worthy substitute for the departed trio, as is shown by the following narrative.[1] 'Cosimo had obliged the Grand Duchess to send back to France all the gentlemen and ladies of her Court, and only one Frenchman, a cook, remained. The Grand Duke gave himself up to devotion and solitude and governed his family, as he did his State, like Tiberius, and allowed his wife no amusement save a small concert for two or three hours every evening.

'The Grand Duchess, who was very young, found these concerts monotonous, or perhaps, being born in France, did not care for Italian music, so as a diversion she used to send for her French cook, who came with his long apron and white cap, just as he was dressed for cooking the dinner. Now this cook either dreaded, or pretended to dread, being tickled, and the Princess, aware of his weakness, took great pleasure in tickling him, while he made all those contortions, cries and gurglings proper to people who cannot bear to be tickled. So the Princess tickled the cook, and he defended himself, shouting and running from one side of the room to the other, which made her laugh immoderately. When tired of such romps, she would take a pillow from her bed and belabour the cook on the face and body, whilst he, shouting aloud, hid himself now under, now on, the very bed of the Princess, where she continued to beat him, until tired out with laughing and beating she sank exhausted into a chair. While these games were going on the musicians stopped playing, and as soon as the Princess sat down they recommenced.

'This noble amusement continued for some time before the Grand Duke was aware of it; but one evening it happened that the cook was very drunk, and therefore shouted louder than usual, and the Grand Duke, whose apartments were five or six rooms distant from those of the Grand Duchess, heard the noise and went to discover the cause.

[1] *Lettere familiare e critiche di Vincenzio Martinelli.* Londra Presso G. Nourse. Libraio nello Strand, 1758.

As he entered the room the Grand Duchess was beating her cook with a pillow on the grand-ducal bed, and the Prince, horrified at so novel a sight, instantly condemned the cook to the galleys (but I believe he was eventually reprieved), and scolding the lady with the utmost severity, with a bearing more princely than marital, he forbade her ever again to indulge in such conduct. The Princess resented being thus taken to task in the presence of the musicians, perchance with less consideration than she thought due to her high rank, and was exceedingly angry.'

On December 2nd (1672), Madame Du Deffand arrived, as she wrote to Pomponne a week later, with all the fatigue imaginable: 'I would take no account of it, if only my coming here could bring peace into this household. Her Royal Highness received me wonderfully, and was very pleased to see me. This did not prevent her from exhibiting her usual strains of passion, especially concerning her resentment at the dismissal of the servants we spoke of when I last had the honour of seeing you.'

To make matters worse, some correspondence fell into Cosimo's hands which Madame Du Deffand thought wiser to conceal even from the King. The Grand Duchess felt she had been caught in a snare, and wrote the following appeal to Nicolas de Gomont,[1] one of the King's gentlemen-in-waiting, the sole person she could think of in her distress:

'*The Grand Duchess of Tuscany to Monsieur de Gomont,*
From Florence, 4th December.

'This bearer will inform you of the way I am treated. To crown all, I have discovered that now they wish to deprive me of Madame Du Deffand; you may judge of the state I am in. I am so convinced of your kind feelings towards me that I beg you, if they are sincere, to prove them by coming hither as soon as you possibly can. I am sure the King will not object, and maybe this is your sole opportunity of rendering me a real service, since I have nothing so much at heart. You will earn my everlasting gratitude. I am sending you a letter which I implore you to dispatch to the King.

'Marguerite-Louise d'Orléans, Grand Duchess of Tuscany. In the name of God do not forsake me.'

[1] Vicomte de Portian, Baron de Las, etc., and later Governor of Montdidier. He was often sent on polite missions to Italy.

Strong evidence, this, of the Grand Duchess's harassed condition, for Cosimo had not wrested Madame Du Deffand from the Duchesse de Guise only to send her back to France, tired and tossed with her recent journey. Even when reassured about the Marquise, she unburdened herself to Gomont in another pressing epistle, almost as disheartened, on December 18th:

'I am persuaded that you still hold the memory of late Monsieur [Gaston d'Orléans] sufficiently dear to watch my interests, for love of him. I have depicted my misery to the King, and beg you to see that he does not forsake me. This is all I ask of you, and to see that His Majesty keeps a French resident, or at least one gentleman by me, who will render him a faithful account of my actions. The only favour I beg of the King is a convent in France, or any place in the world he chooses, even in the Grand Duke's estates; I know not whether I shall obtain it. They will bury me in the course of awaiting His Majesty's orders. I shall no longer be able to give you my news. Pray let me know if you have received this letter. Do not forget me, and rest assured that you could not oblige one more grateful or anxious to render you a service.'

In this forlorn mood she made her supreme resolution. She had become intolerant of half-measures. Rather than continue to live near her husband in the Pitti, she would 'bury herself' of her own free will. All around her she saw oppressors. At first her complaints had awakened pity at Versailles, but with reiteration they had lost their pathos. The Grand Duchess of Tuscany and her domestic trials had become a bore. The Sun King resented disagreeable news, as he could not abide a mournful face. Marguerite-Louise was frittering his sympathy away.

On December 20th (1672), she humbly begged Cosimo's permission to do reverence to the Madonna's girdle at Prato, and afterwards dine at Poggio a Caiano. The roads were almost impassable at this season, and the villa was unprepared for her, but Cosimo consented, since it was for purposes of devotion. Next day she persuaded him to buy her a valuable jewel from a French merchant. He bought it, although he found the price rather high, considering what gratitude he would get in return.

On the morning of December 23rd, regardless of pelting rain, she set forth with Madame Du Deffand, her ladies-in-waiting, and her chamberlain, Marchese Malvezzi; her suite had to wade behind her on horseback. After hearing Mass at Prato, the pilgrimage halted at Poggio a Caiano. There the Grand Duchess dined with immoderate gaiety, and at the time fixed for her departure, announced her decision not to return to Florence, but to remain where she was until the Grand Duke or the King should assign her a more appropriate residence. She despatched Malvezzi with the following letter for Cosimo:

'I have done what I could until now to gain your friendship, and have not succeeded. The more consideration I showed for you, the more contempt you showed for me. For a long time I have tried to bear it, but this is beyond my power. So I have made a resolution which will not surprise you, when you reflect on your base usage of me for nearly twelve years. It is, that I declare I can live with you no longer: I am the source of your unhappiness, as you are of mine. I beg you to consent to a separation to set my conscience and yours at rest. I shall send my confessor to discuss it with you, and shall here await the orders of his Majesty, to whom I have written, craving permission to enter a convent in France. I beg of you the same, and assure you that I shall forget the entire past if you grant me this favour. Do not perturb yourself about my conduct; my heart is as it should be, and it will never let me perform a dishonourable action, seeing that I have the fear of God and horror of this world ever before my eyes. I believe that what I am proposing to you is the surest means of affording us peace for the remainder of our days. I recommend my children to you.

'Marguerite-Louise d'Orléans, Grand Duchess of Tuscany.'

Cosimo answered immediately:

'I do not know if your unhappiness could have exceeded mine. Although everybody else has done justice to the many signs of respect, consideration and love which I have never tired of showing you for nearly twelve years, you have regarded them with the utmost indifference. I ought to be satisfied with universal approbation, but I continue to hope that Your Highness also will recognize this truth. I await the father confessor you are sending, to learn what he has to say on your behalf. I shall acquaint him with my sentiments. Meanwhile I am giving orders that besides proper attendants and conveniences Your Highness will receive at this villa all the respect which is your due, etc.'

These dignified words covered various conflicting emotions, of which wounded pride and desire for vengeance stood foremost. Marguerite's letter, moderate for so impulsive a creature, and containing but a bare allusion to the three children she thought of leaving for ever, almost struck him dumb with fury. She had put him in a painfully ridiculous position. Had she been at the mercy of Cosimo I, she would never have returned to France, dead or alive. But Cosimo III was incapable of ferocity. If he killed his wife, he would kill her by boredom.

Was the Grand Duchess determined to live in retirement? Well, Cosimo would be the last to put an obstacle in her way. He would see to it, moreover, that his wife's retreat should be made as humiliating as possible. His feelings found some outlet in a set of sarcastic regulations he drew up and signed for her benefit. Malvezzi, never to move from Poggio a Caiano, was daily to report on her behaviour. He was to follow her every time she set out on foot, 'to ward off dangers'. She was, of course, forbidden to enter Florence. Did she go on horseback, four stout anspessades (an anspessade was a kind of non-commissioned infantry officer under the rank of corporal) were to escort her. At the instigation of Madame Du Deffand, who 'deemed it good to deprive her of that little diversion', her horses were confiscated. One suspects this was Madame Du Deffand's retaliation for the fatiguing walks Marguerite had inflicted on her 'by break-neck mountain paths'.

Every evening, the footmen, porters and anspessades were carefully to examine all the locks and doors of the rooms she occupied. No attendant or servant of the Grand Duchess, 'whatever his rank or condition', was authorized to leave the villa, either for Florence or elsewhere, without a written permit from Cosimo. If there was need for a workman of any kind, he must come provided with an order from the Grand Duke, or he would not be admitted; nor could he sleep at the villa, however long his labours lasted.

'Italian or foreigner, nobleman or commoner', nobody could gain access to the Grand Duchess or even to her apartment, and this interdict extended to the persons 'most bound to the Grand Duchess by friendship or relationship', unless Cosimo condescended to make an exception. Concerts and balls, assemblies and parties in which peasants danced—all were forbidden. Whenever Marguerite had any observation to make, she was to address herself, not to Cosimo, but to

Marucelli, his chief Minister of State, whose orders she must obey 'as if they emanated from the Grand Duke in person'.

To these regulations Cosimo adds, with studied irony: 'we desire the Grand Duchess to enjoy perfect freedom to come and go, to amuse herself and spend her time, to be obeyed by her servants, and to receive whomsoever it will suit her to receive at all times and at all hours'. He must have gloated on that little tailpiece.

X

*The Grand Duchess Begs Louis XIV to Allow Her Return
– He Sends Her the Bishop of Marseilles – Failure of
Attempts to Conciliate Her*

During the next few months Cosimo and Marguerite were each busy accounting for their conduct to Louis XIV. Both were anxious to win his sympathy. 'Your Majesty,' wrote Cosimo, 'may judge the greatness of the affliction to which I and my whole family are reduced, and from which I can expect no consolation save in the protection of Your Majesty.'

Marguerite hammered away distractedly. 'Sire,' she wrote, 'I beg Your Majesty's pardon on both knees, while revealing how I quitted the Grand Duke, since it was impossible to remain with him. I have done this thing with the minimum of scandal . . . out of consideration for Your Majesty. As for him, he has always treated me so ill and given me such scant consideration that I did not deem it necessary to give him any, but shall continue to do everything that I trust can be agreeable to Your Majesty. I implore Your Majesty to save me from my present misery; and if you happen to be under some obligation to the Grand Duke which hinders you from sheltering me in a French convent, I beg you to allow me to go to the Electress of Bavaria who has a convent near her palace, where I shall be able to live in peace and pray for Your Majesty. She is my first cousin; she has the honour to be yours as well; and her husband is your ally. . . .

'When it is Your Majesty's pleasure, my letters will be filled with expressions of gratitude and joy. Only take me hence, and from the depths of misery I shall rise to the heights of happiness. It matters not whither I go, provided I escape from the hands of my oppressor, who is not in the wrong, since I have made him lose patience. I am assured he pities himself exceedingly, but those who suffer most do not complain, for I do not mention all he has made me endure. These sufferings will end when Your Majesty wishes. I have done penance now for nearly twelve years. This does not prevent me from remembering what I owe Your Majesty, and from nurturing a passion to serve you which will only cease with my life.'

Louis was embarrassed. He did not wish to abandon Marguerite or offend Cosimo; he would not agree that the marriage he had sponsored was a fiasco. His letters to Cosimo were kind but non-committal. He urged him to try every means of making her change her mind.

It seems strange that after his previous experience of Marguerite-Louise he should resort again to the same old method. So many worthy ambassadors and priests had been bundled off to Tuscany in vain. Louis proceeded to send her Toussaint de Forbin-Janson, the Bishop of Marseilles.

The Bishop left for Florence in February, with detailed instructions from the King. Louis's attitude encouraged Cosimo to act as he felt inclined. The rules he had drawn up were obeyed to a certain extent, but there were always loopholes.

Marguerite was constantly ruffled by the petty indignities to which she was subjected. Cosimo made a fuss because her confessor spent too much time in her room. One of her French servants had been so bold as to suggest a fishing expedition. As he had done so furtively, begging the Grand Duchess not to mention that the idea had been his, he was dismissed. 'One can easily spread nets, and fish with a rod,' wrote Malvezzi, 'without wrapping it in so much mystery.'

Vignettes of Marguerite's life in February, 1673, are at variance: in a letter to the Queen of France she depicts herself as 'deprived of every convenience, buried alive in appalling solitude', while the Nuncio's secretary reports that 'the Grand Duchess continues to enjoy the delights of Poggio a Caiano'. Her household actually contained as many as at the Pitti, more than one hundred and fifty men and women. When she complained of solitude she was not literal. She was comparing, thinking of her existence as it might have been. The splendour she might have enjoyed at the Court of France! She remembered those four days at Fontainebleau.

And now life was this: her every step under observation; her every act to be accounted for. But she had her reprisals; and Malvezzi's task as superintendent of that little world was made a fretful one. One day there was an uproar in the kitchen. The scullions, who had been half-starved, sent up a fish without head or tail to the Grand Duchess's table. Malvezzi threatened to expel the pack of them, but they explained that they had no wish to die of hunger: if the Grand Duchess wanted her portions whole, she should keep her scullions alive. But kitchen riots were child's play beside some of the Grand Duchess's. However sad at heart, Marguerite-Louise was determined to appear blithe before her entourage, for it galled her husband to hear of it. Now she would require a fiddler 'to divert her pending the Bishop's arrival'; now she would perform a graceful *pas seul* before her assembled household; or she would command her ladies-in-waiting to dance before her. And Malvezzi was obliged to follow her everywhere—on endless drives through violent downpours of rain—on endless walks which blistered his soles but never seemed to tire the Grand Duchess. Far from being shattered by her private sorrows, her health improved; she seemed to gain vitality.

As soon as she knew of the Bishop's mission, she wrote a determined letter to Cosimo: 'I have just heard that the King has done me the honour of sending me Monsieur de Marseille, a man of singular merit. I think I must acquaint you with my sentiments before his arrival, so that you may make up your mind; no matter what he does, I shall never return to you. It is not that I am ignorant of all I owe the King; his commands will ever be inviolable laws to me; it is because I am convinced that if he saw things close to as he sees them from afar, and if he knew my reasons, he would not constrain me. And if he came himself to lead me to you, I would obey, for he is my King, my father, my master, and my all; but I should never live with you. I believe you understand me and you have so much wit that you must have understood from the past that it is impossible for me to live with you, that I have always done so in spite of myself, and that I could never return.'

The Bishop disembarked at Viareggio with a suite of thirty-three, on March 13th, 1673. Pomponne, while assuring him that Italy was a country where ceremonies were very much observed, had not been able to answer his questions about Italian etiquette, and he had been rather nervous in consequence. But Cosimo's reception put him at ease. First he had to get in touch with Madame Du Deffand. Then he was to see the royal prisoner. The Marquise warned him that the Grand Duchess was hardened as the Pharaoh of Egypt, and that her aversion to Cosimo was invincible. But the bland Bishop entertained a conviction that he must succeed where others had failed. He even inspired confidence in Cosimo. 'In her aversion to the Grand Duke,' he wrote the King, 'there is none of the usual cause for matrimonial dissensions. For as she does not complain of having suffered from the slightest suspicion of jealousy, the Grand Duke on his side warmly assures me that H.R.H.'s virtue is beyond reproach, and everybody here confirms this. All hinges upon the disparity in their temperaments, and their totally different habits. The Grand Duke, naturally melancholy and sombre, leads a private and retired life, while the Grand Duchess is so playful and merry, that it is not strange they should be at variance.' Give way to some of her caprices, and the main thing, that obstinate antipathy, would be forgotten and disposed of. . . .

He betook himself to Poggio a Caiano on March 17th, and like all her superficial observers he found the princess had 'a natural wit': she was 'lively and brilliant, bold and enterprising', even gentle. He had to walk warily with such a penitent. First 'he must insinuate himself into her mind'—flatter her sense of responsibility, surrendering to her whims until some good occasion presented itself, with plenty of leisure to talk matters over and lead her into confidences.

Next morning, before the Grand Duchess was awake, the Bishop had a long conversation with Madame Du Deffand. It was decided that he would pretend to forget his mission to begin with: his only wish, apparently, would be to participate in the Grand Duchess's pleasures. Marguerite-Louise, overjoyed to find a new companion, entered the game with so much spirit that she disarmed the good Bishop. He was given a *Serata d'Onore*. Last Carnival's comedy was revived, and her ladies-in-waiting danced before him. Apparently the Bishop was not altogether pleased, for he remarked that the stage was unworthy of a sovereign. Marguerite-Louise invited him to her table after the performance, and sat beside him, pranked out in her comedy costume. The conversation was enlivened by the presence of Abbate Sacco, a typical specimen of the Tuscan buffooning monk. Marguerite-Louise clapped her hands and laughed, as she did all things, immoderately, louder than the gentlemen in the Bishop's suite, and the prelate began to realize that she was putting him in a ludicrous situation. Next morning he left Poggio to report on his encounter to the Grand Duke. He returned with his tactics revised. This time he would be straightforward. The Grand Duchess appeared ready to listen to him, but scarce had he opened his august mouth when lo! the musicians appeared, followed by her German professor and ladies-in-waiting. The Bishop began his carefully premeditated instruction to the sound of violins. Then Marguerite-Louise herself rose and, after a few preliminary trills, obliged the company with a song.

The Bishop began to take in the measure of that hardness the Marquise had warned him of, her combination of artfulness and tenacity. One by one, all the advances that had been made on his advice to Marguerite-Louise were rejected. The horses Cosimo restored to her she sent back. She declared herself resigned to all things except seeing the Grand Duke.

The feasts began anew. The Grand Duchess called Giusto Sustermans to Poggio, and sat for her portrait in the Bishop's presence, and afterwards persuaded the Bishop to pose, but only for the head and shoulders. There was dancing, we are told, and every kind of noisy distraction. The Bishop concluded that the Grand Duchess was possessed of 'quite an extraordinary firmness'. He sought the assistance of her confessor and French doctor. The confessor asked Madame Du Deffand to tell Marguerite-Louise the result of their conference, but as she refused he had to tell her himself. If, he said, she continued thus to offend against laws human and divine, he would find it impossible to give her absolution and communion the following Easter. Marguerite-Louise replied that as her own conscience was immaculate, the Grand Duke, and not herself, was to blame. She told the horrified Bishop that she had once gone eighteen months without confessing: she would do so again if they refused her absolution.

The Bishop still searched for further ways and means. One of the Grand Duchess's chief subjects of complaint had been her exclusion from the *Consulta*. She blamed the dowager, and not without cause. So the Bishop approached Vittoria and got her to give way on this point. Marguerite-Louise had also complained of the inconvenience of her apartments in the Pitti, 'without even a closet to which she could retire'; of only receiving an allowance of thirty thousand crowns

VEDVTA DELLA PIAZZA DI S.ᵗᵃ CROCE DELLA CITTA DI FIRENZE NEL ATTO DI PRINCIPIARE IL GIOCO DEL CALCIO ST.° J 6 09 09
Alexander Cecchini del

41 *(previous page)* The ceiling of the Sala di Marte by Pietro da Cortona, in the Pitti
42 *(above)* The ceremony at the beginning of a football game (1689) in the Piazza Santa Croce.
Engraving by A. Cecchini. Istituto Germanico

43 *(right)* The Piazza
and church of
S. Giovannino, with the
Palazzo Medici-Riccardi,
the palace of Cosimo
Pater Patriae.
Museo di Firenze com'era

Veduta della Piazza, e Chiesa di S. Giovannino de PP. Gesuiti, e de Palazzi dei SS. Marchese Riccardi, e Panciatichi.
T. XIX

44, 45 *The World in Festivity*, a celebration in the Boboli Gardens for the marriage of
Marguerite-Louise and **Cosimo III**, in 1661. Engravings by Della Bella, 1661
(above) the Mount of Atlas; *(below)* Hercules, with the Sun and Moon

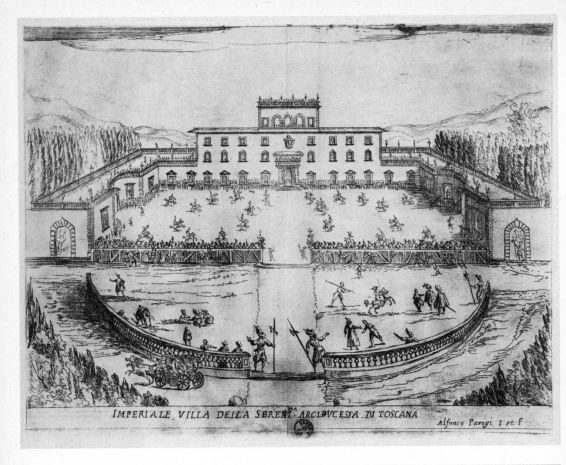

IMPERIALE . VILLA . DEILA . SERENT.ᴬ . ARCIDVCESSA . DI TOSCANA   Alfonso Parigi. I et f

46, 47 *(previous pages)*
Pietro da Cortona:
frescoes in the Palatina
(left) The Golden Age
(right) The Silver Age

48 *(opposite above)*
Poggio Imperiale, engraving
by Alfonso Parigi.
Uffizi, Gabinetto Fotografico

49 *(opposite below)*
Fireworks on the Arno,
drawing by Jacques Callot.
Gabinetto dei Disegni
e delle Stampe

50 *(right)* Marguerite-Louise
d'Orléans, bust attributed
to Giovanni Battista Foggini
(1652–1725).
Private Collection

51 *(opposite)* Ferdinando II on his succession beside the Regents,
his mother Maria-Maddalena of Austria
and grandmother Christine of Lorraine,
by Sustermans. Oxford, Ashmolean Museum

52 *(above)* The yearly *Festa degli Omaggi*, at which
all the Grand Duke's vassals paid homage.
Florentine school, eighteenth-century.
Historical Topographical Museum

53 *(left)* Bust of Vittoria della Rovere
by G. A. Torricelli (1696).
Museo delle Pietre Dure

54 *(below left)* Violante of Bavaria,
medal by A. Montauti. Museo Nazionale

55 *(below right)* Marguerite-Louise,
medal by A. F. Selvi. Museo Nazionale

56 *(opposite above)* View of Florence taken near the Porta alla Croce.
Engraving after Zocchi. Museo di Firenze com'era

57 *(opposite below)* View of Florence taken from the Porta a S. Niccolò.
Engraving after Zocchi. Museo di Firenze com'era

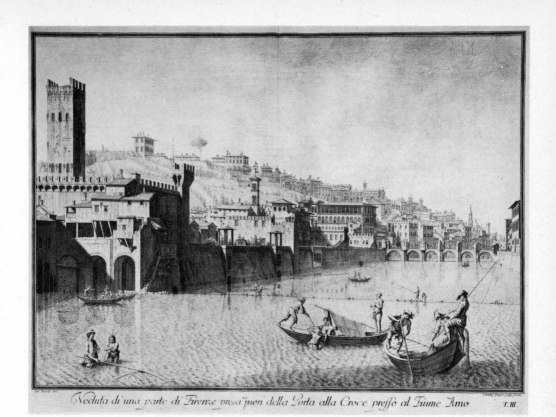

Veduta di una parte di Firenze presa fuori della Porta alla Croce presso al Fiume Arno   T. III.

Veduta di una parte di Firenze presa fuori della Porta a S. Niccolò presso al Fiume Arno   T. IV.

58 Bartolomeo Bimbi: *Still Life with Cherries*. Uffizi

59 The Villa Ferdinanda at Artimino

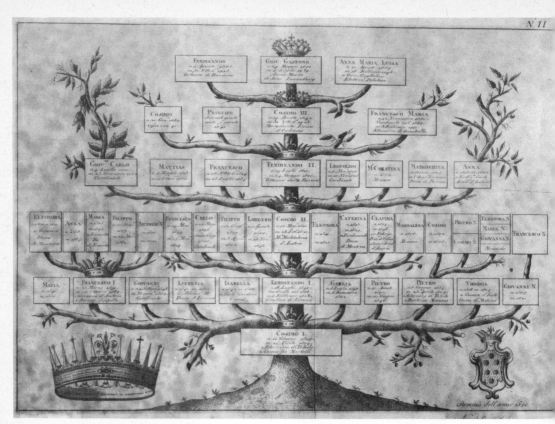

60 *(above)* The Medici family tree by N. Lapini. Istituto Germanico

61 *(left)* Medal with portrait of Francesco Redi, scientist and man of letters, by M. Soldani Benzi. Modena, Galleria Estense

62 *(opposite above)* The gardens of Pratolino, with trick fountains which soaked the unwary. Etching by Della Bella

63 *(opposite below)* Another view of the gardens at Pratolino, showing the fountain walk. Etching by Della Bella

64 Cosimo III as a young man, by Sustermans. Pitti

for clothes and pin-money; and of lacking 'a country-house of her own, whither she could go whenever she pleased'.

For all these grievances the Bishop procured redress. He knew that the Grand Duchess did not trust her husband's promises; but he assured her that the King would guarantee their fulfilment, and offered to remain in Florence until she was satisfied. Having swept away so many obstacles, he now expected Marguerite-Louise to surrender. But she told him, without the faintest embarrassment, that she had only been expressing herself indirectly, as it were. She was undoubtedly grateful, oh very grateful, for all he had said and done, and his reasoning was altogether excellent, but—'having tried in vain for twelve long years to change her feelings, she could not repudiate them now'.

Truly the prelate's optimism was prodigious. He exhorted her, with all his eloquence, 'to make a sacrifice to God of this fatal aversion'. The Grand Duchess was quite unmoved by this, but she became startlingly confidential. Although the question at issue was not new to him, he stood aghast to hear it from her lips.

While the Bishop was rubbing his eyes, the Grand Duke informed him that he, too, had certain declarations to make. These were no less serious and delicate, and added to the complication.

Meanwhile Marguerite-Louise resumed that argument of religious scruples she had found so effective before. She protested that she could not return to the Grand Duke without exposing herself and him to the sin of concubinage. She sent Cosimo a very forceful letter on the subject. In agony of conscience Cosimo consulted his theologians. Their discordant opinions perplexed him all the more. He brooded over them, terrorized by the thought of the sin he would commit in taking back his wife under compulsion. Then he began to dread the success of these efforts to propitiate her. 'The theologians he consults,' wrote the harassed Bishop, 'encourage his scruples, so that he wishes me to cease urging the Grand Duchess to return to him.' But the Bishop's mission was precise, and he could not renounce it—unless Louis XIV countermanded his orders. He informed Cosimo that whatever happened, he would continue striving to restore his wife to him. Nothing daunted, he spent eleven days on end at the villa, from the seventeenth to the twenty-eighth of April.

Partly because she wished to provoke Cosimo to such a pitch that he should long for her departure, and partly because she enjoyed throwing convention to the winds, she invited all her household to her table, even those least qualified to sit there, so that the Bishop was shocked and Cosimo was justified in saying that his wife only enjoyed herself in the company of riff-raff. Finally she availed herself of the horses which the Bishop had caused to be restored to her; and galloped about the country for six or seven hours at a stretch. Only her escorts, as usual, were fatigued. Often the horses came back foundered.

Gradually the Bishop was convinced that nothing on earth could bring about a reconciliation. But before leaving the Princess he thought it his duty to make one last attempt. For several hours he conversed with her alone in her bedroom, told her how sinful her behaviour was, of the remorse she would suffer after leaving her children, and yet again insisted that the King had an insurmountable objection to her return, even to a convent. Furthermore, he declared that if she left Tuscany, Louis XIV would prevent other sovereigns from offering her an asylum. Having administered this final rebuke, the frustrated Bishop definitely took leave of her. He had been butting his head against a wall; and the wall had observed the process of his collapse with amused detachment.

Madame Du Deffand departed with him on May 7th, 1673, and Cosimo was inwardly delighted by their failure.

XI

Louis XIV Opposes Separation; then Acquiesces in 1674
—The Convent of Montmartre Chosen for the Grand Duchess's
Retirement – Her Departure, 1675

'My cousin,' wrote Louis XIV to Marguerite-Louise when in August Madame Du Deffand and the Bishop of Marseilles divulged the 'secret': 'I have received your letters and listened at length to what the Bishop had to say concerning yourself; and I admit that it was not without being touched by portions of his narrative. But the more susceptible I become to all that concerns you, the less capable do I find myself of leading you to expect the separation and departure he spoke of. These are extremities so little worthy of you and of me, that if unhappily you resort to them, you need expect no further consideration or protection from me.'[1]

The secret in question was, of course, the Grand Duchess's innocuous flirtation with Prince Charles of Lorraine. Cosimo had seized several of Prince Charles's letters, passionate in tone; unfortunately he did not possess the Grand Duchess's replies. But he suspected that Prince Charles's feelings were reciprocated from Marguerite-Louise's anxiety to learn German and go to Bavaria, where Prince Charles spent most of his time. Doubtless her German grooms had helped her in this correspondence. Some intercepted notes addressed to them gave ground for most disquieting suppositions.

An amorous correspondence, however lively, would not perturb Louis XIV unless it had an object in the immediate neighbourhood. Prince Charles's letters from distant Germany, under the circumstances, were as good as platonic from his point of view. He persisted in his determination to unite the Grand Duke and Grand Duchess of Tuscany because, if their marriage was annulled by the Church, himself would be partly responsible for an illicit union. Besides, it would cast

[1] August 22nd, 1673.

a dangerous doubt on the validity of most marriages contracted by princes of the blood, even when consecrated by the Church, by time, and the birth of children.

But Cosimo was now quite as determined not to take his wife back. 'If she returned to me,' he wrote Madame Du Deffand in October, 'what sentiments, what union could exist between us, and what would not be the torment of my conscience? I should still be uncertain about the validity of our unfortunate marriage. Whichever side I turn, I only see distress in the future.'

Thus by a singular twist of irony both Cosimo and Marguerite-Louise had to contend against Louis, with different aims but an equal intensity. Neither had any desire to live together, but Cosimo wished his wife to remain a sort of prisoner in Tuscany while she was determined to escape to France.

On May 19th, wishing to change air, she asked to stay at San Cerbone, a villa near Figline, belonging to Marchese Salviati. Malvezzi saw a harder task before him, and implored the Prime Minister to prevent it. He would require months to convert it into such a stronghold as Poggio a Caiano. But Cosimo dared not oppose her, and to San Cerbone she went on June 3rd. Malvezzi had all the doors padlocked and windows barred. It was thoroughly sentinelled and patrolled. As soon as she arrived the Grand Duchess wished to return to Poggio. She was afraid of the purples, she said, and her doctor supported her fears. 'The heat of this place,' he wrote Cosimo, 'will spoil her complexion and inflame her blood.' But the Grand Duke considered the air of Poggio no better, and would not allow her to return until July 27th.

Marguerite-Louise devoted the last days of July to the compiling of a copious memoir, in which her misfortunes were enumerated. Grandin, the cook, who had excited the scullions against Malvezzi, was commissioned to draft it.

Occasional visitors came to brighten her solitude. When Cosimo's Court went to Pisa, she wished to go to Florence. But Gondi wrote Malvezzi expressing a hope that the Grand Duchess would not make arrangements in open defiance of the Grand Duke's will.

She persevered in her attempts to get Cosimo to authorize her retirement to a French convent. But she had not shown enough regard for her religious duties for him to consider her vocation genuine.

Cosimo repeated to Marguerite-Louise 'that she should pray God to enlighten her'. To which she replied that she spent her life in doing so. In order to convince him she began to attend Mass with a marvellous assiduity.

It suited Cosimo's new frame of mind to feign belief in her penitence. Suddenly he declared that 'he mingled his prayers with hers, and laid them at the King's feet'.

She registered this important event in the following words, dated May 15th, 1674: 'The Grand Duke having asked if my vocation to become a nun persisted, and I having answered in the affirmative, he told me that he would beg the King to allow me to enter a convent in France which His Majesty will select.'

Whereupon she sent Cosimo two letters compromising her for all time, 'as a proof of her inability to live in good conscience with him without offending God'. Such was the significance of these letters that when she asked him to return them (prior to leaving Tuscany), the Grand Duke replied that 'he would keep them as a document to assure his peace of mind in future and prove to him, if ever he came to doubt of it, that he had acted wisely, and had not let himself be carried away by impulse'. Besides, he added, it was to his advantage to keep them secret. Then he discovered that certain casuists at Rome, consulted by the Grand Duchess, had decided in favour of the nullity of his marriage, and were even ready to publish their opinions. This brought matters to a head. He commissioned Gondi to persuade the Bishop of Marseilles, Madame Du Deffand and the Duchesse de Guise to 'coach' the King for Marguerite-Louise's return to France. Gondi repeated that the King would never allow it.

Cosimo's lamentations were piteous. Had he not tried every means of inducing his wife to return to him? Must he take her back by force, when his eternal salvation was at stake? Nay: he would never consent, merely to save the King trouble, and lose his immortal soul and his wife's in the bargain. Gondi seemed deficient in zeal, and Cosimo goaded him on precisely as Marguerite-Louise wished him to do. For, though she was longing to leave, she wished to have it said that Cosimo had driven her away.

The King asked why, if the Grand Duchess were so anxious to enter a convent, she did not choose one in Italy. Gondi replied that, in renouncing matrimony, Marguerite-Louise could do no better than put herself in His Majesty's keeping, and that the Grand Duke was anxious to know that she was under his protection.

Finally Louis acquiesced on condition that Cosimo would assure his consort an existence worthy of her rank: she was not to appear imprisoned, even if she lived in a convent. Marguerite-Louise heard of the King's change of mind on June 7th, 1674. Her rapture was ill-concealed. France, Paris, the Court of the Sun King: she would see them all again: her dream would be realized.

There remained all sorts of niggling questions to be threshed out: questions of money, politics, etiquette. Madame Du Deffand alone could contend with them, knowing the secret wishes of both parties. But she was old and her health was failing. She declined another mission to Tuscany. Then the King said he counted upon her; and she was compelled to leave. The heat was intense, and by the time she arrived at Vercelli, she was so exhausted that her servants thought her on the verge of death. A maid of hers called Charenton, and a spy in Cosimo's service, sent him word of her illness, and drugs were hastily despatched from Florence, which enabled her to pursue the journey. When finally she arrived, on October 9th, 1674, she had one foot in the grave.

It was very difficult to select a convent suitable for the Grand Duchess of Tuscany. Either it was infested with ladies of tarnished quality, such as Madame de Longueville and Madame de la Vallière, or infected with Jansenism. The Benedictine convent of Montmartre emerged as incontestably 'superior in rank' to the others.

Both Cosimo and Madame Du Deffand decided in its favour. But when Gondi approached the Abbess, that lady raised a host of objections. She was far from anxious to assume the responsibility of supervising a notoriously turbulent Grand Duchess. Only two apartments in the convent were available, she said: one above the infirmary, the other overlooking a noisy street, where the scum of the district assembled. And though Gondi assured her that the Grand Duke would build a special wing for his wife, which would serve for future abbesses on the Grand Duchess's death, the Abbess would not yield. Madame Du Deffand advised Marguerite-Louise to write her a submissive letter, whereupon she surrendered. The document which was to settle Marguerite-Louise's future was signed on December 26th in the presence of Madame Du Deffand, at Castello. The articles of separation declared that Marguerite-Louise had resolved to pass her future life in retirement in the Convent of Montmartre, near Paris: that she bound herself never to leave it without the King's permission: that she renounced her privileges as princess of the blood; that she would only keep such attendants as were approved by the Abbess: that she bequeathed to her children whatever she might die possessed of; and promised solemnly that her conduct should be blameless.

In return the Grand Duke promised to provide her with a pension of 65,000 crowns for the first year, which had already begun, and 80,000 French livres for the years to follow. He allowed her besides 8,000 crowns for the expense of her journey and installation; 10,000 crowns' worth of silver; two hangings, one of damask and one of tapestry work; and two beds for her use at different seasons.

The moment was appropriately dramatized. 'Such is Madame's desire to serve Your Serene Highness,' wrote Francesco Redi to the Grand Duke, 'that having had a clyster and suffering from cruel torment that made her think she was like to die, she nevertheless insisted on signing this document, which was sealed with her seal in the midst of her screams.' Then she regained composure and her anguish abated. Madame Du Deffand, her work achieved, expired on January 22nd, 1675.

Her maid, Charenton, was taken into the service of Marguerite-Louise. This woman foresaw that Gondi, as soon as he heard of her mistress's death, would be in a great hurry to get hold of her papers. She wrote at once, informing him that these were in a sealed casket of which she alone held the key, and advised him to await her return before opening it. But patience was not among the Abbé's virtues. He proposed that the Marquis Du Deffand should open it in his presence, then seal it up again, after he had extracted the Grand Duke's and Grand Duchess's correspondence. Thanks to the widower's connivance, Gondi already saw himself in possession of Marguerite-Louise's most incriminating letters. Then he remembered that, on hearing the news of Madame Du Deffand's death, he had asked the Duchesse de Guise to affix her seal to the precious receptacle, lest the widower might pick the lock. He regretted this precaution, for now he could not open it without the Duchesse, who rightly mistrusted him.

Although she bore her sister little love, the Duchesse had no desire for her family honour to be smirched. She would let Gondi break the seal only on condition that all the Grand Duchess's letters found within were instantly destroyed. It was almost a repetition of that tantalizing incident after her mother's death, when Gondi had had to see the documents he yearned for consigned to the flames. But the Abbé's hand had gained in nimbleness since then, and, as he admitted not without pride, he managed secretly to filch some dozen letters, which he took home to enjoy. Alas, his alertness was ill-repaid. Only seven had been written by Marguerite-Louise, and their content was trivial.

The Grand Duchess was quite aware that in Florence as in Paris her adversaries were intriguing against her. She dreaded the consequences of remaining 'at the mercy of wild Italians', and begged the King to send her the Comte de Sainte-Même. But Cosimo did not wish it to appear as if his wife had been recalled by the King, and refused to receive Sainte-Même, on the ground that Marguerite-Louise would take advantage of his presence to raise new difficulties. (Later Gomont was sent in his stead, but on the strict understanding that he was not to accompany, or interfere in any way with, the Princess. He was 'to confine himself to witnessing the attentions that were shown her'. But he did not arrive until May 6th.) So Marguerite-Louise was left at this critical juncture with her faithful doctor Pelletier, and her own sagacity. Cosimo had pretended that she was a flutter-pate, but where her own interests were concerned she was impressively practical.

She had a hot dispute with the treasurer Bernardi over the 10,000 crowns' worth of silver that had been promised her, when she learned that she was to receive the equivalent in Italian money. The question of furniture she solved by appropriating it. When Marchese Salviati, the Grand Duke's chamberlain, arrived at Poggio a Caiano, he discovered that all the silver—candlesticks, ink-stands, ewers and chandeliers—had been replaced by crockery. The Grand Duchess had only left an earthenware basin for her own ablutions. A cabinet inlaid with precious stones and a valuable perfume-burner had already been packed off. She was also prepared to take away a fine necklace which Cosimo had given her after her first confinement. For Marguerite-Louise had no intention, as she expressed it, 'of setting forth without her proper wages'. In addition, she claimed a tapestry of damask and a bed, two pairs of sheets, two coverlets, one embroidered, the other of taffeta, a 'foot-warmer' and a 'wallet for when I go to Mass', both of red velvet and in the French style.

So generous was she in distributing alms before her departure that within a few days she had spent all that had been given her for largesse and incidental expenses on the journey. She had to ask for more, not desiring, as she said, 'to find herself penniless on the highway'.

France and Spain were at war, and Cosimo was nervous lest his wife's galleys should come in contact with Spanish ones. Such an adventure would have been welcome to Marguerite-Louise, who said she longed to take part in a naval combat. But Cosimo preferred not to put her valour to the test, and all the members of her suite were provided with Tuscan passports.

As the time of her release drew near, when her suspense was hardly endurable, Marguerite-Louise became very quiet and reserved. The vigilance of her guardians increased. But she for once behaved irreproachably.

It was natural that she should wish to see her children before departing. But Cosimo said it would be unwise to expose them to all the anguish of such a rupture. Marguerite-Louise insisted and prevailed. 'I am waiting impatiently,' she wrote, 'for you to let me know which day my children may come to Castello, and at what hour; I hope it will be early, so as to have more time to see them'.[1] When they arrived she bade them dance before her, after which she abruptly dismissed them. It is improbable that she was deeply attached to them; but her elder son, Ferdinando, at any rate, bore her some affection, and it was partly on her account that he quarrelled in later years with his father.

Her mother-in-law begged to pay her a last visit—a gesture which Marguerite-Louise had forestalled—'being very happy,' she wrote, 'since we have always lived together on good terms, that we should part the same.'[2] Her uncle-in-law, the Prince-Cardinal full-fledged, and her brother-in-law, the Prince-Cardinal in embryo, came likewise to bid her farewell. Only Cosimo abstained. He was afraid of dropping some discordant word, if such an interview took place.

So Marguerite-Louise left Poggio a Caiano on Monday, June 10th, 1675, after having set up a continuous commotion in that peaceful villa.

[1] May 31st, 1675. [2] June 4th, 1675.

On the 12th she was at Leghorn. Her suite consisted of twenty-six servants: she had had over a hundred on her arrival in Tuscany. One Italian soldier was taken on board at her request because he played the lute; also a singer whom she wished to bring to Montmartre.

At the last moment Gomont, defying his instructions, suggested that Marguerite-Louise should send her confessor to Cosimo, begging forgiveness for all the injuries she had done him. She offered to pardon him in return. The trap was obvious. By accepting such an exchange, Cosimo would admit that himself was not without reproach. So he sent a Franciscan friar to say that he was too ill to receive the Grand Duchess's message, but that he would continue to pray for the salvation of her soul.

The externals had been respected, and Pomponne was enabled to write Strozzi that 'the misfortune of this separation was somewhat alleviated by the fact of its having taken place in so decent a manner'.

When the Grand Duchess's departure was proclaimed throughout Tuscany it caused 'a great displeasure' among the people. She had played the martyr with such skill that the Florentines blamed her husband for this separation. Cosimo had alienated all by his morose and peevish self-righteousness; he appeared callous and inhuman. Marguerite-Louise, on the other hand, suggested sympathetic frailty; her blemishes vanished in the memory of her gaiety and light-heartedness.

In the same year, 1675, on November 10th, Cosimo's sole surviving uncle, the cultured Cardinal Leopoldo, died, exhausted by chronic ill-health. He was the last of the nobler Medici, and the last slender restraint on Cosimo III.

XII

Cosimo III's Reaction to His Wife's Departure
— Theological Outlets; Persecution of Jews; Political Ambitions
— The Grand Duchess on Her Return to Paris

After the departure of Marguerite-Louise, Cosimo's first impulse we are told, anxious to disprove the reputation for avarice his wife had given him, was to introduce into his life a new system of what Balzac would have called insolent luxury, such as had not been seen in Florence for many a year. Regardless of calamities, he spared no expense to summon the rarest and most precious condiments from all sections of the globe to his table, whose splendour was increased by the attendance of foreign servants arrayed in their native costumes. The latter he received in exchange for wines and other gifts. Missionaries sent him two Indians from the East, the Czar a couple of Kalmuks, the King of Denmark two Greenlanders, and so on. The richness of his repasts was the admiration of all that were admitted to them, albeit the Grand Duke's intemperance diminished their esteem of his person. That 'paragon of piety' preached abstinence to others, and taxed his subjects heavily so that they might practise it, but himself remained a conspicuous gormandizer.

He would have his fatted capons weighed at the table, and if a pair of these failed to weigh the requisite twenty pounds, he had them removed as if they had given him personal affront. His exotic sweetmeats were washed down with liquors cooled in snow, so that he soon grew disproportionately stout. He suffered in consequence. To reduce his weight, he was advised to take physics which put him in a worse plight, for both his legs began to give way beneath him. It did not look as if he would last long.

Tuscany was mistakenly supposed to have reached her zenith of prosperity. Cosimo III was uncommonly concerned about stage effect, and his expenditure on pomps and ceremonies swelled the legend of his opulence: no prince or ambassador came to Florence but was entertained with Oriental magnificence, and loaded with gifts on his departure. By this unnecessary profusion Cosimo hoped to increase his ever-waning prestige. His mind seemed wholly occupied with trifles.

He ordered, for instance, that the helmet and sword of Guglielmino degli Ubertini, the famous fighting Bishop of Arezzo, should be moved from the church of San Giovanni, where they had hung for centuries by an ancient decree of the Florentine Republic. It was not right, he said, to keep alive in the people's memory the example of a priest who had perished on the battlefield.[1]

Of all the great yearly Florentine festivals, that of *Calendimaggio*, or May-day, was the most prepossessing. Up betimes, the young men went off to hang a *maio* on the doors of their sweethearts. This *maio* was a branch of some flowering shrub, gaily beribboned and entwined with glittering tinsel, or with dainties and sweetmeats attached to it. There were songs in chorus, improvised *stornelli* and *rispetti* to the shapely tiorba, a lute with two necks, followed by such frolicsome dances as the rigoletto, the ring of roses, to welcome 'the year's pleasant king'.

'Enjoy what you can of spring,' said the Tuscan, 'and help others to enjoy it, if it be but with a blossom, or a verse or a pleasant thought.'

Cosimo was suspicious of these simple sentiments. It all seemed detrimental to morality—this crude love of nature. He sincerely wished to wean his subjects from such paganism. So he commanded the 'Eight' to publish an edict suspending the perennial feast of *Calendimaggio*, 'with the penalty of the whip for those girls who go through the streets singing songs of May', as they had done from time immemorial. Happily, Cosimo did not succeed in stamping it out altogether. It is not easy to stop the birds from singing. . . .

While this innocent holiday was suspended, copious others for little rhyme or reason were commanded to crop up in its stead, involving tedious parades and processions, of pseudo-pious nature. In these Cosimo himself was proud to take a conspicuous part.

His theological humour found another vent in persecuting the Jews. He forbade all carnal intercourse between Hebrews and Christians. All Christians, of whatever age, sex, grade or calling, were forbidden to serve in the houses and shops of Hebrews. Whoever broke this rule in-

[1] On the plain of Campaldino, 'at the foot of Poppi', June 11th, 1289.

curred a fine of fifty crowns. Such as had not wherewithal to pay were liable to be tortured twice on the rack; if they were physically unfitted to receive this punishment, the sentence was commuted to four months' imprisonment.

Jews found guilty of visiting Christian prostitutes were even more severely dealt with. In this case each incurred a fine of three hundred crowns. If the woman were unable to pay, the unfortunate Jew had to defray her share. The woman, health permitting, was stripped to the waist, even in mid-winter, and, after being kept warm with lashes, vigorously applied by the executioner, was sent to cool them in prison pending the judge's goodwill. Proclamation followed proclamation; on July 1st, 1677, June 16th, 1679, and December 20th, 1680, respectively. The last is fully the most intricate. Certain Christian and Jewish families, it informs us, had actually dared to live in the same house. To quash this horrible abuse, 'the superior virtue of His Serene Highness' commanded that no Jew or Gentile of any sex, or condition, with or without a family, was to inhabit the same house (even if the apartments were separate and distinct), or share a door, window, roof, terrace, well or any other convenience or method of communication. Disobedience to these injunctions was to be visited by the penalty of five hundred crowns, to be paid by the head of each household. The public treasury, some 'pious foundation' or other, and the sanctimonious spy who had brought the offence to light, would thus be enriched by a thousand crowns.

Florence ceased to be the rendezvous of scientists and scholars, for Cosimo did little to protect them against the Inquisition, 'ever busy in scenting out the taint of heresy in philosophy and science'. The learned Lorenzo Bellini was so persecuted by the latter that Vincenzo Viviani, in alarm, concealed the manuscripts of his master, Galileo, in a haystack. Cosimo sent some of his most distinguished and gifted subjects to foreign Courts: either he wished to be rid of them—else they set out in voluntary exile. Count Lorenzo Magalotti was sent as ambassador to Vienna, where his talents were probably better appreciated than at home.

Others remained in poverty and neglect, deploring the conscientious elimination of progressive elements.

A life without incident is wholesome enough, but needs some flavour to make it palatable, and Cosimo's was seasoned with flattering dreams. He still pictured to himself a glorious future for the Medici. So in a sense he triumphed over fate. Life had broken a few bones, it is true, but it had left intact two very important organs, his self-esteem and his respect for the world's opinion, both of which are essential to the enjoyment of fame. A feeling of satisfaction was always present with him, to relieve the dull routine of his existence.[1]

He dreamt of being acknowledged heir to the Duchy of Lorraine. The present Duke was that Charles (V) who had loved Marguerite-Louise. He married Eleanor of Austria, the King of Poland's widow and Emperor Leopold's sister, and his marriage seemed likely to be sterile. In the natural course of events, if Charles died childless, Marguerite-Louise would be his next heir and, failing her, the Grand Prince Ferdinando, her elder son.

Marguerite-Louise discussed the question at Montmartre with an appalling candour, since Charles's marriage had exasperated her. Gondi wrote secretly to Cosimo on July 22nd, 1678: 'The precise words employed by the Grand Duchess in her conversations with Madame d'Harcourt, a nun of Montmartre, touching the Queen of Poland and Duke of Lorraine can only be obtained from the Abbess. She told me, as she tells everybody at all times, that if the Duke of Lorraine should die without offspring, the duchy reverts to herself. So Madame d'Harcourt was resolved to tell her that the said Queen was big with child, and thus put an end to her hopes. But she retorted that it did not matter. . . . By suborning the midwife it was not difficult to make the infant die. This had happened in one of the Empress's deliveries, when the babe was caused to perish as soon as she gave it birth: she knew the very woman who had contrived this affair. The midwife had been corrupted by a goodly sum of money, and was living at Avignon now. Beside which it was so easy to accomplish: you had merely to prick the new-born's head with a pin for its death to be a certainty. And she discoursed in similar fashion before another nun, who was highly scandalized.'

Cosimo was anxious to have these rights respected at the Treaty of Nymegen. The Emperor seemed to favour him, for he did not wish

[1] These sentences from Italo Svevo's *The Hoax* (translated by Beryl de Zoete) apply perfectly to Cosimo.

Lorraine to go to France. But his favour proved hollow. Then Cosimo's courage hung woefully back: he was too afraid of Louis XIV to insist: his wife alone made him dependent on, and brought him into embarrassing contact with, the Court of France. Magalotti was left to lament the wavering, treacherous compass with which he had to steer, the pusillanimity and inertia of Tuscan ministers. They were, he said, like little children: if you talk of school you put them at once in a rage. The humiliation of his post in Vienna was felt keenly by Magalotti, and he wrote to one of his friends: 'Our greater evil resides in the opinion we have made the world conceive of us, that nothing is to be expected from us but good words and mighty protestations of deference and respect towards all and sundry, while refusing to commit ourselves to the smallest risk whatever happens. The slight notice that is taken of our affairs arises insensibly from this, since it cannot be hoped that anyone should wish to expend either finesse or facility on a house that would rather perish under universal ruin . . . than look ahead and try to save itself by following a definite party.'

The high-flown phraseology of Cosimo's political correspondence caused general amusement. But it did not help him to procure Lorraine any more than the title of Royal Highness or King of Jerusalem, for which he begged the Emperor, 'inasmuch as the possession of Pisa which once dominated that kingdom provides a claim equal to the House of Savoy's on the kingdom of Cyprus'.

The amusement afforded by Cosimo's epistles at Vienna was as nothing compared with that caused by his wife in Paris. It seemed as if Marguerite-Louise, not content with the comparative freedom she had gained, sought to wreak a cruel revenge on Cosimo for those years at Poggio a Caiano.

Gondi, his minister in Paris, had to keep him informed about her daily existence in all its particulars. No tittle-tattle was too finicking for him to report; and each of his letters inflicted a fresh wound in the Grand Duke's hide, which had not thickened with experience.

First came complaints about the Grand Duchess's allowance: the 80,000 livres with which he provided her annually did not suffice to maintain her in a style befitting her rank.

Marguerite-Louise soon showed that she had not come all the way to Paris to bury herself in a convent.

In the beginning her resigned air had impressed those who had known her in early youth. All noticed the change in her physical appearance. Madame de Sévigné remarked upon it to her daughter: 'It seemed to me that ennui was written on her face; she is very virtuous, and of a sadness that makes one pity her.' To Mademoiselle she looked pinched and drawn. The preachers she listened to, Bourdaloue among them, bored her, she said, and taught her nothing. She was given spiritual books, to make her realize the vanity of earthly joys, but these bored her also.

The King invited her to the opera, and even to the balls that were given during Carnival: he allowed her to spend four days at Versailles —a liberty which perturbed the Abbess of Montmartre. 'When the master is pleased to command,' she wrote Cosimo, 'there is nothing but to bow the head and obey. I fear that after these four days her solitude will only seem more frightful and she will bear it with less patience' (January 17th, 1676). Monsieur became her friend and adviser. He shared her love of rouge and frivolous conversation: Marguerite-Louise had become so loquacious that even the King remarked upon it. She never tired of recounting the minutiae of her existence: she chatted about her carriages and stables, her prowess as an Amazon. She ordered masculine attire to ride in—small periwigs, male jerkins and cravats. 'And it is in garb half-feminine, half-masculine,' wrote Gondi, 'and so little proper to a person who has declared her intention to spend the rest of her days in peaceful contemplation, that the Grand Duchess now prepares to exhibit herself!'

It was about this time that Cosimo wished her back in Florence. He feared that in Paris she would obtain more freedom than he had authorized; in Italy he would regain control of her life. Bernardino Guasconi, an unofficial envoy, came to sound her, with promises of power, money and independence; but the Grand Duchess answered that she would not renounce her 'tranquil existence' at Montmartre at any price.

Her sisters and the Abbé Gondi did their best to spoil Versailles for her. In September she had an attack of jaundice which did not improve her beauty. She put on a double quantity of rouge and a bright yellow periwig, hoping to hide the traces, but the King and Monsieur asked her quizzingly if it was the Abbess who had advised her to bedizen herself in this way. She was regarded as an eccentric Bohemian at Court because of her perpetual coming and going with a shabby suite, between Paris and Montmartre. And she was sensitive to their criticism. They accused her of being a timid rider, who had always been so proud of her horsemanship. The fault was Sainte-Même's for, as he boasted to Marucelli, he was careful to exaggerate the dangers of riding.

Lest her love of horses should outweigh his arguments, Sainte-Même wrote: 'I always find some pretext to bring her an unruly horse to suppress this inclination: often my wife and I remind her of the accidents we frequently see happening to ladies who expose themselves in large riding parties.' But he could not stop her from dancing. At the convent she took lessons four times a week from Desairs, the Dauphin's dancing-master, and Gondi had to look on, sick at heart. One day Marguerite-Louise gaily remarked to him that dancing was quite a different sin from riding, and that it was truly comic to have made the Grand Duke pay 50,000 crowns for building a ballroom. To which the Abbé could only retort with some acidity, that 'each takes his pleasure where he finds it'.

Throughout her life, as Rodocanachi observed, 'she delighted and charmed to begin with, but later she bored even those that were most friendly towards her'. In her desire to have confidants, she had admitted people of insignificant birth into her circle, as at Poggio a Caiano. They played charades, the Princess asked them riddles, and afterwards they bragged of the favours she had shown them. She was aware that such behaviour invited scandal, but she did not mind in the least, knowing, as she told Gondi, 'that she was more estimable at bottom than others believed'.

Some said that Charles of Lorraine's marriage had driven her to seek forgetfulness in this deplorable company. Long after she had recovered from jaundice she plastered her face with rouge and patches, and Madame,[1] outspoken as usual, criticized her for doing so before the King, saying that she made both her husband and herself ridiculous. Marguerite-Louise retorted that she was merely copying the Queen and Madame de Montespan: if the Grand Duke found fault with it she was sorry, but she had not left him to consider his opinions on the

---

[1] Charlotte Elizabeth, Princess Palatine, Monsieur's second wife and mother of Philippe d'Orléans, the Regent.

subject. This incident made a disagreeable impression at Court, and prejudiced the King against her.

It was rumoured that she was entangled in a love affair with the seductive Comte de Louvigny.[1] One of her maids, supposedly the go-between, happened to drop a *billet-doux* from her bosom, which was discovered, but others maintained it was an ill-natured trick of the Montespan's. Gondi did not refer to it in his letters to Cosimo: adventures more piquant lay in store for him.

Alexandre, who had seen service in Florence as a groom, had succeeded an adjutant of Monsieur de Luxembourg's guards, and was now retailing the numerous charms of his mistress in the coffee-houses 'in a tone which should not have been employed by a creature of his stamp'. And soon Mérincourt, a lifeguardsman in the same regiment as the adjutant, was boasting of favours which may not have been quite imaginary. Although he was a boozer and a boor, the Grand Duchess took infinite pleasure in his company. She gave orders that no one was to disturb her under any pretext when she was with him in the parlour. Her attendants were warned that whoever spoke ill of either of them, or told any tales of the manner she received him, would promptly be discharged. While he was a guard their interviews lasted till eleven o'clock at night: on other days he slept at the convent. Marguerite-Louise had a bed made ready for him in the Comte de Sainte-Même's apartment. There was no way to stop it. Gondi felt it was hopeless to appeal to the King. 'His indulgence for women,' he wrote Marucelli, 'is such that he easily excuses all they do; and one cannot count on any firmness from that quarter.' Louis XIV not only excused his cousin's frailty; he was entertained by it. One day, however, he asked the Maréchal de Luxembourg to point out the object of the Grand Duchess's esteem. After a glimpse, 'not wishing to retain a man of such base extraction in his guard,' the King had him dismissed.

Mérincourt's familiarity with the Grand Duchess increased. He daubed on her complexion, accompanied her in rides, and became so insufferably conceited that his rival, Alexandre, took umbrage, forgot himself in some impertinent allusion, and was discharged. It was then discovered that Alexandre had been one of Gondi's spies. The Abbess

[1] Later Comte de Guiche on the death of his eldest brother, and Duc de Grammont on the death of his father, the Maréchal.

tried gently to dissuade her from taking Mérincourt into her service, but she answered that if they crossed her wishes she would set fire to the convent.

Gondi's clique managed to remove Mérincourt: apparently he was sent off on one of the Toulon galleys. Despite this minor triumph, Gondi compiled a list of her offences, which the Abbess was to offer the King. But the King's answers only proved his impartiality. The Abbess proposed that His Majesty should cease to allow the Grand Duchess to attend Court save in exceptional circumstances: that he should never grant her the 'apartment' she longed for (i.e., that apartments might be specifically allotted to her in all the country residences of the Court): and that he should forbid her to ride, above all, in Monsieur's company, and prevent bodyguards from approaching her: in particular she would specify Mérincourt, Fayolle, Saint-Germain, d'Achon, Vaccagne, Karff, Durand. . . . The King replied that such measures, however secret, would soon be noised abroad and give rise to further scandals.

Then Marguerite-Louise turned and devoted herself, with overflowing energy, to charitable works. She began to devour those pious volumes she had formerly found so tedious; she fasted and prayed; attended services punctually; confessed to Bossuet; visited hospitals and almshouses, especially the Hôtel Dieu, with her sister the Duchesse de Guise. Gondi looked askance at these activities. He suspected the reason for them was her desire to join her sisters at the Luxembourg.

Her affected austerity did not hinder her from going to Court and gambling there. Gambling would naturally appeal to a woman of her temperament. Lansquenet was the game most in vogue. 'Enormous sums are played for here,' wrote Madame,[1] 'the players being as those possessed; one yells, another strikes the table so hard with his fist that the whole room shakes, a third swears in such a manner as to cause one's hair to stand on end—all seem not themselves, and are fearful to witness.' She played against Madame de Montespan, lost thirty doubloons, and forgot the time. When they reminded her that once she had found the gates of the convent closed on her return, and had had to wake up the entire neighbourhood, she replied that she had no intention of leaving before she had made up for her losses.

[1] Correspondence.

In summer she returned to her chief equerry's château at Sainte-Même, and charitable works; and dancing innocently with her ladies was her sole entertainment during the long evenings.

Then Mérincourt returned and took possession of the Comte de Sainte-Même's apartment. Sainte-Même was too discouraged to object.

Gondi sent in another report to the King, denouncing her familiarity with two grooms, Gentilly and Robert. (Even adjutants were more excusable!) His Majesty questioned the Abbess, who replied that for the sake of the Grand Duchess's children it were better to leave things to follow their natural course. 'A conspiracy of silence,' she concluded, 'is the sole antidote to the depravity and disgraceful excesses of this woman.' Which explains the scarcity of references to Marguerite-Louise in gazettes and memoirs of this period. But for Gondi, whom Cosimo goaded on to pry into all the details of her life, these would have been consigned to oblivion.

XIII

*The Grand Duchess of Tuscany at Montmartre
– Cosimo's Illness and Cure – Alcantarine Friars*

From Gondi's letters it appears that the 'tranquil' convent of Montmartre was a labyrinth of wagging tongues and secret agents. The Comte and Comtesse de Sainte-Même—in whom the Grand Duchess had confided for years—Cinzia, the musician she brought from Florence, Charenton (who had been in the service of Madame Du Deffand), Alexandre, the porter, La Rue—all of them furnished Gondi with reports sooner or later. Outside Montmartre there was Mère Thérèse de Jésus, Mother Superior of the Carmelites in the Rue de Bouloi, whither Madame de la Vallière had gracefully retired and Marguerite-Louise had gone to mingle tears with hers. Extravagant and constantly in debt, Mère Thérèse was all ardour to serve Cosimo; in return for a perfume she had sent him, distilled by herself, he gave her an unguent against apoplexy; in exchange for news of his wife he granted her a salary.

To account for Sainte-Même's attitude, we must remember how inconsiderate and exacting a mistress the Grand Duchess could be. He was old in advance of his years, stiff-limbed and short of breath, and she made him run errands that exhausted him. More than once she had sent him by night to Versailles to beg some trivial favour from the Queen on her behalf: a place at her dinner-table or permission to enter her carriage. On the other hand she would not allow Sainte-Même to take his meals at the convent. He came there too often, she said.

To escape the heat of late July (1679) she set off for his country-house one evening at six o'clock. The groom, Gentilly, had now supplanted Mérincourt and his predecessors in her affections. It was a simple life at Sainte-Même, and Gentilly sweetened and spiced it with his assiduity. For he laced her garters, put on her shoes, pinned and fixed her caps, collars and veils, and dressed her hair with a comb he

always carried in his pocket—just as if he were a maid. At table the
Grand Duchess gave Gentilly her nuts and almonds to crack with his
teeth: otherwise she would not eat them. She kept late hours playing
cards with him, and often contrived that he should win; she also
promised to leave him a large annuity in her will. When she mounted
a horse, she set one foot in Gentilly's pocket, and taking him by the
neck, jumped into the saddle. Her infatuation for him increased, although, wrote Gondi, he is clumsy, ill-made and advanced in years.

In August she returned to Court, to attend the marriage by proxy of
Monsieur's daughter, Mademoiselle d'Orléans, with Charles II, the
imbecile King of Spain.[1] This unfortunate Princess dreaded her departure for the land of bullfights and *autos-da-fé* even as Marguerite-
Louise had dreaded hers for Tuscany. But the King told her intentionally, in the hearing of Marguerite-Louise: 'Madame, I wish to bid you
farewell for ever: to see France again would be the greatest calamity
that could befall you.' The ceremony gave Marguerite-Louise another
opportunity for wounding Cosimo's pride, for she bore the royal train,
with the other 'daughters of France'. Gondi had protested in vain
against this proceeding—a stroke directed against Cosimo, showing
her indifference to her rank as Grand Duchess of Tuscany. While the
young Queen was toying with her wedding-ring, Marguerite-Louise
warned her to be careful not to lose it: if she did, it would be a sure
sign that she would die before her husband, or that her marriage would
be unhappy, since she had lost her own ring in the first month of her
nuptials.

The Church, which had always opposed the Grand Duchess's
separation, made a final attempt to restore her to Cosimo. In her discontented moods she had complained of not being treated in France
with sufficient respect. She had even said in the Queen's hearing that
she had 'an infinite number of obligations towards the Grand Duke'.
Her friends, and chiefly the Princesse des Ursins, encouraged her in this
frame of mind. But Cosimo was always tormented by a dread of
ridicule; and he thought it would make him look foolish to recall his
wife after having released her. He also feared that she would exert a
malign influence on his children, and quarrel again with his mother.
When Cardinal Cibo's nephew, the Prince of Carrara, broached the

[1] August 30th, 1679.

subject of reconciliation, he declared that his wife's character was always that of a dissembler.

Many hoped for a marriage between the nineteen-year-old Dauphin and Cosimo's daughter, Anna Maria Luisa, who was but twelve years old; this, too, might bring about a reconciliation. Marguerite-Louise herself seemed to expect it, and she despatched Sainte-Même to Florence. He interviewed Pomponne, Colbert and the King before his departure; but neither Gondi nor Marguerite-Louise knew the substance of these interviews. Sainte-Même set forth on October 2nd. Whatever the cause of his mission, he acquitted himself to his own advantage rather than to that of the lady he was supposed to be serving.

He told Cosimo that for some time he had applied himself assiduously to ruining the Grand Duchess in the King's esteem, so that he should turn deaf to her entreaties. He asked him whether to inflame or extinguish her hatred of Tuscany. Concerning Gentilly he persuaded him that it were wiser to leave the Grand Duchess to follow her caprice: better this than that she should bestow her favours elsewhere and on persons of higher rank, for then the scandal would become too patent.

Cosimo's reply was characteristic. He recommended Sainte-Même to find a confessor capable of inspiring his wife with the love of God, a respect for her duties, and fear of laws human and divine. He was evasive about the Dauphin's engagement; French marriages did not appeal to him. Finally Sainte-Même expanded about his long and loyal service in the Grand Duke's cause: after further protestations of devotion, he begged him to raise his salary. And although the Tuscan finances were in a wretched state, Sainte-Même's secret pension was more than doubled. On one point Cosimo stood firm: he refused to take his wife back.

Gondi kept whetting his master's impatience for the most trivial details of her existence, thus: when Gentilly was taken ill with a colic, 'the Grand Duchess devoted all her thoughts to him; sending for surgeons and physicians, speaking to them herself; entering into all the particulars, and showing an excessive solicitude. And because the physicians maintained that he sickened because he drinks too much, she flew into a rage with the said Gentilly, and she has now resolved to make him abstain from liquor'. She 'formed the great idea of giving him a clyster, and herself took the care to procure him one'. Since

Gentilly was reluctant, she ordered her gentleman usher, Monsieur d'Etampes, 'to assist at the operation', lest he should wriggle out of it. . . . Undoubtedly there was a motherly element in her affection for the groom.

When she went riding 'she would wait for him to dismount from his horse, to relieve his physical necessities . . . . When he was mounted again she continued on her journey. During their sojourn in this place she openly showed her preference for him. This was witnessed by Cinzia, who told me that she tried to induce him on all occasions to entertain her with his discourse. And because he still had symptoms of dysentery, she set food aside for him at meals, purposely taking chocolate from her own table for him to recruit his strength'.

On January 3rd, 1680, there was a conflagration in the Grand Duchess's quarters at Montmartre. It had started with the basket of her pet dog, which had been placed too near the fire. Everyone remembered her threat; and her behaviour seemed to indicate that the basket had been placed there intentionally, for instead of encouraging people to extinguish the flames, she exhorted all to fly for their lives.

The Abbess pressed Cosimo to pay for the construction of a large reservoir as a precaution against any future accident of the kind. Cosimo complained bitterly to the King. This time Louis could do no less than show her his resentment, and prevented her from appearing at Court. Marguerite-Louise exhaled her rage and despair in several pages, addressed to her husband on January 8th, 1680.[1]

'I can support your extravagances no longer. I know that you are doing your utmost to prejudice the King against me. You attract His Majesty's undesirable attention and that of all his Court by not wishing me to attend it, which I should do constantly to gain the King's protection for all my requirements and personal necessities; and in this way you harm your own children, because if I were continuously at Court your sons would fare better now and in the future. Thus you wrong them as well as me and yourself, for you reduce me to such despair that there is neither an hour nor a day when I do not desire your death and wish that you were hanged.

'You reduce me to such straits that I can no longer attend the Sacraments, and thus you will have me damned; and you, for all your

---

[1] This letter was first published by Galluzzi.

devoutness, will damn yourself also, because one that causes the loss of another's soul cannot save his own. . . .

'What displeases me most in this affair is that we shall both go to the devil, and I shall have the torment of seeing you even there. If you had let me be, I should have dedicated myself to devotion, because I was beginning to be instructed in my obligations towards our Lord and Saviour. By my good works at Alençon with my sister, and by staying with these nuns, who are angels, I should have gone back to my first thought of becoming a hospital nun, because when I am at Alençon I serve the sick every morning, and adapt myself very well to it. If you inform yourself, you will discover that I spend whole days with the sisters of mercy, and that I do the same things as they without repugnance. But now I do not wish to think of doing good any longer, because I cannot succeed, for you reduce me to such despair that I can only think of being avenged, unless you change your method of dealing with me. And I swear to you, by the thing I most loathe, which is yourself, that I shall make pacts with the devil to enrage you, and rescue me from your madness.

'Enough! I shall commit every possible extravagance to displease you, and you will not be able to prevent me from doing so. Do what you will, your devoutness will serve you for nothing, because you are a "flower of rue, which God will not have, and the Devil renounces".

'Now what I require is that you write to the King saying that you cease to concern yourself either with me or with what I do; that you leave His Majesty to govern me in his own fashion, that you refer all my actions to his prudence; and that you beg him to protect me like one of his daughters. If you do this, I promise you to place myself well in God's hands, and perhaps to dedicate myself in the manner I once promised. If you do it not, expect great things from my avenging furies, for you will never be able to change me. And if you think you will make me return to you, it will never happen; and if I should return to you, beware, because you would never die but by my hand. You may prepare to leave this life soon without assistance, because I know that you have only a little while to last. Leave me in peace during the short time you remain in this world, so that I can pray for you after your death, and stay near the King to help your sons upon whose fortunes you have hitherto brought ruin.

'Enough! change your tune. By wishing to rule me straight you will only be ruled yourself, and you will do as those pipers who came to play and were played upon with blows.

'I warn you; these actions are yours: they are no longer mine, because I am already desperate, and have little to lose.'

The original version of this epistle was shown to the King, who was merely amused by it. '*Sfoga o schiatta*,' as an Italian proverb runs—relieve yourself or burst. Marguerite-Louise relieved herself, and soon began to put her threats into execution.

That summer she went to one of Sainte-Même's country houses at Serbonnes, some twenty-five miles from Fontainebleau, and bathed every evening in the River Yonne. Cosimo was a masochist: the more a thing maddened him, the more would he seek the galling knowledge of it. And Gondi never assuaged him: his letters were corrosive:

'Concerning the form and decency with which the Grand Duchess bathed in the river, I cannot say more than what I wrote you recently.[1] The Comtesse de Sainte-Même told me that they went thither towards eventide, and that Mademoiselle de Lebi bathed with her and her ladies-in-waiting, while her servants stood by the river-bank. And they bathed according to the manner of the place, and as all the women do still hereabouts, which is without tents or any other preparation and by entering straightway into the water.' Gondi was loth to communicate all at once to the Grand Duke that while his consort was bathing she was held by Gentilly, 'who stood in the water covered by nothing but his close-fitting jacket, and held her firmly in the water from behind, with his hands on her shoulders'. He waited till November to send him these morsels. But their effect on Cosimo was the same, infuriating and voluptuous.

She persuaded Louis to support an application for an increase of her allowance: if Cosimo would not consent to this, he was to restore the entire capital of her dowry, and turn it into a life annuity. Cosimo flatly refused and repeated his complaints about her scandalous conduct. But Louis had heard these once too often, and when Cardinal Bonsi put forward the arguments in Cosimo's favour, he expressed 'his disgust at such meanness, and at the absurdity of the continuance of such petty family disputes. Since Cosimo had consented to the retire-

[1] July 26th, 1680.

ment of his wife into France, he had virtually relinquished all right to interfere in her conduct; the anxiety he exhibited concerning her behaviour was inconsistent with his usual prudence; and his prosecution of revenge against her could only be attributed to an alienation of his reason.'

The Grand Duke was mortified by this rebuff: it showed him that he was becoming a laughing-stock at the French Court.

Indeed Cosimo was so deeply affected that his health gave way in 1681. It was a sore of his own scratching. For many years he had been leading an intemperate and sedentary life. Suddenly he was attacked by 'an overflow of bile'. Marguerite-Louise was secretly informed of his condition by Prince Ferdinando. She immediately spoke of returning to Florence, and told everyone at the French Court that 'at the first notice of her detested husband's demise she would fly to Florence to banish all hypocrites and hypocrisy and establish a new government, good taste and philosophy there, as in the time of Ferdinando II.'

She wished to have it known that she did not dislike Florence and the Tuscans, as they had been led to believe: 'she would willingly return to a country she loved, to enjoy and improve it'. But all these hopes were dashed, for Cosimo managed to recover.

Cosimo was surprised to hear that his wife had been regaled with the facts of his illness, which he had tried to keep secret, and more surprised to hear of the projects she had formed to follow his funeral. With his well-organized system of espionage he soon discovered her informants. These were the two brothers Lorenzini, 'noted for their talents and expert skill in mathematics', who were in the service of Prince Ferdinando. They had merely obeyed their master in writing to the Grand Duchess. This obedience was magnificently rewarded by Cosimo. The Lorenzini, then in the pride of youth and comeliness, were sentenced to twenty years of imprisonment and thrown into a dungeon in the fortress of Volterra.

He was determined never to fall ill again, and he took the advice of Redi, his trusted physician, the gist of which was to change his diet.

'A severe Pythagorean regimen' was prescribed for Cosimo's salvation. Yet, though vegetables only were served at the grand-ducal table, there was no lack of rare and delicious fruits, salads and aromatic herbs from exotic regions, and products of the most contrary seasons: October pears in April, and strawberries in December.

'One does not grow up in the school of Maecenas without learning the subtle delights of the simple life',[1] and his diet led Cosimo to take an interest in botany. He started to cultivate curious plants; and flowers from the Indies, from America and Asia, were grown in the Boboli Gardens, and in the orchards of his pleasant places. They became a form of physical gratification. They answered his moods; and when he was no longer detained by lugubrious sacred images he would wander forth among the shrubberies of bay and myrtle, to examine some quaint corolla and inhale the scent that hovered as an inspiration and sped to his nostrils like the flesh he could not quite forget, sweet and pungent like his own pride and disappointment. Ah, he would yet live long, these friendly flowers assured him; and he would spite them all: his wife, his wretched people, the vermin who had wished the death of their pious lord and master.

To prolong his life, he combined his 'severe Pythagorean regimen' with plenty of open-air exercise, riding, hunting and visiting his various country houses, preferably those nearest the hills. The villa of Ambrogiana perhaps was his favourite, and since body and soul should be tended with equal care, he added a monastery thereto, and transplanted some Alcantarine friars from Spain to fill it. So he could strengthen his limbs and thumb his beads alternately: when his knees were sore and his body cramped with long hours and lowly attitudes of devotion, he could expand them in the temperate air again.

[1] Norman Douglas.

XIV

Louvois's policy was causing the name of France to become a terror and abomination in Italy. Cosimo III was kept in awe by the French fleet in the Mediterranean; he reinforced his armaments, increased his troops, and fortified his arsenals, especially in Leghorn. The Turks were marching towards Vienna, the Emperor Leopold sent his chargé d'affaires to demand assistance from the Pope, and from all the Italian principalities. When the Imperial envoy applied to Cosimo on May 23rd, 1683, so arrogant was his tone that the Grand Duke took offence. He replied that he could give him no financial assistance; however, as if this were equivalent, he promised to allow a discount on the Emperor's debts. This reply infuriated the minister, who was quite aware that his Caesarean Majesty had never dreamt of discharging his debts. But for all his insistence Cosimo would only promise him four galleys to join those of Portugal, Malta, Genoa and the Pope, and force a landing in the Levant. The Emperor wanted money, and his minister tried to persuade Cosimo to supply a lump sum instead of spending it on a small fleet, but the Grand Duke foresaw that the Emperor would first take the sum, and then oblige him to send the galleys. The minister openly expressed his resentment at obtaining so little from Cosimo, who, 'while showing himself so zealous a Catholic and so attached to the grandeur of religion, refused at this critical moment to send the necessary help to defend it'. But suddenly Cosimo lost the courage of his refusal, and before the Emperor's minister returned to Vienna, hastily dispatched a considerable load of ammunition to Trieste, and renewed his offer to join the league against the Turks.

Vienna was already besieged, when, in March, 1683, the league was concluded between the Emperor, John Sobieski, King of Poland, the Venetian Republic and Tuscany, which prepared a fleet to defend the coasts of Albania and Dalmatia. Finally the siege was raised and the citizens were freed by John Sobieski, and the fleet helped to scatter the Turks. Meister Johann Dietz, the much-travelled and weather-beaten barber, has left a terrible account of these wars in his vivid autobiography.[1] 'I was amazed,' he wrote, 'by what was done, and to see that mankind shows itself far crueller to its own than the beasts.' The Christian soldiers were more than a match for the 'infidels' in cruelty. For instance, Dietz describes as follows an incident in which the Turkish cavalry, during a sortie from Buda, were caught between a line of trenches which they could not cross and a strong force of Belgians and Bavarians:

'They were so distracted and so confused that I myself saw how they sat on their horses, still sabre in hand, although their hands were folded together, with their eyes bent upon the heavens, and so allowed themselves to be shot down. Not one was spared; all were massacred, and most were then flayed; the fat was roasted out and the *membra virilia* cut off, and great sacksfull dried and stored; for of these that most costly preparation known as *mumia* was made. As a general thing, too, they were cut open and their bowels were searched, in case it should be found, as had previously occurred, that the dead men had swallowed ducats.'

A courier, sent by the Emperor Leopold to Cosimo, reached Florence in late September, 1683, with the joyful news that the Imperial armies had totally defeated the Ottomans. Cosimo's elation knew no bounds. He gave orders that the image of the Santissima Annunziata was to be uncovered as a sign of universal gratitude to the Most High. A magnificent *Te Deum* was sung in the Duomo; the city thundered with artillery, bells, drums, trumpets; the skies were ablaze with fireworks from the tower of the Palazzo Vecchio. The head swims, the ears tingle, as one reads of the festivals ordained to follow.

They culminated with that of the clergy of San Lorenzo, on the piazza in front of their church: the machine they set up was to symbolize the Triumph of Faith. Four statues of Turks prostrated themselves before a larger statue of Faith, with a chalice in her left hand, and

[1] *Master Johann Dietz*. Allen & Unwin, 1924.

a naked sword in her right. When the fireworks, artificially concealed inside the machine, were ignited, the Turks were slowly and noisily consumed.

Cosimo wished to exhibit himself again before the world as a foe to all heretics. Looking about him he could only find Jews to persecute. And these were many, if the proverb 'Seven Jews make one Genoese, and seven Genoese one Florentine' was ever to be taken literally. Notwithstanding his previous proclamations 'many scandals and disorders continued to occur in the matter of carnal intercourse between Jews and Christian women, and especially in putting their children out to suck by Christian wet-nurses'. Therefore, he commanded that from that day, November 4th, 1683, no Jews were permitted to have their children suckled by Christian nurses. If, owing to the large number of births or 'other accidents' there were more Hebrew children to suckle than mothers and nurses of their own race could manage, the Jewish father in Florence must have recourse to Senator Ferrante Capponi, Judge of Pardons to H.S.H., and in Leghorn to the Governor, to obtain a licence for a Christian wet-nurse, which licence must be given in writing and registered in a book that was kept in their tribunals. This, however, on the tacit understanding that no Jew or Jewess was allowed to enter for any reason whatever into the houses where these children were suckled by Christian women. Nor were the said women and wet-nurses allowed to enter into the houses of Jews and Jewesses for the clandestine purpose of suckling their children.

Gilbert Burnet, Bishop of Salisbury, writing from Florence on November 5th, 1685,[1] gives a dismal account of it. 'Florence is much sunk from what it was, for they do not reckon that there are above fifty thousand souls in it; and the other states, that were once great republics, such as Siena and Pisa, while they retained their liberty, are now shrunk almost into nothing; it is certain, that all three together are now not so numerous as any one of them was two hundred years ago. Leghorn is full of people, and all round Florence there are a great many villages; but as one goes over Tuscany, it appears so dispeopled that one cannot but wonder to find a country that hath been a scene of so much action, and so many wars, now so forsaken and so poor, and

[1] Some Letters containing an account of what seemed most remarkable in travelling thro' Switzerland, Italy, etc., in the years 1685 and 1686.

that in many places the soil is quite neglected for want of hands to cultivate it; and in other places where there are more people, they look so poor, and their houses are such miserable ruins, that it is scarce accountable how there should be so much poverty in so rich a country, which is all over full of beggars.'

Cosimo was now preoccupied, and long continued to be, with the problem of succession. He dreamt of powerful alliances for his children; above all, he dreamt of an innumerable progeny, to perpetuate his glory through the ages.

His heir apparent, the Grand Prince Ferdinando, had a great affinity with his vivacious mother: though shorter, his features resembled hers, and he solicited and followed her advice even after the Lorenzini catastrophe. He was a rebellious youth, who disagreed intensely with Cosimo on every subject.

Nature had blessed his exterior: he was handsome, a fine rider, a talented musician. At the age of sixteen, he had arranged for an opera entitled *Colla forza di Amore si vince Amore* ('Love is won by the strength of Love') to be given at Pratolino. He sang melodiously, and played the harpsichord with unusual grace. In his early youth a certain Petrillo, a *musico* famous for the beauty of his person, had occupied the first place in his heart. Vain, we are told, was the emulation of courtesans, for Ferdinando loved only his Petrillo, and 'he enjoyed him a long while'. Unfortunately this attachment was sundered by an indiscretion. Petrillo once sang so ravishing an air that the Prince forgot himself and ardently embraced his nightingale. The happy singer, failing to notice the presence of Marchese Albizi, His Highness's tutor, 'closely hugged the Prince in return, and kissed his face'. The tutor felt it his duty to interfere, with a threatening expression, and the Prince took alarm. 'What do you think of that?' he asked Marchese Albizi, exculpating himself at his favourite's expense. 'He deserves severe and exemplary chastisement,' answered the tutor.

Poor Petrillo, who had experienced even greater marks of tenderness beforehand, turned pale at this heartless betrayal. Not knowing what might happen to him next, he departed trembling, and swiftly fled from the Palace and State. Had he humbled himself, the chronicler adds, Albizi would have been obliged to accept his submission, because the Prince extraordinarily loved him. But Petrillo never set foot in

Florence again, greatly to Ferdinando's regret, though decorum had compelled him to support the tutor.

Besides being a musician, Ferdinando had a flair for the fine arts. Notwithstanding his extravagance, in open contrast with the poverty of the people, the young Prince was popular because he looked ornamental, seemed human and was utterly unlike his father. 'If,' as Sir Max Beerbohm finely wrote in an essay on George IV, 'we lay all pleasures at the feet of our Prince, we will scarcely hope he will remain virtuous. Indeed, we do not wish our Prince to be an exemplar of godliness, but a perfect type of happiness. . . . In Royalty we find our Bacchus, our Venus.' Ferdinando was surrounded by a retinue of raffish and frivolous young men who took a pleasure in annoying his father's priestly favourites. The bigots, on their side, were scandalized by the Prince's behaviour. But they had to wink at it, if only for the fact that Francesco Maria, eighteen years younger than the Grand Duke his brother, and seven years older than Ferdinando his nephew, was his boon companion.

Francesco Maria had been destined from infancy to fill the place of his uncle, Cardinal Leopoldo, since the Medici always had at least one Cardinal in the family, to balance the scales in papal elections. But for all his predestination to the purple, Francesco Maria continued in the pursuit of worldly pleasure. He and Ferdinando generally stayed in one of the numerous Medicean country houses, where they galvanized the sleepy neighbourhood, scorning conventions, impatient of etiquette and ceremonial, 'always courted by a band of giddy youths'; and came to Florence in Cosimo's absence, doing as they pleased without respect for the law. Cosimo tried to lessen his brother's influence over Ferdinando by appointing him Governor of Siena in 1682, which did not prevent Francesco Maria from appearing frequently in Florence. Thus it was not easy for Cosimo to impose his will on the Prince. Ferdinando had never been on good terms with his father since the discovery of his letters to Marguerite-Louise, followed by the imprisonment of his secretaries.

When the Grand Duke first broached the subject of marriage the Prince replied that he had no intention of marrying before he had been to Venice. Cosimo was disconcerted, but he did not insist. He merely conveyed his disapproval.

The Prince was bored with the placid entertainments of his home; he was more anxious to meet accomplished Venetian *virtuose* than a virtuous bride. Finally, the Grand Duke promised to allow this journey, on condition that he first consented to marry. Cosimo was anxious to avoid delay, because the other princes of the family gave little promise of fecundity: Gian Gastone was frail, and Francesco Maria, even if he renounced the purple, was burdened with unhealthy corpulence. Ferdinando was offered the choice of five Princesses: the Infanta, sole daughter and heiress presumptive to Portugal, a Princess of Bavaria, two daughters of the Elector Palatine and a Princess of Parma.

He was far too apathetic to raise an objection to any of them. Louis XIV declared in favour of the Infanta Maria Isabella, daughter of Pedro II, King of Portugal. Pedro had no male heir and Louis wanted to give the Infanta a husband of friendly nationality, since the Portuguese Constitution allowed her to succeed to the throne. But when Marchese Lorenzo Ginori, the Florentine consul at Lisbon, opened negotiations with the Portuguese ministers about Ferdinando's marriage, he met with insuperable barriers. The first was a clause that Ferdinando would have to reside at Lisbon, renouncing every right to the Tuscan throne—unless Pedro married again, and male heirs sprang from that union. The second was that if the Infanta became Queen of Portugal, and Cosimo III, Gian Gastone and Francesca Maria died without male heirs, Tuscany should be annexed to the Portuguese crown, and Florence should be governed by a viceroy.

Ferdinando refused to hear of such conditions and, when Louis tried to insist, replied that if the Infanta desired the honour of becoming related to the Medici, she must betake herself to Florence, not he to Lisbon. For once Cosimo had come out of a tangle without losing his dignity; and he retired to the villa of Ambrogiana to benefit by the mild spring weather of that year (1686), and to follow his 'Pythagorean regimen' at ease. But Cosimo was always unfortunate when it was a matter of his relaxation. One day, without any regard for his presence, there was a fierce brawl among the Alcantarine friars he had summoned from Spain for his spiritual comfort. As he had built them a convent near his villa, he was much aggrieved. It was impossible to conceal anything from the Florentines: the rumour of it spread, and awakened their sarcasm, as is proved by a letter written by a friend to Zipoli, the minister in Paris:[1]

'I know not what broil has broken out among the monks of Ambrogiana, to whom H.H. is so attached, but they mauled one another badly, and Father Segneri, the Jesuit, has been sent there to restore order among them. If this be true, H.H. will withdraw his patronage, and all the more because this incident occurred during his residence. No one knows to what expense they have put him, and that they continue tc incur in victuals and various ways, and there is not a monk but costs him 200 crowns a year.'

The next match Cosimo considered for his son was with the Dauphine's sister, Princess Violante of Bavaria. This would procure him the alliance of one of the most powerful Courts in Germany, and strengthen his relations with the Bourbons. Unfortunately there had been a money dispute between Bavaria and Tuscany in the past, which had never been settled. Ferdinando II had invested a large sum (300,000 ungheri[2] in gold) for the Elector Maximilian in the *Monte di Pietà*, or municipal bank, which failed in 1645. As the Grand Duke maintained he had acted in good faith, he refused to reimburse the whole sum. But Cosimo offered to credit the sum claimed from his father by Maximilian in reckoning the dowry, so that obstacle was eliminated. The Dauphine influenced the Bavarian Court in his favour. But after the Portuguese affair it was difficult to overcome Ferdinando's aversion to marriage. As a condition for his consent, he obstinately required his father's to that Venetian journey he craved. Cosimo was forced to acquiesce, and, while doing so, exhorted him to behave and warned him against the disreputable Duke of Mantua.

'I know,' he wrote him, 'that I am bound for the peace of my conscience to assure myself that the Prince keeps an eye to his, when he finds himself in the freedom of Venice, and especially during Carnival. I wish him to promise to abstain from diversions that are damnable to the soul, and neither permitted by the divine laws, nor suited to the condition of a Prince, who should give example to others. And likewise that he will avoid becoming indecently familiar with musicians, comedians (reputed as infamous people) and take no part in

[1] Florence, April, 1686.
[2] The value of an unghero was about five shillings and sixpence.

the conversations, and still less in the entertainments, of courtesans. The Duke of Mantua having forfeited much of that credit which would otherwise be due to his birth and rank, and having contracted various obnoxious attachments in Venice, I intend the Prince not only to avoid his friendship, but also his company. . . .'

Ferdinando set out on this journey in 1687 with a splendid retinue and, although he had now reached the more or less responsible age of twenty-four, accompanied by his tutor Marchese Albizi—no longer in favour since the Petrillo affair. The Venetian Senate received him with signal honour. All the aristocracy competed to entertain him, and he was dazzled and greatly impressed. Here he soon found a substitute for the lost Petrillo. This was Cecchino, nicknamed de' Castris, from his physical condition, for he was, as a polite historian phrases it, 'one of those mutilated human beings that disgrace Italy'. The Prince took the songster into his household and lavished affection on him.

'A passion for music,' adds the chronicler, 'should excuse a more culpable passion for musicians.' The Prince was such a master of counterpoint that when he was at a festa of Venetian patricians and a very intricate sonata for the harpsichord was set before him, he not only played it at sight, but afterwards repeated it faultlessly without looking at the music, and with a skill that astonished his noble audience.

Cosimo's expenses were diminished when Francesco Maria was raised to the purple in 1686, for the new Cardinal was immediately provided with enormous revenues. He thought of initiating Prince Gian Gastone into the ecclesiastical career, to serve France as Francesco Maria served Austria, Germany and Spain. It did not then seem strange that two Princes so closely related should serve different, and often inimical, powers. Spain proposed to make Gian Gastone General of the Sea, to hinder a Medicean Cardinal from protecting the interests of France at the Conclaves. It seemed as if Gian Gastone were much in demand. Even King Pedro of Portugal, after he had fulfilled the wishes of his ministers, married the Elector Palatine's daughter and been blessed with male offspring, came forward to offer him the Infanta Isabella. All these opportunities and alternatives flashed before the young Prince's eyes: none of them developed. His father would not give him a sufficient allowance to marry the Infanta, so Gian Gastone was forced to vegetate. His contemporaries had a high notion of his merits: 'a comely person, agreeable features, docile, moderate, human, and addicted to a studious life'. He deserved a better fate.

While Ferdinando was filling his lungs with Venetian air, his father was resting at Ambrogiana, where peace had been restored among the friars. Daily he devised a fresh match for his favourite child, the Princess Anna Maria. She would have married the King of Portugal had not his ministers, who required a princess of gentle, subordinate character, entirely devoted to Austria, feared that Anna Maria might have inherited some of her notorious mother's defects. In reality it was otherwise. Those who knew her said she was a living image of her father and grandmother, a combination of their qualities.

Cosimo, unbending with his sons, was pliable with his daughter, and flattered her that with France's partiality to the Medici she could nourish the highest of hopes. But that this partiality was an illusion was proved by Louis's support of Marguerite-Louise when she demanded another 20,000 crowns from Cosimo to pay her debts.

Cosimo thought he had smoothed matters down by recalling Gondi from Paris; and he now expected Louis to protect him against his wife's exaggerated claims. Her behaviour had been even more disgraceful since Gondi's departure. She had made friends with Madame de Maintenon, and the King paid no attention to her escapades. Though she did much as she pleased at Montmartre she still considered it a restraint, and left it frequently for the Luxembourg or the provinces. Gentilly always accompanied her on these excursions. She took no trouble to conceal her infatuation for the groom.

The convent of Montmartre became a hotbed of scandals and wranglings, and the Grand Duchess was the torment of all who had dealings with her. 'The Grand Duchess,' wrote the envoy,[1] 'says that when she grows old, she wants to end her days at Martinique. Gentilly remarked to Cinzia in her presence: "You will go there too"; and Cinzia replied: "God has not hitherto inspired me".' She insulted the Abbess and the Tuscan Resident, beat her servants one moment and embraced them the next. One day she summoned her first coachman, a postilion and a valet, under the pretext of moving some furniture.

[1] August 6th, 1685.

'When they were in the spider's web,' as Zipoli phrases it, 'the Grand Duchess took each in turn by the hair, struck them with her fists, tore their tufts out, and knocked their heads against the sharp corners of the door. After which she sent the first two to the Hospital of the Salpêtrière, and dismissed the last.'

She dealt not less severely with her equals. Once, while Mademoiselle de Guise was praying in her room at Montmartre, the Grand Duchess went to visit her, and instead of wishing her a good evening, told her that she would do better to pay her debts, and that if she did not pay the 400 crowns she owed a relation of Pappelard's she would ask His Majesty to give her no more letters and would declare herself her open enemy, and so took leave of her. As soon as poor old Mlle de Guise recovered from her shock she called for the Abbess, who was in the choir. When the Abbess heard of the matter she too was stupefied and at once went and asked the Grand Duchess why she had been carried to such an excess; she should have spent a night like this in meditation, and not in turning the house topsy-turvy. She implored her to change her mind or she would find it a painful necessity to give His Majesty her own account of the affair. She advised her to make it up with Mlle de Guise, who had such esteem and consideration for her; if she wished, she would settle it herself. They stayed nearly an hour together, at the end of which the Grand Duchess agreed to patch it up.

Marguerite-Louise was only gentle with Gentilly. 'I met Gentilly and spoke to him,' writes Zipoli,[1] 'chiefly about his unhealthy appearance. He told me that he had a fluxion in one of his arms which gave him much trouble, and which he kept in a sling. When I had got rid of him Cinzia came to the first-floor grating. She told me that Gentilly's father died some little while ago, and that when the old man was ill he asked to be taken to see him, but Gentilly would not hear of it. When he got news of his death, Gentilly burst into a flood of tears before the Grand Duchess, saying that because he had not been by his father's death-bed he was the loser of a thousand crowns. The Grand Duchess, who is full of charity, said: 'A mere bagatelle! Am I not capable of giving you a thousand crowns?' So he is now triumphant, hoping that she will keep her promise, but everybody knows that his father had not threepence in his purse.'

[1] November 5th, 1685.

Hitherto she does not seem to have suspected the treachery of Cinzia, the Italian maid she had trusted so long. Now her behaviour indicated that she had got wind of it. Zipoli writes on January 21st, 1685: 'Your Highness is aware that among the Grand Duchess's servants Cinzia alone had not been maltreated with slaps on the face. To-day this is not so. Last week as the Grand Duchess was dining and discoursing with her in our language about that famous valet and guardsman of hers, Cinzia observed that Her Highness should not attach any importance to so miserable a creature. . . . The conversation then turned on the Prince of Tuscany, and the Grand Duchess remarked that her son was ever on worse terms with the Grand Duke, and evinced some satisfaction because of it. But Cinzia, who is kind-hearted, and cannot hear such matters spoken of, could do no less than retort that Her Highness could remedy every discord with good advice. The Grand Duchess, who perhaps had been put out of humour either by Cinzia's remarks about the soldier or the Prince, slapped her face and told her she should learn how to talk; so violent was the blow, that not only her hand made Cinzia's cheek very red, but, what was worse, her ring bruised the part near her eye. Cinzia was quite stunned by this unexpected gesture, and observed with some presence of mind that she had never till now seen stars at midday. Then, turning to Her Highness, she said: "Had I thought that Your Highness would take offence, I would not have opened my mouth." The incident, however, was hushed up, and the Grand Duchess has not breathed a word of it to Madame de Montmartre.'

Marguerite-Louise would tolerate no criticism. 'Cinzia told me that the Grand Duchess does not want to bring Mademoiselle de Mainville to Marly because she says that she is loquacious. When she was last at Court this gentle girl spoke warmly in favour of the Grand Duchess, whom she maintained was most devout in her application to good works, and that she thought only of charities. When the Grand Duchess heard of it she said to this young lady, with a very haughty air: "I'll give you a sound drubbing if you mention me again, for I do not wish to be spoken of, kindly or otherwise; and if you speak of me I'll hit you such a rap that you will say I have ceased to be good." '

So the Grand Duchess continued to live, fantastically, with a few occasional pleasures but no satisfaction. She had been profoundly thwarted. After years of scheming, rebellion, argument, endurance, life in her beloved France was 'a discarded play without plot or plan'. The years passed aridly, with this difference: there were no dreams. Now when she lay awake at night it was to ponder how she could pay her debts and extract more money from her husband. *Tout passe, tout lasse.* But she was not weary yet.

XV

Prince Ferdinando's Engagement to Princess Violante Beatrice of Bavaria – Their Marriage, 1689 – Festivities, Carnival, Lent

'I know not by what accident the whole country was covered with a deluge of monks who took up all the easy carriages,' wrote a traveller to Florence in 1688. It was no accident; and this ingenuous remark summarized the situation. At least ten thousand monks and nuns thronged the city. Penitent whores, renegade Turks and converted Jews, beggars, scavengers, paupers and tattered vagabonds completed a rabble which was only exceeded by that of Leghorn in heartless degradation.

The Grand Duke's clerical advisers clutched at all privileges that came their way, while the people bled patiently; the spirit had gone out of them. Anyone who did not kneel down in the street when the bell sounded at an Ave Maria, whatever the state of the weather, was instantly marched to prison.

When Prince Ferdinando returned from Venice, and from all the delusive happiness the world then seemed to lavish on 'men of the mode', he was able to note the contrast next morning, as it were, after his intoxication. He did not take up his former train of life with any fervour. He had little opportunity to emerge and figure in State affairs, as the Grand Duke was determined to be the only master. His talents were wasted, and he continued to lead the vapid existence of a pleasure-seeking dilettante, consoled in fluctuating moods of dissatisfaction by Cecchino de' Castris, whom he had brought as a living souvenir of the floating republic. The gliding soprano, the caressing inflections of the Venetian dialect, were a balm to those melancholy strains that were a portion of his family inheritance.

The courtiers could not endure their Prince's favourite, who was arrogant and meddlesome, like most who shared his physical condition. The Grand Duke was even more displeased, and rebuked Albizi because he had not prevented the Prince from bringing him to Florence. The contract for Ferdinando's marriage to Princess Violante Beatrice of Bavaria was signed at Munich on May 24th, 1688, so there could be no question of withdrawal.[1]

Although he insisted that Princess Violante was to bring no lady-in-waiting or servant, male or female, the whole way to Florence, Cosimo made one concession on the earnest entreaties of the two priests who had helped to arrange the marriage. The Princess was allowed to retain a Turkish girl and two Turkish children whom she had had baptized and educated in the Catholic faith. Perhaps the sentimental memory of his own weakness for Cosimino, the graceful Turkish boy whom he had also caused to be converted, softened the Grand Duke in this respect. The customary portraits were exchanged between the affianced couple, and the Dowager Grand Duchess Vittoria selected the members of the Princess's Court.

Marguerite-Louise had only heard of this through the *Gazette*. When Gondi wrote her an official letter from Florence on the subject, she replied as follows:

'You did well not to apprise me of the negotiations for my son's marriage, because that might have done for you, and I would have been annoyed. But all France is astonished that I have not been consulted before the conclusion of this affair, which would have merely been proper, and they think I should be angry. However, I am not in the least surprised or offended; vexation brings illness and I wish to enjoy good health and long life. I am now in the best of health and disposed to let things slide (*lascio andar l'acqua alla china*); I am the happiest person in the world, and shall not worry so long as the King continues with his kindness to me, and am content because he is flourishing. . . .'[2]

The Grand Duchess was by no means so happy as she pretended to be; in revenge she chose this moment to revive that old question of the validity of her marriage. She presented Father Gondi (the Abbé's

---

[1] The dowry of Princess Violante was established at 400,000 thalers cash down, with jewels valued at an equal sum. If Prince Ferdinando predeceased her, the House of Medici was to restore 200,000 thalers in case she released the jewels in her dowry, or 100,000 if she preferred to retain them. Princess Violante was granted an income of 20,000 ungheri, including the dowry, for which Cosimo gave as guarantee 'the revenue of a city administered by officials named by the Princess'.   [2] From Montmartre, August 8th, 1688.

nephew, who assisted, and ultimately replaced, the resident Zipoli) with a memorial on the subject which he read to the King's confessor, Père La Chaise. 'The latter was so scandalized,' says Gondi, 'that he exclaimed: "Is it true that the Grand Duchess wrote what I have just heard?" "Nothing could be more true," I replied, "and the King has received a copy of the same memorial. . . ." '

'I begged the said father to defer his resentment against the Grand Duchess's so unworthy proceeding until I had read him the letter she addressed Your Highness in Italian, translated so faithfully that not a word of it was added or insinuated.

'Scarce had I read two lines when he interrupted me, saying: "How ill one can judge from appearance. The Grand Duchess seems so gentle whenever we meet and converse; her letter, however, betrays the humour of a mad woman; pray continue."

'And when I had finished he owned that he would never have believed the Princess capable of such black thoughts and evil transports, and that the devil must have possessed her when she penned this epistle, adding that Your Highness was to be pitied for finding himself united to a fury of hell, which he must set at defiance until God has changed her wicked heart.'

On August 2nd, 1688, Cosimo wrote to inform the Senate that Providence had been pleased to hear his prayers, and find his first-born a wife who, 'for the sublimity of her origin, and for the signal virtues of her mind, promises to bring into our States the fullness of celestial benedictions'. Whereupon the whole Senate proceeded to the Pitti, with the apparent motive of congratulating the Grand Duke on so happy an event, but actually to make him a gift of 200,000 crowns (1,176,000 francs) to be raised, or extorted, from his rejoicing subjects·

After an ornamental marriage by proxy, the Princess left Munich towards the end of November, notwithstanding the severe cold. Her Italian Court awaited her at Mittenwald, whence she travelled through the Tyrol. At Innsbruck she was received by the ex-Queen of Poland, on behalf of her husband, Duke Charles of Lorraine, who was ill; passing through Mantua and Modena, she reached Bologna, where her eighteen-year-old brother-in-law, Prince Gian Gastone, came to meet her. Four days were spent at Bologna, amid banquets and entertainments at the Ranuzzi Palace. On December 27th she set foot in Tuscany, stopping at Firenzuola. We may conceive the virgin fears and alarms of this demure little German girl, not sixteen years of age, before she was finally met by her bridegroom at San Piero a Sieve, with every demonstration of gallantry.[1] She fell in love with him at sight. This love for one who proved himself so little worthy of it never left her.

Unfortunately she did not stir the Prince with a similar emotion. His demonstrations were no more than the courtly necessities of rank. He was repelled by her German plainness. From San Piero a Sieve the bride and bridegroom travelled in the same carriage to the superb villa of Pratolino where the Grand Duke and Cardinal Francesco Maria were awaiting them.

If the Prince failed to appreciate her, Princess Violante made a very agreeable impression on the Grand Duke. In default of beauty, she possessed a sweet, ingenuous manner: the antithesis of Marguerite-Louise, she was gentle and pliant. Soon the misanthropic and embittered Cosimo was writing to one of his confidants: 'I have never known, nor do I think the world can produce, a disposition so perfect and amiable as hers, nor a lady whose mind is more candid, who possesses a greater desire to please and to be kind to all, is of more tender docility, or has a greater inclination to piety. These perfections render her the love and delight of us all, so that I am perfectly contented with her, and feel that I am unworthy of so great a blessing.'

And in a contemporary chronicle we read that she soon won the sympathy and affection of the Florentine people. The Grand Duke, the Heir Apparent and his betrothed, and Cardinal Francesco Maria left Pratolino with their retinue on December 29th, and arrived in Florence towards evening. Those who were near Prince Ferdinando could see from his manner that the bride had failed to please him. He took little trouble to conceal it: on reaching the Porta San Gallo, he scarcely saluted her, and instead of entering the carriage where she sat beside Marchesa Bichi, her maid of honour, he went alone to the Pitti. On various pretexts he delayed the official ceremony as long as possible. The Princess arrived in Florence on December 29th; she was not crowned until January 9th (1689).

The Cathedral had been given a new façade. For twenty-seven years

[1] A. Segni. *Recollections of the Journeys and Festivals on the occasion of the Espousals of Violante of Bavaria to Ferdinando of Tuscany.* Florence, 1688, in 8vo.

the old brown walls had been covered by an ugly canvas curtain until at last the wind took pity on the Florentines, as one of them observed, and brought it down in tatters. Cosimo sent for one of those Bolognese 'companies' who from Bigari to Bibbiena were so famous for their perspectives, to cover it with frescoes.[1]

The ceremonies were much the same as on the occasion of Marguerite-Louise's wedding. But there was this difference, and it was almost symbolical: Marguerite-Louise had been married in June, and great awnings of crimson velvet had been raised to shield her from the sun, whereas Violante Beatrice was married in the grip of January, and glass had to protect her against the frost. So intense was the cold that two soldiers who were on parade during the long ceremony outside the Porta San Gallo, fell frozen to death from their saddles. The bride herself, though accustomed to the rigours of her native clime, arrived half numb at the Cathedral. After the function 'she never lifted her muff from her face on the way to the Pitti, and looked so weary and wan, that the sight of her aroused compassion, and she was heard to tell her husband that she had never experienced so bitter a cold on so brief a journey'.

The celebrations for Ferdinando's marriage were the last flashes of that extravagant splendour which had always been connected with the Medici. The city wakened from its torpor: for a short time there was an efflorescence of that gaiety which Cosimo had almost crushed out of his people.

---

[1] From Segni, who wrote the official narrative of the festivities, one gathers that this façade was divided into three sections by Corinthian pilasters, each comprehending one of the three doors, the entablatures of which were extended along the entire length of it. Over each door was a great arch supported by double columns, in the included space of which was depicted one of the three councils held in Florence at various times and presided over by three Popes. The upper order, shaped like a large label or placard, bore the escutcheon of the Most Serene Grand Dukes (the five red balls, 2, 2 and 1, on a gold field, surmounted by a gold lily in the centre of a disc), to correspond with the central nave, and was enriched by seven vases emitting groups of flames. This was so much admired that the Florentines wanted to make it permanent in marble. But the pick demolished the faded and crumbling plaster that was all time and weather had left of it in 1877, when the Cathedral was last encrusted with the marble and mosaic we may appreciate to-day, niched with statues by Passaglia and 'the daughter of the late eminent sculptor, Giovanni Dupré' (The Misses Horner: *Walks in Florence*, 1884), and given the Italian-Gothic front which Commendatore de Fabris designed.

Ferdinando now decided to build a theatre at Pratolino, the big hall there being unfit for the operas he wished to give. He commissioned the architect who rebuilt the Cathedral at Pescia, Antonio Ferri, and an admirable theatre was opened on the third floor of the villa; the Prince himself supervised the painting of the scenery and the making of the stage machines. His visit to Venice, then the most celebrated city in Italy for operas, had fired him with enthusiasm, and he caused the Teatro della Pergola to be rebuilt and redecorated for the performance of *Il Greco in Troia*. The alterations were adversely criticized in Florence because Ferdinando had entrusted them to Venetians: now it was said that a stentorian voice was scarcely audible, whereas originally the acoustics, for which Tacca had been responsible, had been so perfect that a little child whispering could be heard throughout the theatre. Nevertheless *Il Greco in Troia* found favour with the Court and many foreigners who had been drawn to Florence.

It was at this time that Ferdinando began to take an interest in Alessandro Scarlatti, whose voluminous correspondence with him remains one of the few sources of knowledge for students of that great composer, throwing an instructive light on his ideas and methods. Scarlatti's dramatic talent found scope at Pratolino, for which he composed five operas: according to Mr E. J. Dent, the music to these, 'except fragments of the version of *Turno Aricino*, has entirely disappeared, a loss the more to be regretted since Scarlatti evidently took a great deal of trouble over both the last two, and seems to have considered them as the best he had produced up to that time'.

The festivities were all the more gay for being near Carnival, which ended with a splendid joust on Shrove Tuesday, organized by the enterprising Prince. This took the form of a contest between some Asian and European knights on the Piazza Santa Croce. The square was surrounded by wooden scaffolding for the spectators; fine woven carpets and tapestry were hung from windows already compressed with a marquetry of human heads. It cannot have changed much since Callot had engraved similar pageants, and we may trust the truth of Callot's elaborate and sinewy observation. Prince Ferdinando, clad in green satin sewn with pearls and valuable gems, commanded one squadron of nine knights, themselves in green satin, with silver braiding, Turkish buskins, sabres at their sides, and superb morions, or open hat-like helmets with long flowing feathers on their heads—so that the warriors resembled gorgeous crested birds, and the ornithological simile could be enhanced when the buglers blew their piercing instruments.

A burst of applause greeted their spectacular entry to the Piazza; and it was renewed when the squadron of Europe came, led by Prince Gian Gastone, and preceded by two trumpeters. But the crowd applauded the costumes rather than the wearers of them. When the joust was over Marchese Vincenzo Capponi, of the Asiatic party, was declared victor, and the Serene Bride presented him with a prize valued at a thousand sequins.

Having a devotional cast of mind, Princess Violante was enchanted by her new environment. Soon after her arrival, the sisters of the Order of St John of Jerusalem (known also as the lady knights of Malta) invited her to the investiture of a nun in their convent. She accepted with alacrity.

The Princess also found the discipline of a Florentine Lent to her liking, when a picturesque penance began for the mad revels of the recent Carnival. The acutest period set in with the fifth Sunday, when seven thorns from the crown which pierced Our Saviour were exhibited in the Church of S. Pier Maggiore, and later borne in solemn procession through the city. A sermon against blasphemy was delivered in Santo Spirito (where Martin Luther had preached when he paused, as an Augustinian friar, in Florence, on his way to Rome); after which a 'grossone'[1] was exposed 'bearing the images of Jesus Christ and the Virgin Mary'. The legend returns to Empoli on January 17th, 1392. It was said that a sacrilegious gambler, enraged after losing his money, nailed this, his last coin, to the table with a dagger. Whereupon a quantity of blood had gushed from the wounded silver, and it was taken with great devotion to Santo Spirito, and revered as a miraculous relic.

Passion Week was packed with functions, most curious of which was probably the sermon to prostitutes, preached in the Duomo, on Passion Monday. Only women of that class could attend it, as they were obliged to under the threat of severe penalties. But whoever molested them on their way was threatened with penalties equally

[1] A silver coin formerly in use and worth nearly threepence.

severe, by a proclamation which was annually renewed. Many young daredevils paid no heed to this injunction, and tried to endanger the temporary virtue of these trulls with sallies as they fared forth on the road to repentance.

The Matins of Darkness, recalling early Christians in the Catacombs, were held on Wednesday. Gradually, during the singing of the Benedictus, all the lights on the altar save one, a symbol of Christ, were snuffed out. This was removed and concealed behind the altar: Our Saviour's death and burial. The church left in gloom, the clergy and congregation beat the floor with slender rods of willow, whose sound, the *strepitacula*, represents the upheaval of natural forces at the hour of crucifixion. Afterwards the solitary light was restored to the altar, and silently the worshippers dispersed, rapt, muffled, solemn, thinking of death.

People streamed in and out of the churches through Maundy Thursday; the Holy Oils were blessed; all received Communion; the Archbishop washed the feet of twelve paupers in commemoration of that first feet-washing in the upper room at Jerusalem, and the Grand Duke followed suit at the Pitti, rewarding each of those whose feet he had laved with a golden piastre. Interminable were the processions; and some brotherhoods lashed their bare flesh till it bled in the public thoroughfares. Thus Florence must have borne some resemblance, at these times, to certain fanatical cities of the East, and the sects of Christianity to those of Islam; the dishevelled and exhibitionist Aissaoua and Hamatcha—but that the former devour scorpions and the latter burst their scalps with hatchets.

The Grand Duke and his family went separately to visit the churches on foot—it was a duty to visit seven—and not a carriage was to be seen in Florence on that day. For a 'sepulchre' was set up in each church, representing a tomb in a garden with the Host in its midst, surrounded by lights and emblems of the Passion. A ghostly kind of grass called *vecchia*, grown specially in sombre crypts and cellars, and bleached to a pale strange silver from lack of light, was used in the decoration of these sepulchral gardens, and sometimes mustard and cress, and sprouting wheat.

Enthusiastically, Princess Violante suggested that her ladies should visit the churches with her barefoot, but she had to renounce the idea since her ladies showed no inclination, however devout, to risk catching pneumonia. On Good Friday the streets were empty and the churches full, until, at three o'clock in the afternoon, there was a long and loud awakening. The vergers of all churches, convents, etc.—and the number of these was immense—went out with wooden clappers and roused the neighbourhood. This was a signal for all to throw themselves down on their knees and pray, wherever they happened to be, in memory of Jesus, when after three hours on the cross, He rendered up His soul 'in the arms of His eternal Father'. A miraculous figure of the dead Christ was exposed that evening in S. Croce; and His funeral was celebrated with pious pomp. At night the company of Gesù Pellegrino formed a lugubrious pageant. All the streets in the line of procession were illuminated and the houses hung with festoons of black and white cloth. Every portable object connected with the Crucifixion —the cross, scourging post, rods, crown of thorns, spear, sponge, tankard, purple robe, dice, hammers, nails, pincers, each had its bearer. Then came the dead Christ recumbent under a canopy of black velvet and gold; last the Virgin, following him, erect in deep mourning, with a white handkerchief in her hand.

Lent could not finish more gaily than with the *Scoppio del Carro*, the dove of Holy Saturday, and pyrotechnics in broad Italian daylight, about which so much has been written. Altar and throne that had been hung with black, were now covered with cloth of gold. The Piazza del Duomo is still thronged on that morning and, as twelve o'clock strikes, *Gloria in Excelsis* is sung by the Archbishop in a jewelled mitre and crosier, and that artificial *colombina* on whose successful flight the next harvest depends 'still speeds her fiery course down the centre of the old cathedral, and sets fire to the wonderful erection of squibs, crackers and catherine-wheels outside the great front-door, piled up on an old triumphal chariot'. All the bells in Florence, which had their clappers tied up for two days lest the devil should get among them and disturb the holy pause, rang out at once.

Yearly the citizens are thus held in thrall, watching this important little dove like children, with wide absorbed eyes.

XVI

*The Grand Duchess Applies to Cosimo for Funds – Her Appeal to
Prince Ferdinando – Economy in Florence – Marriage of Princess
Anna Maria – 'Trattamento Reale' – 'Villainies of the Virtuous'
– Taxation – Relics: Cresci and Onnione – Penal Justice and
Education*

The exigencies of rank compelled French princesses to be extravagant. Cosimo would not realize this, and when Marguerite-Louise contracted further debts he refused to pay them. In 1688 she found herself in such straits that she was unable to pay her doctor or apothecary; she applied to Cosimo for 20,000 crowns, and the King exerted himself on her behalf. The French minister in Turin was dispatched to Florence, and adding threats to arguments, he obliged the Grand Duke (as he himself expressed it) 'to drink the bitter chalice', and promise to pay. It was a large sum, and the Grand Duke took his time: months elapsed, more debts were piling up, and still it was not forthcoming. The Valenti bank, where the Grand Duchess's pension was deposited, failed in the meantime. Marguerite-Louise vented her spleen in letters to Zipoli, the resident.

'The Grand Duke, who is rich, happy and content, wishes everybody else to do penance; while he lives on the fat of the land, I must fast. When I fast it will be for God, not for him. Unless I obtain the satisfaction I expect, I shall procure the King's authorization to borrow to the extent of the 300,000 crowns I brought him; in short, let him feel that he will get no peace until I receive my money.' (April, 1689.) On June 28th she wrote again:

'I have sold my pearl necklace; Zipoli can testify that I have pawned my diamonds; in short, unless I receive the rest of my due within six weeks, I shall make a violent decision which will astonish the Grand Duke. My good nature, or folly rather, allows him time for the last payment, after which things will go badly for him. . . . My patience is at an end. Tell him that when one is without bread one's blood is on the boil; anything may be expected of me when I am driven to extremities. In fine I want my money, and not to be ruined by the Grand Duke's spending of it. If he had a clear conscience he would not do me the injustices he does: it is the theft of my goods, and unquestionably worse than highway robbery, because he does not risk his life in the business. He is all the guiltier because he does it by reason of his hatred for me, and he will have to render account of it on the day of Judgement. May it please God that all the harm he does me will not cause his damnation; he will never be able to do me as much good as he has done me wrong; he should begin to examine his soul and set his conscience in order.'

Zipoli implored Cosimo to relieve him of his post, 'to escape the furious anger of the Princess'. She had driven her maid Cinzia out of her senses: Zipoli thought she had tried to poison her after discovering her secret dealings with Gondi. The resident's nerves were on edge. Cosimo was annoyed with him for having to pay the 20,000 crowns; Marguerite-Louise for the slowness of their payment. He was eventually allowed to retire in July (1689), and he did so with every precaution. On taking leave of the Grand Duchess he spoke of his departure as but a vague contingency, and even her courtesy seemed the veneer of cunning. Travelling by stage-coach as a private passenger, he took a roundabout route; and thanked heaven for his deliverance when he set foot on Italian soil.

Marguerite's debts and desperation rose, and she now wrote a letter to her son Ferdinando, describing her poverty, and begging him to relieve her. If he was unable to assist the afflicted mother who loved him so tenderly, she desired him to purloin some valuable jewel, and send it to her. This letter she industriously circulated to make Cosimo the object of public dislike. Ferdinando waited nearly three months before replying: 'I regret that I can do nothing with my august father; I too am in such a predicament that I must make a virtue of necessity, and can only dispose of my heart.'

And when at last the 20,000 crowns were paid, the Grand Duchess was no better off: the cost of living continued to be the urgent problem. Father Gondi died soon after taking Zipoli's post in 1690, and the new resident, the vocalist-Abbé Melani ('Il Castrato' as he was called) was wise enough to refrain from criticizing the Grand Duchess: his correspondence deals with political events, and is not, like his predecessor's, an intimate chronicle of Marguerite's existence.

In Florence, too, money was the urgent problem, and Cosimo wished, for once, to enforce economy at home. But all his projects were opposed by Ferdinando, aware of his own popularity and of the Florentines' desire for a change. The Prince refused to make any kind of sacrifice. And when Cosimo said he thought of selling the most precious of his family treasures, the Prince's indignation was roused.

'I shall never change my mind,' he wrote, 'and consent to the alienation of what is most precious in our house, there being a thousand alternative ways of settling these difficulties. Let Your Highness hearken to those who speak to him as men of honour: since more often those who play the saint and scrupler think of themselves before their master in giving counsel.'

Ferdinando appears to have imitated his mother's epistolary style. He accused his father of being responsible for his family's misfortunes. It was not just, he said, that the son should suffer the penalty of his father's errors.

Pressed again to bridle his extravagance, the Prince wrote Cosimo on April 9th: 'Regarding the allowance; so long as Your Highness preserves my letters and I the copies of them, and so long as there are men of honour who know their contents, I shall be justified. I cannot restrict myself. I have always accounted for what I spent, and have not, with ill-considered zeal, given help to others when it was time to put money aside for my nuptials, and for my sister's marriage—I do not say for the journey you had promised me, because it was the first you kept among so many promises. I am unwilling to accept any sort of fixed allowance: I give you my word that I shall account for the money as I have always done, that if you will not give it me you will find me some, and also that I shall answer no further in this matter, because there is no end to such disputes.'

Cosimo saw no other expedient than to apply to Ferdinando's minion, Cecchino de' Castris, who had gained an entire ascendancy over his mind. The virtuoso succeeded where others had failed, in persuading the Prince to listen to his father. Ferdinando consented to receive a fixed allowance of a thousand doppie a month 'solely for his pleasures', and Cecchino took upon himself to promise that the Prince should in future be obedient to Cosimo, and respectful to his ministers. A treaty was thus entered into between the Grand Duke and the hereditary Prince with a eunuch as guarantee to its observance.

Cosimo clung to his neutrality, awkwardly facing the future, pondering which direction the cat was about to jump. There were but two directions, France and Austria. Louis and Leopold bullied Cosimo in turn and then anointed him with some ephemeral unguent, remembering that he could still be put to advantage. The Cardinals of the Medici enjoyed an almost legendary reputation as electors of Popes, and Francesco Maria was 'Protector' of Austria and Spain.

In June, 1689, Duke Vittorio Amedeo of Savoy had astonished the rest of Italy by signing his treaty with Spain and the Emperor, who rewarded him with the longed-for 'Trattamento Reale' (the treatment by foreign powers of himself and his ambassadors as if he were king). Cosimo III remonstrated with the Court of Vienna that mere dukes were of inferior status and should remain so, reminding him that the Grand Duke's ambassadors had always been placed immediately below those of the Venetian Republic, and were covered before His Majesty. Such a privilege granted to his enemy was extremely humbling to his dignity: 'it unjustly exalted,' he complained, 'the minor above the major . . . since the House of Savoy had not increased to the point of vying with kings, nor had the House of Medici diminished in splendour and possessions, so that there was no reason for promoting one and degrading the other.' Cosimo further reminded the Emperor of his frequent financial assistance, of the troops and munitions he had provided at various times.

The Emperor, who feared only that Cosimo would ally himself to France, retorted that his concessions to Savoy did not change the rights and prerogatives of other Italian princes. But Cosimo was dissatisfied; and the Emperor, anxious to avoid friction, proposed that his daughter should marry the Elector Palatine.

Princess Anna Maria had twice been rejected by Spain, once by Portugal, the Duke of Savoy and the Dauphin. On the Dauphine's death (April 20th, 1690) Louis XIV had considered marrying Princess Anna to the Dauphin; his inquiries about her age, character and personal appearance had all been answered to his satisfaction, when her mother ruined the negotiations.

According to Pietro di San Luigi, the Bernardine monk to whom Cosimo had entrusted them, 'the Grand Duchess was afraid of her daughter becoming Dauphine because it might put a restraint upon her freedom and curtail her visits to Court'. Louis XIV allowed the negotiations to drop.

James II of England had proposed that she should marry the Duke of Modena or Parma. But the Princess replied that she considered neither of these appropriate: having aimed at France, Portugal and Spain, it seemed degrading to marry a mere princeling of Italy. She had aimed high, but now she was in her twenty-third year: the match proposed by the Emperor was a matter of necessity rather than of choice. Perhaps it was some consolation that Prince Johann Wilhelm was the brother of two Queens (those of Spain and Portugal) and of one Empress (of Austria). And in his son-in-law Cosimo gained a zealous and active friend: it was the Elector Palatine who finally procured him, on February 5th, 1691, the same 'Trattamento Reale' which had been granted to Vittorio Amedeo. He had not the most distant claim upon any kingdom, but as his wishes interfered with nobody's rights, he received the pompous but empty title, yet not without incessant pains and vast expense. The 'Trattamento' consisted in placing a bar upon his diadem, to be styled Royal Highness, and written to *Serenissimo*, whilst his sovereign brethren in Italy and Germany kept to Highness and Serene, except the Doge of Venice and Electors of Germany: the first was also *Serenissimo*, however, and the latter Electoral Highness.

Princess Anna Maria Luisa was married by proxy on April 29th (1691), and the festivities were but slightly less extravagant than usual. An eye-witness described her as: 'extraordinarily fond of pomp, and very stately. In her person she was tall, her complexion was fair, her eyes large and expressive, both those and her hair were black; her mouth was small, with a fullness of the lips; her teeth were white as ivory; her voice was masculine, and she laughed loud.'

She left for Dusseldorf on May 6th, accompanied by Prince Gian Gastone, but she had the pleasant surprise of meeting her husband at Innsbruck on the way, where the official wedding took place. There were great festivities, both here and at Dusseldorf. The reports of these, however, omit one of the wedding gifts; for soon after the nuptials, the gallant Prince infected his spouse with some of the 'poison he had imbibed from Venus's shell'.

At first Louis XIV had opposed Princess Anna's marriage, for the Elector was a declared enemy, but Cosimo persuaded him to withdraw his veto: 'H.H. submits to Your Majesty's consideration that since the Elector has to marry, it will be infinitely more suitable to your interest and convenience if this Princess becomes betrothed to the said Prince rather than another. Having been educated in a family which glories in its undeviating principles of deference and veneration for Your Majesty, it is certain that, wherever she marries, her foremost care will be to insinuate corresponding maxims in all that can regard the person and concerns of Your Majesty whatever happens.'

A French envoy, Rébenac, was endeavouring to create an anti-Imperial league at the time, but he found that: 'though the Emperor was feared, France was not loved'. Rébenac warned the Dukes of Parma, Tuscany and Modena that the Emperor's present claims were only the thin end of the wedge; that he meant to incorporate Parma and Modena into the Duchy of Milan, and that Tuscany would not escape with independence.[1] Cosimo was conciliated by a treaty signed on October 9th, 1691, by the French, English, Spanish and Dutch consuls, recognizing the neutrality of the port of Leghorn (which Louis had seldom respected), but he would only promise to join an anti-Imperial league if the Pope would do so. A safe enough condition, for Innocent XII refused to commit himself to anything which might lead to war.

The Imperial minister was demanding large contributions under an assumed feudatory right and urging Cosimo to ally himself with Austria. Cosimo explained that he could not join a league against France, for in that case the French fleet from Toulon would descend upon his coast. Other princes were intimidated into paying these contributions, but Cosimo managed to pay only on his strictly Imperial fiefs—far less than Leopold had tried to extort from him. Louis XIV told Cosimo that if he paid the Emperor a single penny above the acknowledged feudatory rights, he himself would force his claim to equal rights of mastery over Italy.

When Cosimo met his obligations the Emperor flattered his vanity

[1] H. M. Vernon, *Italy, 1494–1790*. Cambridge, 1909.

again. This time he sent him a standard conquered from the Turks[1]. It was to be offered, in the Emperor's name, to the Chapel of the Santissima Annunziata, as a token of gratitude for the victory his army had won on August 19th. Cosimo published an edict for the festivities to be celebrated on this occasion. Perhaps the standard was responsible for an access of moral rearmament, for three days after its installation[2] Cosimo issued an edict against 'improper amours':

'Considering that to admit young men into houses to make love to girls, and to let them dally at doors and windows, is a great incentive to rapes, abortions and infanticides . . .' he forbade 'not only youths and maidens, but also their fathers, mothers and relatives . . . to admit youths into their houses, and love-making, with or without permission, at doors or windows by night', under the penalty of severe fines and arrest. The rack was administered to Pompeo Vangelisti, a young tailor, on the Piazza S. Apollinare, because he had transgressed an order of Signor di Lorenzo Frescobaldi, Prior of San Lorenzo, forbidding him to make love to a girl. A crime regarded as very serious, adds Settimanni,[3] by the Grand Duke Cosimo III. Beside this context it is not strange to find that 'a head came to the Bargello and was set up on the usual wall, and underneath it was writ: "This is the head of Angiolo di Antonio della Fonte, which was severed for sodomy."' Thus Cosimo hoped to guard the morals of both sexes. Nobody outside the priesthood was free from the Grand Duke's interference; and the tyranny of his methods was typified in his persecution of Roberto Acciaiuoli and Elisabetta Mormorai. This oft-told, intricate tale is best summarized by Mrs Janet Ross:[4]

'Handsome and brave like all his race, the son of Donato Acciaiuoli had long admired Elisabetta Mormorai, wife of Giulio Berardi, and on her husband's death they agreed to marry. But his uncle the Cardinal had decided that his good-looking nephew was to make an alliance which might be of use to him in his designs upon the Papal chair. So

---

[1] It must have gladdened the eye, an affair of golden stars and half-moons embroidered on green brocade. On the frieze were the thrice-repeated words: 'There is no God but Allah, and Mohammed is his Prophet' (*vide* Dr Lorenzo Cantini's fulsome account).

[2] October 9th, 1691.   [3] January 15th, 1691.

[4] *Florentine Palaces and their Stories*, by Janet Ross. See also Giuseppe Conti: *Amori e Delitti di nobiltà e di plebe.*

he induced the Grand Duke Cosimo III to forbid the marriage and to order Elisabetta to a nunnery. Roberto immediately contracted a canonical marriage with her by letter, and fled to Milan where he published it. At the same time he demanded justice from the Grand Duke, the Archbishop, the Cardinal and his own father. The validity of the marriage was upheld in Lombardy; in Florence it was declared to be a mere engagement and not binding, and the lady was removed from her convent and shut up in a fortress. On the death of the Pope (Alexander VIII) in 1691, Roberto wrote to the assembled cardinals imploring them, and the future Pope, to do him justice. All Italy was interested in the fate of the lovers, and Cardinal Acciaiuoli tried to throw the entire blame on his relations. The Grand Duke set Elisabetta free and she joined her husband at Venice, where Cosimo was openly accused of arbitrary and unjust conduct and of truckling to the private spite of the Cardinal. He thereupon made formal application to the Republic to deliver up Acciaiuoli and his wife on the plea of *lèse majesté*. They fled disguised as friars, but were followed by his emissaries and taken into custody at Trent. Roberto Acciaiuoli was condemned to imprisonment for life in the fortress of Volterra and to the loss of his patrimony whilst Elisabetta was offered the choice of repudiating her marriage or of being confined in the women's part of the same prison. In the hope of mitigating the severity of her husband's sentence she chose the former.'

Roberto died of grief a few months later, and some accused Elisabetta of weakness for not sharing his fate, but she had two children by her first marriage whom she could not desert: it is less easy, as Conti remarks, to practise than to preach these fine romantic gestures. Elisabetta lingered on, a tragic figure, until 1724.

'The villainies of the virtuous: who shall recount them?'[1]

At the same time Cosimo inflicted new taxes to compensate him for his payments to Austria. The land, its produce, labour itself, four-footed beasts which did not cleave the hoof, and periwigs, were among the objects of this extortion. In addition to the prohibitive imposts and octroi dues on the most ordinary commodities of life—a bale of wool sent from Leghorn to Cortona had to pass through ten intermediate customs—everybody with an income of over thirty-five crowns a year

[1] *Alone*, by Norman Douglas.

had to pay half a crown on every hundred he received. Field labourers and peasant cultivators on the *métayer* system, who paid a proportion of their produce as rent and had no other income, were excluded from the tax, as those who did not succeed in earning more than thirty-five crowns a year with the sweat of their brow and, needless to say, the clergy. Finally this edict of June 21st, 1692, warns evaders that informers would help the inspectors to discover and prosecute them.

The clergy, as usual, escaped lightly from the customs. Either the officials forgot their duties at sight of them or they were subtly outwitted. Labat, himself a priest, illustrated this with two anecdotes of ecclesiastical smuggling, after remarking how very civil the inspectors were to his colleagues.

'A band of novices from one of the most famous religious communities in Florence had been to the country for the benefit of their health, and the father in charge of them had bought a copious twist of tobacco at a price much lower than he would have had to pay for it in town because of the octroi dues. Before returning, he distributed the tobacco among the novices, who made themselves girdles of it under their frocks. The worthy father did likewise; unfortunately, however, his own came undone, and when he entered the town behind his tonsured brigade—walking two by two with gentle modesty—an official noticed the end of his tobacco trailing along the ground.

'In any other country the official would have kicked up a shindy; the whole flock would have been arrested and searched, the tobacco confiscated, and all been brought before the law. At the least influential friends would have been called to the rescue and money scattered to hush this affair. Nothing of the kind occurred in Florence. The Christian or Jewish official came up to the father, bowing respectfully, and whispered in his ear that his garter was trailing in the dust. After thanking him the monk bent down, and was astonished to see that it was the end of his tobacco. He blushed, while the polite official, bowing again, retired into his office, thus giving him an opportunity to proceed without further fear. It was a law in the Grand Duke's dominions that customs officials had no right to exact or confiscate anything once the toll-gates were passed without violence.'

And Labat tells the following story to prove it: 'There was to be an important marriage in Florence, and the bride's jewels, in Italy called the *fornimento di sposa*, had been purchased at Leghorn. But the family wished to avoid paying the heavy duty to which such things were liable. How could this be done? Then a certain friend of theirs, a Franciscan friar, came forward and promised he would elude the inspector's vigilance. With anyone else they would have doubted the success of such an undertaking, but Franciscans everywhere are men of wit, resourceful and businesslike. So they entrusted him with the jewels in a red morocco case, and gave him a rolling chaise to carry it to Florence. The customs officials were warned by their spies that the gems had been consigned to a Franciscan friar, who was in a carriage harnessed to two horses of such and such a colour and driven by a postilion they knew as well as themselves. It seemed impossible that they could ever enter gratis.

'A mile from Florence the friar tied the precious parcel to his breeches (covered, of course, by his frock), dismounted, and told his postilion to wait half an hour before following him. Staff in hand he slowly approached the gate like a man just returning from a walk. The customs officials were more alert than usual on that day, but failing to see the carriage, were not so much on guard as to identify the tramping friar with the one they expected. However, as all Franciscans were suspect, they stopped him and inquired if he had anything to declare. Yes, gentlemen, he replied.

'"And what is it?" asked the chief officer. Whereupon the friar laid his hand on that part of his gown where the box was fastened and said to him laughingly: a *fornimento di sposa*. This indecent gesture coupled with words which could be taken in an obscene sense shocked the chaste ears of the customs officials, who indignantly said: "Pass, you scurvy monk; your Superior shall be notified."

'He did not have to be told twice, and went on his way. When he was twenty or thirty paces from the toll-gate he halted, unfastened his box, and raising it for the officers to see, said: "Here it is, gentlemen, I did not lie to you."'

The Grand Duke continued to levy these taxes long after they had repaid him for his contribution to the Emperor. The proceeds were squandered on the purchase of various relics. The hand of such a saint, or the toe of such a confessor, were acquisitions of the utmost importance.

At times it seemed as if Cosimo considered himself a sort of honorary Pontiff: religion (or superstition) continued to play the most prominent part in his life. He employed secret agents in all the Courts of Protestant sovereigns 'to induce them to become Catholics'. He also tried to unite the Greek and Russian Churches to that of Rome; and zealously identified himself with Catholic interests in England and Holland.

Thomas Platt, the British consul in Leghorn, often served as his English secretary and kept him informed of topical trends and events when he returned to England. Born a Catholic, he became a Protestant and did not really gain the Grand Duke's confidence until he was converted in 1687. Sir Henry Neville, a truly Italianate Englishman, fluent in Tuscan, was another unofficial agent. Having been a member of the Long Parliament and an outspoken republican, he was arrested during the Restoration and set free, thanks to his brother, who had fought for the King during the Civil War. He then obtained permission to travel abroad and visited Florence and Rome where he had many influential friends. Though he was not religious he had strong Catholic sympathies. Cosimo often plied him with questions about English policies and personalities: for instance, he was anxious to hear what Sir John Finch, the British resident in Florence from 1665 to 1671, was saying about him in London; he also asked him to investigate the origins of his protégé, Thomas Platt.

Neville seems to have done his best to oblige the Grand Duke, whom he had entertained sumptuously on his visit to England, and his letters were lively and illuminating. Cosimo long remembered the preserved fruit (*geli di frutta*) he had enjoyed as his guest, and sent one of his Florentine cooks to Neville's house to learn the secret of preparing them. Apparently Cosimo made no strenuous effort to convert him, but when he sent him a letter of condolence on his brother's death he told him he would find greater comfort in Catholicism. Owing to Neville's intimacy with prominent Romans he was implicated in the Popish Plot, but he was able to refute the accusations against him. It is doubtful if Cosimo appreciated his English writings, such as *Plato Redivivus*, of which he received presentation copies—Neville had also translated Machiavelli under the pseudonym of John Starkey—but he sent him regularly cases of choice Tuscan wines, as to other English friends of a certain distinction, and on one occasion presented him with enough crimson damask to upholster his bedroom.

In Holland Jan Van Dam of Utrecht was an assiduous correspondent, whose graphic reports of Peter the Great's activities in Amsterdam were supplemented by Thomas Platt's account of the Czar's unconventional doings in England.[1] Apart from these, Francesco Terriesi, his Tuscan agent in London until 1691, kept him minutely informed about the English Court and was loaded with the most varied commissions. The Merry Monarch and his mistresses seem to have fascinated Cosimo far more than they had shocked him, so that he remained eager for the latest titbits of scandal.

While in London Cosimo had been much impressed by the nimble virtuosity of English dancers and comedians, though he could not understand the language. One of the most notorious of these, Joseph Haynes, turned up in Florence in 1686. According to his facetious biographer, Haynes was presented to the Tuscan Court by an English tailor. 'Mr Haynes, says he, you know you had the honour to dance before the Great Duke of Florence when he was Prince of Tuscany and in England. Now there being a ball at Court very suddenly I can procure the favour for you to dance before him. . . . The project took so good effect that Joe was not only admitted to his presence, but had the honour to teach the young Prince and Princess (Ferdinando and Anna Maria Luisa) . . .' In due course—'Coach and equipage were allowed him and everything suitable to the character and greatness of Tutor to the Prince of Tuscany. . . . In short, he rose so high that whosoever desired to obtain any favour of the Duke could intercede with Mr Haynes to accomplish his desire.' This triumph was short-lived, however: he fell in disgrace 'for teaching the Princess he made bold to be a little too familiar.' From the Grand Duke's secretary, Canon Bassetti, who wrote to Terriesi for his dossier, it transpires that Cosimo had taken particular delight in Joe Haynes because he 'abjured his heresy and devoted himself to the Catholic religion, with signs of great piety and of genuine conversion'. But this conversion, alas, was merely another of Joe's comedies, as the Grand Duke was soon mortified to discover. During the reign of William and Mary the mummer made a public recantation and professed his Protestantism in a prologue to Buckingham's *Rehearsal*, in which he played the rôle of Bayes. In his

[1] See Anna Maria Crinò: *Fatti e Figure del Seicento Anglo-Toscano*. Florence, 1957.

youth he had posed as a Count at the French Court, and 'from the same principle of mirth and diversion', he was resolved 'to palm a Convert upon the Pope and Cardinals' in his middle age.

Gondi, the Grand Duke's ex-resident in Paris, of whom we have heard much in connection with Marguerite-Louise, owned some property in the Mugello, where there was a half-ruined chapel containing the bones of two long-forgotten martyrs, Cresci and Onnione. With sound experience of the Grand Duke's idiosyncrasies, he hit on a capital idea. Why not restore the cult of these two good companions? The Archbishop Morigia approved. As for the Grand Duke, he was infatuated with the suggestion. He gave immediate orders to have the little church repaired and embellished. No one could tell him more about these holy men than that they had been martyrs, so he set his theologians to the task of compiling the acts of their martyrdom, and requested the Pope for indulgences on their anniversary.

Unfortunately a Servite monk chose this moment to come forward and challenge their authenticity. Those acts of martyrdom, he said, were entirely apocryphal. Maybe professional pride had taken umbrage at secular interference; one is amazed by his audacity. It did not pay to spoil the Grand Duke's fun; and the ill-natured servant of Mary was banished from Tuscany. The Oratorian Laderchi was appointed to crush him: he was to edit a manuscript containing the records of their martyrdom. Laderchi endeavoured to show that this narrative was drawn up shortly after the events—not indeed by an eye-witness—but from a true and accurate statement. More than one writer had quoted it, he said, and none had ever contested its authenticity. Why should we not accept the beliefs of our forefathers? Besides, the deeds attributed to these Christian heroes were incontestable, for similar facts reported about other venerable personages had been acknowledged as correct.

Several theologians, however, refused to admit these arguments and the controversy was much discussed in the literary academies. It served as an admirable illustration of a topic they enjoyed: the contrast between the credulous man and the thinker. To one a simple semblance of proof is enough; the other is sceptical: he has to be convinced.

The most striking objections to Laderchi's arguments were these: according to the 'acts', Cresci died on October 24th, 249, and several other victims were also put to death with him on that day, who are enumerated. But it is certain that the others perished in the year 250 and not in 249. Heresies, however, are mentioned in the same work, posterior to the date when it was supposed to be written, and Cresci expounds Christianity to a tyrant in language which the primitive Church never used with idolators (who designedly were addressed under an enigmatic form). Finally, it contains locutions unknown to the third century of the Christian era. Cogent objections; but Cosimo's ardour was nowise chilled. Rome remained impartial, and did not pronounce in favour of, or against, Cresci and Onnione. Cosimo adopted the saints as his special advocates. Their festival falling in summer afforded him an agreeable excursion to the Mugello. But Gondi had over-rated their commercial value. Cresci and Onnione savoured too much of preciosity to become popular: they lacked that realism the true pilgrim demands.

The Florentines were not edified. Poverty and sheer hunger drove many to despair; 'crimes were frequent and generally accompanied by atrocities, and the punishment of death became familiar.' The Grand Duke wanted speedy trials and all the paraphernalia to inspire due terror at executions. Penal justice had become even more cruel and arbitrary. The archives abound in examples. In 1672, for instance, a certain Alessandro Cornesi killed his wife and wounded his young nephew. Cosimo, ever an 'epicure of souls', ordered him to be 'executed at the gallows and quartered, and wished to have him tortured with red-hot pincers, but he was advised against this by the examining magistrate because of the disgust that it would give the city to see him thus tormented, whence he was absolved from this form of punishment at the said examining magistrate's request'.

The average petty thief was bound to a column in the market-place and dealt fifty lashes, each numbered by the executioner (*cinquanta frustate ben conte*). Youthful sinners were punished with corresponding severity: in some cases, however, one must applaud the method. Settimanni writes, in October, 1690: 'A peasant boy between five and six years old, from the district of Pistoia, was castrated in the hospital of S. Maria Nuova, for killing a little girl of three with a stone. He had wanted to remove a medal that she wore about her neck, whence she began to scream, and he stoned her to the ground, striking her head in such wise that it killed her. Seeing that she was dead, he dragged her to a ditch, and covered her face with his clothes. For so much craftiness (*malizia*) it was well judged that he should not be allowed offspring in this world, and therefore he was castrated.' Cruelty to animals was also punished in a manner we might emulate: a scoundrel was put in the pillory by the column in the market-place, with a collar and placard, 'for being a murderer of cats', and two of his dead victims were appended on his neck.

The Jesuits controlled education, while the disciples of Galileo kept prudently in the shade, for the arrows against them were still flying. Had he not followed the advice of his physician Redi, Cosimo would have expired ere now, yet his attitude towards science is exemplified in a letter from his secretary to the professors of Pisa University (October 10th, 1691): 'By the Serene Master's express command I must inform Your Excellencies that His Highness will allow no professor in his university at Pisa to read or teach, in public or in private, by writing or by voice, the philosophy of Democritus, or of atoms, or any save that of Aristotle. Whoso shall in any way oppose H.H.'s will, besides incurring H.H.'s displeasure, may consider himself dismissed from his chair. . . .'

He revived an old law of 1626, when his grandmothers were in power—the *Tutrici*, and origins of Tuscany's decline. This obliged all students to attend solely the university of Pisa; under no circumstance were they allowed to study abroad. Cosimo typified the very state of mind that the best philosophers of his age were striving to combat. Yet he had an inquisitive nature; and this is proved not only by his persistent inquiries into all the piquant details of Marguerite-Louise's daily existence at Montmartre and elsewhere. For Settimanni wrote in his diary, on May 23rd, 1683: 'The Grand Duke, desirous of gathering the best knowledge of the affairs, properties and styles of foreign peoples, and an exact and full familiarity with their measures, weights and moneys, their names, qualities, use and value in relation to ours in Italy, has written to all his residents at the Courts of Europe to seek out notices from all parts of the known world reached by commerce.'

And again: 'The Grand Duke having wished to furnish his library with books in foreign languages and commissioned them in various parts of the world, received a coffer full of them to-day at Leghorn.

65 The Villa Medici at Fiesole

66 Fiesole: Villa Medici and the view of Florence

67 Fiesole: a terrace in the garden of Villa Medici

68 *(below)* Alessandro Magnasco: *The Stag Hunt.*
Wadsworth Atheneum, Hartford, Conn. (Sumner Collection)

69 *(opposite)* The Electress Anna Maria Luisa dancing
with her husband, by J. F. van Douven. Pitti

70, 71 *(previous pages)* Castello
(left) the fountain by Tribolo
with Hercules crushing Antaeus
(right) the statue of Oceanus
by Giambologna

72 *(above)* School of Marcuola: Cosimo
Riccardi visiting Gian Gastone in bed.
Museo degli Argenti

73 *(opposite)* Prince Ferdinando, Princess Anna Maria Luisa
and their governess, by Sustermans.
Museo Stibbert

74 *(above)* Florentine tapestry with portrait of Cosimo III.
Museo degli Argenti

75 *(above left)* Soldier, jewel from
Dresden brought back by the Electress Palatine.
Early eighteenth-century. Museo degli Argenti

76 *(above right)* Pendant with siren, probably also
brought from Germany by the Electress Palatine.
c. 1700. Museo degli Argenti

77 *(opposite)* The Cappella dei Principi in San Lorenzo

CASTELLO

78 *(opposite above)*
The main façade of
Cafaggiolo

79 *(opposite below)*
Castello, lunette
by Utens. Museo di
Firenze com'era

80 *(right)* Silver bust of
San Cresci (1703) in
Valcava by Bernardo
Holzmann

81 *(below)* La Peggio
(Lappeggi), lunette by
Utens before its
transformation by A. Ferri.
Museo di Firenze com'era

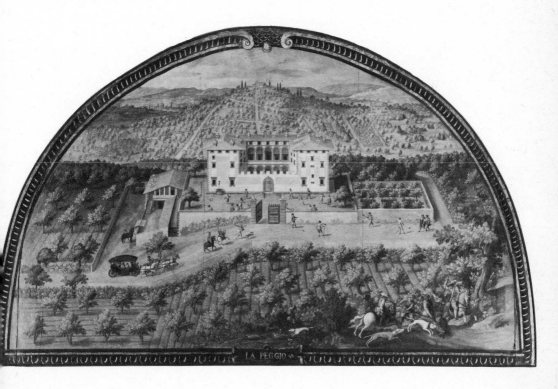

82 *(following page)* Anna Maria Luisa and her husband the Elector Palatine,
by Van Douven. Uffizi

Among them were a Latin, Lithuanian and Polish dictionary, with Bellarmino's Catechism in the Lithuanian tongue; a Russian grammar, and another book which contains the alphabet and principles of the aforesaid Russian language. . . .'

Besides various time-pieces and mechanical inventions Terriesi, the Tuscan agent in London, sent Cosimo long lists of recent English publications which were returned with a cross or two against those which he wished to acquire. Among the latter were the works of Milton, including *Paradise Lost*, of which Magalotti translated the first 234 verses. Sir William Temple, whom Cosimo had met as British ambassador at The Hague, presented him with his *Observations upon the United Provinces of the Netherlands* (1673), and his posthumous *Letters to the King, the Prince of Orange and Two other Persons* (1703), edited by Temple's secretary, Jonathan Swift, were sent to Cosimo in memory of his friendship, with a dedication in Swift's hand. Which shows that Cosimo enjoyed a greater reputation abroad than at home. Sir Samuel Morland, the inventor of a *Tuba Stenterophonica*, 'an instrument of excellent use as well at sea as at land', sent him a chest full of these speaking trumpets and other inventions mathematical and geometrical, with explanations of how to use them.

For a long time after his visit to England Cosimo continued to despatch wines, gloves, perfumes and other gifts to those who had left an agreeable impression on him, especially to famous Court beauties like the Duchess of Cleveland, whose portraits he collected, as did Charles II.

While in London he had posed to the fashionable Samuel Cooper for a miniature, and he urged Terriesi to procure other samples of his art from the painter's widow, but Terriesi thought them too expensive. He commissioned several portraits from Sir Peter Lely, and there was a long and fussy exchange of letters about a portrait of Louise de Kéroualle, Duchess of Portsmouth, which he was determined to obtain in spite of obstacles. In this case the miniaturist, Richard Gibson, proved exasperatingly dilatory. 'The phlegmatic nature of these people is enough to kill one,' groaned Terriesi. But eventually he succeeded in sending Cosimo a miniature of the lovely and exorbitant Louise. Gibson was both a Catholic and a dwarf, so that he would appeal to Cosimo's curiosity irrespective of his talent as limner 'second only to

Cooper'. Though married to a dwarf, he had five children of normal stature. Thus Cardinal Leopoldo's collection of miniatures was increased by Cosimo with several from England, which are now in the Uffizi Gallery.

Missionaries who arrived in Florence from antipodal climes, with a rich repertory of picaresque stories, were assured of an audience at the Pitti, whence they would depart more mellow and more prosperous. A scholar qualified by priesthood, like the Benedictine Father de Montfaucon, was given an exceptional welcome at his Court and expressed his gratitude by dedicating his *Travels* to Cosimo in language worthier of his great ancestors.

'Many congratulated my good fortune,' he wrote, 'when they beheld me not only permitted freely to go into the Laurentian Library, but to have the keys consigned to me, that I might abide in that treasury of learning, and dive into the most secret recesses of it at pleasure. What a singular favour, and token of your extraordinary generosity was it, that you should cause that catalogue of manuscripts, composed by men excellently learned, with great care and industry, whereof there was but one copy, to be delivered into my hands, and permitted to be carried into France! This goodness I am sensible claims immortal thanks, and deserves a perpetual memorial.'

But Antonio Magliabechi, who strangely enough was employed as Cosimo's librarian, 'lamented, most feelingly, the decline of that patronage which he had been accustomed to receive at Florence'.

It was related of him that once, as he was showing the city to a stranger, he remarked in front of the Riccardi Palace: 'Here letters were born again,' and then, pointing towards the College of Jesuits opposite: 'There they returned to the grave.' He told Burnet that there was not one man in Florence that either understood Greek, or that examined manuscripts. And he gave other visitors a similar impression of the state of Florentine culture. Misson writes: 'Mr Magliabechi told me, that it was computed there were 2,300 Oriental manuscripts in the Great Duke's library; and I could have wished also he had informed me what real advantage had been drawn and received from those books for the good of mankind. But he told me, that if it was true, that there was any treasures in 'em, they were hid, for the present, as being laid in the ground.'

XVII

The Grand Duchess Removes to Saint-Mandé – Princess Violante's Barrenness – Melancholy Character of Gian Gastone – Cosimo's Neutrality – Minor Episodes – Popular Discontent

Time had not yet subdued the passions of Marguerite-Louise. 'She has an iron constitution,' wrote Sainte-Même; 'she would suffer all the discomforts in the world without a murmur.'

A new Abbess, Madame d'Harcourt, had succeeded Madame de Lorraine at Montmartre. Madame d'Harcourt was young and inexperienced; and when she complained of the Grand Duchess to Cosimo and the King, Marguerite-Louise was quick to retaliate. One day, when this Abbess dared to rebuke her personally, the Grand Duchess pursued her through the convent with a hatchet in one hand, a pistol in the other, threatening to kill her. Eventually she formed a faction against her in the community, accused her of an illicit intrigue with a financier (and of other infamies besides), and loudly demanded permission to retire from a place where her delicacy and conscience were outraged. This was all part of her scheme to live at the Luxembourg. She even modified her tone in writing to Cosimo:

'In spite of the many differences which have arisen between us, I have always done you the justice to believe that you harboured no rancour against me, knowing the purity of your conscience.' She then described the feverish state of her health; her shame at the Abbess's behaviour, and thus professed the morality of her own:

'I remain here with my holy sisters, and what leisure I have I employ in acts of piety and in attendance upon the sick, having never relinquished my original design of devoting myself to their service; not in attendance upon the hospitals at Paris, because I do not wish to be in a place where I have friends or relations, but a hundred leagues distant, where I am seen and known by no one, where I shall have nothing else to engage me but to think of God and the salvation of my soul. There is no danger of my abandoning this resolution; *I am tired of the world with which I am too well acquainted.* I therefore pray you, not for love of me, but of that God whom we all adore, that you will contribute to the saving of my soul.'

Cosimo only consented to her removal from Montmartre to Saint-Mandé, which was farther from Paris, on the following conditions. She was not to spend a night outside the convent without the King's express permission; consequently she could not travel without her husband's consent; and she was always to have a female attendant as well as a chamberlain approved by him. If she broke these conditions, she was to receive no more than 20,000 francs of her pension.

When Marguerite-Louise refused to subscribe to them, Cosimo suspended the payment of her pension. The Jesuit La Chaise persuaded the King to guarantee them, and on September 19th, 1692, the Grand Duchess was forced to sign what she described as 'the act of her own condemnation'.

After this she underwent a revulsion of character. At Saint-Mandé a new chapter began, with the approach of the seventh climacteric. The nuns shocked her by their irregularities, jumping over the convent walls to join their lovers, while the Mother Superior disappeared for months disguised as a man. All was confusion in what the Grand Duchess styled this 'spiritual brothel', and she set about reforming it with zeal. She had the Superior arrested and removed to a convent where the rules were strictly observed; recalcitrant nuns were expelled; and virtue reigned once more at Saint-Mandé. The Archbishop consulted her and followed her advice, and she found herself mistress of this small community. This did not prevent her from having a lover at the same time, who posed alternately as an artist and soldier, but who in reality was Fra Bonaventura, a renegade monk. We hear little of him; doubtless he was an ephemeral occupation. At last the Grand Duchess began to calm down and her conduct ceased to worry Cosimo.

But his peace of mind was now disturbed on another account, for Princess Violante vouchsafed no signs of motherhood.

'This gracious and gentle maiden,' wrote Paolo Minucci, 'perhaps through inexperience of character and certainly because of her religious education, was incapable of influencing her husband.' Fortunately she had the tact to shut her eyes to his infidelities. She was mortified, however, when Cosimo ordered special devotions for three days, to obtain the desired succession.

He seemed impervious to the ridicule to which his bigotry exposed him. But the poor Princess must have been pained when impostors exploited this bigotry, where her barrenness was concerned. 'To-day the 14th April' (1694), we read in an anonymous codex, 'the base of the column opposite the Via degli Arazzieri, which faces the Via Larga (now Cavour) was begun to be repaired. It had been pulled down when the Grand Duchess Maria-Maddalena of Austria, wife of the Grand Duke Cosimo II, came to Florence, for the function attending her arrival. This is the reason why this base is now being mended: a priest called Filippo Pizzichi has persuaded the Grand Duke that a statue of the Archbishop Saint Antonino blessing the city would look well on this column, for skilled craftsmen existed in Florence who could repair it. Albeit the expense were heavy, he suggested that it should be entirely defrayed with alms. The Most High would assuredly confer progeny upon Prince Ferdinando in return for this pious labour.

'So Cosimo gave Pizzichi leave to collect alms in Florence, and he gathered a goodly sum. . . . Finally, after he had got some thousands of crowns together, the base was finished but there was nobody to set the column up. Pizzichi let the matter drop, always giving hopeful words to those who had contributed towards his project, while he built himself a fine house in the Via Larga. There were several satires against him at the time, among which this couplet was found on the column-base when it was hardly finished:

> *Pizzichi mio, a ingravidar le donne*
> *Ci voglion c . . . e non colonne.'*

The gist of which is that columns do not get women with child.

Although Princess Violante seldom referred to her troubles, they transpired occasionally in her conversation. When one of her ladies begged her to intercede on her behalf with the Grand Duke, whom she wished to protect her against a brutal husband, the Princess replied: 'Madam, I sympathize with you; but under these broad sleeves I hide wounds deeper than yours.' And to a courtier who had been defrauded of his emoluments and sought her assistance: 'I would marvel greatly if matters were properly conducted at Court, while they are arranged by a *castrone*' (wether, or castrated colt)—alluding to Cecchino, whose power had increased since he had ingratiated himself with the Grand Duke.

Certainly Princess Violante disproved the saying that Hell has no fury like a woman scorned. Her private sorrow drew her in sympathy towards her brother-in-law. Prince Gian Gastone cut a pathetic figure; his father took little notice of him: 'the nobility and courtiers only surrounded those in whom the chief authority seemed to reside'; and he was left in the cold, as it were, the dependent, impecunious, just-tolerated younger brother—a romantic temperament, and one neither intelligible nor sympathetic to the tough, rational Florentine of the period. He found an escape in antiquarian pastimes, and lived in seclusion without a retinue—in odd contrast to his extravagant brother and uncle, the jocular Cardinal, who moved in theatrical state between Rome and Lappeggi, with an elaborate train of grooms and groomlings, buffoons and parasites. Cardinal Francesco Maria frequently invited his nephew to Lappeggi: he hoped to distract him from the tonsured tribe at the Pitti, and from that introspective hypochondria which already had a morbid tinge about it. For the young Prince would spend whole hours a-weeping in his chamber, cultivating his misery. Perchance, like Rasselas, he was unwilling to cloud with his presence the happiness of others. In the Middle Ages they would have said he was visited by the *daemon meridianus*: he had all the symptoms of Acedia, that mysterious disease of the will and compound of boredom, sorrow and despair,

L'Ennui, fruit de la morne incuriosité,

which 'took the proportions of immortality' with Baudelaire and the Romantics of the nineteenth century.

'I am very surprised,' wrote the Jesuit Father Segneri, 'to hear that Prince Gian Gastone has now lost faith in everyone. But how can he lose it in his confessor? I know not if the latter has warned him against confessing his thoughts to himself. . . . I never miss praying for him as Your Highness has enjoined me to do: still it is needful that he should help himself.'

Gian Gastone was powerless to help himself. It was hoped that travel might cure him, and when his sister was betrothed he had been allowed to accompany her as far as Trent. But this journey, as Salviati informed Francesco Maria, served him for naught else than to make him believe that he knew more than the rest of the living.

He was not entirely self-obsessed, however, for we are told that he received some solace from antiquarian studies and botany. There is a small round building in the Boboli Gardens which was built for his retreat. A sort of lunary Pierrot he must have looked, anaemic and pensieroso, moping amid the bustle of Lappeggi. But Francesco Maria enjoyed piquant contrasts, and the spectacle of so rare a degree of sensibility threw his own gross gaiety into relief; they both tacitly disapproved of Cosimo's government.

Meanwhile Cosimo made the most of any circumstance that enabled him to stimulate piety. There were no more proclamations against Jews, because he could invent no novel way of persecuting them; his edicts against immorality were still-born. So he must turn such incidents as the following to his account:[1] 'On the second of January, 1693, during the night, an image of Our Lady in that narrow street leading from the Lung' Arno to the small square of Sant' Apollonio was most indecently defiled with mud and other filth. Whence the Grand Duke, after considering the enormity of this excess, issued a proclamation that whoever within the term of ten days knows the malefactor and does not reveal him to the magistracy of the *Otto* shall incur the penalty of death and confiscation of his property, and whoso reveals it shall be rewarded with 200 even up to 300 crowns at the magistrate's discretion.'

Rich and poor alike forgot all else in contemplation of the crime: Cosimo, like the modern newspaper, exploited it for his own benefit. It had happened, most appositely, during a 'silly season'. The proclamation of January 21st, 1693, was worded as one 'of devotion to placate God for the execrable crime committed in Florence against an image of the Blessed Virgin . . . lest the divine vengeance (which for the crime of one will sometimes scourge a nation, more especially in matters of this kind) discharge its blows against ourselves. . . .' The following Friday was declared a holiday, with the usual suspension of work and processions from the Cathedral to San Marco and the Santissima Annunziata. The Archbishop, all the clergy and confraternities were present, with the Grand Duke and Prince Gian

[1] As related in the manuscript diary of a Canon Salvini.

Gastone, 'who had come post hither from Pisa the eve before solely on this account. Notwithstanding the intense cold and wind they wished to accompany the procession on foot, which succeeded in being very decorous. . . . On the following morning the Grand Duke, Prince Gian Gastone and the entire Court returned to Pisa'.

There is no mention, we may note, of Prince Ferdinando and Cardinal Francesco Maria, who kept aloof.

Cosimo's neutrality incurred its disagreeable penalties of contributions to Austria, and France thwarted him in minor ways, chiefly by disregarding Leghorn's neutrality, for Louis XIV was annoyed by the way Cosimo had wriggled out of Rébenac's proposals. But Cosimo relied on a trimming, procrastinating policy.

Another in that series of small sensational episodes of which life in Florence was compact helped citizens to forget their woes. An armless German aged twenty-four 'who did with his feet all that others do with their hands' arrived for the yearly festival of San Giovanni.

He was allowed to build a special booth under the Loggia dei Lanzi at his own expense, wherein he could exhibit himself and his numerous talents to the public, for (with due respect to chroniclers) he wrote, combed his hair, washed his face and achieved most necessary and indispensable things with his toes. A giulio, about fifty-six centimes (and an exaggerated price for the period), was the entrance fee to his booth; it was paid by many, in spite of grumblings, for the curiosity of Florentines had ever been overweening. His fame was soon spread through Tuscany, and drew more visitors than usual to the festival of St John the Baptist. It was but natural that Cosimo, much addicted to the uncommon, should wish to examine him, so there was a command performance at the Pitti on June 30th.

The début of the armless young German at Court was brilliant. On reaching the palace, he was presented to the Grand Duke, who congratulated him. The Princesses, to whom he was introduced, were also very gracious, and deigned to ask him a number of questions on his account. As soon as he saluted an audience of nigh two hundred and fifty ladies and gentlemen, by doffing his hat with one of his remarkable feet, there was a spontaneous burst of laughter and applause. Thus encouraged, he began to thread a needle and sew, holding needle and thread with such adroitness between his toes that they seemed the nimble fingers of some experienced sempstress. He stitched well, and gallantly thrusting forth a foot to some of the ladies standing near him, displayed a fragment of the linen he had sewn; and they were greatly astonished. Then he fixed a quill between his big toe and one of the little toes of his right foot, and wrote a letter in his native language which nobody understood, with the exception of Princess Violante, but all admired the neatness of his calligraphy. The climax came when, after a lengthy repertoire of similar marvels, he extracted various instruments from a case and began to shave. He seized the razor with his right foot, sharpened it on a leather strop, and spread it with a coating of grease on the sole of his left one, so swiftly, so surely, that it was indeed a joy to behold. After he had shaved in a few minutes, and no barber could have done better, congratulations and compliments rained on him like manna, and the ladies grew quite lyrical. Seldom had an entertainment been greeted with such immediate and sincere enthusiasm: the German had given these idle courtiers much food for meditation, and hints of truths unguessed at before, while 'the Grand Duke was so enchanted that he presented him with a fine gold necklace on his departure'.

The city was favoured financially at the expense of the provinces, and the unfortunate peasantry bore the weight of taxation and were crushed between the nobles and government officials. The land about Florence became desolate, for when monopolies and privileges absorbed all profits, it ceased to be worth cultivating. This legalized robbery and bloodsucking of taxation was an incentive to brigandage, with its concomitants of homicide, imprisonment and capital punishment: the record year had been 1683, when public executions in Florence reached the average of six a day.

All the industries were controlled by a few individuals, who obtained a monopoly by paying enormous sums into the Grand-Ducal exchequer. Possibly the most oppressive was that of flour, granted to the brothers Andrea and Lorenzo del Rosso from March 20th, 1676, for nine years, when the contract was open to renewal. Bakers could not buy a pound of flour or grind half a bushel of corn without a special permit. The contractors could choose and dismiss millers at their discretion, and keep *sbirri*, or guards, in the mills to watch the grinding on their behalf. A miller who ground corn for anyone outside his own district without the necessary licence, 'or who, by night, received corn to grind in his mill; or sent flour outside it by night' was liable to be sentenced to the galleys, and the contractor could claim an indemnity three or four times exceeding the loss he had suffered. The tariffs and market-prices were higher than to-day. Foreign corn and salt (which cost less) were forbidden: all were obliged to consume the State salt. When it was discovered that the poor managed to evade this by extracting theirs from the brine of pilchards and anchovies, Cosimo issued a proclamation forbidding this practice under severe penalties.

There were bans on foreign iron, linseed oil, sulphate of copper, silks; there was, in fact, a harmful and exaggerated system of protection. There was but little luxury in Florence, yet Cosimo attributed some of his people's poverty to their extravagant wardrobes. 'As for their apparel or dress, it's commonly black and modest'—as if the generality of men and women were in premature mourning for the Medici, since the era of black was upon them. Yet on December 29th, 1694, Cosimo issued an edict to moderate the luxury of maidens, who henceforth must go simply clad, without embroidery and silver. Young brides might wear brocade for two years only; but widows must always be clothed in black without ribbons or superfluous ornaments, or plumes to their head-dresses. Needless to say, the fair took this edict so much to heart that they soon forgot about it.

The restrictive laws drove many artisans out of work; the unemployed surged before the Pitti and called with threatening fury for bread and work. There is no jesting with a hungry mob; and Cosimo, in sudden panic, 'assumed upon himself the subsistence of the artisans and retail of their manufactures by obliging the chief merchants of Leghorn to receive them'. One of the chief causes of the people's rage was the extravagance of the Court, which had never diminished in spite of Cosimo's projects for economy: like his many edicts, his hopes for aggrandisement and progeny, these projects were doomed to failure.

XVIII

Prostitutes and Priests – Death of the Dowager Grand Duchess – Projects for Prince Gian Gastone's Marriage – Loreto and Venice

To gauge the futility of Cosimo's moral campaign, it is instructive to look beyond the monotony of Court life, occasionally broken by the advent of a foreign princeling or of some grotesque freak, and regard the two poles, to wit, the prostitutes and priests.

There was an Office of Public Decency, the magistrates of which had a special patrol of detective-police agents, known as *Salti* (which we could roughly translate as 'Jumping Jacks'), because they could jump on any poor trollop who was found transgressing the laws regulating her profession. They would hide behind street corners, or in some dark passage, to capture her in *flagrante delicto*; then she was clapped into that dreaded gaol, the *Stinche*. Their victims, hungry rather than vicious, were whipped by the executioner all the way from the *Stinche* to the old market-place, with a great placard tied to their necks, on which was written in large letters 'For Whoredom'. Children often fell in with such lively processions and learnt that their elders, too, could be naughty.[1]

When they could not pay their fines, the women captured by the *Salti* often remained in the *Stinche* for years. So scant was the prisoners' diet that Cosimo, to keep them alive, imposed a tax on the licence to use an arquebus. Such was the chastening influence of the *Stinche* that many died within those massive walls; survivors lost all traces of whatever charm they had once possessed. One course was always open to them on their release: they could take religious vows and enter the convent of Convertites. Some sought refuge there for life, others until

---

[1] Cases such as the following abound in Settimanni's *Diary*: i.e., September 10th, 1681. A woman went on the donkey, whipped by the executioner. Her husband led the animal by the halter; and both of them had defamatory notices on their chests, which said: 'For being pimps'.

they recovered their bloom, 'leaving the Lord to minister again to the devil'. Those who reverted to their former profession were duly taxed to support their penitent sisters. And when they died, the Convertites inherited their property.

Loose women were happily not exempt from those privileges that were the order of the day. On paying six crowns a year they need not register their names in the Office of Public Decency, or wear a yellow ribbon in their hats or hair; they were free from molestation by *Salti* or bailiffs of the Bargello; and they were not 'bounden to live in brothels and premises licensed for the habitation of public harlots'. And if 'they returned to a respectable life', not necessarily among the Convertites, they were exempt from the tax. The six crowns did not exonerate them from having to purchase nightly passports, allowing them to go out after dark, and a licence to be masked; and the magistrates of Public Decency could eject them from their houses, if neighbours complained. Sometimes they were called *torcie*, because those who could pay the dues were allowed to perambulate the streets at night with torches; like modern motorists, they were fined if the police found that they had not lighted them.

But the measures against them were not sufficiently strenuous for the Archbishop Marzi-Medici. 'To safeguard public morals, which were outraged by these women who dared, with their wonted lack of modesty, to flaunt themselves in public places where many are assembled for sacred functions, with the vile aim of procuring lovers and seducing them from pious practices,' the Archbishop fulminated an edict of his own. 'We forbid,' he wrote, 'all women of impure life, be they inscribed or not in the Office of Public Decency, to enter under any pretext the Church of the Santissima Annunziata on all Sundays and Church festivals and Saturdays throughout the year; we forbid them to enter the Churches of Santa Maria Novella and San Marco on all the first Sundays of each month,' etc. They were excluded from some churches at all times and seasons, 'even under the pretext of listening to sermons'. The Officials of Public Decency, who had no wish to seem idle, issued a proclamation of their own, forty days after the Archbishop's. This forbade prostitutes to drive through the city in a carriage, masked or otherwise.

Though the clergy were practically outside the law, an occasional scandal focused attention on their private lives, as when two Franciscans murdered their Superior, and were degraded and beheaded in the presence of four witnesses in the courtyard of the Bargello; or when four monks of the Camaldoli in Florence half-killed an innocent boy, whom they suspected of stealing a brazier, by strapping him in a burial vault, after beating him senseless with a rope.

Such cases were deplorably common, especially where foolish virgins were seduced by priests *via* the confessional. Since the time of Pandolfo Ricasoli, the learned theologian, orator, author of a volume entitled '*De Unitate et Trinitate Dei et de primo et de secundo Adventu Dei*', and canon of the Duomo, who was sentenced by the Inquisition in 1641 to be walled up alive for depraving not a few of the girls whose consciences were laid in his charge, there had been a sad number of sequels.

Giuliano Lucchetti, the parish priest of the village of Serravezza, belonged to the same category. He persuaded his prettier penitents that he was the 'founder of the new law'—of a religion complementary to Catholicism. Its ethics were promulgated in the confessional: needless to say they were applied elsewhere. 'Whereas the Son,' he said, 'had proceeded from the Father Eternal, who took human shape in the Virgin Mary's womb, by means of the Holy Spirit, the moment had now come for the Holy Spirit to emerge in person.'

This new, exciting and mysterious faith gained many female adherents at Serravezza. Some could hardly await the result of Lucchetti's exertions; and he was often at a loss to calm their fervour by saying that 'it was not allowable to go against the decrees of Providence, which might not deem them worthy of so great a miracle'. The strangest meetings were held, at which these possibilities were debated. Some were disillusioned; others, blindly fanatical, hoped yet to engender the Holy Spirit. The mother of one girl, for whom the time 'to take part in the assembly' was past, 'filled with the priest's maxims, slapped her daughter hard because she refused to hear of them, and forced her to yield to him'.

But as the years progressed babes male and female were born in Serravezza, with little to distinguish them from other sucklings. No sign of a Holy Spirit! The parishioners lost patience. 'They began to mutiny against the priest and report on these proceedings to the

Government in Florence'—but not ere the slender population of Serra-vezza was almost doubled, for country minds are slow to act, even in Tuscany. The Grand Duke's Council of Eight referred the matter to the Inquisition, who sent their bailiffs to arrest Don Giuliano. He lingered in the cellars under Santa Croce until his trial in the great refectory (May 21st, 1700). The profligate churchman, now in the hey-day of sixty-three summers, wore a costume painted with flames and demons. With his hands tied behind him, he had to climb a scaffold, hung with black, in the centre of the hall, opposite the bench of five inquisitors who were to judge him. There 'he contritely confessed his bestiality and abjured his abominable heresies'. The pulp of his thumbs, which had been consecrated with oil at his ordainment, was cauterized with red-hot irons, and while he was writhing in agony, the Chancellor of the Holy Office rose and read the sentence. He was to be hanged, burned and his ashes scattered on the wind.

So many others had been let off with five years in the galleys that the verdict caused some astonishment. After ten minutes, an eternity during which Lucchetti could envisage his doom in awful silence, the Grand Inquisitor called the Chancellor aside, and ordered him to read a paper which he consigned to him. By an especial grace, the sentence was commuted to imprisonment for life.

Such cases were generally hushed up. There was another in 1694, when a monk of San Marco deflowered half the girls in an orphanage entrusted to his spiritual care, beginning with the Superior, a French-woman, who procured him the others to keep his affections for herself. After getting five of the girls with child, he absconded to Geneva. His colleagues of S. Marco suspected that something was amiss, and when he disappeared, the Archbishop of Florence appointed another priest to take over the spiritual charge of the orphanage, and investigate the why and wherefore of his disappearance. A glance was sufficient. The new confessor ran horrified to the Archbishop, who scolded the Superior and informed the Grand Duke. But nothing could be done at this juncture: the Abbess and five orphans were despatched to the convent of Orbetello, there to deposit the wages of their sin.

Only the clergy fattened and increased. A chronicler of the late seventeenth century complains that most parents sent their children to the schools kept by Jesuits to save themselves expense: 'the public schools are closing and, what is worse, nobody studies, and few become teachers, because there is no longer any employment for them, and generally boys are taught just enough to enable them to pass examinations and become priests'. The law of primogeniture condemned many younger sons to that profession unless they took to soldiering abroad, for then the only profitable military career for Italians was in foreign service. Daughters could not pick and choose: the nunnery was nearly always an alternative to marriage.

The whole of civic life, wrote one historian, was reduced to a monstrous parody of the monastic; a communal existence in which freedom of action, as of thought, of opinions, affections and habits, was forbidden or regulated by edicts and inquisitorial methods, sanctioned by cruel violence. . . . The people were in perpetual terror of spies and informers. 'When any persons are informed against, the officers come in the middle of the night and carry them away; and no one of whatever rank dare oppose them.' Cosimo paid in ready money for conversions and baptisms, and this industry was frequently exploited by people who regarded it as a lucrative joke.

Matters were not improved by Princess Violante's persistent barrenness. Therewith came the sense of a fatalism hanging over Tuscany. Cosimo became alarmed at the idea of the extinction of his race. Griefs clustered thickly: on March 6th, 1694, his mother the Grand Duchess Vittoria died, aged seventy-two. Until the end her empire over Cosimo's mind had been unshaken. She was not regretted by the people, who attributed most of the evils of his reign to her pride, bigotry and intolerance.

This obese old woman had become the pivot of the family. Her life, like that of most Princesses de' Medici, had not been happy. Sole heiress to the duchy of Urbino, she had been cheated of her heritage by Urban VIII who, taking advantage of the investiture which excluded women, had persuaded her decaying grandfather, Francesco Maria II della Rovere, to cede his possessions to the Church. On her grandfather's death in 1631 she obtained only the allodial estates of the Duchies of Montefeltro and Rovere. Despised by her fickle husband, she had yet maintained a decorous appearance of domestic harmony until their reconciliation, after an estrangement of eighteen years. It was natural that she should take refuge in religion, and one must not judge a mother harshly for devoting herself, even fallaciously, to the education of her elder son. Although 'the benign and generous character of Ferdinando was incapable of punishing others for his own defects, and of victimizing the woman who could not win his love',[1] he had been equally to blame for Cosimo's development.

Sustermans has left numerous portraits of the Grand Duchess Vittoria. She appears in them stately, soberly dressed, with big proud features set in a long head, a pronounced double chin, large and lustrous black eyes, full-blown lips and falling tresses of raven hair. The years puffed out her face and body, until she became the ponderous duenna Carlo Dolci has portrayed: a fungoid growth, a hybrid of toad and tortoise.

Her allodial possessions were bequeathed to Cardinal Francesco Maria, on condition that they served as an appanage for younger sons. Prince Gian Gastone's marriage became daily more necessary, as Prince Ferdinando candidly told those who rebuked him for his treatment of Violante, that she was not pretty or witty enough for him; he had married her merely in obedience to his father.

With his brother's example before him, Gian Gastone, now twenty-three years old, evinced no desire for matrimony. But his father fretted over the succession, and searched for a princess whose wealth might enable Gian Gastone to maintain an establishment without further demands on his exhausted finances. The dowager Grand Duchess's influence over Cosimo, wrote Galluzzi, had devolved upon his daughter the Electress Palatine, and he consulted her now. She proposed a German princess who sounded satisfactory, an heiress, from current accounts. This was Anna Maria Francesca, daughter of the last Duke of Saxe-Lauenburg, and widow of the Count Palatine, Philip of Neuberg, who had left her with a daughter. There were two obstacles: the daughter and Princess Anna Maria Francesca's reluctance to marry again. Her wealth was overestimated, but Cosimo was optimistic: he hoped at least she would bring him grandsons galore. He was prepared to send Gian Gastone to Germany, should the lady prove unwilling to come to Florence. As usual he built himself castles in the air. Already he saw a branch of the Medici established in Germany: he hoped to justify the Princess's claims to the Duchy of Saxe-Lauenburg, and

---

[1] Giovanni Masselli.

enrol Gian Gastone among the princes of the Holy Roman Empire.

The descriptions of this dame are not flattering. She was about the same age as Gian Gastone, and looked older; a surprising mound of bosom and belly—a female colossus that might well inflame a Turk but freeze a Florentine, especially of Gian Gastone's refinement. Yet her aversion to renew the marriage-tie was not easily overcome. She did not care to wed a younger son, when she considered herself worthy of a sovereign. Cosimo needed the Emperor's support; his son-in-law's was not sufficient. Now that the Emperor claimed more contributions, Cosimo did not hesitate to pay them. He would tempt means human and divine for the attainment of this marriage, and with all the pomp imaginable, took Gian Gastone on a pilgrimage to Loreto, to implore celestial aid. Among the gifts he brought was a chandelier of pure gold, weighing eighteen pounds.

As a contrast to this pilgrimage, Ferdinando sought recreation in Venice. There he could shake off the ennui that oppressed him in Florence, and that was chiefly caused by his unhappy wife. He arrived in time for the Carnival. The Venetians remembered and fêted him. But alas! it was on this visit he contracted the disease that shortened his life, and destroyed his future hopes of offspring. It is said that soon after his arrival he formed an attachment with a Venetian lady of ancient lineage. Cecchino de' Castris tried all his blandishments and languishments to distract him, warned him of the dangers to which he was exposed, for he had a rival in the Duke of Mantua. But Ferdinando was undaunted, and the Duke of Mantua made way for him. But the lady was not of easy virtue. Beyond a few caresses she resisted him. One evening he upbraided her coldness. How long, he asked, would she continue to torment the heir to Tuscany? And the lady replied: 'Sir, my family is infinitely indebted to the House of Medici, so I shall never see you betrayed. Know, then, that I am not in a condition to requite you: to do so would condemn you to suffer for it always. Be not dazzled by appearances, which are generally deceptive. And trust one who loves you more than she loves herself.'

But the amorous Prince refused to believe her: 'I am not Gonzaga, Madame,' he retorted, 'but I have wealth and estates no less than his. I perceive it is Gonzaga you love, me you despise.' The poor lady, who reciprocated his passion, was wounded by Ferdinando's interpretation of her painful and embarrassing avowal. She gave herself to him after a final warning: he was not to blame her for the consequences. The Prince obeyed his impetuous instincts, and returned to Florence with what were known as 'manly disorders'. Last time he had brought Cecchino back with him, but his amatory tastes had changed. Now it was a female vocalist called La Bambagia (the Cotton Girl), who gave his wife too severe an opportunity of practising that patience for which she was so eminent.

XIX

*Marriage of Gian Gastone to the Princess of Saxe-Lauenburg
– Existence at Reichstadt – Peace of Ryswick – The Prince's
Escapade to Paris, Debauchery at Prague – Writes a Résumé
of His Troubles to Cosimo*

The matrimonial alliance of Gian Gastone was settled at Dusseldorf on March 4th, 1697: the Princess of Saxe-Lauenburg reserved 'the absolute freedom of administering all her dominions', and Gian Gastone had to assume responsibility for debts, taxes and ground-rent to the Emperor. The future spouse swore loyalty and obedience to Gian Gastone, and promised to leave half her possessions to their first and second sons. It was settled that they should ordinarily reside in Bohemia: the Casino di San Marco was placed at their disposal in Florence. Cosimo wished his son to have political status in Bohemia, but when the local grandees bristled the matter was dropped.

In all that concerned his family Ferdinando had gloomy forebodings: he had watched his father pile mistake on mistake. Clairvoyantly he was against this marriage from the start, and sympathized with the victim. When Gian Gastone went to take leave of him at Poggio a Caiano, 'almost as if he had heard nothing of the matter, he inquired: "Pray, whither is Your Highness about to proceed?" "To Germany, to seek offspring," replied Gian Gastone. Whereupon Ferdinando said with a sigh: "I could prove that for our House Germany is barren. Go forth, marry, and a good journey attend you, though I cannot foresee felicity in that direction." '

Gian Gastone reached Dusseldorf towards the end of March, where the cruel surprise awaited him. For his bride was far uglier than his apprehensions; nor had she charm of intellect to redeem her exterior. If we peruse, in their museums or country houses, the portraits of German ducal families, so many piggy eyes and bursting bodices, it is easy to conceive the pitch of her plainness. Gian Gastone summoned courage to fall into the trap that his father and sister had laid for him, and was married in the Chapel of the Elector's palace at 6 p.m. on July 2nd, 1697, with the Suffragan Bishop of Osnabruck officiating at the ceremony. A pastoral was sung on the following day, which ended, as if ironically, with country dances; Teutonic yokels and hoydens kicking their heels on the sward were an appropriate epilogue to such a wedding.

For Gian Gastone's wife was nothing but a glorified Bohemian peasant. She disliked cities, courts, urbane society and did not conceal her impatience to return to the rustic freedom of her little native vale. While they dallied at Dusseldorf she became daily more peevish. Inured to country life, wrote Galluzzi, her chief exercises had always been riding, hunting and conversing with the horses in her stable.

In September the couple departed for their residence at Reichstadt, not far from Prague. They were ill-assorted to begin with, and every circumstance, apart from his wife's character and physique, contributed to Gian Gastone's disgust. Had Reichstadt been, like many a German hamlet and Schloss, some small imitation of Versailles, inhabited by a few men of culture and refinement, he might have been reconciled to this existence. But it was the very place to breed melancholy in one of its easiest victims: a humble village consisting of hovels, sheds and kitchen gardens in a valley crouching between horrid hills. Their dwelling was situated near the village, on a rugged eminence, and had nothing fine unless in its stable. This was his consort's Paradise, and the stable-yard constituted her *salon*. Had Cosimo wished his son to expire by inches from the severe climate, boredom, solitude and the hypochondria that was already settled in him, he could not have found him a more effective environment.

Gian Gastone had sought solitude in Florence, but at Reichstadt, where it was imposed on him, he had a wild craving for the reverse. His heart sank when he saw himself condemned to live in this wilderness, where he was shown little more consideration than at home, and there was little more for him to do than stay indoors, since he did not share his wife's passion for outdoor sport. It was as if some tropical bird were dropped on a frozen moor. He looked out of the castle windows, and whether the reluctant sun crept through them or they were lashed by rain, the view was equally dispiriting: no formal alleys, terraces and fountains, but sedgy ponds and cow-pastures, with a background of blackish fir-woods. Life became the colour of mould in such surround-ings. The Princess's temper did not sweeten his bitterness. 'She was imperious and voluble, easily moved to paroxysms of rage and tears, greedy, pertinacious and full of mean artifices to turn her own defects to advantage: she seemed an instrument predestined to overcome the strongest will.' From one vexatious tyranny to another! Gian Gastone discovered that his predecessor had been driven to drink by her tan-trums, only surviving his marriage by three years.

To add to this fine state of affairs, Gian Gastone's Florentine suite were always quarrelling with the Princess's; and, among them, Giuliano Dami who, though a lackey of the humblest extraction, now began to exert a magnetic influence on his master. The Prince had first been charmed by Giuliano's appearance when, as a groom, he had accom-panied Marchese Ferdinando Capponi to the Pitti. The Marquis was ready enough to gratify Gian Gastone when he asked him for the menial as a personal favour. So Giuliano accompanied him to Germany. A cunning rascal, 'he could not fail to apprehend H.H.'s aversion to wedlock in general and to his spouse in particular'. So 'he indulged in every way the Prince's irregular inclination for himself, and studied daily to allure him with the beauties of his person, and foremost with those little tricks in which he became a master of his craft'. He had already, we are told, entered upon domestic familiarity with the Prince in Florence. In Reichstadt everything was to promote Giuliano's advancement.

Meanwhile Cosimo rubbed his hands over Gian Gastone's marriage. He thought he had solved the problem of succession. But he was never at rest. If he regained composure, it was only to lose it again.

Peace was concluded, after so many years of war, at the Congress of Ryswick in 1697. The anti-Hapsburg, Italian confederation which France advocated was now impossible. Gian Gastone was not the only Italian prince to be drawn into the net of the Hapsburg marriage alliances. A sister of the Empress and of the Elector Palatine was to marry the Duke of Parma, and a German mate was also found for the Duke of Modena. Imperial influence decidedly outweighed that of France. Austria kept demanding excessive contributions; for the 150,000 crowns the Emperor now imposed, Cosimo saw he would have to turn to the Church, as well as his secular subjects. After much insist-

ence, Innocent XII allowed him to levy from the clergy in his dominions 'only a quarter of what he levied from his other subjects'. Whereupon he issued a proclamation, in which he explained that with the consent of His Holiness, who had reflected on the justice of the cause, he
ordered the clergy of his most happy States to assemble with a ready
subsidy to compensate him for the formidable sums he had had to pay
to avert the horrors of war.

Ecclesiastical possessions in the region under Florentine jurisdiction
were equivalent to twenty-five millions of crowns. While so many were
cramped with want, the clergy lived easy and often frivolous lives, with
comedies and ballets to keep them amused, in which the novices appeared as graceful and ogling ballerinas. In the convents, nuns were
also ready to emulate the theatrical profession and display their charms
before a sufficiently distinguished audience. Yet Cosimo had the
greatest difficulty to squeeze this relatively small tax from them, and
they were furiously indignant with him and the Pope. Meanwhile the
Imperial ambassador to Rome was summoning all possessors of feuds
in Italy to prove the legitimacy of their possessions, or, within a
definite time-limit, take new investiture from the Emperor. This produced the greatest consternation, especially to Cosimo, when he was
informed that Florence had been proved a fief of the Holy Roman
Empire. It came as a flash of lightning in which dire events were foreseen, a prelude to the storm in which Austria would strike at its prey.
Cosimo's readiness to pay the new subsidy of 150,000 crowns made
the Emperor swallow his words. Nevertheless the intention lurked behind them, and a suspicious silence followed. The Emperor became
friendly again. Perhaps he feared that Cosimo would deliberately turn
to France. But the result of his friendliness was that France perpetually
heckled Cosimo about the freedom of Leghorn.

Marguerite-Louise had ceased to torment him, for in 1696 she had
inherited enough from her sister, the Duchesse de Guise, to buy carriages, furnish her stables and reinstate herself in the 'rank in which Providence had placed her'. She had been engaged in several lawsuits with her
relations about this inheritance, in which Cosimo had come to her aid,
so that when she won them she was less aggressive. The fever in her
system had burnt itself out. She had renounced the company of *valets
à tout faire*, and henceforth devoted herself to good works.

But Cosimo was never clear of domestic strife, and he saw that Gian Gastone's marriage was about to follow the tradition of family failures. The Prince, who had managed to survive a severe winter at Reichstadt, cut off from all the amenities to which he was accustomed, showed signs of restlessness and growing impatience. In December he wrote Francesco Maria: 'The news from here cannot be else than frigid, all being shrouded in snow. The sport of sledges has already begun. . . . To-morrow we dine at Zittau, a town belonging to the Elector of Saxony, just to remind ourselves of the kind of place which is made of houses, for it is now three months since we have seen nothing but hovels.' Cosimo tried to console him with pious words: 'It is our duty to do the will of God, who suffered much greater things for us.' Alas, he was not consoled.

By the beginning of spring, in 1698, he could bear it no longer. Without a word of his destination, he left his conjugal retreat. He stopped at Aix-la-Chapelle to see his sister, the Electress, who was taking the baths 'to promote fecundity'. A manuscript tells us that she had twice been pregnant in the first years of her marriage, and both times miscarried. 'These misfortunes, and the extinction of her tested fertility, were due to disorders contracted from her husband, for although he esteemed and loved her well, he was frequently, through the generous warmth of his heart, diverted by irregular amours.' The particulars of these miscarriages were concealed, and the Princess kept her ailing a life-long secret, expressing a wish that her body should not be opened and embalmed when she died. Gian Gastone told his sister that he felt a necessity for change: he was weary of rustic life, and saw no hope of offspring. The truth was that he had not attempted to respond to his wife's demands on his affection, demands that corresponded with her greed and *embonpoint*. She might have remained a widow, for all the attention he paid her.

Such was Gian Gastone's craving for freedom, that he had not written his father about this resolve, since he had received instructions never to leave his wife's side without his consent. After a few days he left Aix-la-Chapelle, without mentioning his destination.

He arrived in Paris towards the middle of May, incognito, as Marquis of Siena. His mother had been told no more than his father about this impromptu visit, and showed not the slightest anxiety to see him. She had left him twenty-three years ago, at the tender age of four and, now that he was in Paris, kept him waiting five days before inviting him to dine with her at Saint-Mandé, and then on a Friday.

Did mother and son console one another about the failure of their marriages? Was Gian Gastone taken to Marguerite's bosom, bathed in tenderness and tears? *La mère coupable* has always been a fruitful theme in romance, and one would fain picture this as a romantic meeting. But Marguerite had changed: her thoughts were wandering towards religion, and she did not care to be reminded of the past. Her coldness towards Gian Gastone was striking. She would not even lend him her horses to go to Versailles; they had taken her to Saint-Cloud the day before, she said, and required a rest.

At the French Court, however, the Prince made an excellent impression. His fine complexion and graceful manners were admired, and compared most favourably with the Duke of Parma, who was in Paris at the same time. He thanked the King for having given him certain letters without which he could not benefit by his mother's will. Louis was pleased by his exquisite deference, and they exchanged the usual compliments. Gian Gastone was not only to consider himself as his near relation, but also as his particular friend, etc. Monsieur took him to the opera at the Palais-Royal, the Comte de Toulouse invited him to dinner; he was shown the Hôtel des Invalides and relics of Saint-Denis. Everywhere he was entertained with polite distinction.

But Cosimo was furious to learn that his instructions had been disregarded, and that his son had visited the most brilliant Court in Europe in a style so little worthy of the dignity and pomp of the Medici. He feared that Marguerite would incite him to greater independence. Gian Gastone's wife raised pandemonium on his departure: she accused her husband of the basest ingratitude, and attributed their lack of offspring to his neglect. Cosimo ordered Gian Gastone to return immediately to his consort. Marguerite did not press him to stay, though he had been in Paris little more than a fortnight. He excused the abruptness of his departure to the King by saying that he had undertaken this journey with the sole object of paying him homage, and that he could no longer abuse such gracious hospitality without becoming importunate, renewing his protestations of gratitude. Louis gave him, as previously he had given his father, a jewelled sword magnificently wrought, and his portrait encrusted with diamonds. His mother gave him nothing.

The escapade, however, was a healthy reaction from all that threatened to suffocate him. He left on June 2nd, returning to Reichstadt by way of Holland, where he received ovations from the learned, as the grandson of Ferdinando II and great-nephew of Cardinal Leopoldo. His wife made an effort to welcome him, but the peace between them did not outlast a few days. The Princess offended his tastes at every turn. First he tried to induce her to spend the winter with him at Prague, but she considered Reichstadt the only place in the world worth living in, and declined to leave it, flying into a rage whenever the subject was mentioned. So he went to Prague without her, accompanied by his Italian suite, and Giuliano Dami.

Before he had left Florence, and even in Paris, he had been voted well favoured as to physique, with his sad eyes and sensual lips, his slender shape and delicate complexion. After his sojourn in Prague he became bloated and unrecognizable. For in the capital of Bohemia Giuliano Dami found it more easy to seduce his master into those profligate courses which were afterwards to set their stamp on him. We will quote from a memoir of Gian Gastone in the *Biblioteca Moreniana* at Florence:[1]

'There were scores of fresh young students in Prague, smooth-chinned Bohemians and Germans, who were so impecunious that on certain days they wandered begging from door to door. In this wide preserve Giuliano could always hunt for amorous game and introduce some new and comely morsel to the Prince. There was also no small number of palaces at Prague belonging to great and opulent nobles. These had regiments of retainers about them in their households, footmen and lackeys of low birth and humble station. Giuliano induced His Highness to seek his diversions with these, and to mingle freely in their midst, so as to choose any specimen that appealed to his singular sense. He encouraged the Prince, moreover, to eat and drink and make free with this *beau monde*, and intoxicate himself in their company. . . . His Highness addicted himself besides to every game of hazard. The Germans, and most Northerners, hold that gambling is permissible and honest. The Prince was wont to suffer considerable losses in no time:

[1] See under *Bibliotechina Grassoccia* in the bibliography, page 313.

it was openly averred that Baron Cunex won and cheated him out of sums exceeding one hundred and fifty thousand crowns at the tables. . . . The details of these, and of infinitely more extravagances, were imparted to his wife, who in turn reported them to his sister, the Electress Palatine. The latter Princess repeatedly admonished him, but all to no purpose . . . he treated her observations with ridicule and contempt. Finally the Electress was compelled, if only in her brother's interest, to render an account to his father. First she called his attention to matters in general, and then came to the particular.

'This piqued the Prince, who soon detected the Grand Duke's informant. He thereupon intensified his diversions instead of diminishing or abandoning them. He became their slave. His noble courtiers sighed in vain. His surgeon and chamberlain, Caldesi, an eminently respectable and well-bred man, and Bartolozzi, a gentleman of great civility, put their heads together to distract him from the course on which he had embarked. Their every attempt was fruitless, for the weak Prince remained incorrigible in his distemper.

'Oftentimes when he went abroad by night, he ran in peril of his life. Setting forth in disguise, he would join the ribald company of lackeys and tatterdemalion wretches that lolled about half-drunk in low haunts and taverns of the town. Infernal broils would not unseldom follow on such occasions, and wounds and slaughter among the topers. Prince Gian Gastone had then to put up with blows, pistol-shots and sword-cuts. In these resorts he grew accustomed to wallow and debauch, smoking tobacco and chewing long peppers with bread and cumin-seed, in order to drink more strictly in German fashion.

'His gambling and irregularities soon drained his purse, although he could still draw money by stratagem, besides his customary assignments from Tuscany. But his expenses were so great that he could hardly pay for so many vices. He was thus reduced to procuring loans from various people, to prolong his absence from his consort and enjoy perfect liberty to revel and carouse. The bills were reckoned with later, on his departure from such places, when his debts would be discharged by the Grand Duke his father.'

That low life has often appealed to the fastidious is a platitude proved, in England, by the rakes at Charles II's Court, such as Buckingham and Dorset, Etheredge, Sedley and Rochester. Our English rakes, however, were gay and thoughtless; Gian Gastone was neither: he wished to drown the thoughts that oppressed his whole being. Nevertheless, as Robiony[1] said, 'from time to time Gian Gastone's keen and witty Tuscan spirit caused him to treat facetiously even the dismal circumstances in which he found himself'. He seems to have extracted a kind of sly, dry Florentine fun out of his horrible wife. To his father's scolding letters, which were the result of his visit to Paris, and of his wife's and sister's denunciations, he replied:

'Your Highness will forgive me if I beg to remind you that on account of women's humour you have also been compelled to take measures against your will. If the motive in my case was not so cogent, the solution has been more agreeable, since I have returned to my spouse.'

Cosimo, as all his actions show, was uncontaminated by a sense of humour, and such letters incensed him. It was all the more necessary to keep Gian Gastone harnessed to the bridal couch, now that Ferdinando had lost his health—the consequence of his affair with the Venetian lady. Cosimo's threats and lack of sympathy had driven Gian Gastone to Prague; he also made excursions to Leipzig and other German Courts, only returning occasionally to his wife's Bohemian fastness. Angry letters continued to arrive from Florence. On April 18th, 1699, Gian Gastone excused himself with an enlightening account of his matrimonial existence:

'Your Highness must learn that nineteen days after the marriage ring was given, if not earlier, my Princess began to give me samples of her capriciousness, peevish faces and sharp words, because I would not leave Dusseldorf, now and then saying a number of impertinent things about me and my people; and, with slight respect to the Elector, showing that she could no longer remain there. Then there were more grimaces, tears and tantrums on our journey to Bohemia; she approved of nothing that was done, although the entire journey was made at my expense. She has persisted in this tenor till now, although I have done all in my power to adapt myself to the sweetness of her disposition, even when contrary to my own convenience, decorum and interests, yea more than I have done for Your Highness, and suffered more disgust and affliction for her in these two years, than for my own soul. . . .

[1] Emilio Robiony. *Gli Ultimi dei Medici.*

'She is haughty and vain enough to trample on everybody and lord it over everybody, believing that she is the greatest lady in the world, because she owns these clods in Bohemia. She is irreconcilable in her hatreds and aversions, and all my servants are witnesses to her ill-usage of her own *usque ad desperationem*, who remain here because they cannot find a livelihood elsewhere.

'This seems to me the condition on which we can live together henceforth, and I see no other. . . . A little in the country with her and a little in town, for I could not continue ten months of the year in the country as she does, or ten months running alone with her after all the scenes that have occurred between us . . . because of her miserable character I have just described, which makes those who live with her miserable, it would certainly be impossible for me to stay with her in the most delicious spot in the world. . . .

'This appears the only way I can live with my wife—not better, but not worse, and none can amend it. For according to her servants she has always been the same, in widowhood as in wedlock with my predecessor, who was despatched into the other world by excessive drinking to dissipate the rage and disgust he suffered on her account. Let us continue to hope for the best: in time many things are broken and many patched up. For the present it would be downright impossible to take her to Florence; first, because she cannot leave her estates; secondly, because she hates Italy and Italians with an extraordinary hatred, and before she married me she said that she would never be able to suffer Frenchmen and Italians in her house. But lastly because in Florence . . . I would have to endure her ravings morning, noon and night, she being unable to repair to her estates, as she has done hitherto, and leave me a little in peace; and I would have to seek a tonic elsewhere, since she is not a diet to be taken twelve months of the year.'

XX

'Fin de Siècle' – The Grand Duke Goes to Rome for the Jubilee, and Becomes a Canon of the Lateran – Death of Pope Innocent XII – Charles II of Spain and His Will – Election of Clement XI – Cardinal Francesco Maria and Lappeggi

As the seventeenth century waned, Cosimo lost most of the men who were sincerely attached to him. Francesco Redi, the eminent physician, scientist and poet, who had prolonged Cosimo's existence by sensible advice, died in 1698.

After Redi, Father Pennoni, Cosimo's special theologian, died in 1699. One who did not share the Grand Duke's affection for this priest painted a picture of the devil's abode with Father Pennoni at the window and Cosimo knocking at the door. 'May I?' requests the Grand Duke. 'You may, you may,' replies Pennoni, as he always did when Cosimo asked him if he could impose an extra tax on his people. The caricature was attached to the font before the Pitti Palace, where it was seen by the Trabanti bodyguards, who took it to the Grand Duke. Cosimo sent for the chief constable and secretary of his police, the 'Eight of the Balia', and told them to search for the cartoonist. But they could only find a tattered old cloak hanging under the rope that was used for executions in the Bargello, together with a rhymed placard wishing them every calamity and bidding them hang the cloak.

Apart from his family misfortunes, Cosimo was upset because neither France nor Spain would take any notice of the Emperor's diploma, while they allowed royal honours to the Duke of Savoy, who had assumed the style of King of Cyprus. He was further mortified because the Duke of Lorraine, who had recently recovered possession of his States from France, christened himself King of Jerusalem without any opposition. The Dukes of Savoy and Lorraine were his most obstinate antagonists in refusing to acknowledge his royalty. It was only in Rome that Cosimo was treated as the Duke of Savoy's equal.

His brother's prodigality and power as Protector of Austria; the large sums he distributed annually among Cardinals and prelates and his readiness to oblige them; the blind deference of his government for the Papacy; had retained his family prestige. But this was not enough: he wanted the world to address him as Royal Highness. Towards the middle of 1699 he sent Marchese Vitelli as ambassador extraordinary to Rome, with the ostensible purpose of thanking His Holiness 'for certain graces bestowed upon the Order of St Stephen'. Cosimo's vanity was flattered by the result of this expedition, for Vitelli was given the same reception as the ambassadors extraordinary of kings.

The imbecile Charles II of Spain was on his deathbed, with Louis XIV and the Emperor Leopold intriguing over his moribund body. Louis claimed the throne for one of his grandsons; Leopold, for his second son, the Archduke Charles; war was inevitable. The Italian Princes tried to form a defensive league to oppose French or German occupation, but Venice refused to join it, and Vittorio Amedeo was reserved, waiting for the turn of events. Cosimo decided to consult the Pope, not unwisely, for the political importance of the Papacy 'lay in its position in the Italian State system, and its part in the Italian balance of power'; yet, 'fearing war all the more because he has never seen it', he really meant to be neutral.[1] Cosimo set forth on a pilgrimage to Rome, with the pretext of gaining the indulgences and other spiritual advantages of the centenary jubilee. He left Leghorn on May 15th, with a retinue of sixty, though travelling incognito, as Count of Pitigliano. He reached Porto d'Anzio after twenty days of navigation. Here he stopped to admire the waterworks that Innocent XII had constructed at great expense: approaching the Pope's fountain he reverently kissed it and drank from it, then proceeded to Rome by Albano and, entering the city quietly, went to the Villa Medici on Mount Pincio.

In Rome he floated about in a continual vapour of ecstasy. The Pope welcomed him as a brother. He visited all the churches, confessed and attended Communion daily, but still his devoutness was not satisfied. For he yearned to embrace the *Volto Santo*, the holy handkerchief which Our Saviour was said to have used on his way to Crucifixion, and upon which the features of His face were miraculously imprinted. This was only displayed on certain privileged occasions, and then from

[1] Vernon. *Italy from 1494 to 1790.*

so high a tribune that only such as had exceptionally clear vision could distinguish anything save the general contours. Only the Canons of San Giovanni in Laterano were allowed to show this relic and mount the tribune. But Cosimo was not to be discouraged, and entreated the Pope to make him a Canon of the Lateran. He had been separated from his wife for many years, so to all intents and purposes was a widower. Hence Innocent gave him a brief appointing him a Canon of San Giovanni in Laterano.

This was the climax of all felicity Cosimo was to attain to in this world. Garbed in a costly chasuble, he displayed the sacred linen, and to prove his authority, the Pope's brief was read to the multitude. To gratify his vanity still further he was permitted in this new rôle to impart his blessing to 70,000 devotees who stood beneath him, which he did with great unction and solemnity.

While he was prostrate before the high altar of the magnificent chapel of Pope Pius IV he perceived His Holiness, the sovereign Pontiff, approaching; so leaving his station, he crept upon his knees to the papal chair. Innocent requested His Royal Highness to rise. 'Nay,' replied he, 'permit the Grand Duke of Tuscany to adore the Vicar of Christ, with that veneration that is due to him.' No sooner had he left the church than he sent the Pope a picture of the Annunciation valued at two hundred thousand crowns.

If the Cardinals could not pay the Serene Canon their respects because of his incognito, they did not fail to court him in the churches he visited. 'This sovereign prince who degraded himself to the condition of a common priest', was regarded in Rome as a phenomenon deserving of attention. It was said that a lady, seeing him before the altar of a church, and finding upon inquiry that he was a Florentine of distinction, solicited in the most earnest manner that he would intercede with the Grand Duke, her sovereign, to repeal the sentence of banishment passed upon her husband. The supposed Count promised his interest on behalf of the unfortunate gentleman, who soon received a pardon. Another time, acting in his clerical capacity when a fair penitent confessed the ill life she had led and expressed the earnestness of her desire to reform, he ordered her five hundred crowns to procure admission into a convent.

But he paid handsomely for these canonical pastimes, and was most munificent at his subjects' expense. He left Rome loaded with relics, rarities and spiritual favours, elated with his increased reputation for holiness and grandeur. If he had not preached a sermon, he had at least raised his pale hands in benediction above a surging crowd of worshippers. He had just received a portion of the newly-canonized St Francis Xavier's intestines,[1] when he was wakened from his fanatical reveries by the news of the King of Spain's death in November, after signing the testament which plunged Europe for fifteen years into the War of the Spanish Succession.

The dying Charles II, the last, most characteristic Hapsburg of the Spanish branch, his morbid superstition played upon by Cardinal Porto-Carrero, bequeathed his whole monarchy to the grandson of Louis XIV, Philippe d'Anjou. Louis XIV had of late years been militantly orthodox, while Austria's chief ally was William III, who represented the leading Protestant powers. Austria once established in Italy would reassert Imperial claims, which would seriously inconvenience the Papacy. Hence the Papacy's attitude.

Innocent XII died on September 27th, 1700; and when Charles II's death followed, the Cardinals had been shut for a month in the Conclave, awaiting that event. Cardinal Francesco Maria's position, as Protector of Austria and Spain, was made exceedingly difficult, but he decided to support Cardinal Albani, that able politician who had inspired Innocent's advice to Charles II. By Gianfrancesco Albani's election as Clement XI (November 16th), the Curia declared in favour of a French policy. As soon as the new Pope was installed, Francesco Maria returned post-haste to Florence. He was in a hurry to be back at his beloved Lappeggi again.

Tuscany might have fared better had the brothers exchanged rôles, had the sybaritic Francesco Maria been Grand Duke, and Cosimo bulwark of the Church. It would have been a more cheerful finale, since the Medici were doomed in either case. Francesco Maria was seldom in Rome: Cosimo, had he been given the opportunity, would never have left it. The Cardinals of the family had always been bon-vivants, and

---

[1] In return for his gifts to St Francis Xavier's shrine in the Church of Bom Jesus at Goa—three tiers of jasper and marble sarcophagi, the upper one decorated with inlaid panels of Florentine mosaic, representing scenes from the life of that saint (1696).

Francesco Maria carried on the epicurean tradition. His chief personal characteristic was corpulency. Adipose tissue influenced his outlook, hence he was open and cordial, 'all upon the broad grin'.

Fagiuoli has recounted the delights of Lappeggi, and the doings of the Cardinal and his motley Court there, in several poems; Redi, the marvels of its vintage. When Lappeggi came into his possession it was a modest country house. Prince Mattias, its previous owner, had seldom stayed there, since he was Governor of Siena, and Marguerite-Louise had disliked it even more than Poggio a Caiano. The Cardinal wished to emulate the wonders of Pratolino and lay out the gardens on a grander scale. He employed the Court architect, Antonio Ferri, to make several designs for its improvement. When he had chosen the most magnificent, he asked what the cost would be. 'To make it durable,' answered Ferri, 'you would have to spend eighty thousand crowns (scudi) on it.' 'And if I only desire to spend thirty thousand,' the Cardinal inquired, 'and yet have my villa built according to this design, how long would it last?' On the architect replying that he would guarantee it for eighteen years, the Cardinal exclaimed: 'Then you may proceed. If it stands eighteen years, that is enough; that will serve my time.'

From the *Rime Piacevoli* one would infer that Fagiuoli too had been consulted as to the planting of the grounds. The poet strongly recommended bay trees: 'they are evergreen, but not funereal like cypresses, and so noble that kings make crowns of their leaves; and above all they avert thunderbolts, which are frequent at Lappeggi. But,' he continues in facetious numbers, 'plant what you will, everyone is sure to praise your work, for a Prince can do no wrong. Should he by chance commit some gross error, liars and courtiers will make it out a miracle; so that if you plant a pumpkin to-morrow they will all exclaim: "What a beautiful outlandish fruit." Or if you sow a bean—a common enough thing—you will hear: "What a glorious plant, what a show it makes, what taste the Cardinal has." '

The villa was soon finished; after the Cardinal's death it began to crumble away. But while it lasted it was a Theleme, exactly such as poets assign for the resort of happy spirits. Ease and hilarity prevailed. His Eminence was in the plenitude of his power and enjoyment of unrivalled influence. There was a *perpetuum mobile* of poets, musicians, actors and artists. Everybody ranged according to his fancy through the arched green avenues, or played at pallone with His Eminence, while others preferred to sit in the shade and gossip about their neighbours. At sunset they would return to the house and play basset, until the curtain rose in the little theatre. The Cardinal required his actors to declaim with lightning rapidity, else he would fall asleep. Fagiuoli relates in his diary that the Cardinal would often send his carriage to Florence to fetch him and, upon his arrival at Lappeggi, would order him to find a plot for an impromptu play. On the spur of the moment he had to write out the acts, distribute the parts, rehearse, revise and have it ready for the same evening.

Things of the other world were said and done here, another contemporary relates; women disguised as men, boys dressed as girls waited at table, at balls and in the bedchamber, and courtiers of the lowest rank were encouraged to enjoy themselves at the Cardinal's expense. His pot-bellied Eminence wished to feel as if the elixir of life, not his own sluggish blood, was coursing through his veins. For the joy of watching his grooms and lackeys rolling about on the lawn and wrestling with the neighbouring peasants, he would scatter inordinate largesse from his balcony, sometimes up to two hundred packets, each containing ten crowns' worth of crazie (a crazia equalled seven Italian centimes). Thus he could passively share their expenditure of physical energy, and under the swell of this succulent illusion, his sense of vitality was heightened, his gout forgotten. It is not to be wondered if he often found his finances in distracted state, though he enjoyed a revenue of more than 120,000 crowns; if there were times when he could not pay his retainers, and had to pawn some of his most valuable possessions. His servants robbed him, and he knew it, but it did not trouble him: he almost encouraged their pilferings. At Easter he would summon them all to assemble, from the major-domo to the stable-boys, and beg his pardon on their bended knees. Afterwards, half in fun, half in earnest, he would harangue them thus:

'Now then, accomplished knaves that you are, run quickly and confess. As for me, I absolve you from all your robberies and present you with what you have taken.'

This ceremony was repeated every year, and there is little doubt that the scoundrels took advantage of it. Once he was seen to deposit two rolls, each containing a thousand gold louis, in a drawer of his writing-table. When he looked there again, he found two rolls of silver money in their stead. This amused him vastly. Evidently, he observed, the gold had undergone the transmigration taught by Pythagoras. Henceforth he would believe in that wondrous philosophy. Again, when the villa was closed for the night, the Cardinal consigned two large boxes of his finest chocolate to the porter before retiring to bed. These were to be despatched on the morrow to some of his Roman friends. Next morning the porter discovered the boxes half empty, and raised an outcry that alarmed the entire household. The Cardinal appeared on the scene and asked what the noise was about. 'And is that a reason to despair?' he exclaimed when he was told. 'Take the rest of the chocolate and calm yourself, you booby.'

Never a day went by but something disappeared, especially when the rooms were full of gamblers, and the dissolute, deft-fingered young men who formed his Court and were allowed the free range of his domain. The Cardinal gave strict orders that he was not to be disturbed by any tales of what was missing.

A bold, facetious little valet of his called Bista di Spaurito was dusting the Cardinal's room one morning in his absence. When his master returned, Bista pretended not to see him. A fine tray and silver candlestick had disappeared from a table, so while dusting he soliloquized in audible *sotto voce*: 'Last night I left a tray and pair of silver candlesticks here; now I can only find one candlestick. Thieves have the run of this place, and my fool of a master won't allow any notice to be taken of it. God's faith! How can it last, as Giambracone says. At the end of the psalm comes the gloria. . . .'

The Cardinal drew near and asked what he was muttering. 'Nothing,' said Bista, 'I never opened my mouth.' Whereupon his Eminence remarked: 'I understood you perfectly, you rogue. Take the other candlestick and stop mumbling.' He added that if Bista wished to please him he should always treat him in this way. Such frankness was highly commendable. . . .

For all this eccentric humour, the Cardinal had a sound basis of practical sagacity. He was a passionate hunter of stipends; for him it was one of the chief charms of religion. As soon as a prelate died, he wrote in a hurry to Rome for particulars. Were his abbeys and benefices 'of royal or papal nomination?' Was there any chance of his presenting himself as a competitor? He had talent for intrigue and perspicacity *in eligendo et vigilando*, 'and the indestructible faith that ginger is hot in the mouth'. With the laziness that was a result of his extreme obesity, he entrusted his affairs to a posse of strenuous and vulpine secretaries: he would allow no business to stand in the way of his pleasures. And his chief pleasures were of the table: he undermined his constitution by emetics to increase his prodigious appetite. He was no intellectual; patronized the theatre only as an amusing pastime; and to indulge his craze for perfumes maintained a private distillery in his palace at enormous cost. The mania was not peculiar to His Eminence, however, for there was an invasion of perfumes in Florence at this period, and even an Academy of Odorati Cavalieri. It was the fashion for each to concoct an aroma of his own. Magalotti, who envied dogs their keener sense of smell, wrote a graceful dithyramb on the orange-blossom, but honeysuckle, says he, was even more popular. 'Gloves, purses, fans, vases, powder-puffs, pastilles and pomatums—these for strength and those for love—all diffuse the odour of this flower.' And Magalotti further distinguished himself by inventing a fragrant clay, which perfumed the room as well as the water in vessels made of it.

In addition to these, the Cardinal was inordinately fond of those practical jokes (*beffe* or *burle*) which were a common sport of Florentines from the earliest times of their history. This voluptuary was in his seventh heaven when some mischievous practical joke was being perpetrated.

Fagiuoli records a specimen of the Cardinal's in a racy burlesque. An ass's foal arrived at Lappeggi, and His Eminence had an inspiration. He bought and gave it to Monsieur Niccolò, his chef, saying: 'I want you to prepare a delicious feast from this little donkey for to-morrow. Mind you don't blab about it. Season the dishes according to your taste and fancy, and you will be richly rewarded.'

Next day the guests, including Senators, State Councillors, magistrates, dignitaries, poets and the usual coterie of courtiers, sat down to dine with hearty appetites. After a course of boiled meat, a stew was brought in, then a pie, followed by a fricandeau, then tongue *à la suisse*, and, finally, a splendid roast. Never, it seemed, had Monsieur Niccolò devised a more varied repast. So delighted were the guests that they wanted to call the cook in to congratulate him, as well they might, on his powers of invention. When all had eaten their fill, the bleeding hoofs and hairy head of the little donkey were solemnly placed on the centre of the table. Rising, His Eminence then cheerfully addressed the company: 'Gentlemen, you must excuse my foolish butler who has brought in last what should have come first. But it's an ill wind that blows no one any good! Until now we have warmed our bellies with donkey's meat, let us cool them with the savoury viand before you, which will crown the repast.' Whereupon it was handed round, but it passed untasted, for none had strong enough stomachs to help themselves to it. Some of the party were so affected at the sight that they had to leave the room, but most of them laughed, or pretended to laugh, at the Cardinal's wonderful wit. Fagiuoli decided that for his part he preferred the long ears.

The Cardinal would have been thoroughly at home in the Tuscan Renaissance; Lorenzo de' Medici had played pranks equally fantastic on his acquaintances.

All the Medici—even Cosimo III—loved the splendour of gardens, encompassing them with box-hedges that were cut into elaborate broderie patterns, with ilexes and evergreens, to make walks for every season. Architecture prevailed, and the tints of weather-stained statues and equivocal green (for it might be blue or black) of cypresses: fountains were a substitute for flower-beds. The broad lush *tapis vert*, the rolling even lawn, on which the gardeners of France and England relied for their effects, was non-existent here unless there was a heavy rainfall; in summer the grass was burned to the neutral cinammon of the soil beneath it. Cardinal Francesco Maria was not satisfied with this restrained palette: he demanded variety and contrast in his garden as at his dinner-table. Strangers of note often came to pay him their respects and view his exotic plants and odoriferous trees. The latter were of equal dimensions with the exception of one, the Cardinal's favourite. Visitors usually paused before this, lost in admiration, and superlatives exhausted, would disregard others quite as remarkable.

Once, hidden in a corner close by, the Cardinal overheard these exclamations of wonder and was provoked because nothing was said about his other plants. As soon as the visitors left, he told Bista di Spaurito to take a saw and hew the tree down. The poor fellow hesitated, thinking that his master must have suddenly lost his wits; he refused to obey. 'Chop it down, or I shall have your head chopped off!' cried His Eminence in high dudgeon. So trembling Bista sawed through the trunk, and the tree came crashing to earth with a noise of thunder, while the Cardinal and Bista hurried back to the villa without anyone perceiving them. The gardeners scampered off in terror lest they should be dismissed. When they came to tell their master of this catastrophe, they threw themselves blubbering at his feet. His Eminence mischievously inquired which of them was the delinquent. There was an awful pause. They swore they did not know, and each protested his innocence. 'I alone am the culprit,' the Cardinal serenely explained to them, 'return to your labours in peace. I beheaded that tree because it made visitors overlook all the others.'

Lappeggi was an oasis to hide in, when the Angel of Death was passing over Tuscany.

XXI

Cardinal Francesco Maria Becomes Protector of France and Spain – Cosimo Recognizes Philip V – Gian Gastone's Married Life – The King of Spain at Leghorn – Gian Gastone Returns – Père Labat's Account of Cosimo III

C osimo had now lost the respect of his humblest neighbours. The Lucchese (whose three principles, according to Montesquieu, were: no Inquisition; no Jesuits; no Jews) were indignant when two of their subjects suspected of crimes committed in the Grand Duchy were imprisoned across the frontier at Pietrasanta. A band of patriotic ruffians scaled the prison walls and succeeded in setting them free. As soon as the suspicious characters were safe on their own territory, they received an ovation; hung ex-votos in the churches and celebrated their escape.

Cosimo was exasperated by this affront: Ferdinando proposed that he should send an armed regiment to Lucca, and force an immediate reparation. This was Cosimo's nearest approach to war, and he vacillated. He demanded that besides the delinquents and accomplices in their escape, two representatives of their community be surrendered to him as hostages; he would release them in due course, after this act of submission. But nothing happened. When the period assigned for reparation was over, the Florentines made a reprisal. The small republic, alarmed lest Cosimo should follow his son's advice, implored assistance from the Pope, the Emperor, the French and Spanish monarchs. The latter, and Prince de Vaudemont, the Governor of Milan, were only too eager to interfere. Cosimo hushed them; so trivial an incident, he declared, did not even deserve their notice: retribution was due to him in the name of Justice, and admitted of no prevarication.

The affair evaporated amid the suspense that followed Philip V's election. The Pontiff was exhorting Italian Princes to settle their quarrels. Austria was preparing for a struggle, since Leopold was

231

determined that his younger son, the Archduke Charles, should be recognized in Philip's stead. France was urging the Italian States to form a defensive league against an Austrian invasion. Cosimo foresaw further extortions from Vienna, though France, having conquered Milan and Mantua, might prevent the Austrians from entering Tuscany. His coast was exposed to the French fleet; Spanish garrisons were just beyond his frontier: Tuscany would be occupied by both these powers on his first step in Austria's direction.

Cardinal Francesco Maria, as Protector of Austria and Spain at Rome, found himself in an awkward predicament. If he openly declared in favour of Bourbon, he would lose the patronage of the Hapsburgs; and it was not safe to trust France's promise of indemnity. So Francesco Maria behaved rather like Reynard the fox: 'he covered the arms over the entrance of his palace, a custom usual with the Cardinals. When these became uncovered again, the arms of both France and Austria appeared quartered in the shield. Neither was entirely pleased. Austria thought she was insulted by having the eagle appear in a lower part than the lilies of France, and Louis was dissatisfied that the eagle made its appearance anywhere.'

The Cardinal was snubbed for his duplicity. The Austrian ambassador's wife 'pretended to be under great concern, lest the Cardinal's visiting might give offence to France. He replied "his Catholic majesty's livings were too valuable to be thrown to cocks". She retorted, his frugality was suitable to that of his family, who owed their elevated rank to it.'

Louis XIV proposed that Francesco Maria should substitute the spiritual protectorship of France and Spain for that of Austria. He decided to accept an offer which added so much to his revenue. Cosimo, for all his caution, had been beguiled into recognizing Philip V, and lost no time in sending Marchese Orazio Pucci to pay the juvenile monarch his respects. But Marchese Pucci found it uphill work to obtain an audience; and when he finally had access to the King, he could not hear a word of the royal speech: Philip V drawled in such a low monotone. Madame de Maintenon had written of him to the Duc d'Harcourt: 'His voice and the slowness with which he utters are very disagreeable.'[1] His character was in keeping with his voice.

---

[1] Lavallée. *Correspondance de Madame de Maintenon*, iv, 350, letter of December 3rd, 1700.

83 Illustration for *Il Greco in Troia* (1688),
by A. Van Westerhout. Biblioteca Nazionale

84 Two views of a grotto at Pratolino.
Engraving by Della Bella

85 The house and garden at Pratolino.
Engraving by Della Bella

86 *(left)* Anna Maria Luisa
by Van Douven. Palazzo Pitti

87 *(below left)* Anna Maria Luisa,
medal by G. Fortini.
Museo Nazionale

88 *(below right)* Cosimo III,
medal by M. Soldani Benzi.
Modena, Galleria Estense

89 Decorations for the funeral of Vittoria della Rovere,
by A. Ferri. Biblioteca Nazionale

La Real Villa di Careggi.

31.

90 *(opposite)* Careggi: dwarf in the garden

91 *(above)* Careggi, engraving after Zocchi

92 *(overleaf)* The Medici coat of arms:
Gian Gastone's version by G. B. Termini based on
an anonymous sketch. Galleria degli Arazzi

Hard as it had been for Pucci to obtain an audience, it was even more difficult to obtain a reply to his credentials. The Court of Madrid refused to recognize the royal status of Prince Ferdinando and his wife. A long correspondence was opened on the subject with the Grand Duke's ministers. Pucci was told that His Majesty might deign to treat Princess Violante as a cousin instead of as an aunt, which would entitle her to be addressed Royal Highness, but that it would be useless to claim such an honour for Ferdinando. Cosimo replied that the Court of Madrid might do as it pleased, but he would not allow his son to be treated differently from his daughter-in-law, since it was his duty to guard his family prestige. This firmness won him a courteous reply to Pucci's credentials.

On Pucci's return, Cosimo took official investiture of Siena and Portoferraio from Philip, as feuds of the Spanish crown. The Bourbons were gratified, but obstinately refused to grant him the 'Trattamento Reale'. The Emperor politely asked him for a subsidy, and Cosimo had only himself and his ostentation to blame if people wrongly believed him to be rich.

Gian Gastone's marriage was disastrous. He gambled his money away, was fleeced on every side; borrowed, got into debt and the clutches of extortionate moneylenders. Such were his straits that he pawned some of the jewels he had given his wife for less than half their value. To Cosimo he justified this indelicate action by saying that he had to provide some security against 'eventual losses or unfortunate surprises', and his wife's avarice. Cosimo approved, but the Princess had a very natural feeling of resentment, and expressed it loudly in the law courts of Prague.

When Ferdinando heard of his brother's plight, he urged Cosimo to recall him to Florence with his wife. But Cosimo was slow to follow advice. First he sent various agents to collect information at Dusseldorf and Prague, and settle Gian Gastone's debts. In 1702 Marchese Rinuccini went to visit the Bohemian couple; and he confirmed that the bored Prince was trying to kill time in the company of disreputable adventurers. The Prince's bonds were eagerly bought by Jews, from whom Rinuccini failed to discover the full amount of his debts, because they had no intention of reaching any settlement. Even the venerable Archbishop of Prague was among Gian Gastone's creditors. Rinuccini was shocked by the Prince's demoralization.

The Princess had welcomed him with unexpected courtesy, and was most effusive about the cultivation of her land and all the improvements she had in mind for its administration. Apparently she prided herself on her housekeeping, for she showed him her chamber, cabinet, wardrobe, kitchen, and, finally, that *sanctum Sanctorum*, her stable. She waxed eloquent about her horses, and after opening their mouths and patting them, proceeded to show him her jewels, drawing special attention to the absence of those her husband had given her.

On the subject of Gian Gastone she unbosomed herself. He scarcely ever came near her, whereas she expected greater marks of tenderness than Italian ladies were accustomed to.

Rinuccini took advantage of these revelations to persuade her that she should come to Florence. He promised her a warm reception there, and that Gian Gastone would become a model husband in that milder clime. She pretended to be flattered by Cosimo's invitation, but had no intention of accepting it. All sorts of reasons, she maintained, kept her an unwilling captive in Bohemia. Rinuccini already perceived that nothing would entice her to Florence.

Cosimo urged Gian Gastone to affect the utmost tenderness towards his spouse; doubtless he made himself as agreeable as possible, but his efforts were repulsed. She declared that she would never abandon Bohemia. A mule is a sturdy beast. The more Cosimo implored, the more she persisted in her refusal. He pulled the usual wires, but the Princess was as deaf to Jesuits as to the Empress of Austria. Her confessor, a German Capuchin, had his private reasons for wishing her to stay. Not only did he advise her to stand firm, he inspired her with hatred of Tuscany and terror of the Medici. He told her, dwelling on the most gruesome details of their domestic tragedies, the fate of Isabella Orsini and Eleanor of Toledo—and convinced her that all the Princes of the Medici either poisoned or strangled their wives.

The Emperor and Empress exhorted Gian Gastone 'to try and overcome his great aversion to living with his wife in that horrid solitude'. So the sorry Prince returned again to Reichstadt. Mrs Sullen's dictum[1] ('Tis a standing Maxim in conjugal Discipline that when a Man would enslave his Wife, he hurries her into the country; and when a Lady would be arbitrary with her husband, she wheedles her Booby up to

[1] Farquhar's *Beaux' Stratagem*.

Town') was reversed in Gian Gastone's case. Failing always to wheedle his Princess up to town—whether to Prague or Florence—the Prince was hurried, by general conspiracy, back to the country again.

'Touching the persuasion of my well-beloved,' he wrote his father on this occasion, 'I have considered approaching her through her Capuchin Father to the best of my ability, so that he may solicit her on my behalf. She has not answered me yet, but through this inter-mediary she is apt to be more expansive, and at least offers arguments good or bad. To me—apart from her ill-humour—she replies so curtly that I can accomplish nothing, nor even await a favourable opportunity, for she is a woman, and a German woman, which signifies more than a woman. I have used such finesses and blandishments to propitiate her as nobody else in my position would tolerate. I demand nothing from her, though my claims are ratified by the pacts that were signed at my marriage. I suffer her to call me thief in public with inimitable patience; contrary to custom, I always yield her precedence in everything. Everywhere I give her my arm on leaving her carriage as if I were one of her gentlemen-in-waiting, which is not done here by any German prince, even by those who pamper their wives; and do a thousand other things which inconvenience me to soften her for love of you, and because your Royal Highness desires it', etc.

Cosimo's political ambiguity had lost him the Emperor's kindly intervention in Gian Gastone's affairs. Gian Gastone was probably relieved. He was still heavily in debt, and the prospect of returning to Florence with his uncouth and ungovernable spouse had no charm for him. After another couple of months' penance at Reichstadt, he betook himself to Hamburg.

There he remained from October, 1703, until February, 1704, leading the life of some intoxicated butterfly. When he returned to Prague, he dropped off again into one of his spells of hypochondria; indecision and inertia prostrated him. In September (1704) Count Martelli, the Florentine ambassador to Vienna, paid him a visit. He found that the Prince's 'chief diversion is to remain at a window during most of the day, watching the people pass, pondering and turning over his thoughts, in which His Highness informs me that he finds his whole pleasure.'

Martelli stayed for some time in Prague, studying the Prince's character, and gently trying to reform it. He must have realized he had to deal with a case of mental aberration. He described his impressions to the Grand Duke. The Prince could be pliable enough, he discovered, when handled with patience and tact. But the Prince did not know what to do with himself. To achieve anything it was necessary to avoid pressure, to negotiate with him when he was in the mood. 'The Prince does not lack spirit, activity, diligence and self-possession: he fears God and loves his neighbour, but you must know how to take him.' Martelli could never persuade the Prince to sit down and discuss even his most important affairs deliberately in his study: he would only discuss them while walking, or in his carriage.

He would have liked to instil into him a greater love of writing. 'Often His Highness cannot bring himself merely to sign a letter already written by his secretary, who has told me with much feeling that many letters His Highness receives, even from distinguished personages, are left unanswered, because he refuses to sign them.' This was not due to cunning, he observed, but to a peculiar horror of his writing-table. . . . Writing might serve him occasionally for a pastime, likewise an interest in politics, especially in the present crisis. And finally, 'he needs some sort of serious occupation, for it is sloth that drives him to gamble, and makes him frequent certain rascally boys and others of low condition.' Martelli appears to have exerted a restraining influence on Gian Gastone, for he actually summoned enough energy to write Cosimo in October, 1704: 'Another prodigal son, I throw myself at my father's feet, most humbly to beg your forgiveness for all my youthful errors.'

Florence was fortunate in being situated beyond the arena of French and Austrian activities. In 1701 Prince Eugene, the strong commander of the Austrian army, had seized several fortresses south of the Po, blockaded Mantua, and invaded Ferrara and Parma, declaring Parma to be an Imperial fief. In January, 1702, he nearly took Cremona by a night attack, and captured the French general, Villeroi. But soon the Duc de Vendôme arrived with eighty thousand troops, and drove Eugene, who had only twenty-eight thousand, from Mantua.

Louis XIV considered this a good opportunity for the young King of Spain to receive his baptism of fire and learn the art of war under Vendôme's guidance. So Philip V reluctantly left his kingdom fifteen months after his accession, and his young wife five months after his marriage, arriving in Naples on April 17th (1702). When Cosimo discovered that the Pope was sending a Nuncio to meet him, he dispatched Cardinal Francesco Maria with a fleet of Tuscan galleys to pay him his respects. As the Cardinal was spiritual protector of Spain, Austria could not accuse him of partiality.

Morose and sullen as Philip showed himself to the Neapolitans, he seems to have given the Cardinal a pleasant reception. Leaving Naples, Philip sailed slowly to Leghorn, accompanied by Francesco Maria. Everyone said that a Franco-Tuscan alliance would soon be announced. Cosimo left Florence on May 21st with his most precious plate, his finest tapestries and coaches of grand gala, an army of lackeys and postilions in pompous liveries, determined to impress the King of Spain.

Leghorn was then a modern city corresponding to Marseilles, a cosmopolitan emporium and free port created by the Grand Duke Ferdinand I. The trade, however, was largely in the hands of the English and Dutch: Florence profited little by it. In 1644 Evelyn had described it as: 'such a concourse of slaves, Turks, Moors and other nations that the number and confusion is prodigious; some buying, others selling, others drinking, others playing, some working, others sleeping, fighting, singing, weeping, all nearly naked and miserably chained. Here was a tent, where any idle fellow might stake his liberty against a few crowns, at dice or other hazard; and, if he lost, he was immediately chained and led away to the galleys, where he was to serve a term of years, but from whence they seldom returned: many sottish persons, in a drunken bravado, would try their fortune in this way.' By this time (1702) it contained about 22,000 Jews. They regard Leghorn and the rest of the Grand Duke's States as a new promised land, wrote Labat.[1]

'They wander free, wear nothing to distinguish them from Christians, are not segregated in a Ghetto as elsewhere, thrive by a very extensive trade, own nearly all the government contracts, and are so well protected that it is become a proverb in Tuscany, you may hit the Grand Duke rather than a Jew. Consequently they are all the more odious to

[1] Labat (Jean Baptiste) de l'Ordre des FF. Prêcheurs. *Voyages en Espagne et en Italie*, 1730.

the rest of the community, but they are quite indifferent to this, and I do not think there is another corner in the world where they are more arrogant. . . . You need not ask on entering a house, if it is inhabited by Jews, for a sniff will soon detect them. They love to appear opulent, especially on the occasion of nuptials. One of the richest begged the Grand Duke and all his family to pay him the honour of assisting at his son's marriage. The Grand Duke had his reasons for not doing so, but allowed Prince Ferdinando to be present. The Prince did not eat with them, but honoured the married couple by attending the ball which followed their banquet; and he was as much astonished as his Court by the magnificence of the household, the tapestries, damask, velvets, the fine embroidered beds, the plate, and especially when it was pointed out to him that the married couple's room, ante-room and great hall where they danced, were paved with silver bricks of a thumb's depth, which the bridegroom's father had ordered to replace the earthenware tiles with which they had been paved prior to this event.'

Labat found the Turkish baths a consolation for this lamentable state of affairs: 'one feels so light afterwards that it is as if one had left one's body behind and become all spirit.'

On June 8th the King of Spain's galleys were in sight. All the Tuscan soldiery, with fresh uniforms and fluttering banners, were marshalled from the royal palace to the port, and the fortresses resounded with salvoes. Crowds had come from Pisa, Lucca and the neighbourhood to enjoy the pageantry. The Court was assembled under a great pavilion to await the King's disembarkation, for which an elaborate bridge had been constructed.

First the Governor of Leghorn went to welcome His Majesty, receive his orders for landing, announce that the entire Court awaited him, and that the Grand Prince of Tuscany himself would go to meet him. But when the Governor returned from the royal galley, it was to convey the strange news that the King would not land. Philip had taken umbrage because the old Grand Duke had not exerted himself to pay his respects in person. So Cosimo, Ferdinando and Violante had all to climb on board his galley. Philip received the Grand Duke with ostensible coldness, 'at a stately supercilious distance, and never asked him to be covered, though the grandees of Spain, of the most illustrious rank, constantly appear with their hats on before the Catholic majesties'.

After a brief conversation of the utmost formality the King expressed a desire to be left alone with his aunt, Princess Violante; whereupon Cosimo and Ferdinando had to retire and content themselves with the society of some grandees until the King finished what he had to say to the Princess.

Cosimo swallowed his mortification, and sent the royal fleet 'magnificent and exquisite gifts for their refreshment and delight'. The King's galley lay anchored by the mole, which was illuminated throughout the night. Those of the Spanish retinue that landed were sumptuously entertained. On the morrow the Grand Duke, his son and daughter-in-law, returned to wish the King a good journey, and the sulky sovereign deigned to profess some satisfaction for all their obsequious attentions; he promised Cosimo to accord the Duke of Savoy no higher honours than to himself. This was one of the causes of the famous breach between Philip and his father-in-law. But after Cosimo's exertions and heavy expenditure, he must have felt that from a spectacular point of view, this visit had been a failure. The fiddles had played; the scene had been painted with every rich accessory, but the *jeune premier*, in petulant caprice, had refused to make his appearance.

Cosimo was still 'balancing himself on his insecure seat of neutrality; by maintaining the freedom of the port of Leghorn, and thus giving Austria a naval refuge in the Mediterranean, he did not please France'; by refusing to recognize the Emperor's younger son as Charles III of Spain, he did not please Austria. He even failed to please himself; for he dreaded annihilation. He continued to urge Gian Gastone's wife— that hardest of metals, as Martelli called her—to come to Florence; for he still had an obscure feeling that in Tuscany the Princess might bear fruit, like some hidden plant transported into the sunshine. The Princess prevaricated, first accepting his invitation, then finding excuses for delay, then leading him to expect her with the following words: 'I hope that two years hence I shall be in Florence to kiss the hands of Your Highness' (August, 1704).

Gian Gastone returned in June, 1705, after lingering at Vienna, Innsbruck and Venice on the journey, because of that recurrent inability to make up his mind, while his father kept urging him to expedition. He was more merry than usual on his arrival, exhilarated by bachelordom regained. Meanwhile his spouse was supposed to be setting her affairs in order. In a year's time he was to fetch her from Reichstadt.

Cosimo never departed from his rôle of zealous patriarch. Labat, as a priest and missionary, could see the Tuscan sovereign only through rose-coloured spectacles, yet even he was struck by his rigid conservatism.

'The Grand Duke,' he wrote, 'who combines a true and sincere piety with great wisdom and all the other royal virtues, provides his people with a rare example of devotion. Unless he is so ill that he cannot leave his palace, he never fails to visit daily the church where the Blessed Sacrament is exposed, our Convent of St Mark where lies the body of St Antonino who belonged to our Order and was Archbishop of Florence. . . .

'I have often seen him at these holy exercises. Several monks met him at the church-door, and the Superior offered him holy water. The monks ranged on either side saluted him, and he returned their salute very graciously. He conversed with the Superior before the Blessed Sacrament was exposed until he reached the praying-stool prepared for him before the altar. They led him back with the same ceremony, except that they did not present him with holy water again, because in Italy it is the reasonable custom not to take any while leaving the church, since you are obliged to do so on entering.

'The Grand Duke knows all the monks of St Mark at least by sight, and when he notices a stranger among them, inquires who he is. This happened to me: he stared at me fixedly and, concluding that I was a foreigner from my habit and sunburnt skin, asked the Prior who I was and whence I came. When he heard that I was French and came from America, after a long sojourn there, he ordered me to be brought to the palace before his dinner on the morrow.

'In appearance he was tall and stoutish, his expression Austrian, with a protuberant lower lip, his upturned moustache white and heavy. Intelligence, nobility and kindness were in his features: he wore a close-fitting suit of black cloth entirely buttoned, a neckband folded so as to form a kind of cravat, a longish sword, silk stockings and shoes of Morocco leather, a cloak of black cloth, and a big skull-cap which covered his white hair. He only had eight or ten guards or cavalry officers, about the same number of footmen, four little pages and a pair of two-horse carriages. He was alone in the first; there were four officers in the second and twelve Switzers with halberds march on either side of him. The Switzers, footmen and pages go on foot, and have no difficulty in following or preceding the carriages, which keep a slow pace. They do not cheer him when he passes, but whoever happens to be in a carriage on the way descends and salutes him, and he acknowledges their reverence with much courtesy. Pedestrians pause and do likewise: when these are ecclesiastics, monks or people of distinction, he never fails to return their salutation. Ladies do not descend from their coaches, but their bows are sure to be repaid with interest.

'I have been assured that he takes particular care of all his servants, and especially of his pages. These are children of the aristocracy, and some from foreign lands. He makes them render an account of their studies, and sometimes attends their exercises. He provides for them magnificently, spares no expense to procure them excellent masters and all the education becoming to their birth. He engages them very young and keeps them in his service until they are of an age to follow a suitable career: whereupon they are recompensed in royal style. Should it rain when he is out, he has the kindness to admit these children into his carriage. . . .

'He has travelled much, seen all the Courts of Europe and studied their languages. This is an advantage for strangers who go to pay him their respects. He receives them according to their rank, always with extreme politeness, and speaks their native tongue with marvellous facility. He is learned and curious; enjoys accounts of distant lands and can perfectly distinguish the good from the mediocre. Audiences are easily granted: you need only apply to his Chamberlain to be admitted to him with great courtesy. There are special occasions for these. He desires nothing to interrupt him on his way or prevent him from doing what he intends at the self-appointed hour. As soon as the Chamberlain calls *Il servizio di sua Altezza Reale*, that is, his carriage and suite, all those waiting in the ante-rooms who have not to accompany him, must retire forthwith. It is a polite form of dismissal.

'*A propos* of this rule I shall here relate what happened to a Tuscan bishop, concerning whom there had been several complaints to the Grand Duke. Albeit an honest, virtuous man who took great care of his flock, he had the misfortune to like innovations and endeavour constantly to substitute new practices, good in essence, but differing from the old ones. Italy is more guarded against change than the rest of the world put together. The Grand Duke summoned him to his Court, resolved to mortify him a little and teach him to observe the ancient customs. As soon as he appeared in the noblest of the ante-rooms, the Chamberlain called in a loud voice, *Il servizio di sua Altezza Reale.* It was a civil command for all to retire, and the bishop had to obey like the rest. There was no alternative: it was an ancient custom which nobody was allowed to violate. This continued for nearly six weeks.

'Finally, when it was considered that the bishop had had a good lesson that old customs must be religiously observed, the Chamberlain pretended to catch sight of him for the first time, came up to him, inquiring about his health, since when had he arrived, and what affairs had led him to Court. The bishop returned his compliments and told him he had been at the Court these last six weeks by order of His Royal Highness, without ever being able to obtain the honour of an audience. That is a pity, said the Chamberlain, for I know how highly His Royal Highness esteems you, and that he will be overjoyed to see you. A moment's patience, and I shall admit you to him.

'The Grand Duke received him with even more than his usual politeness. After conversing of indifferent matters, he asked him if he had read the Life of St Eloy. On reflection the bishop replied that he had not. I am surprised, said the Prince, for there are some very fine passages in the life of that saint, who, like yourself, was a bishop. He was also a farrier; and one must admire him especially for the fact that he never pricked a horse while shoeing it. Will you tell me the reason why?

'The bishop, who failed to see whither his discourse was trending, answered that being a skilful craftsman and shedding the light of his intellect on the practice of his craft, it was not strange that he did not fall into those errors you find in less spiritual and less experienced artisans.

'That is not the reason, said Cosimo. I shall now tell you for your own advantage. It is because he always put the new nails in the old holes: by this method he ran no risk of bungling. Do likewise in your diocese and everyone will be satisfied; you are at liberty to return there when you please.'

XXII

Gian Gastone Returns to Florence Without His Wife in 1708
– Francesco Maria Renounces the Purple to Marry Princess
Eleonora of Guastalla – The King of Denmark Visits Florence –
Death of Francesco Maria, 1711

The Emperor Leopold died in May, 1705, and the succession of
Joseph I gave greater energy and cohesion to the Imperial
policy.

'Cosimo, having compromised himself by recognizing Philip as
King of Spain, thought it best not to complicate matters by acceding
to the Emperor's demand that he should recognize another King, the
Archduke Charles. Fortunately he had powerful friends in Germany,
especially his son-in-law, the Elector Palatine. But after the Battle of
Turin, an Imperial envoy came to Florence to demand a huge contribution (300,000 doubloons) from Cosimo's Imperial fiefs, and winter
quarters for three cavalry and three infantry regiments. He was ordered
to recognize the Archduke Charles as King of Spain, and to ask for
investiture of Siena from him. The vengeance of the English and Dutch
fleet was threatened should he prove contumacious. Cosimo managed
to wriggle out of most of the conditions, and did not recognize Charles.'[1]

Joseph I looked forward to the extinction of the Medici, and the
prospect of taking possession of Tuscany. Prince Ferdinando was
generally lying in a semi-coma; he had lost his memory, and could not
recognize those who came to see him.

Gian Gastone returned to Reichstadt in May, 1707, to induce his
wife to keep her promise. Wild horses, it seemed, would not drag the
Princess of Saxe-Lauenburg to Florence. Cosimo begged the Pope to
use his influence: Clement XI sent her an eloquent brief exhorting her
to obedience, and wrote the Archbishop of Prague to do likewise. But
the Princess held her ground. She told the Archbishop that she failed

[1] Vernon. *Italy from 1494 to 1790.*

243

to understand why she should go to Florence, when the present Grand Duchess of Tuscany had left her husband at a time when she could still bear children; yet the Pope had not obliged her to be reconciled to Cosimo.

It is a clear proof of Cosimo's lack of wisdom that while he was lavish in grovelling to the King of Spain, he was close-fisted with the only son who seemed likely to survive him. Gian Gastone expressed himself mordantly on the subject to his sister, the Electress.

'I am fully aware that I must set my affairs in order, but this cannot be done without money; and where I might expect relief I discern such strange economy that it seems almost more possible to fly than reach any settlement.

'I can tell you now, in case you are not informed, that we have no money in Florence, or at least if we have any it is like those spirits which everybody speaks of but none has ever seen; for not a German has been to Florence but maintains that there are millions in the fortress of Belvedere. The proof is that our family is so riddled with debt and each member of it in particular, that there is always an outcry when Prince Ferdinando's have to be paid. Once, in an emergency, I asked for a bagatelle of ten thousand, and fine phrases were all the answer I had; now we are so reduced that even with continual reminders two or three quarters of my pension are fallen in arrears.'

Cosimo requested the Pope to turn the screw of his authority on the Princess: the Archbishop of Prague was bestirred to recall her to her duties as a wife. A final interview ended in further revelations. The Princess did not spare the crudest details to prove that it would be impossible for her to bear this husband children . . . through no fault of her own. She told him of the violent scenes they had had, which rankled in her to such an extent that the mere thought of a journey to Florence was odious. She wished the Pope and Grand Duke both to be acquainted with these details, which explained why it was useless for her to comply with their wishes. Thus the Princess of Saxe-Lauenburg remained in Reichstadt, a voluntary grass-widow.

The Archbishop's letter opened Cosimo's eyes to the hopelessness of a reconciliation. He urged Gian Gastone to return alone. 'Come quickly,' he begged him, 'for I desire to embrace you again before I die.' But Gian Gastone froze with resentment against that reproachful, imploring figure. Even his nostalgia for his native land evaporated. He loitered at Prague, unmoved by his father's letters, brooding and yielding to alcoholic lusts. At length he pulled himself together; in 1708, very gingerly, Gian Gastone returned to Florence alone, a not very well preserved old gentleman of thirty-seven. But he chose to live in seclusion with a restricted Court, dominated by the lackey, Giuliano Dami.

His drunkenness regaled a cynical public: often he fell from his horse, and after dinner, we are told, he was always fuddled. His almost pathological love of solitude, so un-Latin a trait (as Norman Douglas has remarked), his noctambulous habits, suggested a streak of insanity.

'He spent whole nights alone at the Isolotto, or in the Cascine, or at Argingrosso, leaving Cavaliere Giudici and his darling Giuliano behind him to gaze at the moon. Then, almost at daybreak, he would betake himself to Florence. From the curious reflections and facetious remarks he would sometimes let fall he kept everyone in a prodigious perplexity.' Yet there was method in his madness and a humour more subtle than his uncle the Cardinal's.

Seeing a ballad-monger on the Piazza de Pitti he beckoned to him, and giving him six sequins, told him to leave his wares at the house of a swollen-headed senator who prided himself on his knowledge of law, with an injunction 'to study them and become a scholar'.

Again, when a peasant was selling brooms, the Prince bought all his stock and ordered his father's ministers to store them for future use. They will eventually serve to sweep the offices, he said, in the city and its neighbourhood.

It seemed improbable that the Medici should produce any male heirs. Austria rummaged for pretexts to occupy Tuscany. The Emperor benevolently hinted that Cosimo's subjects would revolt against him as soon as the heir apparent, in whom they put all their confidence, gave up the ghost. Whence it would be necessary, he urged, to prevent disturbances which might expose Tuscany to foreign invasion. For the Austrians had ceased to consider themselves foreigners in Italy.

Then Cosimo hurled a bombshell in their midst. Resolved to leave no method untried to obtain an heir, he persuaded his brother to obtain dispensation from Holy Orders and marry. An uncle might yet succeed where nephews failed.

Francesco Maria was most unwilling to secularize himself: it would mean the loss of all that made life worth living—the 'ever new and better ginger'. Philip V had offered him the Archbishopric of Toledo as soon as it was vacant—an offer which would not entail any journey to Spain. He had acquired great wealth, power, prestige; and he was no longer young. But there was no escape from duty's call; family must needs prevail. The Pope, and the Kings of France and Spain, would allow him to keep his pensions if he resigned, on condition that his hat was transferred to Monsignor Salviati. The lord of Lappeggi had to bow his head; and it is related that from that moment he was never seen to smile again. Adieu to the frisking nymphs and fauns, the Bacchic noise and bachelor nonsense of Lappeggi! The broad face, the copious look, the strutting belly, the jolly mien, had left Francesco Maria.

The difficulty was to find him a suitable partner. Fertility was the prime requisite; and a maiden was required whose alliance would not involve the Medici with any of the warring powers. Princess Eleanora, the daughter of Vincenzo Gonzaga, Duke of Guastalla and Sabbioneta, appeared likely to satisfy these requisites. Various agents had been sent privately to reconnoitre. These ascertained that she enjoyed perfect health; that she was tall, nicely proportioned and carried herself well; that she had a fine skin, vivacious eyes, a full mouth with cherry lips, breasts firm, round and well developed, a slender waist, and that she was agile and quick in her movements. . . . Trusting to such evidence, the physicians proclaimed that she gave promise of fruitful maternity. She was just over twenty.

Prince Francesco Maria was forty-eight, his whole being encased in rolls of flesh; and it was feared that marriage would ruin his enfeebled constitution. He had overtaxed his digestive organs, and suffered, besides gout and catarrh, from a variety of questionable diseases, which he seems to have borne with exemplary good humour. The Medici did all they could to coddle this pivot of their expectations. His niece, the Electress, wrote him frequent letters, coaxing, imploring him to take care of his health. Her correspondence with him reads like that of some affectionate nurse to a spoilt child. 'Look after your health,' she wrote, 'that soon you may give us the consolation of a little prince, and that I may feel the affair is settled and congratulate you upon it; do everything judiciously to obtain the heir we long for, and try to keep your wife content, for this will contribute largely towards it. I believe that when you change your vestment there will be rare comedy in your chamber.'

When he recovered from his catarrh, she wrote him again to be cautious. 'You are evidently subject to such distempers and must look after yourself, because you can play the gallant no longer, and must bethink yourself of providing us with a little cousin.' The Electress recommended him to avoid cold, heat, snuff, tobacco. The *cuginino* stood foremost; the *cuginino* that was now the obsession of the whole family. 'You will say that I am become your doctor, and I beg your forgiveness, but you see that it is all zeal for your welfare and ardour for the little cousin. . . .'

Pending the marriage treaties, Cosimo heard that Frederic IV, King of Denmark,[1] after being in Venice for the Carnival, wished to come to Florence (1709). In addition to the various calamities that beset Tuscany was that of 'an extraordinary frost, quite unknown to the Italian climate'. This had destroyed the crops, especially the olives, which, with wine, were the chief source of Tuscany's income. But when he was to be flattered with entertaining a king, Cosimo forgot all else.

Frederic had visited him before, in 1691. Then, as a crown prince travelling incognito, he had fallen in love with Maddalena Trenta, the daughter of a Lucchese nobleman. The story has its pathos. Maddalena was beautiful and intelligent, and her father had promised her in marriage to a Count Ercolani. But the Danish Prince had aroused her hopes in another direction; perhaps the girl was ambitious and aspired to a throne. She broke her engagement to the Count, and the Prince left Lucca. Then, after waiting three years in vain for news of her beloved, she sought refuge and consolation in the convent of Santa Maria Maddalena de' Pazzi. Though he did not correspond with her, Prince Frederic was kept informed about her actions. When he heard that she had taken the veil, he was smitten with a safe desire to see her again. This was said to have been the cause of his second visit.

The aristocracy gave balls in his honour, at which he surprised everyone by his powers of resistance, 'since he continued to dance until five o'clock in the morning, without ever sitting down'. There were

[1] *Relazione di tutti le Cerimonie, Feste e Trattenimenti seguiti in Firenze l'anno 1708 in 1709, nella venuta di Frederigo IV, Re di Danimarca e Norvegia.*

festas and picnics; the fountains played in the Boboli Gardens, where torches and lanterns of many colours splashed the terraces with light and made the cold stone statues glow, while slim pages wandered about with sorbets and candied fruits. At Poggio Imperiale young groups of peasants danced far into the night.

Francesco Maria begged him to honour Lappeggi with his presence, and invited ten ladies of the aristocracy, chosen for their fluency in French, to meet him. Prince Gian Gastone accompanied him to his uncle's villa, where the ladies curtseyed to His Majesty at the door, and at dinner they and Prince Gian Gastone sat at the King's table; the Cardinal was kept away by a bad attack of gout. He was present in spirit, however, for at the dinner 'one cloth after another was removed, and towards the end came a course of sweet dishes of various kinds; after these had been tasted, sugar-plums piled in pyramids and many sorts of liqueur were placed on the table. A large coffee-pot, in the shape of a fountain with four jets, was set before the King, and at the sides of the table were four golden dishes, two containing three cups of chocolate each, the other cups of water. The space between the golden dishes was covered with Savoy and other biscuits, and when the coffee-pot was removed, an epergne of bottles of San Lorenzo and other rare wines took its place, and all the goblets were of the finest engraved Bohemian glass.' During dinner there was a concert, and the same musicians followed the King throughout the day, always ready to oblige him with a tune at every halting-place.

After the banquet the King withdrew to play card games until four o'clock, when he drove about the grounds and visited the farm. A sumptuous cold repast awaited them in the orange-garden, confections of cream, capons in jelly, iced fruit and sweetmeats diversified. The iced fruit (a dish novel to the King and his retinue) delighted them all so much that His Majesty asked permission to present some to his dwarf, who was of noble birth, a great favourite and trusted counsellor. On a table apart stood small flasks of the choicest Tuscan vintages, so highly extolled by Redi in his *Bacco in Toscana*. The King and all the company sat down and ate heartily, then a dance was proposed; the King set the pace, but as night was approaching and dew began to fall, it was considered prudent to retreat indoors.

The King of Denmark we are told, wished to waive etiquette and be treated familiarly: with a coolness that astounded the Florentines he would enter Princess Violante's apartments when she was in her dressing gown, chatting and embroidering with her maids of honour. At first his impromptu visits surprised her, but the King took no notice, sat down and stayed a couple of hours, prattling and praising their needlework. Sometimes—an unheard of thing in Florence—the Princess had to beg leave to dress in his presence, and the King would hand her the pins. Ferdinando was too ill to appear.

The King's desire to see his old flame again caused some consternation. He sent word to the Superior of her convent that he wished to have a *tête-à-tête* with Sister Trenta. But the Superior replied that she could not consent without a dispensation from the Archbishop. Disconcerted, he approached the Grand Duke, but Cosimo excused himself: he could not meddle in the Archbishop's affairs. Even the Archbishop faltered: nobody wished to assume such a grave responsibility. The Mother Superior was told that she might allow the King an interview with the nun 'without any reference to the Archbishop'. The Superior was frightened but unable to refuse: she begged other convents to join in common prayer and exorcise the dangers that threatened Sister Trenta.

A king is generally obeyed, as the Archbishop said, and Sister Trenta was allowed to lift her veil during the interview, though a nun was posted within earshot to catch their conversation. She could not understand much because they spoke in French. It was afterwards discovered that the King had sent her his miniature portrait, which she had returned with a crucifix, telling him that this was the husband of her choice, to whom alone she intended to remain faithful. Sister Trenta's last words to the King, which were understood and reported, were 'that he would be damned unless he became a Catholic'. To which the King rejoined, 'that his religion was nearer Catholicism than all others, and therefore he still had hope of being saved.'

'*Chi sa*—who knows?' he murmured as he took his departure, promising that he would always wear the crucifix she had sent him. It was noticed that his eyes were swollen, and that he could not check his tears.

But he soon recovered his gaiety, and joined the ladies playing lansquenet at Marchesa Altoviti's or handed pins and addressed compliments to Princess Violante. All this happened during Lent, and it was observed that 'vanity and ambition had overcome Cosimo's hypocrisy'. Even on Good Friday, the royal guest, kept indoors by rain, amused himself as he sat at a window by throwing coins to the poor, who scrambled in the street for them 'with such unseemly din bringing discredit on that day when the whole city should have been at its devotions'. When Frederic was shown the grand-ducal jewels, amongst which was the famous Medici diamond and the choice topaz, Cosimo, *with a politeness unusual to him*, said: 'The former was a *fidei commis* from my ancestors; I purchased the topaz, and hope Your Majesty will honour me by accepting it.' The royal Dane expressed his thanks, but declined the glittering gift, and retired. Cosimo struck a medal in memory of this royal visit.

The news of Francesco Maria's engagement caused a public sensation. Monsignor Manieri was dispatched to Rome with his hat, to make a formal renunciation to the Pope on his behalf. Two hundred carriages sent by Cardinals, prelates and members of the Roman nobility, assembled for this function, as if Francesco Maria were there in person.

If the ex-Cardinal waddled to his marriage as a victim to the sacrifice, the young bride was no less reluctant to yield him his rights after the ceremony. For the Prince's appearance, the bilious eyes popping from that puffy face, the capacious paunch, the blotched and pock-marked skin, filled the young bride with a trepidation which nobody had foreseen. Besides, she was twenty-five years his junior. She refused to submit to his embraces. No love-philtre could be found. Priests were called in to persuade her; her old confessor was summoned from Guastalla; her father and Cosimo joined the chorus. Her resistance, it was thought, was due to virgin innocence and excessive modesty, but she explained —somewhat to their amazement—that it was chiefly due to physical repulsion and a dread of 'contracting shameful diseases'. Her husband treated her with great indulgence, and she finally submitted to the dismal consummation. But nothing came of it. Princess Eleanora found every possible pretext to elude Francesco Maria. She drank immoderately, feigned illness, and when she recovered, danced and joined in all the recreations that were given to distract her.

Francesco Maria was mortally afflicted by his failure. He had sacrificed his position, peace of mind and public decorum; he had lost his gargantuan appetite: what had he gained but ridicule? Tormented in mind and body, he actually expired of the dropsy, 'in the arms of Emmanuel, the Moor he had baptized', on February 3rd, 1711. He had not survived two years of matrimony. So the last hope of the Medici had blazed for a moment in a Cardinal, an *ignis fatuus*.

A draught of misfortune seemed to blow through the Pitti Palace; outside it the discontented people either cried for 'Bread or Work' or sang ribald and threatening songs. Already, in May, 1710, a placard had been found attached to the Pitti, with the words:

> '*Appigionasi in quest' anno*
> *Che i Medici se ne vanno.*'
> (To Let this year
> When the Medici disappear)

Now there was another fastened to one of the columns supporting Francesco Maria's gaudy catafalque in San Lorenzo, which said:

> '*E morto l'Idropico*
> *Sta male l'Asmatico*
> *Peggio l'Etico,*
> *E ci rimane l'Eretico.*'

> (Dead is the dropsical [Francesco Maria]
> Sick the asthmatical [Gian Gastone]
> Sicker the hectic [Ferdinando]
> Remains the heretic) [Cosimo]

The same board with 'To Let' was found again that morning in front of the Pitti Palace.

Like his uncle, Cardinal Gian Carlo, Francesco Maria had left so many debts that there was a public sale of his effects in March. 'And at this time,' wrote Settimanni in his diary, 'the Grand Duke began to chastise a number of the late Prince his brother's lackeys, pages and grooms, most of whom had been cherished in their youth by the said Prince for their comeliness, and after they had grown to man's estate continued in enjoyment of his favour, serving him as pimps and procuring him other handsome lads and companions in this infamous vice, in which the Prince took such delight, especially (so that Dante's words in the *Inferno* should be verified) while he was Cardinal. He vastly enjoyed watching others perform, and the Villa of Lappeggi was their gymnasium. Some were expelled the State, others sent to the galleys. Among the exceptions Settimanni notes a Roman abbé, 'who had no punishment although he richly deserved it'; instead he was given a secretaryship by the Grand Duke (because he happened to be the nephew of a well-known Barnabite friar). Cosimo could always forgive and forget his clergy's peccadilloes. But one wonders what became of Bista di Spaurito, that bold, facetious little valet. . . .

XXIII

The Last Phase – Problem of Tuscan Succession – Death of Grand Prince Ferdinando, 1713: His Achievements – Cosimo Declares His Wish that the Electress Anna Maria should Ultimately Succeed

With the death of Cardinal Francesco Maria, a period of the history of the Medici closes. Cosimo enters the last phase: the sere and yellow leaf. He begins to sense the earthiness of the grave about him. His many-stringed efforts to provide himself with a grandson had finished on a shrill note of ridicule, and the proud, stubborn, bigoted old man must have experienced all the misery and shame of his frustration. He, of all his contemporaries, might have compiled a homily on the Vanity of Human Wishes. Old age's awakening must ever be more painful than that of youth. He had dreamt of magnificent alliances: the marriage of each of his progeny in turn had been treated as an affair of vital import to Tuscany and the world. Yet in his utter disillusionment he summoned all his tattered dignity. The noble family of merchants was struck with sterility: it had nothing better to do than descend with decorum into the tomb.

No heroic sunset; a dark sulphurous glow from which Cosimo emerges, nevertheless, as a being refined by misfortune. Who should succeed when all the Medici were dead? The problem had been considered, even with the birth of the new century.

'The Chapel of St Lawrence will be perhaps the most costly piece of work on the face of the earth when completed, but it advances so very slow, that 'tis not impossible but the family of Medici may be extinct before their burial-place is finished,' Addison had remarked,[1] adding: ' 'tis not impossible but in such a conjuncture, the commonwealths, that are thrown under the Great Duchy, may make some efforts towards the recovery of their ancient liberty.'

---

[1] Addison (Right Hon. Joseph). Remarks on several parts of Italy, etc., in 1701–1703.

The thought which had troubled the first Cosimo *Pater Patriae* when, walking through the empty halls of his palace in the Via Larga, he exclaimed: 'This is too large a mansion for so small a family,' was worrying the last Cosimo, most fatal of all the Medicean sovereigns. After more than two centuries the thought recurred, mingled with despair and remorse, that these citizens who had become a domestic appanage of the Medici, were destined to fall into some other's hands—whose, he knew not, nor could anyone foretell. He knew, however, that the watchful speculators in the European market were ready to evoke the dreaded formula: Feud of the Empire.

'The Duchy of Florence had been settled by Charles V upon Alessandro de' Medici. When he was assassinated, the Florentine Senate elected Cosimo I as Duke, and Charles V had confirmed the election in 1537. But, in spite of Charles's interference on these occasions, Florence had always claimed independence of the Empire, and the Medici had constantly insisted that it was not an Imperial fief. Thus it seemed as though, on the extinction of Cosimo's line, sovereign rights should return to the city which had itself conferred them on the Medici. There was this obstacle: Siena and the grand-ducal possessions in the Lunigiana were undoubtedly Imperial fiefs (although the Emperor had invested Spain with the overlordship of Siena), and consequently beyond the Grand Duke's disposal.'

Would it have been possible for Florence to rise, phoenix-like, from those republican institutions which had lain buried for two centuries? Would Florence yet recover her departed greatness? The elements needed for the restoration of a republic now seemed to be extinct. The finer fibres of public life had long disintegrated.

Cosimo hoped that Tuscany would not become the prey of contending claimants after his death, but that the question of Succession might be amicably settled at the pending peace negotiations. His conscience, so acute on some points, but roused rather tardily on this one, and the advice of his Council, led him at first to adopt the view that the sovereignty of Florence should return to her citizens. As his spokesman to the Powers, he sent Carlo Rinuccini, who bore a name famous in its association with Florentine republicanism, to the peace conference at Getruydenberg. Rinuccini infected the Dutch and English with his own enthusiasm. This project was about to be approved, when Cosimo could not help spoiling it. He suddenly made a reservation that if he and both his sons predeceased the Electress Anna Maria, the immediate succession should devolve upon her, and the Republic be reconstituted after her death. Heinsius, the Grand Pensioner of Holland, and Lord Townshend, the British ambassador to the Hague, who had both been favourable to the idea of a republic, were alienated by this. Could not the Electress be sacrificed? Surely Cosimo must realize that she would cause endless complications. Kinsmen of the Medici by marriage would soon be plaguing them with their rights to succeed by her example. Remote pretenders would join in the contest. Without that reservation the affair could be settled; Florence would regain her independence, and the Grand Duke's conscience might lie at rest.

But Cosimo's altruistic impulse flickered out. His family came first, and the Electress was his favourite child. What would it avail Tuscany to become a republic again, he asked. Without Siena and the Lunigiana, it would be reduced to a paltry State, incapable of enjoying freedom. As if it had enjoyed much during his reign! Rinuccini begged him in vain to bequeath Tuscany to the Florentines. Cosimo was impervious to such idealism. Then the Emperor Joseph I died in April, 1711, and the Tuscan question was shelved while more important matters were sifted to suit new conditions.

Although the Electress was older than Gian Gastone, she flattered herself that she would survive him. With her domineering character, she looked forward to the prospect of returning to rule over Tuscany. The princes and electors of Germany supported her, for they considered her as one of themselves. But the House of Hapsburg, accustomed to a free hand in Italian affairs, would brook no interference from any quarter. It was necessary for the Electress to have an interview with the new Emperor, Charles VI, and she obtained one in December, 1711. The Emperor was affable, and the interview closed with a promise that he would examine the question and give a definite answer to Cosimo's proposals.

When the reply came, both Cosimo and the Electress were aghast. Charles VI was willing that Anna Maria should succeed, provided that himself succeeded after her death. Perhaps he realized that he had gone too far, for, on January 9th, 1712, Count Zinzendorf wrote the Elector Palatine that he would accept Cosimo's project, if the grand-ducal Court did not dispose of its States to enemies of the Hapsburgs. Evidently this letter was intended to be non-committal, containing mere overtures for treaties, 'floating particles in the stream of talk'. But Cosimo and the Electress took it seriously. Hence, when the formal peace conference opened at Utrecht in 1712, Cosimo told Rinuccini to stand discreetly aside. 'Look much and listen much . . .' he wrote him on May 31st, 'all depends chiefly on Divine Providence, circumstances not being disposed so that human measures can be of any assistance.' The result was that Tuscany missed those international guarantees which would have been extremely useful to her, apart from Article 3 in the treaty between England and Spain, in which Spain was pledged not to molest Cosimo because he had received the investiture of Siena from Austria, and to concede the investiture of the feud under discussion to the Electress.

It was a period of funeral orations. Cosimo had pronounced Tuscany's in his words to Rinuccini. The question of Succession was left to doze through 1713, until Prince Ferdinando died on October 30th. Health had been ebbing from him for eighteen years, the last four of which had been dragged out in all the horrors of premature decay, ranging from epilepsy to dementia. During these years Princess Violante had nursed him with remarkable devotion after all he had made her suffer; she had scattered alms, she had besought the convents and monasteries to pray for him, she had prayed assiduously herself. His death was announced to her as she lay in bed, first by a discalced Carmelite, and then by the Franciscan Brother in whose arms the Prince had given up the ghost. The corridors of the Pitti were a-buzz with friars. Shortly after, Cosimo entered her chamber with Gian Gastone, whereupon the Princess, covering herself hastily, fell on her knees before her father-in-law, who immediately helped her to rise, comforting her and telling her to trust in his affection and that of his son. Then the bereaved Princess was bled from one of her feet, by order of the Court physician. On the first day of her widowhood Cosimo presented her with a fine set of sapphires, as a mourning gift. Ferdinando's remains were embalmed, according to the family custom, twelve hours after death. Then they were dressed up for the lying-in-state on the ground floor of the Pitti, where several altars were erected, for Masses to be said until midday. Two days later he was buried in S. Lorenzo.

Ferdinando had been, as a contemporary phrased it, a martyr to Venus, and a disciple of the Graces. It were idle to speculate on what he might have achieved in a different environment. The misfortune for Tuscany was that his will was weak. He had that impulsiveness which is a feature of the artistic temperament; and shared with Gian Gastone the pessimism of most hedonists. Cosimo could rely on his faith, but both his sons were cynics, Ferdinando even to a more marked degree than Gian Gastone. 'We have exposed the crucifix here,' he once wrote Francesco Maria, 'in order to have some rain. Shortly we shall be praying for the rain to cease.' He had always despised his father's mode of life; he had a clear insight into the hypocrisy of his Court, and the wiles of the tonsured herd which surrounded him—'bf,' or *baronfottuti*, he dubs them in his letters—but he had no counteracting stamina.

At the age of seven he was said to have been the image of his mother. From Marguerite-Louise he derived his independence, his love of riding and volatile companions, his passion for music; from his father his listless desponding moods. He was intelligent enough to be dissatisfied, but not intellectual enough to overcome his dissatisfaction. Yet he was one of the greatest patrons of the fine arts then living: a dilettante in the good sense of the word; in this he compared with his most illustrious ancestors. He added to the collection of self-portraits which Cardinal Leopoldo had begun, and in an age when there was more flamboyancy than discrimination, he showed a nice personal taste in all he purchased—whether it was an engraving or a piece of majolica.

Cosimo would acquire an object because it appealed to his curiosity, like those life-size portraits of double-headed sheep and calves, rare birds, quadrupeds and monstrous fruit with which he filled the rooms of Ambrogiana; or because it excited religious emotions, like those swooning Madonnas, weeping Magdalens and martyrdoms by Sassoferrato and Carlo Dolci. It is significant that the sole artist to whom Cosimo extended the fullness of his protection was Gaetano Zumbo, the Sicilian modeller in wax (1656–1701), the character of whose work must have appealed to him profoundly. Zumbo had a predilection for the macabre; the sufferings of Purgatory, the tortures of Hell, the dead body of Christ, the effects of the plague, were all portrayed by him with a most horrible meticulous realism.

Of his rendering of the gradual putrefaction of the body, even Keysler, who belonged to a merrier epoch (1756), wrote with enthusiasm:

'On one side of this admirable piece sits Time, with an old torn folio at his feet, and the whole consists of several figures. The first is an inflated female corpse, near which lies another of a sallow hue; after this is seen a child, whose body, being marbled as it were with blue and yellow, indicates a nearer approach to putrefaction. The fourth figure is full of suppurating ulcers, with worms crawling out of them. The rest exhibit the increasing ravages of worms, with the gradual progress of putrefaction on the human body, till at last it terminates in a bare skeleton. However disagreeable such a spectacle may be to timorous self-love, the execution of it is so natural and delicate, that a person is never tired with viewing it.'

Tastes have changed, and most modern visitors to the Bargello would rather not enter the forbidding little room where Zumbo's masterpieces are preserved.

Ferdinando was a connoisseur: he bought Madonnas by Raphael and Andrea del Sarto, and even went to some trouble and litigation to procure them, as when he added the masterpiece of that under-rated genius, Parmigianino, the so-called Madonna of the Long Neck, to his collection.

His patronage of contemporary painters throws an even clearer light on his original flair: Giuseppe Maria Crespi was long employed by him at the Pitti, and spurred on to some of his finest achievements. And it was Ferdinando who organized the first public exhibition of fine arts to be held in Florence (1705, in the cloister of the SS. Annunziata).

Among poets he befriended Vincenzo da Filicaia and Benedetto Menzini—both of whom have survived their period—and founded an Academy of Nobles, a society of dilettanti, which actually indulged in masques, festivities and sport rather than in intellectual pastimes. Scipione Maffei's dedication to him of the *Giornale de' Letterati* (1710) is a proof of Ferdinando's widespread reputation: it is doubtful whether the author of *Merope* would have dedicated his review to Cosimo III.

But his accomplishments were mainly musical. He had studied counterpoint and the harpsichord under Gianmaria Paliardi of Genoa, various bow-instruments and probably the violin, under Piero Salvetti.

Music prevailed at his receptions and filled his correspondence. Musical critics—Leto Puliti and Piccini (Jarro)—agree that he exerted a notable influence on the musical culture of the Settecento: the latter wrote that his theatre at Pratolino had for years an importance comparable to that of one of the greatest theatres in the world to-day.

Among the musicians he invited to Florence were Alessandro and Domenico Scarlatti, Giacomo Peri, Bernardo Pasquini, Handel, and Bartolommeo Cristofori, who perfected the harpsichord and is said to have invented the pianoforte. He took the most detailed personal interest in operatic performances, selecting the librettists himself, and giving minute directions to the composers as to the style in which he wished them to be set to music: he wanted an all-round perfection, and, to improve the theatres of Florence and Leghorn, commissioned Giovanni-Maria Galli (Bibbiena) and Antonio Ferri to design the scenery. Thus an army of singers and composers were in his pay, and several critics, whose duty it was to travel from city to city in search of fresh talent. Every year saw the birth of at least one new opera; Alessandro Scarlatti composed no less than five for Pratolino, and his correspondence with the Prince is voluminous. Amid much florid adulation expressed in typically Seicentesque metaphor we occasionally glimpse the composer at work, and the Prince as an exacting critic.

'I shall be very pleased,' wrote the Prince to Scarlatti, 'if you make the music [of *Il Gran Tamerlano*] rather more easy, and noble in style; and if, in such places as is permissible, you will make it rather more cheerful.' Scarlatti did his best to follow such directions, but we still find Ferdinando complaining of the melancholy nature of his music, as well as of its difficulty, while Scarlatti protests that the operas in question [*Lucio Manlio* and *Il Gran Tamerlano*] contain nothing melancholy, 'even in the places where it seems that such a character is indispensable'. One gathers that the Prince vaguely wished to escape from the rigid *opera seria*—but, as Vernon Lee has pointed out, 'until quite late in the eighteenth century, the Italian comic opera was not only totally distinct from the serious one, but of much lower artistic standing, and its performers were a class wholly apart and decidedly inferior. A long comic opera like the *Matrimonio Segreto* or a semi-serious one like *Don Giovanni* was equally unknown'; and perhaps these were really what Prince Ferdinando was hankering after.

In Florence itself the Prince had had to make concessions to the prevailing bigotry. 'I had the good luck,' wrote Addison, 'to be at Florence when there was an Opera acted, which was the eighth that I had seen in Italy. I could not but smile to see the solemn protestation of the poet in the first page, where he declares that he believes neither in the Fates, Deities or Destinies; and that if he had made use of the words, it is purely out of a poetical liberty, and not from his real sentiments, for that in all these particulars he believes as the Holy Mother Church believes and commands.'

Ferdinando himself composed, with what success we cannot judge, or with what assistance from his protégés. There is a letter extant, dated 1698, and signed Amalia, Princess of Brunswick, in which, after thanking him for some music he had sent her, she says: 'I vastly enjoyed reading the fine compositions that issue from Your Highness's brain, so beautiful and luminous, and I assure you with all candour that I seem almost to enjoy the satisfaction of your own society, having near me such worthy fruits of your high virtue.'

This explains why warblers, male and female, retained their influence over him, their melodies echoing in his diseased and broken memory until he died. He had loved their atmosphere: they had evoked the pathos and iridescence of pleasure which is timeless. Ferdinando escaped with them from the acrimonious bigotry of his age, from his father and unfortunate wife: he had loved *Fêtes Galantes* and lived in an artificial paradise; it is fitting perhaps that he should have expired 'a martyr to Venus'. After his death the theatre of Pratolino was closed for ever.

This seemed the right moment for Cosimo to announce his intention regarding the Electress Palatine. On November 26th, 1713, he declared that if Gian Gastone and himself predeceased her, she was to succeed to all the States of the Grand Duchy. Next day his decree was submitted to the Senate's approval. Private feelings on the subject must have been mingled: perhaps, in the dying hour of that family which had ruled and misruled them for so long, the Senate could summon a sentimental enthusiasm, which blinded them to all else. Perhaps something approaching awe hung over them, for Florence without the Medici must have been hard to conceive: almost the two words had become identified. Apparently the motion was greeted with joyous acclamations, even with gratitude, but the Senate was a mere shadow of what it might have been. Cosimo III was as absolute a despot in Tuscany as Louis XIV in France: in old age, when Louis too had become a devotee, the lesser was but a caricature of the greater.

Charles VI expressed his indignation at the news. He wrote the Elector Palatine on May 25th, 1714, that the Grand Duke had absolutely no right to take this measure; his States were Imperial feuds, except for what small portion of them depended on the Church.

Meanwhile Louis XIV sent General Albergotti to condole with Cosimo on Ferdinando's death, and to praise his and the Senate's decision regarding the Electress. Anna Maria was no longer young, and Louis wished Cosimo to peer even farther into the future, and choose an heir who, as he phrased it, would uphold the glory of the Medici, and the peace and prerogatives of the Grand Duchy, with superior strength. But Cosimo was not to be caught by this gilded fish-hook: he replied that he was powerless to decide until peace was settled between Charles VI and Philip V.

To complicate matters, Philip V was now engaged to Elisabeth Farnese, who as a great-granddaughter of Margherita de' Medici (Ferdinando II's sister) was a direct heir to Tuscany as well as to the Farnese property. The Emperor was even more annoyed by this freshly cemented relationship between Spain, Parma and Tuscany: it looked as if he might become violent. Cosimo hurriedly despatched Rinuccini to London to gain England's support of the Grand Duchy's independence, now seriously threatened. On June 10th, 1715, the Tuscan ambassador was assured by General Stanhope:

'Le Roy embrassera avec plaisir cette occasion et toutes autres que les conjonctures pourront fournir pour appuyer vos prétensions, et cependant l'on est assuré qu'un Prince aussi éclairé que Monsieur le Grand Duc ménagera les choses de manière que rien ne puisse diminuer le poids des offices et des démarches que Sa Majesté est très résolue de faire toutes et quantes fois elle en sera requise par Son Altesse Royale.'

Stanhope's phraseology is amusing when we consider the monarch he served. There was little in these assurances, but they gave Florence a vague feeling of security—Austria would think twice before executing her threats, though she employed all her industry to procure documents which might establish her claim, and Zinzendorf insulted Marchese Guadagni, the Tuscan ambassador.

Suddenly, in May, 1716, there was a change in Vienna's tactics, for a son had been born to the King of Spain in January. Charles VI's minister, Count Stella, coolly pretended that the Emperor's reply to the Electress had not meant that he wished to acquire Tuscany for himself. Far from it! The Electress's succession, he continued, presented no great difficulties, but they must soon reach an understanding, satisfactory to both parties, about the family to succeed after her death. If, as he hoped, they could agree upon this point, the Emperor hinted that he might even enrich the grand-ducal dominions. Cosimo saw that this was no time to spurn Austria's proposals, for eventually the heir to a Farnese could amalgamate the crowns of Spain and Tuscany, which would mean the end of all independence for the latter. He thought it more prudent to agree with the Emperor, and appoint an heir who would preserve the traditions, and at the same time be agreeable to the house of Hapsburg. But in May, 1716, none could foretell which dynasty would be likely to fulfil these conditions. Cosimo was elated—even at this stage of his life—by the possibility of increasing his dominions. Yet this was the very year of Brandano's prophecy:

> *Nel mille sette cento sedici,*
> *Tutti sani, non più Medici.*

'The Florentines were hoping to see this accomplished,' wrote Guyot de Merville,[1] 'and when the year elapsed they were exceedingly surprised that Brandano's prophecy had not been fulfilled. Marforio, equally astonished, consulted Pasquin, who gave him the following reason:

> *Per non morir prima di Papa Albano,*
> *Cosmo a fatto bugiardo anche Brandano.*

('So as not to die before Pope Albano, Cosmo has even made a liar of Brandano.') But if Pasquin asserted that Clement XI and the Grand Duke were contending for precedency in this respect, the Florentines depicted them at variance on another matter. They showed a cartoon of

---

[1] M. Guyot de Merville. *Voyage historique d'Italie.*

Clement XI, Cosimo and a Jesuit—all three bowing to each other before the gate of hell, but none wishing to enter first. Whereupon Pluto arrives with a three-pronged fork, and prods them in simultaneously. Several copies of this were exhibited about the town, with explanatory verses.

'You see,' exclaims this writer, 'to what extent the Florentines hate their sovereign. Yet if you examine the facts impartially, you will have to admit that he does not deserve such treatment. It is true on one side that he burdens his people with taxes, but on the other he guarantees them from war, which would be worse. If he lavishes money on the Jesuits, he does no less for the poor. In fact he has a heart so tender that (if such an expression be permissible) he would not even hurt a fly. In his youth he was very fond of shooting, and nearly every day he would set out for one of his preserves: it is said, however, that he never wished to kill his quarry, but was content to watch it run or fly. When a bird started up before him he was wont to take aim as if about to fire, but after repeating the word *poverino* (poor creature) several times in succession, he withdrew his gun without discharging. This gave rise to the saying "to go shooting like the Grand Duke", whenever a sportsman returned empty-handed. Nevertheless the Grand Duke eats game with relish, and pheasants in particular. That is why it is strictly forbidden to kill any, and the penalties for doing so are extremely severe.'

XXIV

The Electress Anna Maria Returns to Florence – The Problem of Tuscan Succession Continues Unsolved – Triple and Quadruple Alliances – St Joseph – Contemporary Accounts of Cosimo III in Old Age – Decay of Tuscany – Last Years and Death of Marguerite-Louise (1721) – Cosimo's Final Protest to the Powers of Europe and Death in 1723

T he Elector Palatine died in June, but Anna Maria remained another year at Dusseldorf. She did not wish to betray her anxiety to return, and assume the rôle she yearned for. She was packing up the treasures she had amassed during her husband's life and sending them to Florence.

With Ferdinando's death it could surely be said that his widow had risen on a better morrow. After all these years she had become deeply attached, as so many Northerners do, to the Florentines and their ways; she had built up her life, her personality, in Florence: and now she had no desire to go back, a stranger, to her native land. Cosimo did not wish to be left with only one Princess at his Court, his brother the ex-Cardinal's bibulous widow, and pressed her to stay. He appreciated her virtues, and she added to his prestige by her active correspondence with princes, church dignitaries and the most important families in Italy. Violante also had a reserve of common sense, for she stipulated that her allowance was to be paid in hard cash, and that she should hold a Court of her own, entirely selected by herself. Besides her apartment at the Pitti she was given Lappeggi, which henceforth became a sort of literary academy, for Violante loved literature and extempore recitations as much as her husband had loved music.

Among the poets she encouraged who specialized in various styles of extempore recitation were Ghivizzani, Lucchesi, Morandi, all flattered in their day but now forgotten—with the exception of Cavalier

93 Violante of Bavaria, medallion by B. Permoser. Museo degli Argenti

94 *(above)* La Magia: the staircase in the garden

95 *(below)* La Magia, engraving after Zocchi. Museo di Firenze com'era

96 *(opposite)* The courtyard of La Magia, designed by Buontalenti

Villa della Magia del Sig. Pandolfo Attavanti.

97 A theatrical performance, engraving by A. Cornacchini.
Biblioteca Marucelliana

Veduta del Palazzo del Sig.r March.e Strozzi, del Centauro, e della Strada, che conduce a S. M.a Nouella

98 *(above)* View of the Palazzo Strozzi and the Centauro.
Museo di Firenze com'era

99 *(below)* View of the Piazza della SS. Annunziata. Engraving after Zocchi.
Museo di Firenze com'era

Veduta della Piazza della SS. Nunziata, Statua Equestre di Ferdinando Primo, Fonti, e Loggie Laterali

100 *(above left)* Cosimo III, medal by Filippo della Valle.
Modena, Galleria Estense

101 *(above right)* Gian Gastone, medal by Filippo della Valle.
Modena, Galleria Estense

102 *(below)* Villa La Petraia, lunette by Utens.
Museo di Firenze com'era

103 *(opposite)* Festival for the canonization of S. Andrea Corsini,
frontispiece engraved by Della Bella

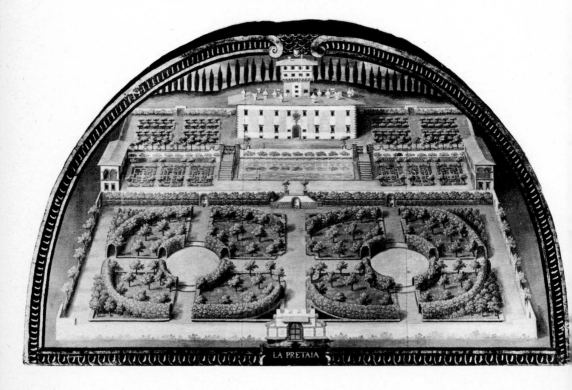

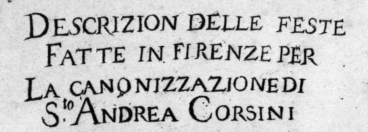

DESCRIZION DELLE FESTE FATTE IN FIRENZE PER LA CANONIZZAZIONE DI S.to ANDREA CORSINI

In Fiorenza nella Stamperia di Zanobi Pignoni
con licenza de SS. Superiori
1632

104 The Belvedere and Pitti, lunette by Utens. Museo di Firenze com'era

Veduta del Reale Palazzo de Pitti Abitazione de Regnanti Sovrani.

T. II.

105 The Pitti Palace, engraving after Zocchi. Museo di Firenze com'era

106 *(above)* Medal commemorating Antonio Magliabechi,
Cosimo III's librarian

107 *(below)* View of the church and Piazza S. Pier Maggiore,
engraving after Zocchi.
Uffizi, Gabinetto di Disegni e delle Stampe

Veduta della Chiesa, e Piazza di S. Pier Maggiore

108 *(opposite)* Cerreto Guidi, staircase leading up to the villa

109 *(above)* Ambrogiana, lunette by Utens. Museo di Firenze com'era

110 *(below)* View of the Badia and the Bargello, engraving after Zocchi.
Gabinetto di Disegni e delle Stampe

Veduta della Badia Fiorentina, e del Palazzo del Potestà presa dalla Piazza della Chiesa de PP. dell' Oratorio

111 (above) Medici arms on a gate
at La Petraia

112 (left) Francis of Lorraine,
medal by Lorenzo Maria Weber.
Museo Nazionale

113 (opposite) Decorations for the funeral
of Gian Gastone, by F. Ruggieri.
Biblioteca Nazionale

ARCO *inalzato dalla* NAZIONE BRITANNICA *dimorante nella Piazza di* LIVORNO
in occasione del solenne Ingresso fatto in quella Città dall' Altezza Reale del Serenissimo Principe
DON CARLO INFANTE DI SPAGNA, DUCA DI PARMA, PIACENZA, E CASTRO, &:
E GRAN PRINCIPE DI TOSCANA,
seguito il dì XXVII *Dicembre* MDCCXXXI.

114 *(previous page, left)* Anna Maria Luisa by Van Douven. Palazzo Pitti

115 *(previous page, right)* Triumphal arch in honour of Don Carlos (the future
Charles III of Spain), designed for Florence by V. Ruggieri.
It was eventually erected in Leghorn.
Biblioteca Moreniano

116 *(above)* Gaetano Zumbo: *The Triumph of Time* (stages of human decay).
Waxworks. Museo Nazionale

Bernardino Perfetti, to whose extraordinary talent the Président de Brosses has left so glowing a testimonial.

Perfetti was of noble Sienese descent, a knight of the order of St Stephen, and a professor of jurisprudence, who seems to have improvised merely for pleasure and glory. Many of these extempore poets, however, came of humble stock. One of Princess Violante's favourite protégées was a peasant girl from Legnaia, Maria Domenica Mazzetti, called Menica for short. This girl had a remarkable gift for *terza rima*, and after a competition with the polished Ghivizzani, Violante decided to have her taught reading, writing, Latin and music, all of which she learnt with ease. This did not deaden her inspiration: her natural gifts were improved by study to such an extent that Princess Violante took her to Court and afterwards to Rome. The poetess never lost her head in this environment, so different from that to which she was accustomed. Only—she no longer wished to be called Menica!

Cosimo, who enjoyed shooting in spite of his unsportsmanlike reputation, laid aside his gun for ever after January, 1717, when he killed a man by mistake. He was so upset by this accident that he wished to be tried by a Council of twelve knights of St Stephen, which condemned him to grant five scudi a month to the dead man's family, and to navigate for several years. In execution of the said sentence, wrote Settimanni, His Highness substituted a knight who was to navigate in his stead, and thenceforward abstained from shooting.

Gian Gastone, now past forty, kept away from the Court as much as possible. Their contemptuous treatment of him in his youth had made him dislike the aristocracy. Violante was the only member of his family he cared for. After the Elector Palatine's death it became evident that his widow would return. Violante knew her sister-in-law's imperious character: foreseeing that her own position might become unbearable, she decided, against her will, to retire gracefully to her brother's Court in Munich. One respectable Princess at the Pitti was sufficient, so Cosimo put no obstacle in her way. But Gian Gastone was determined that Violante should remain, if only to spite his sister.

It was plain that the two Princesses, the one who had been first lady in the land, the other who regarded herself as her superior, would never co-exist in Florence without friction. So Cosimo proposed to appoint Violante Governor of Siena. She was relieved to accept this offer, which would not have been made but for her request that her position be clearly defined before the Electress's return.

Even so, since she would be certain to meet the Electress at official functions, careful regulations were laid down for the precedence of their coaches, and so forth, and it is amusing to note that in these allowance was still made for the long-absent Grand Duchess Marguerite-Louise.

Celebrations were prepared for the Electress as if a radiant bride, rather than a middle-aged widow, were coming to gladden the city. She arrived on October 22nd, 1717; and Cosimo awaited his favourite child in the SS. Annunziata, where the miraculous image was uncovered. He had not seen her for twenty-six years; and his subjects were given a theatrical display of his paternal affection. Princess Violante had been invited to take part in the rejoicings, but the Electress had come to supplant her and she could not help resenting it. So she pretended that she had to fulfil an important vow to the Virgin of Loreto. The inevitable disputes arose when they met, for nothing would induce either of them to surrender on any point of ceremonial. Anna Maria behaved as if she were Grand Duchess, and always assumed her superiority when they were together in public. Cosimo had ceased to take part in many functions. Gian Gastone, who had quarrelled with him, usually stayed at Pescia, and since ceremonies bored him, he asked the two punctilious Princesses to represent him on St John the Baptist's day, when the race of barbs was run.

The Electress was to give them the signal to start, and the Governor of Siena claimed that her sister-in-law should consult her, at least out of courtesy, beforehand. But, without a word to Violante, she ordered the race to begin. Violante took offence, and ceased to appear with her henceforth.

Meanwhile the problem as to who should succeed the Electress was being weighed, measured, sounded and turned inside out. Cosimo was ready to do anything the Emperor wanted, provided that the Emperor would grant him Piombino and the Presidii. But in Vienna such demands appeared excessive. So the diplomatic scuffle went on. The

Emperor thought Cosimo should make the first proposal, but Cosimo preferred to leave it to the Emperor. Finally the Imperial Minister Stella lost patience, and told Cosimo's envoy Marchese Bartolommei that if Cosimo obstinately withheld his opinion nothing could be done—the Emperor would never pledge himself to bestow a gift (i.e., Piombino and the Presidii) on a person who could not make up his mind (March 20th, 1717).

After further hesitation, Cosimo adopted the Imperial attitude. In June, he declared that his own choice fell on the Modenese House of Este. Duke Rinaldo had married Charlotte of Brunswick, sister to the Dowager Empress Amalia, Joseph I's widow, who naturally used all her influence in Vienna to favour the Estensi. Cosimo's proposal was approved, but Charles VI went back on his vague promises about Piombino and the Presidii: he now told Cosimo he could never part with them. The Medici had coveted these possessions for one hundred and fifty years, and Cosimo was furious to have them thus flashed, a tantalizing mirage, before his eyes; more furious when, just as Spain conquered Sardinia, Count Stella coolly informed Bartolommei that the Emperor would never tolerate the union of Modena and Tuscany. How could anyone deal with these shifting tactics? Meanwhile, the fate of Tuscany was being settled in London.

England, France and Holland, joined later by Austria (April 4th, 1718) now decided that Philip V and Elisabeth Farnese's firstborn— the very one on whose account Cosimo and Charles VI had drawn together—was to succeed the Medici and Farnese. The decision of these Powers had been due to George I and the French Regent, Philippe d'Orléans. The Triple Alliance had been signed at the Hague in 1717 between England, France and Holland to preserve the peace of Europe and see that the Treaties of Utrecht and Rastatt were respected. George I, bound by his German interests to the Emperor, had suggested that the Infant Carlos should succeed to Parma, while Charles VI should have the right to dispose freely of Tuscany.

All this when Cosimo was counting on England's support, and the English ministers were so generous in their promises to the Tuscan envoys! It was not until March 25th, 1718, that Marchese Neri Corsini, his ambassador to London, awakened him with a jolt. But he guessed there would be some opposition. It was unlikely that Spain would

be satisfied by an offer which included such a humiliating condition as that the Infant should become an Imperial vassal. Austro-
Spanish distrust and suspicion would probably release Cosimo from
the mortal coils in which he seemed about to be suffocated. When the
Triple Alliance submitted its decision to Madrid, Cardinal Alberoni
refused to consider it. And the Spanish ambassador in Florence maintained that Tuscany was exempt from feudal ties.

Cosimo's ministers tried to play one against the other as usual.
During April and May (1718) Bartolommei was writing from Vienna
that the Emperor would do his utmost to deny the Infant Carlos the
promised investiture, and prevent Elisabeth Farnese from establishing
Spanish garrisons in Tuscany and Parma. While Corsini was pointing
out to the Spanish ambassador in London that it would be ignominious
for the Infant to acknowledge Imperial suzerainty, Bartolommei in
Vienna was drawing the Austrian Cabinet's attention to the dangers of
Spanish garrisons in Tuscany and Parma. Corsini and Bartolommei
were pleased to observe, moreover, that each of their interlocutors
agreed with them.

On July 1st the Spanish troops landed near Palermo. The Sicilians
were preparing to receive them with enthusiasm, when Admiral Byng,
acting as the Emperor's auxiliary, appeared with an English squadron
and destroyed the Spanish fleet off Cape Passaro (August 11th). On
August 2nd the Quadruple Alliance was concluded in London as between Great Britain, Holland, France and Austria. Spain and Savoy
were offered three months in which to adhere to it. The Emperor was
to have Sicily, and Savoy to receive Sardinia in exchange; the succession to Parma and Tuscany might be settled on Elisabeth Farnese's
son. Cosimo, Gian Gastone, the Electress, were completely disregarded.
Corsini protested in London, Bartolommei in Vienna. The Quadruple
Alliance had assumed that Tuscany was an Imperial fief, and had suggested that Elisabeth's son should succeed to it and to Parma under
Imperial suzerainty. But both Cosimo and Elisabeth herself refused to
acknowledge such suzerainty, while the Emperor was not reconciled
to the idea of establishing a Spanish Bourbon in Italy even as his own
vassal.

The Quadruple Alliance had infinite difficulty with Spain, whose
Prime Minister Alberoni's ambitions were 'to restore Spain to her

former greatness by reconquering all that Philip V had signed away at the Peace of Utrecht, form an alliance with the Turks against the Emperor, gain Holland by concession to remain neutral, cripple England by arming the Pretender for a fresh attack on the Crown, stir up Civil War in France, deprive the Duc d'Orléans of the Regency and set Philip V in his place, and finally hand over the whole of Europe thus conquered to the Duke of Parma with himself for Prime Minister.'

Alas for Alberoni, the country he dominated had neither the means nor the energy to accomplish such vast designs. Holland joined the Quadruple Alliance, Byng destroyed the Spanish squadron off Syracuse, the Pretender was driven by a tempest from the coast of England, Cellamare's conspiracy against the Regent was discovered, and an army sent by the Duc d'Orléans successfully invaded Spain. Alberoni was banished in December, 1719; and eventually Philip V was induced to sign the Quadruple Alliance (January 26th, 1720).

Three years of idle discussion at Cambray followed. What mattered most to Cosimo was that the declaration of Tuscany's feudality should be cancelled and that his freedom in choosing a successor should not be coerced by the Powers. The old game of pitting Spain against Austria's inflexible claims to feudal dominion continued.

But small to greater matters must give way! Apart from politics, Cosimo had been concerned with electing another heavenly Protector for Florence; as Noble words it, having made some feeble remonstrances against this infringement of the rights of independent sovereigns, Cosimo then sank into his usual strain of religious folly. St Joseph, he thought, was needed to reinforce the others in this hour of emergency, the others being St John the Baptist and St Zenobius (mere contact with whose corpse had caused a withered elm to burgeon into leaf); to whom St Mary Magdalen dei Pazzi was added on extraordinary occasions. The new patron was publicly elected by the Senate in December, 1719, amid the processions and festivities that had become almost a daily feature of Florentine life. A medal was struck with St Joseph's head on one side, and, on the other, six little angels upholding the balls of the Medici escutcheon.

Two years later, some zealots having drawn his attention to their impropriety, he ordered Bandinelli's marble Adam and Eve to be ejected from the Cathedral where they had stood by the altar, naked and unashamed, since 1551. They were removed at dead of night, thus drawing everybody's attention to the fact. Even the nude statues in the Uffizi worried Cosimo's conscience. The priests continually told him, wrote Montesquieu, that in their confessions they learned the pernicious effects of these nudities. There was in Florence at that time a canon so foolish that he wished to put breeches on a crucifix.

Guyot de Merville, who was then in Florence, wrote: 'Verily Cosimo should entrust his son with the government, but the breach between them is too far gone. It is enough to be in the Prince's good graces to fall immediately from his father's, and this often exposes the Prince to affront. It is but a week ago since he suffered a most unpleasant one.

'The Grand Prince (which is the title they give him) had asked Bettino Ricasoli, the Captain of his father's guard, to receive a Swiss protégé of his. Ricasoli declined under the pretext that he was not tall enough. Stung by his refusal, the Prince got the man a uniform and sent him thus accoutred to the Captain, to show that he had it in his power to admit him without his consent, and that if he had asked Bettino in the first place it was only to do him honour. But Bettino, instead of acknowledging his mistake, had the man stripped and threatened to imprison him if ever he had the effrontery to wear that uniform again. In short, the Prince had to give way, because the Captain reported the incident to the Grand Duke, who took Ricasoli's side instead of his son's. This public mortification contributes not a little to the people's discontent, for they expect to be happier under the Prince's government.

'Gian Gastone, however, does not appear capable of any great exertion. Perhaps the chagrin he experiences from his father's ill-treatment accounts for his singular apathy. He carries this so far that it is even said he never opens a letter, to avoid having to answer it. This course of life might bring him to a very advanced age, did he not suffer from asthma and aggravate his infirmity by the quantity of potent cordials he consumes. Some fear he will predecease his father, which would not be surprising, because the Grand Duke has a robust constitution and takes great care of his health. His son, on the contrary, seems only to accelerate his death.'

Edward Wright, who saw Cosimo in 1720, describes him as follows:

'His Royal Highness was about eighty years old: his state of health was then such as would not allow his going abroad; but whilst he could do that, he visited five or six churches every day. I was told he had a machine in his own apartment, whereon were fix'd little images in silver, of every saint in the calendar. The machine was made to turn so as still to present in front the Saint of the day; before which he continually perform'd his offices. His hours of eating and going to bed were very early, as was likewise his hour of rising. He never came near any fire; and at his coming out of his bedchamber, had an adjacent room warm'd only by the breath of such attendants as were to be always ready against his rising. His zeal was great for gaining proselytes to the Romish Church; and he allowed considerable stipends to some of our nation, that had been brought over by that expedient.

'For the last twenty years of his life, his constant beverage was water. His food was plain: he ate of but one dish, and always alone, except upon the festivals of St John, and other peculiar days, when his family were summoned to join him. Like his father, his time was divided between Florence, Pisa and Leghorn.'

His religious monomania became ever more pronounced: 'His Highness diverts himself with teaching the Christian doctrine to three Cossack boys, from the ages of seven to twelve, who have been sent him as a gift by the Bishop of Cracow, and although they are very insolent, His Highness tolerates them with wonderful patience, and the pious supposition of the merit he acquires, by leading this triad of souls on the way to God.'

The Grand Duchy was as decayed as its sovereign; on every side of him there was a lamentable spectacle of dilapidation and senility. This state of affairs was reflected in the army. In 1718 it was divided into regulars (*permanenti*), the garrisons of Leghorn, Portoferraio and Grosseto, and of the companies of cuirassiers and light cavalrymen. There was also a reserve (*in congedo*). The main force comprised the two garrisons of Leghorn, 1,711 strong, and of Portoferraio, which had a garrison of 703; that of Grosseto was insignificant. It was assumed that seventeen companies of light cavalrymen and five of cuirassiers formed the cavalry, but of these only the frame survived. Four times a year they were mustered for review. Then came a select contingent, the kernel of the army, destined for the sovereign's bodyguard. This consisted of a cavalry unit eighty strong, officially named the Company of German Cuirassiers, and an infantry unit, called the Trabanti Guards. A nobleman was always appointed to command this 'crack' regiment.

The fortresses of the Grand Duchy, great and small, were forty-three in number, of which Leghorn and Portoferraio alone had sufficient garrisons. The Florentine Fortezza da Basso, largest in the State after those of Leghorn and Portoferraio, had only a garrison of a hundred men who, among other duties, had to attend to the 165 cannon with which the fort was armed. Most of the forts, like S. Miniato, had but a custodian in charge of them and 'an artilleryman who cost the State twelve *scudi* a year'.

About half Cosimo's soldiers were married; in 1723 the garrison of Leghorn consisted of 944 bachelors and 767 married men; the wives of the latter lived with their husbands in the barracks, and it is easy to imagine the disorders that occurred. A large proportion of Cosimo's soldiers were doddering veterans. In a curious document, dated October 21st, 1700, there is a catalogue of the disabled soldiers in the garrison of Leghorn, with such indications as the following:

'Domenico Campana, pay 5 *scudi*, age 70, 34 years of service; does not see owing to advanced age, and walks with a stick.

'Gio. Battista Leonardi, pay 4 *scudi*, age 70, 40 years of service; has lost his sight.

'Michele Ricci, pay 7 *scudi*, age 80, 59 years of service; old and decrepit, walks with a stick.'

Three armed galleys and a few unserviceable ships which never left Leghorn were all that remained of the Tuscan fleet, and the total crew consisted of 198 men. As for the glorious Order of Santo Stefano 'whose banners long feared and respected had waved over the Mediterranean, and which had registered so many successful deeds of daring against Turks and Corsairs off Cyprus, Famagusta and the Albanian and Algerian coasts' (providing such painters as Bernardino Poccetti, Matteo Rosselli and Antonio Tempesta with subjects for their masterpieces, and Callot with that of his rarest etching[1]), it had long lost the seafaring habit.

The future lay elsewhere; only the past survived in Tuscany. Cosimo

[1] *Rivista d'Arte Anno VIII*, 1912, p. 115.

was eighty; Marguerite-Louise lived on in close competition, but had long survived every one of her attachments. The only one of her children for whom she had any affection was dead, and with the death of Louis XIV (September 1st, 1715) it must have seemed to her as if true royalty were departed and the world must inevitably fall in with a crash of thunder.

The Grand Duchess had been struck by apoplexy at the Palais-Royal in 1712. Her arm had suddenly stiffened while opening a snuff-box; she wanted to speak, but only a white foam gathered on her lip, and her ladies saw that the Princess was paralysed. Her left side was quite inert, her mouth all twisted, her left eye shut. The doctors did not think she would live, though she dictated her will to two notaries, who declared her sane in mind, memory and judgment. Her self-possession was astonishing, and she slowly recovered. She was anxious to hear from the envoy Melani whether her accident had created any sensation in Florence. He tried to conceal from her the fact that it had created none whatever.

The following years were spent between the Convent of Our Lady of Lepanto at Picpus and various watering-places. She had a second attack in 1713, when her mouth went crooked and her left eye closed again: she could only express herself with difficulty. Thanks to a dose of viper's powder, grains of amber and vinegar, she recovered again and insisted on going out, even in the coldest weather. Cosimo told his agents to keep watch on her possessions. After cures at Mont-Dore and Vichy, she wished to reside in Paris. The Regent allowed her to buy a house in the Place Royale (actually number 15 in the Place des Vosges), where she had a private chapel and gallery of pictures. Here, half-crippled, she spent the last years of her life, a great devotee in her own fashion, said Saint-Simon, much addicted to charity and never weary of recounting her former life to whomsoever would listen.

Madame, the Regent d'Orléans's mother, had now become her confidante. 'Nobody approved,' she wrote, 'of the Grand Duchess leaving her husband, and the more because she speaks so well of him, and describes the life she led in Florence as an earthly paradise. But she does not in the least regard her change of position as a misfortune, and all the splendour she enjoyed in Florence does not seem to her to compare with the freedom she has now. She is amusing when she tells her history. I often said to her: "Do you realize, my cousin, that you are speaking against yourself?" "Ah!" she replied, "I care little about that, so long as I never have to set eyes on the Grand Duke." '[1]

In Paris she was almost as forgotten as in Florence. Occasionally the Court was reminded of her, as when Mademoiselle de Valois, the Regent's daughter, was engaged to the Prince of Modena. The Grand Duchess, we hear, 'says that she is unwilling to receive Mademoiselle, for she has a fair knowledge of Italy, and believes that Mlle de Valois will never become accustomed to their strange ways. She says that she fears, should Mademoiselle take it into her head to return to France, everyone would say: "Here comes the second edition of the Duchesse de Toscane", or that every time the bride does something foolish: "Ah! this is owing to the instructions given her by her aunt, the Grand Duchess", would instantly be said. So she has made up her mind not to speak to her about her future life. . . .'[2]

Every year she became feebler and less articulate. Cosimo, foreseeing the end, sent his new representative Pennetti precise instructions, for it was generally believed that she would leave everything to the Regent. 'The Grand Duke is artful,' wrote Madame,[3] 'he imagines that his wife will soon die, and that he will thus be saved from paying what he owes her; besides which he is always in arrears with her pension. . . .'

She clung to life until September 19th, 1721, when she succumbed at the age of seventy-six, and was buried at Picpus. Her legacy proved her persistent hatred of the Medici. She left her property to Princess d'Epinoy, a distant relative, thus violating the compact she had signed at Castello, wherein she had agreed that all she might die possessed of should descend to her children. Marguerite-Louise must have foreseen the tedious lawsuit this would involve. Even if Cosimo won it (as he did) she wished to annoy him after her death, and bequeath him some bitter reminder of the past.

To the titles of Royal Highness and Canon of the Lateran, Cosimo could now add that of widower. Instead of arranging for a *Te Deum*, which, as Conti remarked, would have been a more sincere expression of his feelings, he commanded that his wife's glorious memory be honoured with solemn pomp in S. Lorenzo. Gian Gastone attended on a throne; the Princesses Violante and Eleanora were in a balcony

[1] May 19th, 1716.   [2] June 25th, 1720.   [3] May 13th, 1718.

facing the catafalque. But the Electress refrained from paying her mother the posthumous compliment of attendance, even though the ceremony was one of mere formality. As for Cosimo, he stayed at home.

The Florentine diplomatists were getting worried: towards the end of 1721 it did not seem as if their game of playing Spain against Austria could continue. Spain appeared shrunken after Alberoni's disgrace: Elisabeth Farnese, wishing to make sure of her son's inheritance to Parma and Tuscany, thought it safer now to acknowledge feudal submission to the Empire; once the Austrian ministry had given their formal assent they could not easily revoke it. There was considerable agitation in Florence until Spain defined her policy. Memorials about the freedom of the Florentine State were distributed among the Courts of Europe; Austria retorted with contradictory arguments based on an academic discussion at Leipzig. Neri Corsini then arranged that Giuseppe Averani's treatise '*De libertate civitatis Florentie eiusque Dominii*' should be printed secretly in Paris, with the false date 'Pisis, 1721': a pious fraud, as he confesses, 'to look as if it were printed prior to the one from Leipzig, even if none believe it'. Their ingenuity was misdirected: the great Powers paid scant attention to these dim scholarly debates.

Austria spoke of sending Bavarian garrisons instead of Swiss ones to Tuscany, as had been decided in London; and the Electress was swept completely off the board. All seemed inextricably tangled. Austria, after trying to make Spain accept a diploma (December 7th, 1722) in which the Infant Carlos appeared little better than a vassal, was compelled by the Powers who had signed the Treaty of London to substitute a more moderate one, without, however, destroying the idea of feudality. According to Corsini, Spain had come round to the view that a declaration of feudality would be a quick solution. Cosimo made his final protest, through Marchese Corsini, on October 25th, 1723. In substance, he said, since the Congress wished to establish general peace, and a lasting peace required that the rights of each be respected, the Grand Duke demanded:

'I. That no step be taken at this Congress to change the statute calling the widowed Electress Palatine to succeed to the ancient State of Florence.

'II. That no measure be taken to extend this statute or prevent the Grand Duke and Grand Prince his son from fixing the Succession and government in the manner they consider best adapted to their people's tranquillity.

'III. That the Powers meeting at the present Congress shall guarantee through their ministers what wise provisions their Highnesses are prepared to make.

'IV. That no offence be done nor allowed to be done to the independence of Florence and her dominions, and that these shall come into possession of whomsoever the Grand Duke and Grand Prince of Tuscany appoint to inherit them, with the same titles, pre-eminence and prerogatives as the House of Medici hitherto.

'Under these conditions only the Grand Duke and Grand Prince his son will contribute to the general peace and to that of Tuscany in particular, taking measures in agreement with the Powers contracting to establish the Succession, and to ensure that this be effected only by laws that are just, valid and indisputable.'

Sad protest, in its impotence and dignity: a protest of some battered ruin against the winds! 'If the face disappears no respect is left for the nape of the neck.'

In spite of the Pythagorean regimen he strictly followed, Cosimo had fallen a victim to the infirmities of old age. He seldom left the Pitti; when he did, vast crowds collected to catch a glimpse of him. He had become an object of curiosity, a sort of relic. Gian Gastone was summoned from his seclusion at Pescia to take over the government when his father was stricken with a slow fever and erysipelas—then called the Rose, or St Anthony's fire.

As Regent, Gian Gastone already showed flashes of intelligence and reassuring tokens of goodwill. He had begun to deputize for his father at the *Consulta* in July, 1722, and he brought wit and gaiety with him. There were masques and balls, symphonies of various instruments on the Piazza S. Spirito and elsewhere; ladies appeared in their coaches and on foot 'not without the amazement of many not used to seeing so much freedom in the city of Florence'. When Gian Gastone sat on the throne to receive homage on St John the Baptist's day, he turned to those near him and jested, 'as was His Highness's wont on all occasions', saying that he seemed to be playing the part of King in a comedy.

Until his final collapse Cosimo remained jealous of his authority: he still wanted to do and see everything for himself, indefatigable in what he believed to be his duty, corresponding with his ambassadors, directing each of them personally. On September 22nd, 1723, while sitting as usual at his writing-table, he had a fit of trembling which lasted two hours. He recuperated, but it was a warning of the end. The clergy did their utmost to prolong the life of their patron; all the convents and monasteries read special prayers for his recovery: the Miraculous Virgin of Impruneta was brought out, the body of St Mary Magdalen de Pazzi was exposed. Cosimo selected Monsignor Francesco Frosini, the Archbishop of Pisa, to minister to him on his death-bed. They held frequent conversations, and after one of these the Archbishop declared, on leaving the Grand Duke's chamber, 'that this Prince required little assistance in order to die well, for he had studied and cared for nothing else throughout the long course of his life, but to prepare himself for death'. The Archbishop's remark is profound: although he did not intend it as such, it was at once a criticism of Cosimo's life and reign, a condemnation and an epitaph.

Memento Mori, Mort m'est Vie, was verily his motto, for to his mind death was the central and dominating theme. Cosimo's reign, longer than that of any other Medici, had been but a preliminary for it—he had fostered and nourished death—and that of Tuscany besides his own. What remained for Gian Gastone and the Electress Palatine after so consummate a preparation? What could they undo?

There was many an anti-climax before the catastrophe: he asked the Archbishop of Florence to convey his regret to the people for having failed to edify them by a good example. He made a similar request of his confessor, to crave forgiveness of all his familiar servants for the bad example he might have set them. While the body lingered on, sending forth unctuous messages, waiting in superstitious awe, it yet found strength to sign a proclamation, a last souvenir of his affection for his subjects, imposing a new tax of five per cent on their incomes or earnings.

On the fifty-third day of his illness, the Nuncio and Archbishops of Florence and Pisa were summoned again to his bedside. The Nuncio conferred on him the Papal blessing *in articulo mortis*, after which they left him with his confessor, who gave him the form of absolution usually imparted to the third Order of Franciscans (i.e., those not living a cloistered life), among whom Cosimo had been registered. The Sacrament was exposed in the Duomo and elsewhere; and the prelates returned with various prayers to succour him as he was about to expire. The Nuncio prayed for his soul again at two o'clock in the morning, after which the Archbishop of Florence offered up an orison in honour of St Joseph; scarce was this recited when Cosimo breathed his last, on the vigil of All Saints, October 31st, 1723.

The panegyrics were many: from some it would appear that the entire population of the bereaved city was plunged into a Malebolge of despair, but after fifty-three years of such a disastrous reign they could not mourn him sincerely. Cosimo's death was assuredly no shock. The general feeling was rather of intense relief. They came cheerfully to inspect his corpse in the Pitti; the pomp of his burial was gorgeous: the bells of the Palazzo Vecchio and all the churches tolled for six and a half hours, but the funeral seemed gay, the tolling rapturous. Already the citizens anticipated a livelier scene, breathing an air no longer thick with incense.

XXV

'It would not be easy to find a greater contrast in the character and habits of two princes succeeding one another in any country,' wrote Lord Brougham, 'than the third and fourth Georges of England presented to the eye of even the most superficial observer.' This remark might be extended to Cosimo III and Gian Gastone de' Medici.

Cosimo III had reigned for fifty-three years, and died on the fifty-third day of his illness. Gian Gastone, the last male of the Medici, quietly succeeded him at the age of fifty-two, jaded and old in advance of his years, a degenerate sot, according to some—and yet, in spite of apparent indolence, canny and benevolent. It could not be said that at any time he showed anxiety to rule; he cared little for power, and would have gladly been left alone. He had been obliged to witness the political prostration of his country; his married life had been a failure, and he tried to drown the consciousness of this in wine. The habit was formed by now, he could not discard a remedy grown despotic: too long he had lived a recluse, with Giuliano Dami as pander-companion. Gian Gastone could not alter, but his latent resources were now displayed, and there was a pleasant reaction in the fourteen years of his reign, as if autumn had suddenly burgeoned into spring. In November, 1723, the Serene Grand Duke ordered all his attendants to dress in French style, and the whole city began to imitate the Court. He abolished Cosimo's 'Pensions on the Creed' to Christianized Jews and Turks, converted Lutherans and Calvinists, as well as that espionage over private lives which had been a salient characteristic of his father's rule.

Travellers have left a sombre picture of Florence at the time of Cosimo's death—a place vowed to lethargy, sunk in superstition and squalor, swarming with beggars, who were chiefly old women.

'The declining state of this city is very visible, a great deal of the ground within the walls being unbuilt, and many of the houses ill-inhabited, so that it is not very populous; nor are the inhabitants useful, the clergy making up the bulk of the people. . . . I counted above 4,000 monks and friars in a procession, besides the secular clergy who are reckoned about half that number. The sick and infirm must also be very numerous where there are so many aged persons.'

The appearance of this city, wrote another, suffers considerably from the great number of oiled paper windows in the houses, which were apt to be torn. As at Rome, however, only foreigners were struck by the decadence around them.

Gian Gastone could hardly be expected to reform all the vices of the administration, but he acted as a wholesome corrective. He lived in a private manner, with very little appearance of a Court about him, had no love of splendour, nor desire to impress, and therefore did not indulge in extravagant ceremonies. Cosimo had long preached economy, but Gian Gastone practised it. With all his lechery and bibbing, even beneath his scepticism, one feels that mayhap he had sounder ideals of holiness than his pious father, who had annually sacrificed fabulous sums for mere display, and scattered indiscriminate largesse to the clergy and converts to the faith, leaving the State on the verge of bankruptcy.

Violante had left Siena, and henceforth the public audiences were generally given by her. 'She is of a cheerful disposition,' wrote Keysler, 'yet with a prudent reserve that she may not give offence to her sister-in-law, who was oftener seen at convents and churches than at Court.' The Electress had fallen into the background: Gian Gastone would never forgive her the part she had taken in his marriage. The spirit of Cosimo III survived in this Princess, who had to look on at changes she abhorred, at a whole movement in contemporary life that was profoundly distasteful to her. Gian Gastone was taking his revenge with ironical relish; he rejoiced in her discomfiture.

During the first years of his reign Gian Gastone still appeared in public, but gradually his taste for solitude grew upon him and he did not even trouble to appear at the time-honoured functions. On December 31st, 1725, 'being the last day of the year, on which according to custom, a solemn *Te Deum* is sung in the Collegiata of S. Lorenzo, to render thanks to God for the benefits received in the past year with all the magistrates present, the Serene Grand Duke did not attend as he had done heretofore, and as Cosimo III had done invariably, showing thereby that he took little pleasure in pietistic practices'. The people, however, appreciated the humanity of this recluse who abolished the death penalty; and lit bonfires of joy because he had lowered the price of corn, reducing it to four *paoli* a bushel. What did it matter to them if their sovereign was cynical about religion, appearing among them drunk as usual (*S.A.R. al solito stravizzò alquanto*, or *bevve assai*): they were no longer at the mercy of spies, the load of nervous apprehension was removed, the burden of taxation lightened. And Florence benefited by a breathing-space from the baleful influence of hypocrites.

Soon after his accession Gian Gastone abolished some of the most onerous taxes, such as the *collette*, and took in hand the shoals of beggars 'both hale and infirm' infesting the city, establishing a workhouse where they could apply themselves to any trade they were capable of. The poor did not consider themselves so very unfortunate. They were unconscious of their degradation. Sufficient alms were distributed to content appetites long controlled by hereditary frugality and sobriety. The steps of the myriad churches provided them with couches, and cool seats for siestas on hot afternoons. Only in winter did they suffer hardship. If they fell ill, they need only knock at the door of one of the numerous hospitals. They loved festas, they lived for them. They possessed, moreover, 'the faculty of making much of common things and converting small occasions into great pleasures'. On the whole, as in Rome, poverty wore a smiling aspect: hardly a day passed but there was something to amuse and interest the eye. Add to this that their faith was profound, accommodating, unperturbed. 'Provided they regularly attended religious functions and habitually pronounced certain pious words, they had Paradise in store for them.' Such, at any rate, was their belief, and they lived without anxiety.

The nobles kept up the grand palaces of their ancestors, but their ostentation was generally a sham. Strangers were impressed by the multitude of lackeys in their ante-chambers. In reality these domestics were neither lodged nor fed in the household. They were there on show for a few hours, and their wages were absurdly small, but they could count on the noble's protection and occasional gratuities. The entertainments of the aristocracy were limited to *conversazioni*, with card-playing—generally Ombre or Taroc, a game with seventy-two cards, in suits of suns, moons, devils and monks—for modest stakes, tempered with 'iced fruits and other pleasant rinfrescatives'. Few of them gave dinners; generally their own meals were brought in from a neighbouring cook-shop and they were fed for a crown a day.

'There is no town where men live with less luxury than Florence,' wrote Montesquieu in 1728: 'with a dark-lantern for night and an umbrella for the rain, one is completely equipped. It is true that the women are slightly more extravagant, for they keep an old carriage. It is said that they spend more in the country; and also at baptisms and weddings. The streets are so well paved with broad flagstones that it is very convenient to go on foot. The Grand Duke's Prime Minister, Marchese di Montemagni, has been seen sitting by his street door, swinging his legs. . . . As I went out with my small lantern and umbrella, I thought that the ancient Medici must have left their neighbours' houses in this wise. There is a very gentle sway in Florence. Nobody knows or is conscious of the Prince and his Court. For that very reason this little country has the air of a great one.

'Italian families spend a great deal on canonizations. The Corsinis of Florence have lavished above 180,000 Roman crowns on the canonization of a Corsini saint (St Andrea Corsini, A.D. 1373). Old Marchese Corsini used to say: "My children, be virtuous, but do not be saints." They have a chapel where their saint lies, which has cost them over 50,000 crowns. Few knaves have cost their family so much as this holy man.

'They also spend much on Church burials. In short, all forms of magnificence will open an Italian's purse more readily than comfort: every Italian loves to be flattered.

'Wood brings a good revenue in Florence. General economy has produced a principle that it is injurious to the health to warm oneself in winter; but it is the fire at home they consider injurious, not the fire they find elsewhere.'

Gian Gastone's chief desire was to avoid the humiliation of Spanish garrisons and the presence of Don Carlos in Tuscany, at any rate provisionally. He appeared ready to accept the Austrian proposals. He knew that various disputes were bound to arise between Austria and Spain about the garrisons, and the regents to be elected if Don Carlos were to succed when still a minor. And he was convinced of the advantages to be gained from lying low and biding his time: Austria's delay suited him. Father Ascanio, the Spanish ambassador to Florence, gave vent to his exasperation in a letter to the Duke of Parma, dated January 2nd, 1725.

'To the Grand Duke's physical stupidity,' he wrote, 'which has been seen on divers occasions and over a long period, lying motionless as a lunatic, is added his political stupidity, in which H.H. perseveres no less than his government, ignoring all that happens in the world relating to this Court, believing this to be the best policy, to avoid any engagements and enjoy the benefit of time.'

Diplomatic relations between France and Spain were broken in the beginning of 1725, and no more was said about the Tuscan Succession for the time being. Impatient for an heir, Louis XV, a well-grown boy of fifteen, had repudiated his betrothal to the little Infanta Maria Vittoria, who was under seven, to marry a riper, if obscurer, Polish princess. This unexpected event wholly changed the situation. Spain was drifting towards Austria under the influence of the new Prime Minister, Ripperda, and in April, 1725, the (first) Treaty of Vienna was concluded between them, guaranteeing the succession of Parma and Tuscany to Don Carlos while assuming an Austrian preponderance. The Maritime Powers, which had for years striven to reconcile the Emperor and Spain, were far from pleased when they settled matters for themselves, suspecting dangerous hidden clauses in the treaty, clauses which actually existed. Its first result was the Treaty of Hanover between France, England and Holland (September, 1725); this led to a new secret agreement between Austria and Spain, by which a war with England and a marriage between two of Elisabeth's sons and two Archduchesses were planned; and it looked as though war between the two groups were unavoidable. But the alliance between Spain and Austria did not continue; Ripperda fell in disgrace; the Emperor recoiled from the actual establishment of a Spanish Bourbon in Italy and would not carry out the proposed marriage arrangements, nor join in a war against England. He even tried to settle the succession by arranging a marriage for Elisabeth's uncle, Antonio, the reigning Duke of Parma. If Antonio had a son, he might also be proclaimed heir to Tuscany.

Cardinal Fleury now found it easier to restore French influence in Spain. He promised Elisabeth that Spanish garrisons should be introduced into Parma and Tuscany, and that Don Carlos should hold these States free from Imperial suzerainty. Accordingly, when England negotiated the Treaty of Seville (November, 1729), which included France, Holland and Spain, it guaranteed all Fleury's promises to Elisabeth, and the allies promised to go to war if the Emperor refused to acquiesce. The Emperor's reply was to pour troops into Italy. Charles VI even told Gian Gastone that he would send them into Tuscany, but the Grand Duke managed to avoid this: his ministers intrigued and promised, twisted and turned, negotiating with all parties at once.[1] None would suspect the slightest activity, however, from Gian Gastone's manner of life in Florence.

'He is a good Prince,' noted the author of *L'Esprit des Lois*, 'endowed with brains but very lazy, rather addicted to the bottle. He has no confidence in any minister and is often sharp with them: probably the effect of his vinous hours. Otherwise, the best of men. Somebody was seized and condemned to the galleys for publishing a libel against the ministers in which the Grand Duke was included. The Duke, who has to confirm the sentence, refused to do so. A senator expostulated with him: "But, Sire, we must make an example of him: he has dealt rudely with a senator." "And with me, too," said the Grand Duke, "but he has told the truth, and I do not wish to punish him for that." He is nearly always with his domestics. . . .'

As an example of his extreme laziness, Montesquieu relates that on his return from Germany some of his suite had their clothes packed among his luggage. 'Although this was about twelve years ago, the trunks are still unpacked and the clothes moth-eaten. He puts away everything he is given—even game and fruit—and it is left to rot after he has had it valued and given a gratuity corresponding with the cost. He is a good prince, however. A Marchese Gerini has a post worth 2,000 crowns, which the Grand Duke his father bestowed upon him

[1] H. M. Vernon, *op. cit.*

in spite of the Prince, who hated him, and was so incensed because of it that he retired from Court. When he became Grand Duke he did not deprive him of the post.' Beside mere laziness, his indecision made him an easy prey to unscrupulous adventurers. Gian Gastone prevaricated and jested while the wheels of his small, independent universe continued noiselessly to turn. *Laissez faire! Il mondo va da se*, was his constant refrain: the world governs itself.

Meanwhile he retired to bed, first for weeks, then for months, and finally for years, and what he did there with those domestics of his was an open secret. Giuliano Dami, their chief, the typical wily Tuscan peasant, knew how to feather his nest. Even before Cosimo's death the most respectable of senators and ministers had begun to seek his friendship. Now he became the supreme dispenser of favours, 'the despot of Gian Gastone's Court, and absolute master of his desires'. Giuliano was well bribed by anyone who wished to approach the royal recluse; his income and power increased accordingly. Amongst other family instincts Gian Gastone had inherited that of acquisition. He lacked his brother Ferdinando's connoisseurship, however, and much worthless bric-à-brac was palmed off on him by the antiquaries at exorbitant prices, from which Giuliano pocketed a correspondingly high percentage. The Grand Duke usually consulted his favourite about these purchases, and 'it sufficed his darling dissembler to praise the stuff and say it was beautiful, making a show of much marvel, for him to be seized with an overweening desire to possess it'.

A propitious moment was chosen to tempt the Grand Duke, generally when he had left 'the dull shore of lazy temperance'. Like his uncle, Cardinal Francesco Maria, he seems to have taken a perverse pleasure in being cheated. He bartered the objects already in his possession: the dealers offered him theirs for fabulous prices, underrating the value of those they took in exchange. Time would elapse, and they would return with the latter, as if the Grand Duke had never set eyes on them before. He bought them just the same. One day he recognized a snuff-box which had been brought back to him in this way. His only remark as, mildly surprised, he purchased it, was: 'Faith, who dies not is often to be met again!'

But acquisition was not only a question of inanimate objects: the instinct was extended to human beings. He must run the full gamut of his passion for the strange and unfamiliar. Giuliano Dami, who had every reason to foster this passion, collected a regiment of males and females whose entire business was to pander, however grossly, to the Grand Duke's caprices, and mitigate the asperities of the political situation and the monotony of his daily life. Their salaries varied with the antics they performed; often he required them to insult him and knock him about like a clown; from the fact that they were paid on Tuesdays and Saturdays in ruspi (a ruspo being a Florentine sequin formerly worth ten francs) they became notorious as *Ruspanti*. They were generally recruited from the lowest classes ('it mattered not from what gang of vagrant knaves and mongrels, unruly and unclean, provided they were graced with an alluring eye and the countenance of an Adonis'), though knights and citizens, and many foreigners figured among them. Soon they usurped the Grand Duke's time almost to the exclusion of everyone else: their prominence embarrasses the polite historian, though he may not cancel the rôles they played in Gian Gastone's latter years. Necessarily their presence must cloud the perspective, while investing it with a deeper pathos.

We know that Gian Gastone invited Alessandro Magnasco to the Pitti, who resided there several years practising that cunning in which his patron rejoiced on a range of melodramatic canvases, where Jewish synagogues, crazed ascetics, sorcerers, gipsies, beggars and scenes of monastic life were delineated with quivering staccato restlessness. Gian Gastone's admiration for 'il Lissandrino' throws an effective light on his taste, for already, as Lanzi wrote,[1] this artist was more esteemed by foreigners than by his own countrymen; 'his bold touch, though joined to a noble conception and to correct drawing, did not attract in Genoa, because it is far removed from the finish and union of tints which these masters followed.' Magnasco's macabre humour, dark and repellent to modern critics even, might occasionally serve as an illustration of Gian Gastone's: both stood remote from the threadbare conventions of their age. It is a thousand pities that Magnasco left no portrait of his snuff-besmeared patron, recumbent in bed with nightcap or tattered periwig: what a masterpiece he might have made of it! Gian Gastone in the midst of his *Ruspanti*. Magnasco would have done visual justice to its fantasy.

[1] Abate Luigi Lanzi: *The History of Painting in Italy*. London, 1847.

The Grand Duke's levee was at noon, when those who had business with him were summoned to his bedchamber. He constantly dined at five o'clock in the evening, and supped at two in the morning. He always ate alone, and generally in bed. The history of one day is the history of a year. In summer he lived on the ground-floor of the Pitti: every year a donkey came laden with peaches for the Grand Duke— a gift from the community of San Gimignano—and it was Gian Gastone's humour to have the donkey ushered into his bedroom. Every winter he was carried in a sedan-chair to an apartment above, and those who carried him were generously rewarded for doing so.

Giuliano and the *Ruspanti* knew more about him than his ministers; but his jokes were widely reported, and he joked on every subject. 'He would entertain a dozen dissolute boys to sumptuous dinners, and one by one he would call them by the names of his most prominent men of state. With these he would hold his nightly conference.'

At this time he seems to have wished one of Princess Violante's nephews to succeed him. The Grand Duke would set in for a jovial evening by asking the opinions of these pseudo-ministers, and each proceeded to pronounce some impudent judgment on the matter. One more wily than the others happened to guess where his preference lay. To put his Prince in a good humour, he answered with some astuteness: 'All Europe and Tuscany wants the cloth of Spain, yet to me 'tis as clear as daylight that Bavarian tissue will supplant it.' The Grand Duke rejoiced at this reply, and toasted the health of Prince Ferdinand of Bavaria and his sons. He remunerated this noble councillor more generously than the others, and dismissed that distinguished Council of State at dawn. And since he abhorred the aristocracy, when he gave feasts for his male and female *Ruspanti,* he would call those doxies and drabs by the names of the first ladies of the land, and those rogues and vagabonds by the names of his foremost knights. He would have them all stand in attitudes of stiff reserve, as if they were true aristocrats, and drink to the health of Marquis So-and-so, and Marchioness Such-and-such. He would laugh incontinently at these appellations, and after supper would say: 'Now Marquis X, does the Marchioness Y appeal to you? If so, proceed to business; away and forge ahead!' Unspeakably revolting scenes were said to have followed and though we may not give credit to them all, as the saying goes: there is no smoke without fire. The news of them, besides, was spread abroad by the *Ruspanti*, who boasted vaingloriously of their activities.

In April, 1727, Pope Benedict XIII notified Gian Gastone that as a token of His Holiness's esteem for the Medici, he was bestowing on Princess Violante the Golden Rose. . . . When the Senator and Prior Montemagni, first Secretary of State, wished to discuss with Gian Gastone a suitable function to follow the Rose's arrival from Rome, H.R.H. replied: 'You will have to discuss this matter with Rapa (head gardener of the Boboli), who has a good knowledge of roses; as for me, I know little about them.'

Following Cosimo III's example, the Princess had gone to Rome for the Jubilee of 1725, and Benedict XIII had been impressed by her virtue. The occasion was perhaps even more memorable because she had sent for Cavalier Bernardino Perfetti, the greatest of Italian *improvvisatori*, who excited such admiration by his improvising at the Clementine College, at the Palazzo Madama where Violante was staying, and at the palace of Cardinal Polignac, the French ambassador, that the Pope decided he should receive the crown of the Capitol.

On her return from Rome, Violante tried to wean Gian Gastone from the *Ruspanti* by banquets which often lasted till daybreak; the guests, besides Gian Gastone, who always attended them 'glass in hand', were four ladies, three of whom varied every time, but one remained the same, to wit Mistress Maria Anna Valvasoni, wife of the Bali Baldassare Suarez, a star of the first constellation of female wits at this period, and the toast of Florentine society. This year Gian Gastone also attended Marchese Riccardi's annual dinner in his garden at Gualfonda, followed by a canta with several airs, sung by the already celebrated Neapolitan Carlo Broschi, better known as Farinelli.

But even at these *petits soupers fins* the Grand Duke was apt to mortify his hosts. At one of them, says the chronicler—probably at Lappeggi—many Florentines of the first quality were present, and the Grand Duke's tongue was so unloosed by wine that it uttered the foulest words imaginable, as his head wagged heavily to and fro and lolled upon his shoulders. In the middle of it all he disgorged into his napkin, and anon, as he continued to shock the company with constant belching and atrocious talk, he puked again, and wiped his mouth with the tumbling curls of his periwig, which was much disordered. The Princess, who could no longer endure it, urged her maids of honour to depart, and signalled to the others to do likewise, asking if their carriages were ready. The Grand Duke ordered his coach also, besotted and slabbering as he was, and when it arrived, he was lifted like a bundle of hay by four of his brawny attendants, taken home, and flung upon his bed all covered in vomit.

The *Ruspanti* increased, and Gian Gastone 'enjoyed the benefits of time' in his own strange manner. On Holy Thursday, 1729, there happened to be some Poles in Florence with three bears, which they had trained to dance for a living to the sound of drums and trumpets. While the Electress and Princess Eleanora were at Mass in their private chapel, the Grand Duke summoned these men into the courtyard of the palace, where they made the bears dance before him with a great flourish of wind and percussion. Afterwards H.R.H. wished the said Poles to come up to his chamber and, drinking with them copiously, became intoxicated and, as drunkards do, began to throw the glasses and wine into their faces, and the Poles did the same into his. Fortunately some of his chamberlains overheard the hubbub, and when they entered the room discovered the Grand Duke locked with them in a close embrace and in danger of being hurt, unless they were separated at once.

'It is impossible,' says one historian[1] of Gian Gastone, 'to give much of the personal history of a Prince who, from mere indolence and sloth, was never dressed for the last thirteen years of his life, and who never left his bed for the last eight. His appearance was singularly whimsical; he received those whom he suffered to approach him, in his shirt, without ruffles, a cravat of considerable length, made of muslin, none of the finest, and a night-cap; all of which were besmeared with snuff. The late Earl of Sandwich acquainted this writer (the Rev. Mark Noble) that this "filthy" habit so far grew upon Gian Gastone towards the latter part of his life, that to stifle the disagreeable smells of his bed, the room was covered entirely, when his lordship was introduced to His Royal Highness, with new-gathered roses.' Others have compared the room from which Tuscany was governed to a cell of the *Stinche*, the nightmare prison finally abolished in 1835. In the July of 1729 he stumbled and dislocated an ankle, but one of his chamberlains,

[1] Rev. M. Noble.

289

Zanobi Amerighi, happened to be a surgeon, and promptly operated on him. 'The Electress severely reprimanded Amerighi because he had dared to lay hands on H.R.H. when she did not consider him sufficiently experienced in surgery. Without this immediate operation he would have been crippled for life.'

There was an earthquake in August, and many feared it was a judgment from heaven for the extreme libertinism that had lately been introduced into Florence, especially in the highest circles. Whereupon thirty foreign women of loose life were banished, and these, wrote Settimanni, were probably far less wicked than the Florentines. Commenting on the fact that few Florentines had good eyesight—*Fiorentini ciechi*, or blind Florentines, was a common jest—Keysler wrote: 'They are, even to a proverb, addicted to that atrocious and unnatural vice which brought down the divine vengeance on Sodom and Gomorrah. Thus it is not at all strange, that with such lascivious inclinations the Florentines should not have the best eyes: immoderate and frequent acts of venery being very pernicious to the sight; and at Hall in Saxony, about twenty years ago, a common prostitute in *ipso aestu et actu venereo* became irrecoverably blind.'

XXVI

Rare Excursions – Second Treaty of Vienna – Death of Princess Violante – Don Carlos Enters Florence, 1732 – The Grand Duke Bedridden – War of Polish Succession – The Duke of Lorraine to Succeed to Tuscany – Death of Gian Gastone, 1737

Florence during Gian Gastone's reign might aptly be compared with Paris during the Regency. Florentine society was imitating the French. In France 'the flaunting vice of a clique is often represented as a natural reaction against the austerity of Louis XIV's later years'; in Florence it was the inevitable reaction against a whole century of gloom and bigotry. Gian Gastone was not solely responsible for this epidemic of licentiousness.

The Regent d'Orléans, wrote Saint-Simon, was bored with himself from birth. He sought relief in wine and witty women; vice with him was neither passion nor fashion, but the tiresome habit of a tired man. Substitute *Ruspanti* for witty women, and the same applies to the last Grand Duke of the Medici.

Gian Gastone's final appearance at a public function was in 1729. There had been many rumours of his lying on the verge of death; he was persuaded against his will to emerge and dispel them at the festival of St John the Baptist.

He drank heavily to fortify himself for the occasion: Bacchus, he felt, would lend him a protective armour to meet the gaze of his subjects, that scrutiny he dreaded. It were well to skate over the rest—how the inebriated Grand Duke, as he was driven in gala through the streets of Florence, turned now and again to vomit out of the chariot window, while his peering people bowed or curtseyed or doffed their hats. This bloated, broken-looking bibber: was this the last male descendant of a family which had embodied the perfection of human culture?

At the Prato gate he was helped on to the terrace whence yearly the

Grand Dukes had witnessed the races of barbs. His humiliated courtiers stood as far as possible out of the royal reach, but Gian Gastone was evidently enjoying himself in spite of his puking, for he kept raising his querulous voice and calling to them incoherently, hic-coughing deplorable remarks at the pages and ladies-in-waiting. Then he fell into a dozing torpor; his servants deposited him furtively in a litter, and carried him back to the Pitti. At the Pitti he remained.

After this catastrophe Gian Gastone was almost permanently cloistered there; any excursion, as rare, was worthy of note, as eccentric, was a topic of conversation: his character was a psychological riddle, baffling and entertaining. In February, 1730, at two o'clock after sun-set, he left the palace in a sedan-chair for the Baths of S. Sperandino, accompanied by four lancers and pages, holding torches, and there he stayed until seven; he gave the keeper ten sequins, and one for each of his assistants, besides a commission to the keeper's brother. This curi-ous excursion of H.R.H. excited much comment, for he had not left the Pitti since the feast of St John the Baptist, and the more because there were luxurious baths in the palace. A perusal of Cecchi's comedy *Lo Stufaiuolo* would cast a Petronian light on this excursion. In Luca Landucci's *Florentine Diary*, on November 13th, 1506, we read: 'at about 24 in the evening (8 p.m.) at San Michele Berteldi, it began to be said that an image of Our Lady, which is over a door, had miraculously closed its eyes, the one opposite the *Stufa* (Steam-baths). It seemed as if she did not wish to see the sins that are committed there. Before a day had passed, numerous candles were lighted, and great veneration was paid to it, so that a wall was built in front of it like a church, and if it had not been unfitting for women to go to this place near the *Stufa*, many women would have gone there. . . .' Significant snippets, even if out of date.

Only one other excursion is recorded, five years later: July 5th, 1735. The Grand Duke, who had not left his Pitti Palace for many years, was unexpectedly transferred at $21\frac{1}{2}$ o'clock to the delicious villa of Poggio Imperiale whither he was conducted in a litter by way of the Boboli, wearing a dressing-gown and a straw hat on his head, ac-companied only by Count Canale da Terni, his gentlemen-in-waiting and two chamberlains, and preceded by his guard. This impromptu decision set the whole of Florence in commotion, and everyone was delighted that H.R.H. was beginning to move about and let himself be seen after such a long time.

According to the memoir previously quoted, his courtiers had persuaded him in vain to wear more dignified apparel. A party was then in progress at the neighbouring Villa d'Elci, and when the company heard that their sovereign was expected, they went forth to meet him with blazing torches, for it was night. But the Grand Duke caught sight of them and began to scold and shout: 'Away with lights! Out with every one of them!' They were forbidden to approach, and he condescended to explain the reason for this interdict to his familiars. He was suddenly ashamed of appearing in public so improperly garbed.

The question of the Tuscan Succession seemed settled in 1731. The crisis came with Antonio Farnese's death in January. His widow believed herself to be with child, but diplomatists were sceptical. Charles VI occupied Parma nominally on behalf of Don Carlos. The Maritime Powers offered to guarantee his Pragmatic Sanction, and in return he made the second Treaty of Vienna, to which Spain acceded in July. Spanish troops were to be introduced, even if the widowed Duchess should give birth to a boy. The Imperial investiture was to precede possession of the Duchies by Don Carlos. Spain confirmed the terms of the Quadruple Alliance and of the first Treaty of Vienna of June 7th, 1725.

The second Treaty of Vienna was made without consulting Gian Gastone, who by now was more concerned to end his days in peace than interested in any special heir. He drifted on, as it were, shutting his eyes, averting his head, hardening his heart. Princess Violante died in May: her death was a real loss to him, but he would not show it. Away with grief and mourning, and *memento mori*.

'While the Princess lay a-dying she implored him to come and pay her a farewell visit, but no argument would persuade him to do so. . . . And when she had passed away, and her corpse was ready to be taken to its tomb, a crowd assembled on the Piazza de' Pitti to watch the pomp of her funeral. Some obstacle happened to delay the procession and a clamour arose in consequence. Meanwhile the Grand Duke's chamber was filled with youths of venereal, rather than martial, prowess, who were detained there by the tumult, and the Grand Duke himself was sending repeated messages to speed the corpse upon its last journey. Finally the Grand Duke lost all patience. In a towering rage he sent forth to hurry the procession, and it is said that he broke into infamous invective unfit for the lowest of harlots, let alone for that gentle high-born Princess.'[1]

Not a few have censured Gian Gastone's conduct on this occasion, accusing him of callousness. One is astonished by their lack of insight. It was as plain as an aching nerve to the Grand Duke that he had not long to last: the Powers of Europe were drumming it daily into his ears. For all the *Ruspanti*, he lived in greater self-absorption and isolation than ever. His impressionable mind could not but be haunted with ideas of death. His outburst as his sister-in-law's corpse seemed to lie for an eternity outside his bedroom window was the spontaneous outburst of one who would cling to life with a clutch indifferent to dignity. With a phalanx of youth around him to recall those pleasures which age had disqualified him from enjoying, it seemed monstrous of Violante, for whom he had entertained a genuine affection, to remind him so cruelly of her actual, and his impending, dissolution. Surely in view of such circumstances, we should not judge the Grand Duke harshly.

It only remained for Don Carlos to enter his Duchies. The Infant was not unacceptable; he had been brought up largely by Italians, and had many of their characteristics; the Spaniards were not unpopular, and the Infant's succession at least made it certain that the Emperor's suzerainty would not be more than nominal. It would give Tuscany the support of the Bourbon Powers, while union with Parma would greatly increase its importance. Accordingly, Gian Gastone made a private arrangement, quite satisfactory to himself, with Spain, in which all mention of the Imperial suzerainty was carefully avoided. Don Carlos, still a minor, was to remain under the guardianship of the Grand Duke and of the Dowager Duchess of Parma. 'They do us the favour of appointing me tutor to this Prince,' remarked Gian Gastone, 'and at the same time put us back into pupilage' (alluding to the garrisons). But he tried, as usual, to extract some gleams of mirth therefrom.

'Now,' he croaked, 'you will see an old man of sixty become the father of a bouncing boy.'

The Spanish troops did not arrive until October, 1731. Meanwhile

[1] Settimanni.

the *Ruspanti*, some 370 strong, were becoming a public menace: even Spanish soldiers were less feared than this rowdy gang of bullies. Every time they came for their wages beneath the colonnade in the courtyard of the Pitti, there was an uproar. On the evening of August 25th, 1731, writes Settimanni, the Grand Duke's *Ruspanti*, who since a fortnight had not been paid for their good services to H.R.H., betook themselves in great number to the old market and tried to obtain food from the cook-shops without money to pay for it; but the shopkeepers resisted them, and a scuffle ensued with knives and stones a-flying. Nothing of the matter came before the courts of justice, however, from due regard to the favour this rabble enjoyed with H.R.H. Such scenes were of daily occurrence. And in September, the *Ruspanti* shouted insults outside the windows of the chamber where H.R.H. slept, and even tried to enter it and see whether His Highness were alive or dead, having forced their way through the gate of the Boboli Gardens. After this a sentry-box was built to keep armed guards there during the night, who were ordered to tell anyone approaching the said windows to withdraw, and if they disobeyed, to fire immediately. The Serene Electress also, fearing similar insults from the *Ruspanti*, doubled the guards to her apartment.

A more exact version is told in the reliable MS. memoir in the *Biblioteca Moreniana*: Giuliano Dami had ceased to encourage the Grand Duke's disorderly routs from fear of the Electress, who regarded him as their instigator and pursued him with a deadly hatred. The Grand Duke abstained from them in consequence, for he adored and valued Giuliano more than his own eyes. After a time, however, he could forbear no longer, so great was the delight he took in these assemblies. Without informing Giuliano he arranged with ten or twelve of his *Ruspanti* that they were to enter the Boboli Gardens by a gate above the large piazza, which always remained half-open with a single sentry to guard it. A secret door from the garden would admit them to the palace, whence they could easily gain his apartments. They reached this gate at the appointed hour, wearing grotesque masks and dominoes, but as the sentry turned them back they set upon him and put him to flight with a volley of stones. This obstacle overcome, they entered the garden, but could not find the secret door, for darkness was gathering. In the meantime the sentry had warned the bodyguard.

Torches were lit, and ten stout soldiers fully armed set after them.

The *Ruspanti* were groping in the dark, unable to find the door. When they saw the torches of the bodyguard approaching, they moved some distance from the palace to avoid suspicion. But instead of escaping, as they could have done easily by one of the side-alleys or shrubberies, they came forth pluckily to meet their adversaries. The guards were ready to charge them, but as the *Ruspanti* appeared unexpectedly in a compact body with pistols and drawn swords, they had to let them pass. They were merely escorted, unrecognized, out of the royal gardens. Bettino Ricasoli suspected they were thieves, and gave orders that in future all members of the bodyguard were to use muskets with bayonets attached to them by night. . . . Had any but the *Ruspanti* been responsible, the whole city would have been overturned to discover the culprits. But the incident was hushed up, and no steps whatever were taken to investigate. When the Grand Duke was informed, his delight was unbounded. He summoned his hectic young heroes, and wished them to render him a full account of their adventure. He lauded their courage, and made them bountiful amends.

The same memoir relates that the Grand Duke knew that his sister had a horror of the *Ruspanti*, and that she was informed of all his dealings with them. He was aware that on their pay-days she stood watching them from a remote balcony, and to afford her extra pleasure, he would have them kept waiting for three or four hours. One Saturday he had allowed a week to elapse before they received their wages, and a noisy band of three hundred and fifty was assembled below. The *Ruspanti* on their side despised this Princess utterly. Antonio Frilli, their chief, would ride about the city in a suit of yellow buckskin with silver lacings, so that he appeared as a noble knight, and with pistols in his saddlebow. Thus mounted and equipped, he met the Electress one day near the Riccardi Palace in the Via Larga, and stopped to see her pass at a few yards' distance, staring at her fixedly the while. He did not even bow or raise his hat. Perhaps, they said, when H.R.H. is acquainted of the slight, Frilli will have a double-entry to his graces.

On September 13th (1731), the Duke of Parma's widow made a public declaration that she had been totally deceived about her pregnancy. The Florentines did not dread the advent of Spaniards: they rather looked forward to it as a novelty. Life must have been sufficiently monotonous in a town where the still-birth of a double-headed infant, the happy delivery of a woman past fifty, miraculous cures and occasional falls into wells and apoplectic strokes had to console the population for receiving but little political news, and that little from six weeks to two months old. The Spaniards were expected as some vast troop of comedians to entertain them.

On October 25th a multitude of every rank left Florence for Leghorn, whither, besides Tuscans, many Lombards and foreigners also betook themselves to watch the arrival of the Anglo-Spanish fleet. The cost of living in Leghorn became excessive; a gold guinea a day was charged for a single bedroom; a thaler (7 lire 35) was charged for a capon, and other victuals likewise, although innumerable barges laden with copious provisions had been sent from Florence. Don Carlos landed two months after his garrisons, on the night of December 27th, 1731, and passed through illuminated streets to the cathedral. He caught the smallpox soon afterwards, and it was not until he had fully recovered, on March 9th, 1732, that he made his formal entry into Florence. Everywhere he created a favourable impression by his youthful gaiety, and his eagerness to learn. He was his mother's son, an Italian more than a Spaniard. 'The Spaniards had been furnished with money to lavish and orders to be conciliatory; the Italians were ready to be conciliated, and Don Carlos made an easy conquest of all hearts.'

Sovereignty had become connected with crabbed age and disease: at those brief intervals when the Grand Duke exhibited himself, it was the apparition of some bloated phantom rather than of a human being. So frequent were the rumours of his death—for months together he was supposedly moribund—that occasionally, as in November, on the vigil of All Saints, 'he let himself be seen from a balcony with universal admiration from the people so little accustomed to the sight of this Prince'. Florentine society was yearning for a figurehead. At the coming of a young man full of life, the blood flowed faster through the city's arteries. It was in truth as if an old man of sixty had become the father of a bouncing boy. Don Carlos loved falconry and the chase: he shot and fished in the Boboli; hunted in the Cascine; every day there were military parades and bands in the Piazzas. But the Florentines looked down their noses at his suite, most of whom struck them as Philistines.

'Among other instances of foreign barbarism,' says Grosley,[1] 'they make themselves very merry with the behaviour of Don Carlos's confessor at the door of the Medicean library. This confessor, a Cordelier, attended the young Prince when he went to take possession of the Tuscan dominions. Being the only person in the suite the cut of whose vesture promised some scholarship, the librarian, concluding he must long to see one of the most splendid monuments which the munificence of princes has dedicated to literature, immediately waited on him with a very respectful invitation. He received the compliment tolerably well, and a day was fixed. The director had got together all the most eminent scholars in the city; and the confessor, after partaking of a very genteel collation, moved towards the library, followed by such a respectable company. On coming to the door, he stopped, and gazing round the ample salon, he called out to the director: "Mr Librarian, have you got the book of the Seven Trumpets here?" The director made answer in the negative; and the whole company owned, with some confusion, that they knew nothing of such a book. "Well, then," said the confessor, turning back, "your whole library is not worth a pipe of tobacco." No time was lost to get an account of this book, which was found to be a collection of pious stories, all manifestly apocryphal, and put into Spanish by a Franciscan, for the use of the very lowest people.'

The Spaniards certainly were unpredictable. In October, 1732, a sergeant in the Regiment of Castile who had served fourteen years in the Spanish army suddenly gave birth to a son while 'he' was on guard at Leghorn.

Gian Gastone was delighted with his heir: he presented him, amongst other things, with a parasol embroidered with gold and a small open carriage upholstered with velvet and ornamented with silver. The Prince used to drive it with two little donkeys through the alleys of the Boboli Gardens. In the evening he attended the opera in Via della Pergola, but he seldom had the opportunity of seeing more than one act. 'This evening the opera began with the second act which the Prince has not yet heard, because he must always return early to the palace.' On the feast of St John the Baptist, Gian Gastone, without consulting the Emperor, allowed Don Carlos to receive homage from

[1] *New Observations on Italy and its Inhabitants,* written in French by two Swedish gentlemen. Translated into English by Thomas Nugent, LL.D.

the Tuscan provinces. Gian Gastone had been very ill in May: so weak was his pulse that it was feared his life was in danger, 'to the great alarm of his subjects, who learned that H.R.H.'s death would not be to their advantage at this time'. His sixty-second birthday, on May 25th, was celebrated with enthusiasm; and it is strange to find that there was a pompous gala at Court to celebrate the birthday of his ever-absent wife. The Grand Duke felt that he could now enjoy those benefits of time which fate had conceded him, and the *Ruspanti* increased. He did not seem aware of his tragedy: his indifference was surprising, even shocking, to those of his contemporaries who considered it.

'It seems to me,' wrote von Poellnitz, 'that this Prince, when he sees his family extinct, and his estate pass into the hands of foreigners, ought at least to eternize the glory of his ancestors, by publishing an inventory of the vast wealth which they have acquired, and transmitted to their posterity. 'Tis 150 years ago that St Lawrence's Chapel has been building, and yet it wants two-thirds of being finished. If it were lawful to criticize the conduct of princes, I must say it again, that the Grand Duke, who sees that his greatness and his family must end with him, ought to put the last hand to this monument of the magnificence of the Medicis: for can he hope, that if he himself neglects to transmit the lustre of his family to posterity, his successors will think to do it, who are nothing to him, or at least but very little. But such is the humour of John Gaston, Grand Duke of Tuscany; he is so indifferent and unconcerned about everything, that he sees foreigners dispose of his dominions and nominate his successor, and the courtiers ready to abandon him; and to worship the said successor; and yet the prospect, how disagreeable soever it may be, does not seem to give him any uneasiness. And he said some days ago, after he had signed his last Will and Testament, declaring Don Carlos, Infant of Spain, his successor; that he had just got a son and heir by a dash of his pen, which he had not been able to get in thirty-four years' marriage.'

Oliver Goldsmith, in an essay on Happiness, remarks: 'I remember to have once seen a slave in a fortification in Flanders. . . . He was maim'd, deformed and chained; obliged to toil from the appearance of day till nightfall, and condemned to this for life; yet, with all these circumstances of apparent wretchedness, he sung, would have danced, but that he wanted a leg, and appeared the merriest, happiest man of all the garrison. What a practical philosopher was here! . . . Everything furnished him with an opportunity for mirth; and though some thought him from his insensibility a fool, he was such an idiot as philosophers might wish in vain to imitate.'

Gian Gastone, the haunted, solitary pessimist, had come to possess this happiness of temper. To paraphrase Goldsmith's words, the most calamitous events, either to Gian Gastone himself or others, could bring no new affliction; the whole world was to him a theatre, on which comedies only are acted. All the bustle of heroism or the rants of ambition served only to heighten the absurdity of the scene, and make the humour more poignant.

Don Carlos applied for permission to occupy the Duchies while still under age, and for immediate instead of eventual investiture. Charles VI, annoyed at the oath to him taken by the Florentine Senate, refused. Upon this Don Carlos made a formal entry into Parma, and assumed the unauthorized title of Grand Prince of Tuscany. An open quarrel threatened, but England intervened; and, to please George II, Charles VI granted the dispensation of age, and immediate investiture, if Don Carlos would drop the title of Grand Prince. Then, on February 1st (1733), Augustus II of Poland inopportunely died.

For fifty years Europe had been preoccupied with moribund sovereigns and the division of their property. The succession to Poland was of no moment to Spain, and of little to France, but served as another pretext for all to air their dissatisfaction. The restless Franco-Spanish-Sardinian group wished to humble Austria, tear up the Treaty of Vienna and the Pragmatic Sanction; Louis XV's father-in-law, Stanislas Leczinski, must be King of Poland; Don Carlos must have Naples and Sicily, and his brother Don Philip the Farnese and Medici inheritance; the King of Sardinia, Milan; while France might secure Savoy for herself in exchange. All this was confirmed by the Treaty of Turin, between France and Sardinia (September, 1733), and the Treaty of the Escurial, between France and Spain (November 7th).

Yet again Gian Gastone would have to face the eternal question of the Tuscan Succession, and keep neutral with everyone fighting around him. In a few months, almost in a few weeks, Don Carlos was master of Naples: there was a series of indecisive battles between the French and Austrians in the North. Fortunately for Gian Gastone, Austria and France were tired of the campaign, after two years of needless bloodshed. Whenever the French and Spanish co-operated with any success, Carlo Emmanuele held back, shifty and inconstant: it was felt he might be bribed to change sides at any moment. Knowing that such strange allies could not hold together much longer, and that Elisabeth was privately trying to make terms, Fleury had decided to steal a march upon them, and secure a peace satisfactory to France. The Emperor expected to get better terms from France alone than from her allies, and he was not disappointed. On October 3rd, 1735, peace preliminaries between Austria and France were signed; the siege of Mantua was abandoned, and the Spanish army had to retire into Tuscany.

France had taken clever advantage of her opportunity, since it was arranged that the Duchy of Lorraine, which she had long coveted, was soon to be made over to her, while its Duke was to be compensated by being made heir to Tuscany. As Francis of Lorraine was the affianced husband of Maria Theresa, this arrangement suited the Emperor because Tuscany would, in future, belong to his family; Parma and Piacenza were to be his immediately, in exchange for the two Sicilies which Don Carlos was to keep, in addition to the Presidii. The Emperor was also to recover the Milanese, but Carlo Emmanuele was to choose for himself two amongst its three Western provinces, Novara, Tortona or Vigevano. Besides which, France promised to guarantee the Pragmatic Sanction.

The fate of Tuscany and Lorraine was thus changed without either being consulted. The Duke of Lorraine did not like giving up his ancient home for a foreign principality where he was a complete stranger. Nor was Gian Gastone pleased: he regarded Don Carlos as his near relation, almost as his lawful heir. Of the Duke of Lorraine he knew nothing, but that he would probably be the next Emperor and would look upon Tuscany as a mere dependency, and send hated Germans to rule it.

When, in February, 1736, Spain unwillingly acceded to the peace preliminaries, Gian Gastone asked humorously 'whether the monarchs would make him a third heir to his dominions, requesting to know what child France and the Empire would next beget for him'.

The final peace was not yet signed, however, for Spain raised endless difficulties, especially about withdrawing her army from Tuscany, and there was a lively quarrel between all the parties over the large allodial estates and private property of the Medici. Gian Gastone tried once more to insist that Tuscany was not an Imperial fief, but while he could get no satisfaction on this point, he obtained a compensating clause that, if Francis became Emperor, Tuscany should be settled on a younger member of his family, and at least have a Duke of its own. The prospect of peace was to some extent assured by the stipulation that the Duchy was never to form part of the hereditary dominions of Austria; female succession was made legitimate in the absence of male heirs to the Grand Duke and his brother; and Tuscany was exempt from obligation to support the Pragmatic Sanction. Nothing was settled about the Medici property until Gian Gastone died. Europe was eagerly awaiting this event. Lorraine had been evacuated by its Duke, who was pensioned from March, 1737, until Tuscany should fall in.

In January, 1737, the Spanish garrisons were withdrawn from Tuscany. Having received an oath of allegiance from Generals Wachtendonck and Braitwitz, commanding the Austrian troops that took their place, Gian Gastone began to die. The agony was slow. In June he sank into an extraordinary languor. The Prince de Craon, as the Duke of Lorraine's representative, arrived in Florence that month, on the 8th of which he wrote his master: 'I found this Prince in a condition worthy of pity; he could not leave his bed, his beard was long, his sheets and linen very dirty, without ruffles; his eyesight dim and enfeebled, his voice low and obstructed, and altogether the air of a man who had not a month to live.' He could digest nothing, but never lost his presence of mind. On June 21st the Electress, whom he would never allow to see him, made her way through secret doors to his bedroom, but as soon as Gian Gastone caught sight of her he ordered her to be gone, calling her by all the most opprobrious names he could think of. Later on, when told that she was weeping bitterly because of this reception, he softened towards her, and sent word that she could visit him at any hour she pleased in future. Whereupon the Electress tried to convert him, and he was altogether too weak to resist. The best doctors could do little but move him into a cleaner bed.

The record of Gian Gastone's death-bed conversion is even more painful than that of his nocturnal entertainments: on the morning of

July 10th, when there was but little strength left in him, he summoned Prior Ippolito Rosselli of the parish of S. Felicità. Then, turning to him with great humility, he said: 'You see, we all must die.'

The priest took this very suitable occasion to inspire him with Christian sentiments, to which he listened with great earnestness and attention. He expressed his entire conviction of their truth and a desire to confess and receive the Blessed Sacrament at the earliest opportunity. Later in the morning Prior Rosselli was again introduced into his chamber, and he confessed with sincerest penitence, and begged to be given the Holy Eucharist. This was administered to him in the presence of his sister, the Electress, and his intimates. His midnight acts of devotion, his supplications to God for mercy and forgiveness, stirred the compassion of all that stood around. Meanwhile Senator Pier Francesco Ricci arrived at the palace to confer the Cross of St Stephen on H.R.H. as Grand Master of that holy and military order. He was thus enabled to share the special indulgences conceded to it by the Pope. When this was explained to him, he evinced his satisfaction. On the next midday he was given the Holy Oil in the presence of the Electress and her gentlemen-in-waiting, and again he displayed a genuine piety. Not only did he offer his limbs spontaneously to be anointed by the priest, but afterwards, fixing his eyes upon the Crucifix, he said in a languid audible voice: '*Sic transit gloria mundi.*'

When this function was over, he wished to show what spiritual consolation he had derived therefrom, as well as his gratitude to the clergy. So he said to one of his attendants: 'Go, tell them I beg the Lord God to reward all those priests who are helping to save my soul.'

He gladly welcomed the three prelates that came to succour him. These were Monsignor Gio. Francesco Stoppani, Archbishop of Corinth and Papal Nuncio, Monsignor Giuseppe Maria Martelli, Archbishop of Florence, and Monsignor Francesco Ginori, Bishop of Fiesole. The first gave him the benediction and Papal absolution *in articulo mortis*; the Archbishop of Florence followed with recommending his soul, and while he was reading suitable prayers from the ritual, Prior Rosselli was prompting the sick man with ejaculations and passages from the Scriptures. These were begun by the parish priest and ended by the Prince with considerable spirit. Later in the day he seemed to gain relief, and it was thought advisable to let him rest.

Towards night the prelates retired to their dwellings. Prior Rosselli lingered with some other ecclesiastics in case they were suddenly called for. When the Prince was asked if he desired further absolution for his sins, he replied 'yes' with the little strength that was left in his feeble voice. So cordial and moving was his contrition, that all about him fell a-weeping when they heard it. Shortly after midnight, the signs of his approaching death were manifest. The sick man knew it, for he was heard constantly commending himself to God with all his heart and soul.

Early next morning the prelates returned, and all the churches were directed to pray fervently for the dying Prince. In his last hours he was continually assisted by these, together with his chaplain and other holy fathers. The Electress, and his chief ministers and courtiers stood by him. At twenty minutes past two in the afternoon he peacefully breathed his last, after a reign of thirteen years, eight months and nine days.

The Prince de Craon took immediate possession on Gian Gastone's death. After condoling with the Electress, he read to her the full powers of Francis Stephen, the new Grand Duke, with part of his instructions, from which it appeared that H.R.H. elected a Council of Regency to govern for him, composed of the said Prince de Craon, the Grand Prior del Bene, Marchese Rinuccini, Prior Giraldi and Antonio Tornaquinci. On July 12th the Senate of 48 and Council of 200 swore solemn fealty to the new Grand Duke before his substitute the Prince de Craon, and an Imperial diploma was read which gave Tuscany in feud to Francis Stephen of Lorraine. A shower of silver money was let loose on the mob. The new Grand Duke was fighting Turks in the Balkans: he did not enter Florence until January 20th, 1739, and then it was to stay there for three months only.

XXVII

Reforms Under Gian Gastone – Horace Mann and the New Régime – Last Years and Death of the Electress Anna Maria, 1743 – 'And No Birds Sing!'

About forty years had elapsed since Cosimo III first tried to solve the problem of the Tuscan Succession; the fate of Tuscany was sealed by the diplomatists of Europe against every intention of the last two Medici, and the wishes of their subjects. Though peace was guaranteed, and with the benefits of peace it was possible to foresee an era of prosperity, it was an ignominious climax for a city that will ever be unique in history—'the most important workshop of the Italian and, indeed, of the modern European spirit'.

The era of prosperity would come, but historians would forget that Gian Gastone had paved the way for it: the house of Lorraine would be given all the credit. The strange thing is that Gian Gastone's aversion to government, even his bouts of drunkenness, did not prevent him from doing what he could for Florence when everything had sunk to its nadir. He had no high-flying aspirations and ideals, no meditated programme of reform. But he was guided by a remarkable common sense, fortified by a keen intolerance of ecclesiastical abuses and sympathy for men of culture. His first measures had been to separate the functions of Church and State, free the latter from ecclesiastical tyranny, and rid his Court of the churchmen who had governed it under Cosimo III; he abolished the Council of Four (*Giunta Quadrumvirale*) and re-established the old *Segretaria della Giurisdizione*, showing no small penetration in his choice of ministers to preside over it: first Filippo Buonarroti, who died in 1734, and then Giulio Rucellai, who stuck to his post under the House of Lorraine until his death in 1778. When Clement XII demanded Rucellai's dismissal, Gian Gastone refused, without even condescending to discuss it. When in 1732 Archbishop Martelli of Florence wished to publish the acts of a diocesan Synod which infringed the secular rights, Gian Gastone (influenced by Buonarroti) forbade them to be published or executed: 'Monsignor the Archbishop must understand for once that he cannot interfere in affairs other than spiritual and pertaining to his ministry; that we do not wish him to proceed against laymen with temporal penalties, whatever causes he may allege.' Shortly after, there were furious protests and a general panic among the churchmen because the first Freemasons were allowed in Tuscany. But Gian Gastone gently dismissed the Inquisitor who appealed to him, saying that he could see no harm whatever in the meetings of Freemasons.

Gian Gastone's attitude towards education was also the antithesis of Cosimo III's: deaf to monkish murmurs against the 'new philosophy', he restored Pasquale Giannetti to the philosophical chair of Pisa, revoking the provisions which confined him to teaching medicine; he allowed the entire works of Gassendi to be published, edited by Niccolo Averani in 1727—and allowed solemn honours to be rendered to Galileo in Santa Croce. The Jesuits pronounced the University of Pisa to be a nest of all the most dangerous heresies. As Rucellai explained after Gian Gastone's death: 'one sole obstacle, the University of Pisa, prevented Tuscany from being reduced to that state of ignorance in which nearly all the rest of Italy has been suffocated'. In June, 1735, with a spirit of tolerance quite new to the Medicean dynasty, he published an edict forbidding all persecution of the Jews.

The same characteristics occur in economic legislation. He abolished the deleterious tax on beasts of burden; and greatly reduced the taxes on their export and import. In August, 1726, he forbade the import of corn, there being abundance from the present harvest ('to maintain a just level of prices'—i.e., a fair one to producers and consumers). Until 1727 all his subjects without distinction had to pay an annual tax called the *colletta*. Even the clergy, though privileged, had to contribute their share; only the poor who existed on alms were exempt. The poorer peasantry, small freeholders, minor artisans, were forced to pay this tax as well as the rich landowners, merchants and bankers—quite irrespective of the fact that the former had to suffer from considerable taxes non-existent elsewhere, and complicated rural rights, such as forced labour, rights of wood-cutting, pasturage and so forth which reduced them almost to serfdom, and burdened agriculture. Henceforth *mezzadri*, labourers, artists and others 'who received but scant gains from their industry were exempt from paying the *colletta*, and likewise those earning less than 100 crowns (scudi) a year'. Thus the condition of the peasantry was much improved. Even the national debt, which had attained the enormous sum of twenty millions of crowns at the end of Cosimo's reign (if we are to believe the Spanish ambassador, Father Ascanio's information), was considerably reduced under Gian Gastone's government. Ascanio says it fell to fourteen millions: perhaps the figure is exaggerated, but the fact remains that a Grand Duke regarded as little more than imbecile[1] by historians did exert himself to diminish a fantastic national debt, as well as the taxes, and even trade revived a little.

A year after Gian Gastone's death Sir Robert Walpole appointed young Horace Mann to the British Legation in Florence, where he was destined to remain for nearly half a century. The new régime is graphically described in his correspondence. The absentee Grand Duke left the Prince de Craon in charge of his affairs, and all the good posts were given to Lorrainers. The Prince de Craon's father, a certain M. de Beauvau, had been the 'trusty servant' of the Grand Duke's father (Duke Leopold of Lorraine); himself had rendered the Duke Leopold a double service by marrying his mistress and tutoring his son, Francis. When the latter became Grand Duke he obtained the elevation of M. de Beauvau to the dignity of a Prince of the Holy Roman Empire. The Princess de Craon, it was said, had originally been espied by Duke Leopold as a buxom girl driving turkeys in a field: this was the dame who now gave tone to Tuscany—and a curious tone it was, that of a musical-comedy Court in a mere province of Austria. Masquerades, earthquakes, the Prince de Craon's itch and his Princess's *lavements*, intrigues, serenades, duels, theatricals, are the themes of these twenty-eight years before the arrival of that energetic reformer, Peter Leopold.

Even in Gian Gastone's time there had been more outward dignity at the Florentine Court. The Prince de Craon, whether 'staying at Petraja to scratch himself', or supping in the grand-ducal box at the opera, appeared in a light that was generally ludicrous. 'The Prince,' wrote Mann, 'came behind me, and with his hands on my shoulders, prevented my turning so as to see who it was. "*Devinez*," says he, "*qui*

---

[1] Roscoe's *Life of Lorenzo de' Medici*: 'the imbecile hands of Gaston de' Medici'.

je suis, vous me connaîtrez par la chaleur de mes embrassements." All I could answer on the sudden was: "*Ha, ha; mon Prince; oui, je vous connois.*" What else can one say to such things?'

The Prince was too amiable to be disliked, but the Austro-Lorraine officials and soldiers were loathed. Many would have preferred Don Carlos, but a wiser citizen said: 'I prefer the Lorrainers to the Spaniards, because, though the former would take my clothes (property), the latter would deprive me of my skin (liberty of thought) also.' 'The Tuscans,' wrote the Président de Brosses in 1739, 'would give two-thirds of their property to have the Medici back, and the other third to get rid of the Lorrainers. They hate them as the Milanese hate the Piedmontese. The Lorrainers ill-use, and what is worse, despise them.' These simple words are a testimonial to the Medici: after usurping the government of a free republic, they had made their loss lamented.

The last representative of the Medici, the widowed Electress Palatine, lingered on, a pale shadow of their ancient pomp and power, an alien from her native land, a guest in her magnificent palaces. She was offered the position of Regent, and although she haughtily declined it, was left in undisturbed occupation of her apartments at the Pitti. The founders of the new dynasty had nothing to fear from her, and created a good impression by their tactful obsequiousness. Anna Maria's reception of them was merely formal, but she was not proof against their manifest desire for a good understanding with her. 'In the latter part of her life she was the reverse of that good-humoured sloven, her brother. Then, indeed, she never so far lost her dignity as even to smile.'

'The furniture of her bedchamber was all of silver: tables, chairs, stools and screens. More rich, singular, extraordinary, says a noble author, than handsome. She never went out for some years before her death, except to church, or sometimes to see Florence in the evening; at these times she was drawn by eight horses, and attended by a guard. The present Earl of Orford informed the author,[1] that he once had the honour to pay his respects to her. She received him under a large black canopy, she stood indeed, but after a few minutes' talking, she assured him of her good wishes, and then dismissed him; nor did she see anyone but in this ridiculous way.'

She was redeemed from despair by a deep inward faith which re-

[1] Rev. Mark Noble. See also the *Letters of Thomas Gray and Horace Walpole.*

moved her far from the existing order, and farther from the spirit of the age. While she lived she would still maintain the splendid illusions and conventions, receiving her few privileged visitors erect, a grave and solemn pillar of deportment, under a large black canopy. She had been forced to drink deep of every dishonour, but the bitter cup had left her with a thirst for punctilio. She spent enormous sums on charity; apart from this her chief occupation and expense was to complete the family mausoleum. Ferdinando I had begun it in 1604, but funds had run short, the work had languished; more than a century passed and the Electress pressed the workmen on with 1,000 crowns a week. It must be ready for her burial. Ridiculous she may have appeared to the Earl of Orford, cobwebby, yet, confess it, something approaching awe must have hung over the proud poise of that aged unbending figure, the refined composure of that parchment face: here was consummate dignity, a *grande dame*, and nothing to titter at.

Very soon she too would disappear. In January, 1743, Sir Horace Mann writes that the Electress is much out of order again. 'She has a fever with an oppression upon her breast, and a sore leg. People don't seem to apprehend her to be in any immediate danger, but as she is of late so much decayed, many fear she won't get on this winter. She has been a good deal touched with the news of the death of the Elector Palatine, which was announced to her two days ago, not for any love she had for him, but by the reflection, I suppose, that an Electress may de too.' The theatres were totally deserted and masks were not admitted to them 'so as not to disoblige the Electress, who will be most extraordinarily devout'.

Then, on February 18th, Mann writes: 'All our jollity is at an end, our Carnival overset and all the masking schemes disappointed; the Electress died about an hour ago; the poor remains of the Medici is soon to join her ancestors. . . . The common people are convinced she went off in a hurricane of wind; a most violent one began this morning and lasted for about two hours, and now the sun shines as bright as ever, this is proof; besides for a stronger, just the same thing happened when John Gaston went off. Nothing can destroy this opinion which people think they have been eye-witnesses to. All the town is in tears, many with great reason, for the loss of her; it is very visible; however, it would have affected many much less, had she staid till the beginning of Lent. Nobody apprehended she was so near her end; her courtiers were last night at the Opera. In the night she grew bad; this morning at 16 took the sacrament and an hour after had the extreme unction. I am really sorry for the country; there will be no more disputes about the Jewels; nor will the Grand Duke have anybody to dispute with him about anything he likes to do; what that will be everybody is impatient to see. . . . The death of the Electress employs the discourse of the whole town; it has made us forget the Spaniards, but they who remember them think it is most fortunate they have been routed before the other happened, and 'tis hoped they are not in a condition to come here to make good their pretensions to her great inheritance. The instant she expired, the gates of the town were shut and not a creature permitted to go out, so that many hundred people from the country were obliged to stay in Florence all last night, even the French courier was not permitted to go. These precautions were interpreted that the Spaniards might not be apprised of it. The guards were tripled in and about the palace, and last night late there was a Council what to do.'

It was a second death: she had been dead to the world since Gian Gastone was laid in his grave in 1737. The Mausoleum of San Lorenzo was never finished, but her last valediction is not over: the famous will in which Anna Maria bequeathed the allodial and personal property of the Medici, the greatest art collection in the world, to the new Grand Duke and his successors, on condition that none of it should ever be removed from Florence, and that it should be for the benefit of the public of all nations. Redundant it were to repeat, and stress again, the incalculable importance to Florence, and to all who love art, of the last clause.

Avoiding empyrean flights, we had better cling to worldly Horace Mann, the reporter on the spot. 'People who pretend to know, assert that for a considerable time past, she has given to charities 1,000 zecchins a month,[1] and it is well known, the beginning of her illness, that in one month she distributed 9,000 zecchins. I don't hear she has left anything to the poor, for which they are all in despair, and firmly persuaded that the Devil came for her in the *Temporale* which

---

[1] As three zecchins, or sequins, made £1 sterling, this represented £4,000 a year, worth much more at the present value of money.

happened so suddenly at the time of death, and ended with it. She certainly did not expect to die so soon, nor did anybody else. The fryday before the monday she died, she was so tollerably well that the Physicians made her encrease her diet, and she told Mgr Ugoccioni that she was perfectly easy. On the Sunday night she had a more than usual oppression on her breast, for which they blooded her, and to which many attribute her death. On the monday morning her Confessor by a stratagem was carried to her, for she would not have him sent for, and about 17 hours, he was bid tell her she must soon dye, to which she answered by asking him with some emotion, "Who told you so?" he said: "her physicians".

' "Very well, then let us do what there is to be done; and do it quickly." So they brought her the Communion. She afterwards made a Codicile to her will, but could not sign it; but 3 people and a lawyer attached what she ordered. She was sensible to the last, but did not speak for about an hour and a half before she died. . . . 'Tis said about the town that there's a legacy for *il Re d' Anghelterra* [*sic*] but I am afraid it is for one she calls so, at Rome; but I have not thought proper to make any enquiries for it yet. Her orders were, not to be embalmed, but they were interpreted as being given out of modesty only, and so not complied with. She has lain in state in the great hall of the palace since thursday morning, and is to be buried to-night. . . .

'Sunday morning. There was nothing extraordinary in the funeral last night. All the magnificence consisted in a prodigious number of torches carried by the different orders of priests, the expense of which in lights, they say, amounted to 12 thousand crowns. The body was in a sort of a Coach quite open, with a Canopy over her head; two other coaches followed with her ladies. . . .

'By degrees, I got out of the Prince [de Craon] a certainty about the legacy I mentioned for *il Re*, 'tis as I expected, but mind with what delicacy and circumspection—a Ring—"for the Prince, son of King James the Second of England".'

Were there so many tears for the last of the royal race of Medici? A paragraph from one of Sir Horace Mann's letters again provides an answer: 'We should have more amusement during Lent than we had in the Carnival. Filippo Medici, who was almost ruined by his cousin's death, being Impresario for the little Theatre, has now begun an

Accademia in a large room close to it, where I find it will be greatly the fashion to go. He said publickly there on Monday night: "The Electress hated masks so heartily that she died on purpose to put a stop to them!" and afterwards: "By such a step she found the only means to make the House of Medici weep!" It was vastly applauded, but you must know he is not the least related to her family. . . .'

BIBLIOGRAPHY

A bibliography of the Medici would fill a big volume by itself: Moreni's *Serie d'Autori di Opere Risguardante la celebre famiglia Medici*, published in Florence, 1826, fills 391 pages. I have therefore made no attempt to compile any complete list of documents, authorities and books consulted in the formation of this one, covering the period from Ferdinando II to Gian Gastone.

The most useful and important are marked with an asterisk.

R. Archivio di Stato di Firenze.

*Diario fiorentino del Settimanni, recording the most notable happenings in Florence from 1532 to 1737 under the absolute rule of the Medici.

Diario di Corte del Tinghi.

*Bibliotechina Grassoccia, a rare series of volumes published by the *Giornale di Erudizione* in Florence, edited by Filippo Orlando and Giuseppe Baccini, contains brief accounts of the following, drawn from an unpublished MS in the Moreniana entitled *Storia della nobile e reale casa de' Medici:*

1. *Vita di Ferdinando II Quinto Granduca di Toscana.* 1886.
2. *Vita di Gio. Gastone I Settimo ed ultimo Granduca della R. Casa de' Medici, con la lista dei provvisionati di Camera, dal volgo detti i Ruspanti.* 1886.

   (Of this a translation by Harold Acton, with introduction by Norman Douglas, was privately printed for subscribers by G. Orioli, Lungarno Corsini, Florence, 1930, resulting in a small judicial comedy; see Richard Aldington: 'Books and Bookmen', *Sunday Referee*, December 28th, 1930, and February 22nd, 1931.)

3. *Vita di Cosimo III Sesto Granduca di Toscana.*
   Vita del Principe Francesco-Maria gia Cardinale di Santa Chiesa.
   Vita del Gran Principe Ferdinando di Toscana. 1887.

4. *Vita di Tre Principesse di Casa Medici* (*Violante, the Electress Palatine and Princess Eleanora*). 1887.

34–35. *Margherita Luisa d'Orléans, Granduchessa di Toscana. Documenti inediti tratti dall' Archivio di Stato di Firenze con un discorso proemiale di Giuseppe Baccini.* 1898.

Acton (William). *The traveller in Italy. A new journal of Italy; containing what is most remarkable, etc.* 1691.

Addison (Joseph). *Travels through Italy and Switzerland.* 1705.

Allodoli (Ettore). *I Medici.* Florence, 1928.

*Baccini (Giuseppe) see: *Bibliotechina Grassoccia.*

Baldinucci. *Notizie de' professori del disegno da Cimabue in qua.* 1768 ed.

Baretti (Joseph). *An account of the manners and customs of Italy.* London, 1768.

Bautier (Pierre). *Juste Sustermans, peintre des Médicis.* Bruxelles, 1907.

Benvenuti (Edoardo). *Agostino Coltellini e l' Accademia degli Apatisti.* 1910.

Bourdin (C.). *Voyage d'Italie.* 1699.

Bromley's Remarks in the Grand Tour of France and Italy. 1691.

Brosses, C. de. *Lettres historiques et critiques sur l'Italie.* Paris, 1799.

Buondelmonti (Abate Giuseppe). *Delle lodi dell' Altezza Reale del Serenissimo Gio. Gastone.* 1737.

*Burnet (Gilbert), Bishop of Salisbury. *Some letters containing an account of what seemed most remarkable in travelling through Switzerland, Italy, etc.* 1689.

(and: *Three Letters concerning the present state of Italy, written in the year 1687, being a supplement to Dr Burnet's Letters.*)

*Caggese (Romolo). *Firenze della decadenza di Roma al Risorgimento d'Italia.* Florence, 1921.

Cambridge Modern History, The. Vols. IV, V, VI.

Carmichael (Montgomery). *In Tuscany.* London, 1901.

Chantelou. *Journal du Voyage du Cavalier Bernin en France.* chez Stock. Paris.

Clenche (J.). *A tour in France and Italy made by an English gentleman.* 1676.

Colbert (Jean Baptiste). *L'Italie en 1671.* 1867.

Conti (Giuseppe). *Amori e Delitti di nobiltà e di plebe.* Florence. (No date.)

*Conti (Giuseppe). *Firenze dai Medici ai Lorena.* Florence, 1907.

Coulanges (Philippe Emmanuel de). *Mémoires de M. de Coulanges suivis de lettres inédites à Mme de Sévigné.* 1820.

Crinò (Anna Maria). *Fatti e figure del Seicento Anglo-Toscano.* Florence, 1957.

Dati (Carlo Roberto). *Prose Fiorentine, etc., 1661–1723.*

Dent (Edward J.). *Alessandro Scarlatti: his life and works.* London, 1905.

Doran (Dr), F.S.A. *Mann and Manners at the Court of Florence, 1740–1786.* London, 1876.

D'Orléans, Madame, Duchesse. *Correspondance complète, traduction entièrement nouvelle de M. G. Brunet.* Paris, 1912.

Eachard (Laurence). *The History of England.* 1720.

*Evelyn (John), F.R.S. *Diary.* The Globe Edition. London, 1908.

Filicaia (Vincenzo da). *Poesie Toscane.* Florence, 1823.

Forsyth (Joseph). *Remarks on Antiquities, Arts and Letters during an excursion in Italy in the years 1802 and 1803.* London, 1835.

Freschot (C.). *État ancien et moderne des duchés de Florence, Mantoue et Parme, etc.* 1711.

*Galluzzi (R.). *Istoria del Granducato di Toscana sotto il governo della casa Medici.* Leghorn, 1781.

Garnett (Richard). *Italian Literature.* London, 1911.

Gondi (Jean François Paul de). *Memoirs of the Cardinal de Retz.* English translation, 1723.

Gori (Cav. Pietro). *Il Palio de' Cocchi.* Florence, 1902.

Grangier de Liverdys (Balth). *Journal d'un voyage de France et d'Italie.* 1667.

Gray (Thomas). *Letters, selected by John Beresford.* Oxford University Press, 1925.

Guyot de Merville (Michel). *Voyage historique et politique d'Italie.*

*Hare (Augustus J. C.). *Florence*, revised by St Clair Baddeley. London, 1907.

Horner (Susan and Joanna). *Walks in Florence*. London, 1884.

Hutton (Edward). *Country Walks about Florence*. London, 1908.

Imbert (G.). *Francesco Redi uomo di corte e uomo privato*. Florence, 1895.

*Imbert (G.). *La Vita Fiorentina nel Seicento*. Florence, 1906.

Inghirami (F.). *Storia della Toscana*. Florence, 1843.

Keysler (Johann Georg). *Travels through Germany, etc., 1756–57*.

Labat (Jean Baptiste). *Voyages en Espagne et en Italie*. 1730.

Lalande (Joseph Jerome de). *Voyage en Italie, etc., 1765 & 1766*.

*Lanzi (Abate Luigi). *The History of Painting in Italy*. London, 1847.

Lassels (Richard). *The Voyage of Italy, 1670*.

Leader (John Temple). *Life of Sir Robert Dudley, Earl of Warwick and Duke of Northumberland*. 1895.

*Lee (Vernon). *Studies of the eighteenth century in Italy*. London, 1881.

Lungo (Isidoro del). *I Medici granduchi*. 1896.

Mabillon (Jean). *Correspondance inédite de Mabillon et de Montfaucon avec l'Italie*. 1846.

*Mann (Sir Horace). *Letters to Horace Walpole*.

Martinelli (Vincenzio). *Lettere Familiare e critiche*. London, 1758.

*Maugain (G.). *Étude sur l'Évolution Intellectuelle de l'Italie de 1657 à 1750 environ*. Paris, 1909.

*Menzini (Benedetto). *Satire*.

Mercey (F. B. de). *La Toscane et le Midi de l'Italie*. 1858.

Misson (Maximilian). *A new voyage to Italy*. 1714.

Montesquieu (Charles de Secondat, Baron de). *Voyages*. 1894–96.

Montfaucon (Father). *Travels from Paris through Italy*. 1712.

*Montpensier (Mlle de). *Mémoires*. Amsterdam, 1746.

Morgan (Lady). *The Life and Times of Salvator Rosa*. London, 1824.

Mutinelli (Fabio). *Storia arcana ed aneddotica d'Italia raccontata da. Veneti Ambasciatori*. Venezia, 1858.

Napier (Henry Edward). *Florentine History.* 1846–47.

Noble (Mark), Rev. *Memoirs of the House of Medici.* 1797.

Northall (John). *Travels through Italy.*

Nugent (Thomas), LL.D. *New Observations on Italy and its inhabitants,* transl. from Grosley. 1769.

Palagi (Giuseppe). *La villa di Lappeggi e il poeta G. B. Fagiuoli.* Florence, 1876.

Pepys (Samuel). *Diary.*

Peruzzi (Bindo Simone). *Esequie di Gio. Gastone.* 1737.

*Pieraccini (Gaetano). *La Stirpe de Medici di Cafaggiolo.*

Poellnitz (Carl Ludwig, Baron von). *Memoirs,* transl. by S. Whatley. 1745.

Prezziner (Dottor Giovanni). *Storia del pubblico studio e delle società scientifiche e letterarie di Firenze.* 1810.

Ranke (Leopold von). *History of the Popes.*

Ray (John), F.R.S. *Travels through the Low Countries, Germany, Italy and France.* 1738.

Raymond (John). *Il Mercurio Italico, communicating a voyage made through Italy in the years 1646 and 1647.*

Redi (Francesco). *Osservazioni intorno alle Vipere.* 1664.

Redi (Francesco). *Poesie Toscane.* Florence, 1822.

*Repetti (Emanuele). *Dizionario Geografico Fisico Storico della Toscana.* Florence, 1836.

*Reresby (Sir John). *Memoirs and Travels.* London, 1904.

Ricci (Corrado). *Architettura Barocca in Italia.* Bergamo, 1912.

Robertson (J. G.). *The Genesis of Romantic Theory.* London, 1923.

*Robiony (Emilio). *Gli ultimi dei Medici.* Florence, 1905.

*Rodocanachi (E.). *Les infortunes d'une petite fille d'Henri IV, Marguerite d'Orléans, Grande Duchesse de Toscane.* Paris. (No date.)

Ross (Janet). *Florentine Palaces and their Stories.* London, 1905.

*Ross (Janet). *Florentine Villas.* London, 1901.

Ross (Janet). *Old Florence and Modern Tuscany.* London, 1904.

Schillmann (F.). *Histoire de la Civilisation Toscane (traduction de Jacques Marty).* Paris, 1931.

Scott (Geoffrey). *The Architecture of Humanism*. London, 1914.

Scotti (Francesco). *Il nuovo itinerario d'Italia*. Rome, 1717 ed.

Segneri (P.). *Lettere inedite*.

Smollett (Tobias George). *Travels through France and Italy*. London, 1766.

Solerti (Angelo). *Musica, Ballo e Drammatica alla corte Medicea dal 1600 al 1637*. Florence, 1905.

Taylor (I. A.). *Christina of Sweden*. London. (No date.)

Toffanin (Giuseppe). *L'Eredità del Rinascimento in Arcadia*. Bologna, 1923.

*Vernon (Mrs H. M.). *Italy from 1494 to 1790*. Cambridge, 1909.

Weld (Charles Richard). *Florence, the New Capital of Italy*. London, 1867.

Wright (Edward). *Some observations made in travelling through France, Italy, etc., in the years 1720, 1721 and 1722*.

*Young (Colonel G. F.). *The Medici*. London, 1909.

*Zobi (A.). *Storia civile della Toscana dal 1737 al 1848*. 1850.

INDEX

DATE DUE